Taming EdTech

Also Available from Bloomsbury

Reinventing Pedagogy of the Oppressed, edited by James D. Kirylo
Reimagining Childhood Studies, edited by Spyros Spyrou,
Rachel Rosen and Daniel Thomas Cook
Pedagogies of Taking Care, Dennis Atkinson
Capitalism, Pedagogy, and the Politics of Being, Noah De Lissovoy
Knowing from the Inside, edited by Tim Ingold
Deweyan Transactionalism in Education,
edited by Jim Garrison, Johan Öhman and Leif Östman
A New Perspective on Education in the Digital Age,
Jesper Tække and Michael Paulsen
Philosophy and the Metaphysical Achievements of Education,
Ryan McInerney
Hopeful Pedagogies in Higher Education, edited by Mike Seal
Posthumanism and the Digital University, Lesley Gourlay
Politics and Pedagogy in the 'Post-Truth' Era, Derek R. Ford

Taming EdTech

Why Children Stand to Lose in an Unregulated Digitized Classroom

Velislava Hillman

BLOOMSBURY ACADEMIC
LONDON • NEW YORK • OXFORD • NEW DELHI • SYDNEY

BLOOMSBURY ACADEMIC
Bloomsbury Publishing Plc
50 Bedford Square, London, WC1B 3DP, UK
1385 Broadway, New York, NY 10018, USA
29 Earlsfort Terrace, Dublin 2, Ireland

BLOOMSBURY, BLOOMSBURY ACADEMIC and the Diana logo
are trademarks of Bloomsbury Publishing Plc

First published in Great Britain 2025

Copyright © Velislava Hillman, 2025

Velislava Hillman has asserted her right under the Copyright, Designs and
Patents Act, 1988, to be identified as Author of this work.

For legal purposes the Acknowledgements on pp. ix–x constitute
an extension of this copyright page.

Cover design by Chris Bromley
Cover image © Artem via Adobe Stock

All rights reserved. No part of this publication may be reproduced
or transmitted in any form or by any means, electronic or mechanical,
including photocopying, recording, or any information storage or retrieval
system, without prior permission in writing from the publishers.

Bloomsbury Publishing Plc does not have any control over, or responsibility for,
any third-party websites referred to or in this book. All internet addresses given
in this book were correct at the time of going to press. The author and publisher
regret any inconvenience caused if addresses have changed or sites have
ceased to exist, but can accept no responsibility for any such changes.

A catalogue record for this book is available from the British Library.

A catalog record for this book is available from the Library of Congress.

Library of Congress Control Number: 2024942946

ISBN:	HB:	978-1-3504-3980-1
	PB:	978-1-3504-3979-5
	ePDF:	978-1-3504-3982-5
	eBook:	978-1-3504-3981-8

Typeset by Integra Software Services Pvt. Ltd.
Printed and bound in Great Britain

To find out more about our authors and books visit www.bloomsbury.com
and sign up for our newsletters.

For my family.

Contents

List of Figures		viii
Acknowledgements		ix
1	Introduction: Why a Book about Taming EdTech?	1
2	Digitizing the Classroom: What Is the Problem?	25
3	Infrastructure Capture: What Is the 'Big Picture' of Digitizing Education?	59
4	Automation: What Are the Risks of Automating Children's Education?	89
5	Voice: What Do Children Say about the Digitized Classroom?	113
6	The Good Intentions of School: Why School Matters?	141
7	Governance by Distraction: What Guarantees the Benefits of Digitizing Education?	165
8	Licensed to Operate: How to Fix a Fragmented Governance of EdTech?	195
Notes		222
Index		277

Figures

1.1 and 1.2 Nvidia Canvas transforms squiggles into realistic images   6
2.1 Digitized education becomes part of larger digital infrastructures   30
3.1 Labour (re)production through the means of digital infrastructures integrated in public education   62
3.2 Interoperability enables data-driven decisions that transcend sectors. Those with control of such data interoperable systems can influence decisions and influence populations   72
3.3 Platformization of education: From digitization to datafication to automation to prediction   77
3.4 Interoperable learning record protocol, simplified concept from the original   78
3.5 Data-driven, cradle-to-career pathway development; interoperable learning records for streamlining what industry needs in terms of skills and competencies and what education should 'produce'   81
8.1 Minimum principles and standards that EdTech operators should meet in an ideal 'license-to-operate' scenario   207
8.2 How to ensure that EdTech mediate and influence teaching and learning to the benefit of children?   209
8.3 Cyclical audit of EdTech operators   210

Acknowledgements

I am grateful to many people who contributed to this project in various ways. First, I would like to extend a big thank you to all the parents, children and young people I've spoken with over the years from various parts of the world, including the UK, EU and the United States, as well as to school leaders, governors, data privacy officers and practitioners who have generously shared their insights on EdTech, schooling, the risks and challenges in education, and important topics relating to children – from the world of work to well-being. Additionally, I am grateful to Sara, Kate, Laura, Cheri, Kelley, Jeff, Melissa and their communities from various corners of the United States for their extensive research and valuable contributions way before this book regarding data surveillance of children in education.

I wish to thank several special places and organizations that have been warm and welcoming and supportive in all my work that has led up to this book. I am grateful for the London School of Economics and Political Science and the Department for Media and Communications, Prof. Nick Couldry, Prof. Sonia Livingstone, Prof. Bart Cammaerts, as well as Emma Goodman, Ruhi Khan and Emily Cousens. I express gratitude and thanks to the Berkman Klein Centre for Internet & Society at Harvard University and the Children and Screens institute, with special appreciations to Dr Pamela Herst-Della Pietra, Kris Perry, Kate Blocker and Camara Brown. Big thanks to Dr Andrew Wilkins, Dr Dan McQuillan and Dr Nigel Guenole for welcoming collaboration. My thanks go to Francis and Caroline, and the whole teaching team at Goldsmiths, University of London, where I immediately felt like part of a family, who reminded me that the sense of belonging and socialization are fundamental to both learning and teaching.

I express thanks to many friends and colleagues: Nick Couldry, Mitzi Laszlo, Russel Newman, Gregory Narr, Priscila Gonsales, Emmanuel C. Ogu, Samantha-Kaye Johnston, Rina Lai, Gergana Vladova, Jamie Manolev, Elana Zeide and Priya Kumar. Special thanks to the incredible legal scholars from University of Vienna, Katarzyna, Hande, Clara, Emily and Tima. Big thank you also to Eftim Zdravevski and Evan Radkoff for showing me how advancing technologies like machine learning and AI can be used for good and also their limitations. Special thanks to the GESS working group, in particular Steve, Anthony, Martin and Tony. Immense thanks for the collaboration to Michael Forshaw. I am grateful for Lula Dahir's friendship and insightful discussions on EdTech in Africa. Many thanks to Lord Vaizey and Robin Walker for recognizing the issues around EdTech.

Acknowledgements

My heartfelt thanks to Molly Esquivel for her endless encouragement, love and going over many of the issues raised in this book. My understanding of school governance, fostering nurturing learning environments, and highlighting the crucial role of teachers in children's lives has been greatly enriched by visits to schools in South and Eastern Europe, Africa, Asia, the United States, and most recently the UK. I am grateful for all the schools, leaders and teachers who have opened doors and spoken with me.

A big thank you to the GEM Report team at UNESCO and especially Anna and Manos. I also wish to thank Juliette, Roy and Borhene from the Broadband Commission. With ongoing discussions around governing EdTech, much of the work has reached out to the Far East, and I have had the opportunity to present these ideas thanks to Open Development Cambodia's executive director Thy Try and his team, to Dixon Siu, Keiko Tanaka and Kohei Kurihara including in Japan and Cambodia. Similarly, the MyData Global team starting with Paula Bello has been supportive and providing their platforms to express my critical voice and proposals.

For the friendship and love I thank Joana, Stacey, Lorenzo, Stella, Mario, Aideen, Kristina and Mina.

For meaningful conversations and insight from the EdTech and investment space, I would like to express my appreciation to Richard Taylor. For the advice and confidence in my work, big thanks to Prof James Curran. Sincere thanks to my publisher at Bloomsbury, Mark Richardson, and for the great editorial support from Elissa Burns.

To my friend, mentor and project partner Ronald Hepburn I thank with all my heart for his faith and dedication (onwards and upwards!). Finally, to my family – thank you for all your love and support.

All the mistakes are my own.

1

Introduction: Why a Book about Taming EdTech?

A Stranger walks into a school

In the small town of Willowbrook, nestled amidst rolling hills and earthly landscapes, there was a primary school called Oakwood Elementary. It was a small school of around 300 children, whose laughter filled the hallways as they skittered around their daily learning activities. Every day was fun, carefully curated by the dedicated teaching staff. Except one October Tuesday. As the sun peered through the fluffy clouds, casting a warm glow upon the school, a stranger walked into its gates, unnoticed. At class 4T, Mr Thompson's fourth graders were taking turns in reading. Elly's turn was next. As Mr Thompson called her out, he noticed a stranger peeking through the classroom door window. It was the same stranger that had walked into the school gates and had now made his way in and stood still in front of Mr Thompson's classroom. The stranger was staring back at the children, fixated, but as soon as he saw Mr Thompson charging towards him, he ran off and disappeared. Visibly concerned about the intruder, Mr Thompson ordered the children to stay in class and then dashed out to chase the stranger.

This story is only half true. A stranger did walk into my youngest child's primary school once. Nothing bad happened except that a stranger who lost his way entered a safe and special place, specially dedicated for children. The thought of unchecked strangers walking into a child's school would be disturbing for any parent. My child's school has put solid iron gates since. They stay locked until parents' pick-up time. Today, what with school shootings in the United States, the buildings are a barbed wire away from looking like prisons. Not to stop those on the inside from getting out but from letting outsiders getting in. The strangers can be those lost in the neighbourhood. But they can be strangers with ill intent. They may want to harm and wreak public disorder. They can also be ones that try to sell drugs to children right by the school gates[1] or radicalize them.[2] But can they be those sitting behind digital systems collecting sensitive data about children every single day? Most likely – and hopefully – not. It seems innocuous that a computer system designed for some kind of educational purpose may also have devious intentions. Yet they do – from commercializing children's data to developing products without their parents' consent and influencing education with little regard for whose interests are being served.

The global digital corporations we know today have built their dominion on such practices as harvesting sensitive information about everyone and mediating public and private lives.[3] First they aim to convince a critical mass into buying their ware and then gradually integrate the rest.

Today, tech companies continue to exploit our personal data even when we have asked them not to.[4] People have been deceived; targeted through discriminatory and gender-biased information; had their privacy violated; coerced into harmful products through manipulation; undermined individual autonomy and basic human rights. In education, tech companies have misused children's data. They have continuously exploited their privilege of access to children's sensitive information by tracking and sharing it with data brokers and advertising companies.[5]

Despite considerable and continuous attention from lawmakers and academia regarding these unfair and unethical practices, much-needed change is coming too slowly. Only in June 2023, Microsoft, with world dominance including in education, was fined[6] by the US Federal Trade Commission for exploiting children's data via Xbox, the video game. In May 2023, Edmodo, the Chinese-owned K-12 platform with over 100 million pupils and teachers worldwide was also fined $6 million for unlawfully using children's data for advertising purposes. Edmodo, the self-styled 'Facebook for schools', has reportedly shut down since.[7] However, it will not be a first for a business to merely undergo a name change, restructure or sell its leftovers to another commercial player, the way Naviance, the education data-collecting platform, was sold by the UK *Daily Mail* and General Trust to PowerSchool, the US education technology behemoth, back in 2021[8] (with no public knowledge about the fate of the previously collected pupils' data).

Digitizing education is a highly profitable market. Since the early 1960s, to stimulate future product sales, the computer industry has been extensively providing their products to universities and schools across the United States at reduced prices – and even for free.[9] The computer boom quickly extended to France, Japan and the UK. Meanwhile Soviet computer advancements were frequently highlighted by media as a cautionary signal for the West. Mass media publications, too, boomed with futurist talk about the endless potentials of the computer. The *Family Computing* magazine published in 1983 aimed 'to lead families into personal computer acquisition and help them through those early years of ownership'. There were the *Teaching and the Computer* and the *Electronic Learning* magazines, the latter described as 'the bible of the educational computer field'[10] by its publisher.

Free or at-reduced price has also been the sales model for tech companies half a century later. The recent Covid-19 health pandemic appeared to offer a commercial opportunity. Without hesitation, tech giants Google, Apple and Microsoft offered free devices or heavily discounted software in the United States.[11] In the UK, Microsoft and Google signed deals with government to provide online schooling[12] to the extent that schools today call themselves a Google or a Microsoft one, while in the United States – an Apple or a Chromebook one (Google's digital tablet).

Many educational technology start-ups followed a similar sales strategy hoping that once computers and tablets are purchased, there is no turning back. Around the time of the pandemic, the quantity of laptops and tablets sent to primary and secondary schools in the United States almost doubled, reaching 26.7 million from 14 million.[13] This indeed sped the uptake of digital products and the digitization of education. Low regulatory barriers and the same sales approach have led to massive efforts to digitize the poor regions of the world, too. Projects like GIGA aim 'to connect every school to the internet and every young person to information, opportunity and choice'[14] and the Gateways Initiative to 'establish and iteratively improve national digital learning platforms with high quality, curriculum-aligned education resources'[15] to low-income countries. One may argue that in their effort to educate the world's children, tech companies are tying them first to their commercial products. This is not to deny just how remarkable computers and the internet are. But much of these efforts have been aggressively market driven and continuously infused with exaggerated claims about the omniscience and omnipotence of digital technologies.

But what is the guarantee that digital technologies purporting to improve education and empower learners do indeed contribute to their welfare, safety and future accomplishments? Who are the *strangers* behind the products and what gives them the licence to discuss education problems and how these should be solved? Who checks on them and validates their intent and their behaviour as software businesses? Despite new legislature in developing geographic regions like the European Union and the minefield of frameworks and guidelines for ethical and lawful practices addressing digital technology companies and their developers, we continue to see data misuse, overabundance of production – from the very hardware to software applications – and marketing hyperbole. What is needed to prevent such practices and ensure that digitizing education truly benefits all children equally? These are the types of questions this book seeks to answer especially for those coming into the field of education, digital media, childhood studies, pedagogy and education policy.

From the computer merchants to the data capitalists

Much of the thinking and arguments expressed in this book are preoccupied with how data has taken central place in policy discourse and decision-making. The possibilities from data are, indeed, vast. In the daily classroom, digital technologies have offered opportunities to identify what novel interventions work on making learning diverse and innovative. Many institutions, even in developed countries, are cautious about commercial platforms and the negative effects of data-driven decision-making and screen time. It is important to acknowledge the positive intentions of digital technologies and their potential to benefit teaching and learning. Data can provide valuable insights for teachers, aid resource allocation, and enhance creative teaching methods.

Data from different software and platforms can be assembled and re-purposed well beyond the 'schools' needs'. Algorithms can execute tasks that are associated with commercial objectives by engaging users and maintaining their attention more on the application or platform. That is, in fact, how radicalization can take hold,[16] which often starts online.[17] Selling drugs and promoting eating disorders and suicide are also done through algorithmic manipulation. These implications of digital technologies and data generated from their use do not necessarily relate to education. One could argue that such risks cannot occur on school premises. However, they can, and they do. That is why, for example, schools in the UK are obliged by law to provide duty under the Counter Terrorism and Security Act 2015 and have 'due regard to the need to prevent people from being drawn into terrorism'.[18] This shows that schools are responsible for much more than children's academic attainment. Schools are a whole ecological habitat with their physical, pastoral, social, academic, cultural, as well as political, financial, structural, organizational and now digital topographies, needs and challenges. As a friend in a large US district once told me, '[t]eaching and learning are only a fraction of what schools deal with'. A big part of schools' role as a habitat is to ensure children's safety. There is tremendous amount of effort put into safeguarding and for that a tremendous amount of governance to see it being implemented effectively. As education becomes increasingly mediated by digital systems, their functionalities are hard to understand and often impossible to know who is behind their development, administration and commercialization.

This makes it much harder to ensure that same ecological habitat is a safe and sacred place. Therefore, it also becomes essential to establish reliable structures that oversee and hold accountable the tech industry – the strangers – as their influence in education grows.

Media and much scholarly discourse have been long persistent in saying that children have 'special affinity' to digital technologies. They are 'digital natives'. They are 'tech savvy'. The digital evangelists speak convincingly about 'the *natural* affinity of children for computers [which] can be a powerful tool for teaching the information skills needed for life in an information society'.[19] Today, the same is said of the Digital Age. 'Digital learning will empower the poor' and 'revolutionise education'.[20] Over 800 business, education and non-profit leaders in the United States signed in 2022 a 'bipartisan message about opportunity and the American Dream' urging school governors and education leaders to 'update the K-12 curriculum in each state, for every school to have the opportunity to learn computer science' because, the letter states, it will help them to 'outperform in school, university and beyond'.[21]

But some questions escape this urgent demand: What happens to the US economy if the roughly 55 million students[22] do indeed outperform? Is that even a realistic target? Who will provide the computer science courses for all of them? Until recently much of the encouragement from industry was for educational institutions to teach children computer programming languages. It is unclear which language out of all and how does one choose over another? Is it even realistic to expect that all children will excel in coding or in mathematics, if an educational technology product claims that they will? It certainly is exciting to entertain the thought of such possibilities. And undoubtedly there are students who excel in such subjects as maths and computer science and generally have an affinity towards computers. But there are many others who do not. For some have affinity for dancing or building model airplanes. Some may also be exceptional swimmers or want to learn the violin. Certainly, most public schools cannot afford pools and what government funding goes into digitizing public schools will never be spent on equipping it with string instruments. Alas, that is what bipartisan messages like the 'American Dream' do: they influence the direction of the funds.

Digital technologies are also changing at an incredible speed. Bootstrapping a simple application today can take anyone minimal time to build; ignore scripts of code and create a simple maths, word game or shopping applications – all with a backend connected to hosting, data analytics, commercializing plugins and more. Even creating Metaverse spaces is available without necessarily knowing any programming languages. The user interfaces are like picking up Lego bricks and building virtual worlds – game rooms or classrooms for commercial exploitation or learning, whatever the heart desires.

Nvidia, a US technology company, offers free tools (some functionalities for now) for everyone to create with no understanding of code. With its AI functionalities Nvidia Canvas allows users to click using simple brushstrokes which the AI converts into life-like images. On the left-hand side of the digital canvas, one draws a grey vertical blob; on the right, the blob instantly transforms into a realistic rock next to a just-as-real-looking beach[23] (Figure 1.1). You squiggle with your finger on the left of the digital canvas and a realistic path in just as real field materializes (Figure 1.2).

Many of these tools come for free (so far). How come? How many of the educational technologies that schools use today are also built with 'free'

Figures 1.1 and 1.2 Nvidia Canvas transforms squiggles into realistic images.

components, hosted on third-party platforms and given for free to children? What does 'free' even mean? As a business, how do these providers sustain financially? Are they built with any consideration for children's privacy, learning needs and well-being? Is there a bigger hidden ambition by those who develop and promote these products as the prerequisite to success in the digital age? Most of these questions do not have a simple answer and one that fits all commercial set-ups. Instead, we see more policies suggesting what educational institutions should do about the digital realm they have been asked to transform into and what children should be equipped with. We also see an overwhelming number of guidelines, standards and frameworks for the EdTech and tech industries generally to guide their development and designs – then hope for the best.

Much public talk about digital marvels occupies the public attention more than about poverty despite poverty remaining the single most prevailing factor influencing education outcomes globally.[24] Poverty can affect important cognitive functions and lead to a self-reinforcing poverty trap, out of which there is little chance of exit.[25] Following the pandemic, the digitization of education was envisioned as the way forward, but it seemed more like adding Band-Aid on one's body, without knowing why, where or whether a Band-Aid is what is needed.[26] Substantial evidence has emphasized that the most impactful factors to school success are the home environment and even more so children's experiences in their early years of life. But this evidence does not typically mix with the usual discourse about digitizing teaching and learning.

Creating an 'ideal' adaptive environment thanks to EdTech and AI is the great sell today. As educator and philosopher Gert Biesta argues, 'the most effective way to achieve success in education would be to take children away from their parents at an early age and put them in' such 'an "ideal" environment'.[27] However, societies generally discourage this kind of intervention as the most effective. This means that there are no definitive, fixed methods for achieving success in school. Consequently, there is a lack of substantial 'basis for decisions about educational action'. The keyword in this, Biesta highlights, is therefore whether 'particular interventions are *desirable*'.[28]

The same can be asked about the digitization of educational processes. Is it *desirable* to provide digital tablets in the classroom if it leads to children getting distracted, subsequently needing the use of classroom management software for teachers to manage this distraction and attending to children's well-being in the digital environment? And so, *Taming EdTech*, the book's title, means that there is a need to educate EdTech companies about this key difference of what is desirable.

Inadequate governmental oversight of educational technology companies has allowed these commercial entities to acquire significant influence over pedagogy, regulations and norms within the education sector. The potential of such products to improve learning for everyone sounds great. But so far there has been little substantial evidence. Instead, a new ecology has emerged in schools – where datafication (turning all human actions into data) and surveillance are normalized.

To avoid the worst outcomes of total digital dependence and governance of education by proprietary algorithmic systems, this book proposes three arguments. The first one is empirical: educational technologies, digital systems and infrastructures are not necessarily improving education *equally* for *all* children and across all educational processes. I will draw from the growing evidence to support this argument. There are higher chances for children to lose in this digital experiment. In the digitized classroom, algorithms are also learners – invisible ones whom no one monitors, scrutinizes and holds accountable. Artificial intelligence is advancing rapidly, making it progressively complex to grasp and manage. There are higher chances for children to lose in this digital experiment for two reasons. First, because algorithms, as the invisible learners, at some point *will* become better trained and even harder to understand and control. See what happens with one experimental chatbot – the ChatGPT – launched only in November 2022. By December 2023, it is said to have been able to write classroom assessments,[29] develop apps, create investment term sheets and even draft legislation. What will it be capable of doing in a month's time or by the time this book is published? And second, because of the possibility that educational technologies may not become better tools for learning but yet another distraction just as the excessive information glut endlessly outpouring from digital media.

Mathematician Warren Weaver once said that explaining 'the strange way in which … the word "information" is used is "surprising but true that, from the present viewpoint, two messages, one heavily loaded with meaning and the other pure nonsense, can be equivalent as regards information"'.[30] By this logic mis- and dis-information is equal in terms of data, once transformed into electrical bits and used by large language models (LLMs) such as ChatGPT. At least there is no easy way to corroborate that as far as educational technologies are concerned; they make clear distinction between 'type' of information that they mediate and push into students. As librarian Jesse H. Shera has argued over fifty years ago, it has become impossible to distinguish between data systems designed for transmitting and receiving *signals* and *idea* systems meant for the shared exchange of *thought* through interpersonal communication.[31] Then how is a child, a teacher or even a policymaker supposed to know or distinguish between valuable information and beneficial tool and what is transmitted in the classroom via such ever more sophisticated systems?

And so, working on the side of caution may be a more reasonable way to go with the digitization of education. The assertion made by educational technologies that learning can be 'accelerated' and that children can be 'empowered' and turned into high achievers holds little significance until proven otherwise; until these systems are thoroughly examined; until the business intentions behind data processing and algorithmic manipulation are known. Until then, children and teachers should have alternatives to the data-driven automation of education.

The second argument pertains to the values of societies that are not only mirrored in education but are also anticipated to be nurtured through education. Improving education is not merely about efficiency, which is educational technologies' most prominent market offer. Instead, educators, policymakers and societies at large should ask: What kinds of generations educational institutions should be bringing up and creating to ensure that advancing technologies are put to good use? In that sense, we should add: Whom does the outpouring of education data and the digital technologies processing it serve and to what end? In the words of Shera, 'Data, data everywhere, but not a thought to think',[32] we should enquire: What is the outpouring of data *for*? In a sense therefore *Taming EdTech* seeks to find a calm space in the cacophony of data discourse and the perceived range of urgencies from digitizing and datafying educational processes to the more recent urgencies of 'confront[ing] the new realities'[33] of generative AI so we can see more clearly and make better judgements about how to prepare children to really benefit from such technologies.

I often hear and read work by distinguished scholars, domain experts and successful entrepreneurs who argue for the beneficial use of AI because human and machine can be so much better together. Collaborating with AI human and algorithm can write, play, design, learn better together and so on. Domain experts like the chess grandmaster Garry Kasparov[34] and separately the Google elites, former CEO, Eric Schmidt, and former director of Google Ideas, Jared Cohen, wrote resounding books[35] about how societies will benefit from thought-control motion technologies, efficiency and accelerated productivity. But the problem with such extravagant arguments is that a grand master still takes endless hours of reading and chess playing until he becomes one, although even the harshest of regimes cannot guarantee anything. And to create Google (as Sergey Brin and Larry

Page) and sell its story convincingly to the world still took some kind of schooling, strong social networks, good mentors, possibly privilege and a range of external factors like the right market climate and others.

Even if IBM Watson or any AI can enhance your chances with your next chess move, it is futile to play if you have no knowledge of chess whatsoever. The computer may teach you to play it, yes. But is that everything that a computer may be able to teach children? You still must know what you *want to do with* it. Just like learning *R Studio*, *JavaScript* and the numerous other fascinating computer languages, programs and applications. What then? This brings us to the question of the purpose of education which should be to teach children to think and develop ideas. Not merely to code and learn *R Studio* and so on. It is our thoughts and ideas in exchange with others that we begin to make a difference with the tools that become available to us, that we master (with or without a teaching machine's help). The question shifts away from *what* to think or work with to *why* we are thinking or doing something. Then as the old adage goes, the pen is mightier than the sword as long as one is literate and has an idea what to write; we will have an idea of what to code. Why we should bother is then a whole other story that can take one's lifetime to figure out.

And the third argument is about governance. In the case of the UK, there are sufficient institutions and mechanisms in place to demand greater accountability from the EdTech sector. Indeed, my contention is that if performativity, accountability and measurement are so ingrained in education systems like the Anglo-American and 'Global North' contexts, why not establish analogous systems capable of benchmarking and mandating accountability from EdTech and the businesses behind them?

Measurement and accountability have been articulated as the main catalyst for improving schools' 'outputs'[36] in both the United States and the UK. Measuring both students' performance and teachers' professionalism has been pushed since at least the 1970s. As Steven J. Ball elucidates, '[a] whole new lexicon of policy' was introduced 'to "apply" to education, as a way of rethinking it in terms of accountability, benchmarks, performance monitoring, national standards and school failure and so on'.[37] Schools are in constant fear of being labelled as 'failing', of being shut down. It is simply unfair to exempt digital technologies from responsibility when students are increasingly required to devote more time to using EdTech as part of their learning, especially if their 'performance' is affected. The responsibility around success should at least be shared. And so should accountability and therefore auditing.

Gaining a licence to play a part in education about what would work will not limit technological innovation, as one high-level official once told me.[38]

Governance is not about restrictions or prohibitions although some rules and conditions may be much stricter than they are now. For example, why should digital technologies label students or represent them into green, orange and red boxes (as I describe in Chapter 2) to express how well or poorly behaved they are in class? What good does this serve anyone? This is not only reductionist; it is unnecessary. In the bigger picture, however, this leads towards a *synthetic* world where children are increasingly being streamlined, categorized and reduced to what can only be likened to manipulatable items or, ironically, programmable machines.

The broader context is that we are transitioning from the digital age to the datafication age and from there – to an *Age of Synthetic Existence*. Here we will no longer speak of distinct human individuals with diverse cultures, rich histories and idiosyncrasies but about *personas* derived from well-defined data sets, each possessing 'its' own distinct ontologies and calculable profiles, all curated and governed by an algorithm on established geo-digital data markets.

One of the liabilities of data processing models, Theodore Roszak argued almost fifty years ago, is simplifying things for analytical purposes. All scientific models do that. The danger in this is that the model 'will become reified and be taken seriously'.[39] Taking data about students' behaviour and simplifying this into data models are capable to produce diagnoses, labelling them as 'depressed' or 'likely to cheat' or 'lonely'. The difference between having a bad day and being labelled as 'depressed' is not only huge it is inadequate. In a word, *Taming EdTech* is for protecting the human aspects of education.

Taming EdTech

The Shakespearian overtone about *Taming of the Shrew*, the play, is intended to imply the frivolous behaviour of much of the tech industry. Big Tech's famous 'move fast, break things' motto has propelled digitization in every domain including education. Much of this ethos has been speculative in nature yet very successful in that networked technologies have long become integral to both people's habitus and habits.[40] *Taming* is synonymous with many words that work well in articulating the objectives of this book. Taming can mean calming and controlling but also mastering, domesticating and educating. All these, combined, converge into *governing* EdTech and the businesses, designers and developers of such products.

Taming EdTech is hybrid in approach. It blends academic, practical and policy perspectives. The aim has been to still follow a familiar academic structure, which involves defining and analysing present issues, offering some critique and reflections, and trying to address a possible 'so what' with a 'what's next' proposal for practical solutions.

I am optimistic for education and its stakeholders based on my observations and interactions during this project. I am determined not to reach a point of indifference or harbour a sense of doom although confusion and pessimism occasionally catch up with me. Technologies are highly vulnerable. Planes will not fly; the banks will not work; and emails will not get sent if there is digital failure. Technologies are susceptible to error and crime. Why make education reliable on such vulnerable products? In education, they promise efficiency, choice and empowerment, things that often come to mean nothing to a struggling family where a child may not even have a bed to sleep on.[41]

As Neil Postman reminds us,[42] digital technologies provide great opportunities that overcome space and time where, say, little Mary can now study algebra in the middle of the night way beyond the confines of school if she wants to. But if we look deeper into these narratives, perhaps Mary is not up all night because she wants to polish on her algebra but because she is hungry or she does not know who her father is or if she does – where he is.

The book covers various aspects in education including policy, the EdTech industry and even educators' and students' voices, some evidenced from more recent scholarly work and my own research. As I write, I continuously return to the question of the purpose of education to critically examine how digital technologies align with it. However, this becomes harder as technologies encroach on education.

Digital data-intensive and often proprietary technologies have become so inextricably linked with education that policymakers and international organizations are willingly allowing schools, teachers and students to be validated by them. We now have whole digital ecosystems offering online schooling to children. As I will describe what many students, parents and teachers think, these new conditions are not always as conducive and motivational as they promise to be however great potentials and certainly numerous opportunities digital learning and collaboration promise.

The EU envisions the EdTech sector as the 'key driver in the European digital education ecosystem'.[43] A European alliance of EdTech companies positions its own members' importance by adding how EU acknowledges their 'immense potential to drive forward the digital transformation and innovation of European education and training. By creating innovative hardware, software, and content, the sector is transforming the way learning and teaching takes place'.[44] But who validates this *potential*? In response to this question, the book targets the EdTech businesses and calls on policymakers to tame both in how these businesses articulate their offerings and what they do in reality.

Theodore Roszak regards the digital merchants' narratives about computers as the Emperor's new clothes: 'overdressed in fabulous claims'.[45] Hoping on technologies' potential is as unproductive as is the fear that media, policymakers and equally EdTech themselves tend to emphasize that children will be excluded or disadvantaged if they lack understanding in the latest technology. On the contrary. In the pursuit of upholding fundamental human rights and liberties, EdTech should not create dependencies and environments for children where there is no exit and no alternatives for them.

Taming EdTech is a call for stricter scrutiny and better governance of the technologies permeating classrooms. '*Ed*' and '*Tech*' are capitalized because I look at the wider capabilities of digital technologies (general Tech) and not specifically those designed with education needs in mind. Microsoft manages students' assignments, communication and more, while its suite of products and many like it have been originally designed for managing enterprise supply chain distribution or business sales. I used to sell Microsoft Dynamics NAV twenty years ago when it was still called Navision (an enterprise resource planning software) and see its replication in many EdTech products. These undeniably facilitate a more efficient running of schools. However, a fine line is crossed along the way of running schools like businesses and turning them into businesses that struggle to survive, which has implications for the quality of education they actually 'produce'. 'Produce', in fact, becomes the central word in this transition of schools-run-as-businesses. As policy demands accountability for what is being 'produced', EdTech are not responding to it but are also making the transition between education and the world of work or labour market demands, thus providing opportunities to reframe education as an instrument for labour (re)production through the means of data and analytics. Therefore, from its client, schools become their product.

Which *Tech*?

The technologies I focus on, as Neil Selwyn puts it, are 'not simply a background feature or narrow technical concern'.[46] Ironically, they *are* simultaneously becoming a background feature. As in, not being noticed. This should make them of particular concern that is beyond the technical. Technologies are *disappearing* into the unknown critical conscience of its users and simultaneously into a relatively little scrutinized space where what they do and how they do it is obscured from public eye. The widespread adoption of digital technologies in all aspects of life has rendered them 'invisible', seamlessly blending them into the fabric of our world and almost making them a 'natural' element of our existence.

Mark Weiser calls invisible technology that which is 'so embedded, so fitting, so natural, that we use it without even thinking about it'.[47] In *The Computer for the 21st Century*, Weiser coined the word 'ubiquitous computing', saying that 'the most profound technologies are those that disappear. They weave themselves into the fabric of everyday life until they are indistinguishable from it'. This thinking led Weiser to spearhead a new era of computing by embedding software into various objects, ranging from coffeepots to ID badges, infusing them with interactive capabilities. What we now call the Internet-of-Things. However, not only have technologies been interweaved into the everyday fabric of society; they are also bending living and doing things down to their own conditions and limitations. Indeed, as Steve Jobs, the founder of the Apple computer, once put it: from a servant, the computer will become an 'agent'.[48] And agency computers wield – not on their own but through the strangers who design and program them.

This same agency and influence are steadily seeping into the classroom where technologies have the capacity to steer and influence what children should learn next, how they should learn and what sort of learners they are. As Weiser imagined, with ubiquitous computing there will be 'less strain and mental gymnastics'[49] because technologies will have infinite capacities to know 'that suit you looked at for a long-time last week because it knows both of your locations, and it can retroactively find the designer's name even though that information did not interest you at the time'.[50] These types of technologies are now available in class, following children's gaze, typing speed or pulse rate to infer about their motivation and control it. These are the technologies and their owners that should be tamed in what they promise will happen after they are unleashed.

These products are both software applications but also part of larger systems and connections. Together with the granular data they collect and process, they present complex digital infrastructures.

Occasionally, I will call them software applications or *apps*, but I may also refer to the digital systems or platforms which process and manipulate data to perform various tasks, instructions and functions. I will also discuss and even dare draw the larger digital infrastructures that emerge from these technologies as they stack together to open up greater computational capabilities. From singular use to larger enterprise resource management-type systems, technologies merge into more complex socio-technical synthetic ecosystems along with scientific expertise, data collection and processing, business interests, philanthropic as well as public support, all of which 'constitute[s] the new data-intensive learning sciences'.[51]

Taming EdTech also speaks of those systems that Shoshana Zuboff describes as instruments of surveillance capitalism. These instruments can be individual 'elements' of a larger 'well-functioning machine'. Each individual element of that machine 'is subordinated to the knowledge of the system as a whole'. Out of it, 'instrumentarian power' is born which 'aims to organise, herd, and tune society to achieve a similar *social confluence,* in which group pressure and computational certainty replace politics and democracy extenuations the felt reality and social function of an individualised existence'.[52] In other words, while digital technologies providing, enhancing or supplanting educational processes are the starting point and promise better educational experience in the future, they are not the entirety of it as they relate to the ambitions of those who *own* and can *control* them.

There is always a bigger picture. The technologies I examine are also unique in their computing power and the speed and direction at which they evolve. For instance, technologies specifically designed for education aim to 'individualize' the learning experience and 'adapt' it to each individual learner's styles, needs and contexts. The imagination can run far by drawing a picture of children in their own personalized bubble domes with the unique educational experience designed just for them. In fact, little imagination is needed since social media platforms and even basic search on Google already demonstrate the bubbles we are ascribed to, based on the data collected about us. The same models of 'personalization' are being applied through 'adaptive' technologies.

Yet many other questions emerge with regard to the ethical, societal and even developmental implications for children as a result of what all these types of technologies promise to *do.* Of the more frequently asked are: How do we ensure the privacy and data security of children using these technologies? But also, how might overreliance on technology for education affect in-person social interactions? Who supervises technology companies to verify that they do not exploit children's data for commercial purposes? How is algorithmic bias prevented? Educational technologies deliver content, connect, communicate, assess, organize, analyse, recommend, predict, monitor, assign, manage, store, surveil and more. Who determines which products will mediate children's education? Who is held responsible if or when these products fail? How are educational technology providers governed?

As Audrey Watters argues[53] in *Teaching Machines: The History of Personalised Learning,* there is no need to write a lengthy anthology of all the theories and 'teaching machines' or technologies that are applied to educational settings. Instead, I reserve this space to discuss the *stranger* that has walked into public education, to critically examine how education can transform for the worse *if* there is no scrutiny and proper oversight of its intent, capabilities and fast advances.

Taming EdTech also means calming down the sense of urgency to digitize education and playing catch-up with technological acceleration. Learning takes time. Ask any violinist, chess player or dancer. Schools are also a place to socialize, to learn to collaborate, to cooperate and to co-exist with others. Technologies would not 'care' if none of this happens as children are placed in front of a device with a learning app. And so *taming EdTech* should also mean educating the EdTech industry about these fundamental lessons children should not miss out on. As Robert Fulghum says in *All I Ever Needed I Learned in Kindergarten*,[54] it is the most basic but the most important lessons that children learn in kindergarten. They learn about sharing, playing fair and cleaning up their own mess and more. Certainly, many of these habits would take longer to internalize, possibly well beyond the kindergarten years. And precisely because learning takes time, it is imperative to reduce the prevailing sense of urgency to play catch-up with the tech industry. Instead, there is a constant rush and the perception of immediate necessity surrounding the global AI race – an acute need for upskilling, reskilling and 'lifelong' learning as though what one knows is never good enough.

That *Taming EdTech* calls for better governance of EdTech does not mean that the message is intended for a narrow group of policymakers. On the contrary, chances are that a typical politician would pay attention to the problems for an average of three to five years, although according to the speed at which technologies evolve, it may be significantly less than that. The book instead speaks to the communities of educators, graduate and undergraduate students and research scholars to critically think about the quality and sovereignty of education being subjected to algorithmic manipulation and control and what lax governance of them may mean for quality education and human futures.

EdTech has so far been permeated by a neoliberal governance specifically in the Anglo-American contexts that much of the arguments of this book stem from. The predominant focus in such governance has so far been on free marketplace and maximizing efficiency.[55] Lax governance and prioritizing the well-being of the market have also led to the influx of digital products and with it, constant data extraction, the normalization of digital surveillance, bias and discrimination, cyber *in*security, overreliance on technology, privacy loss and more.

Good governance exists – be that in one's family, in a business organization or in a school. However, it takes more than drafting policies and designing guiding principles. In my experience as one who works at the intersection of academia and industry in the context of governance often finds it challenging to align all stakeholders and foster collaboration with industry. For instance, EdTech providers do not see the commercial incentives to prioritize things such as cybersecurity in their product designs.[56] On the other hand, academia tends to view the challenges of digitizing education from various angles and prioritize different criticalities, say, pedagogy over cybersecurity. Funding has also often been predominantly concentrated around the murky 'what works' question, as in 'what works in education with EdTech'. The so-called randomized controlled trials (RCTs) are well known in the field and increasingly attracting private, non-governmental philanthropic and public funding.[57] But 'what works' has undermined the assessment of fundamental requirements related to technological security, data privacy and human rights considerations, even the cultural, individual and collective social impact of these technologies.

It remains a challenge to have industry allow external evaluators or auditors to assess their inner workings, inspect software and performance before they are launched in classrooms. What company is ready to strip itself down and show all its flaws and liabilities? Having said that, there is much more evidence for the need to build trust through transparency and greater scrutiny. I collaborate with market evaluation organizations in the UK and the EU. Their networks comprise over 4,000 schools in the UK and across the EU and are advocating for a reliable assessment that independently checks which products prioritize student data privacy, safety and well-being. That schools seek greater transparency and safety verification about the technologies they adopt and invest in can only attest to the fact that any existing governance of the EdTech market is insufficient. A recent report by UNESCO[58] confirmed the fragmented governance, too, having analysed the state of the digitization of education globally.

Voices and views

I write this book drawing from various roles I occupy, including research at industry level and schools; engaging with policymakers, international educational organizations; participating in working groups, publicly funded projects relating to the digitization of education, education data governance, digital content,[59] EdTech procurement, and children's well-being in a digitized education.[60] *Taming EdTech* is the result of fieldwork with schools, teachers, students, policymakers, parents, data privacy officers, legal scholars, data privacy activists, researchers and privacy experts, data scientists, as well as with EdTech companies and software developers from all over the world. Additionally, research and development with a European Horizon project have been instrumental in enhancing my understanding of data privacy and security risks and challenges (broadly and in educational settings), in developing frameworks on contextual social, ethical, human rights and accessibility requirements for building technologies that prioritize children's needs and well-being. All of this work has led to this book and its key message: that EdTechs must be licensed to operate, and technological scrutiny is highly necessary to protect children's basic human rights to education and well-being.

My academic background is in media and communications, while I have also occupied most of the past ten years in understanding, researching and working at the crossroads of education, policy, children, AI and EdTech. The field of media and communications however is useful to examine how thanks to digital ubiquity and connectivity, we witness a constant outpouring of information. This is an important point to make in education because information has increasingly become indiscernible from knowledge, which is problematic especially when discussing information access and knowledge as data and power in educational settings.

My attention has also been on understanding how children articulate their thoughts and ideas through the use of digital technologies. In classrooms, I have witnessed how children's voices are not always given attention by teachers. And so, I have seen digital technologies as tools for communication, for creative self-expression and for self-navigated discovery beyond the confines of curriculum or classroom.[61] Technologies can be valuable tools for children to convey their thoughts and ideas creatively. Technologies can help children with disabilities;[62] provide global reach and, in Ivan Illich's words – enable convivial learning.[63] In that regard, education data too can be harnessed for good as it can advance education theory, optimize resources, enhance efforts around school safety and more. I have witnessed first-hand how data helps teachers navigate through their pedagogic methodologies or how safeguarding is achieved with excellence.

On the other hand, as more EdTech integrate into school activities – from apps that survey children about their thoughts and feelings, monitor their content and behaviour – the 'right to remain silent' may transpire as the best option for students under constant surveillance.[64]

For healthy development, children require an environment that protects them from harm but also allows for exploration and discovery even with certain level of risk. However, much more effort is needed to prevent the risks digitization and data extraction can pose on the developing child. Software that scans students' Microsoft and Google accounts and homework, combined with machine learning, aims to detect 'kids in crisis'[65] promising timely interventions for those in or causing trouble. The risks of harms from such surveillance practices themselves remain an afterthought[66] – their effectiveness unclear.

I also write with experience from the corporate world where I have savoured a wide spectrum – from working for commercial software companies (over 20 years ago) to setting up my own media organization and publishing magazines including one dedicated to youth (which unfortunately did not survive the 2008 economic crisis[67]). The priorities of the corporate world contrast sharply with those in education. Additionally, I am a parent governor of a public secondary school in the UK. According to the GovernorHub Knowledge Body that leads, manages and sets the standards around such roles, a parent governor is one whose role is 'to bring a parental perspective to the issues discussed … no different from other governors'.[68] In that regard, effective governance 'provides strategic direction and control to schools … It creates robust accountability, oversight and assurance for their educational and financial performance and is ambitious for all children and young people to achieve the very best outcomes'.[69] The role has helped me understand the inside-out of how a school is run to a certain degree, the achievements, challenges and the huge human effort that it takes to maintain schools safe and conducive environments for children and young people to learn and thrive. The role also carries responsibilities not least because of the continuous training governors are expected to undertake including safeguarding, data privacy, cybersecurity, ethical, financial, academic, pedagogic, organizational and governance – amounting to a full-time job. The role is also an eye-opener.

A big part of the book's rationale is drawn from this role to advocate that EdTech providers should be met with similar governance that expects of them accountability, training and commitment to quality education and the safety, privacy and security of children (their data and futures). EdTech providers are the strangers, just like a school governor, entering the school gates. Unlike a governor, however, they have commercial interests in education. Unlike a governor, they do not undergo much scrutiny or educational training or at least there is no easy way to know.

Besides my voice and experience, the book brings the voices of other experts who say and demonstrate what is known and what is not about the digitization of education. For instance, it is not known what training EdTech providers' staff undergoes as much as it is not known where their staff resides, who accesses the education data their product generates, who is the helpdesk and back-office management, and are they even available for support or questions? Schools recently complained about faulty Oxford entrance tests, criticizing the online assessment platform as a 'complete shambles' with inadequate support and non-functional helplines (although this newspaper omits to name the product).[70]

The biggest technology companies like Google, Microsoft, Amazon, Apple, Meta and many others providing educational digital products (for instance, Class Dojo, Naviance, PowerSchool, Nearpod, Blackboard and others) operate internationally and are used by millions of students and teachers. They provide insight and navigate the learning experience and decisions. But what insight do we – on the user's end – have about the products and the people behind them? We knew that Google, for instance, had an ethicist but then she was fired[71] for saying that their AI was biased. Facebook, too, had a product manager who said that the company uses 'profits over safety'.[72] Some of the biggest companies like Facebook reportedly have engineers who do not even know what they do with people's data.[73] What about the small EdTech companies who may not even have an administration office? Such insight is necessary in order to have some understanding of the systems and how data is managed but also knowledge about the organizational ethos, personal values or business ambitions. Such knowledge is not seen as necessary competencies or skills for students and teachers but as a way of governing these systems and their owners in light of what they are doing or promising to do in schools.

What we do know from research and end-user voices is that their products are starting to influence educational processes – teaching, learning, judgement around attendance and judgement around children's well-being and personality; teachers' decision-making; and even children's futures! What we know is that these strangers make grand promises about improved educational outcomes and even future job prospects for those students who follow the educational pathways as suggested by algorithmic optimization systems.

What we also know is that often policy decisions are also influenced by these promises and without any thorough checks and balances between the promise and the reality in the classroom. We have come to a point where EdTech are acting as the de facto pedagogic authorities in education, having a central role to the extent that schools having electric power cut end up unable to carry on schooling as usual. This book reflects on these voices – from research, privacy, policy, industry, users – and speaks with critical voice for better governance.

Digitizing education should not be a zero-sum game – why this book?

The goal of *Taming EdTech* remains on the practical. I aim to bring many of the concerns around EdTech that are increasingly raised through scholarship over the past few years. Having these resources in one place can serve as a practical starting point for practitioners, policymakers, EdTech developers, and both undergraduate and graduate students to explore, compare, and build on with further research. The products and the problems I describe may not have a long shelf life, and so they are not the sole focus alone. For that, the book has a second objective. It advocates for stricter scrutiny over the private sector of digital offerings.

At this secondary level, the book has the objective, as its title suggests, to tone down the market hyperbole around digitizing education – whatever that really means. The tech industry has been effective in conveying a convincing tale about the digital age and the urgency about children needing to be equipped for it. Its most avid evangelists promise prosperity and abundance *only if* children embrace the digital through digital learning, and digital, AI and data literacies.

Policy measures and supranational effort through public-private partnerships have centred around delivering digital accessibility as the means to support underprivileged populations and bridging inequality gaps. Digital accessibility has become synonymous with equality – access to EdTech, with the right to education. Being part of the *Digital Age* has become a precondition to 'expand economic opportunities for everyone';[74] for 'inclusive and accessible digital education';[75] the main means to participate in the 'digital economy' and to 'lead in digital spaces'. This sounds like a zero-sum game. It sounds as though without digital technologies the entire opposite of inequity, poverty and exclusion awaits. One would hope not.

The first task of this book is to describe the risks of harm in the absence of stricter scrutiny of EdTech. Chapter 2 contextualizes the realities, promises and challenges of the digitized classroom but also the bigger picture that is forming as larger data systems, interoperability and AI capabilities enable complex analytics, prediction and adaptive learning.

Chapter 3 examines the digital infrastructure encapsulation not only by Big Tech companies offering hosting, cloud, education and AI services but by a wide variety of EdTech products and advancing digital services, some of which have been recommended by governments[76] globally. The growing dependence on such systems suggests that they gain powerful access to important societal structures and processes. They mediate all educational processes – from the delivery of content to assessing and monitoring students and teachers, to their greater socio-engineering capabilities.[77] These capabilities draw a much bigger picture about education and societies which is not entirely driven by what is desirable and beneficial to them.

Educational processes have already been subject to automation for some time. However, Chapter 4 unpacks how advancing systems in education propose automation in more advanced and unprecedented ways. This chapter asks how technologies that process education data produce 'insights' and suggested career pathways, grades and even labels about students' current well-being or what they are likely to do next.

Data-intensive algorithmic systems have the capacity to override human decision-making including children's rights and freedoms to develop autonomy, personhood and character and to have the choice to opt out of such systems and still have access to education. This chapter is based on substantial desk research of national policies and strategies around cradle-to-career longitudinal data collection and aligning industry demands with education, white papers, and marketing discourse, in the US,[78] the UK[79] and EU[80] contexts. I map the techno-solutionist 'stack' that is transforming education. This 'solution stack' envisions aligning industry labour market demands with the 'skills of the future'. National policies aim to standardize data collection with the goal to achieve digital credentialing, align learning to workforce needs, and scale the talent ecosystem. However, these policy strategies can hit the less privileged and immigrant families particularly hard.

Drawing from human rights,[81, 82] Chapter 5 focuses on children's voices about EdTech and the digitized classroom.[83] Technologies' capabilities along with policy drives for data collection have led to the increased data harvesting from every experience a child has in the classroom. This, however, is a contentious reality in which policymakers demand more data while digital technology businesses respond by providing it.

Chapter 6 recalls the good intention of School, the purpose of education and the importance of childhood. Particular attention is made to school governance structures[84] as spaces where good practices can be derived for governing the digitization of education.

With critical view of current EdTech procurement and governance in the Anglo-American and other contexts in the Global North, Chapter 7 reviews the growing number and variety of governance proposals, standards, frameworks, toolkits, directives and laws[85] addressing the digital technology sector. This minefield of proposals and frameworks has not been helpful for either industry or educational institutions. Instead, they have created a patchwork of efforts in which teachers and students are often not clear what products they use, how they are beneficial or not, and how their privacy, safety and futures are protected.

Chapter 8 seeks to provide some answers about how to fix a fragmented governance of the digitization of education. I make reference to two specific systems as a point of reference: education governance itself and the online gambling industry. First, I worked briefly in the gambling industry as a cloud provider when it was in its nascence back in 2000s. Today, in many jurisdictions the sector is highly regulated with strict licensing regimes and scrutiny being imposed. The sector is lucrative (just as the EdTech industry is) and carrying ranges of risks for people (just as digitizing education is for children). Yet both sectors are facing different barriers to entry and oversight. I have chosen to draw this parallel when thinking about how to respond consciously to the digitization of education. The second reference is made with education governance itself. The audit culture in which schools operate should encompass the EdTech sector and subject it to rigorous actionable measures and scrutiny just as educational institutions have been a subject to for a long time.

2

Digitizing the Classroom: What Is the Problem?

EdTech platforms offer 'magic' for everyone

NetSupport School is a classroom management system, which, according to its website, serves over 9 million users globally.[1] It advertises itself as 'classroom and corporate software ... award-winning solutions for schools and businesses worldwide'. The very confluence of school and business is already problematic, but more on this later. A small deviation: There are many platforms with NetSupport School's provisions. Here, as with other applications I describe throughout the book, I have used the so-called walkthrough method,[2] which is an established genre of cultural practice with both pedagogical and commercial value.[3] The method involves directly interacting with a software to explore its technological functions but also its pedagogic and even cultural underpinnings through design and functionality to understand how these direct and influence end-user experiences. Vernacular walkthroughs unveil granular details about a software. Pertinent to the accelerated transformation of education through digital technologies is to walk through the individual software. Walkthroughs allow for capturing the nuanced narratives, the discursive and ideological subjectivity that may exist in designs and operations. The method helps to identify possible bias and injustice that may be baked in these products as a result. It also allows to contextualize any critical pedagogic evaluation of how these products shape teaching and learning. Doing so, I do not single out a specific product for any particular reason except that along with another product I describe later these products serve to describe some of the emerging challenges in public education.

Some of NetSupport School's features, its website promotes, include saving time, reducing costs and increasing security. To save time in the classroom the platform 'equips' students with a single click to provide their work files and get instant feedback with auto-marked tests. NetSupport School imagines the classroom entirely through its solutions. Video tutoring, manuals and other free material flood its corporate website and YouTube to explain, describe and convince the future user, teachers mainly, that this is the right tool for managing their classes and students. In one of them, its chief executive officer describes how the teacher is represented with their screen, and so are the students through their devices on the teacher's screen. Starting a new class is easy 'with a click; a new Class Wizard will automatically record the *relevant information*' and 'as if by magic we have some lesson objectives added'.[4] A power mode allows the teacher to turn on or off her students' devices. 'Magically', the voice goes, there is now a room created with several devices and students represented as 'thumbnails' on the teacher's screen. Now that all students are 'available in the classroom', there is an interactive monitoring mode. The teacher can control or 'keep an active eye' on what the students are doing at any time on their screens. A feature called 'student feedback mode' allows teachers to 'gauge feedback from the students' by using 'several visual indicators'. Students can self-report how they 'feel' about a topic and choose between a green, yellow, orange and red emoji, each representing a feeling or confidence level. A digital dashboard presents the compiled feedback with colourful bar graphs. Most responses are in green as shown in the video, with recently updated features.[5] The voiceover cheerfully reacts: 'lovely, lovely … so far the majority of my class which is lovely to hear from me as a teacher are feeling really quite great but I'm being mindful that three of my class are actually feeling a bit low for *whatever reason*'[6] (emphasis added).

What can the teacher do with such options? The tutorial reassures, the teacher can control their classroom activities in 'real time'. Yet the capacity of the software to allow the teacher to conduct such operations 'real time' such as lock students' screens takes a few seconds to update, the tutorial clarifies. A minor delay: *almost* real time for something that is otherwise already happening in the physical real-time classroom. The functionalities of this classroom management platform are almost endless: it allows for keyboard monitoring; targeting inappropriate word lists when students type, where words can immediately be highlighted to the teacher as 'green-target' or red, as in inappropriate. The platform also allows to 'reward' students for good behaviour. Students' voice and audio can be recorded and monitored, and all the coursework or task exchange between students and teacher is rationalized as though all students are one person with the same abilities and characteristics. NetSupport School can also connect to any devices and allow student information system (SIS) integration via platforms such as ClassLink, One Roster or Google Classroom. Each of these is a proprietary commercial product.

The second product I describe here is Blackboard, a learning management platform. In 2020 Blackboard merged with Anthology, a provider of software solutions for higher education. Anthology, itself a company that emerged through the merger of three other EdTech businesses, Campus Management, Campus Labs and iModules, claims to have over 150 million learners,[7] educators and administrators using their services. Anthology is also owned by Veritas Capital, a private-equity firm which invests mainly in technology-focused products and services, including ones for government and commercial enterprises globally.

Veritas Capital has a long history and invests exclusively in companies that support government-influenced markets and specifically in areas such as aerospace, defence, education, energy, health care, national security and software. Their assets approximate $45 billion. Their portfolio includes not only Anthology, and now Blackboard, but also companies like one of the 'big four' in the publishing of educational materials Huffington Mifflin Harcourt,[8] including companies that specialize in big data analytics.

In 2022, the Federal Trade Commission (FTC) heard from a parent[9] how students and parents are rarely notified of corporate mergers or what happens to children's data in such cases. Students, the parent attested, do not have a choice when an EdTech decides to or is bought by or merges with another private company. The amount of sensitive data such companies acquire is immense and with long-term commercial potential. In that regard, what happened to the previously collected student data when Blackboard merged with Anthology is anyone's guess.

As an EdTech platform Anthology, similarly to NetSupport, provides near 'magic'. It asks: 'What if you could meet each of them [students] exactly where they are on their unique journey, deliver the personalized experiences that set them up for success, and make the best decisions for your institution's future?'[10] Anthology calls itself a 'holistic EdTech ecosystem', which includes a customer relationship management (CRM), SIS and a learning management system (LMS) put together. It is useful to provide some more definition to what all these systems are before proceeding. These are all software systems used by schools to manage and maintain relations with students, parents and various other stakeholders. However, these systems have long existed before, and they derive from commercial enterprise management.

CRM systems like Salesforce, for instance, are intended for managing customer relationships and sales processes. Today many of these are integrated into managing schools, staff and students. Project management tools (PMTs) like Asana and business intelligence and analytics platforms like Google Data Studio and Microsoft Power BI have all been at the service of industries and for processing business data. There is a whole business notion of value creation for education through software development. Much of these technologies are a mash-up of other existing 'building blocks' – technological components – which can be put together like in a jigsaw puzzle. The premise is that if they help in, say, the pharmaceutical or car manufacturing industry or support companies with maintenance tracking or analysing customer experience and production planning, and if schools are seen as such enterprises where maintenance and a production need optimization, then any software that helps produce cars will help produce 'educated students'.

CRMs allow to track interactions, communications and engagement with the various education stakeholders. Others like SISs are database-driven software applications for managing student-related data such as student enrolment, class schedules, grading, attendance, demographics and more. LMSs are also software applications for managing and delivering course material. LMSs are used both in educational settings and corporate training environments (like CRMs) as explained in Chapter 1. Learning management systems (LMSs) provide a single point of contact and access to course materials and interaction with teachers and students to manage homework and assignments. Anthology offers all these in one. The data that streams from each application is then utilized through a complex layering of computational capabilities – or 'intelligence'.

Anthology consolidates education data from various silos and integrates it with layers of reporting, analytics, insights, and predictive capabilities. That is, the company's ambition is to go beyond the access to data by educators and schools. Their layers build from data access to contexts whereby summarized data is available to students and instructors. The 'context' is now created and redefined by the platform, the collected data and the platform's computational capacities. The top layer is the 'intelligence' layer where data is converted into suggestions, recommendations and automating specific actions. The granular data collection, at the primary level of the system, builds into a so-called 'data lake' – a common objective in the tech realm to build centralized repositories which can store and process data in its native format and coming from different silos or applications.

Whatever applications students use, 'ideally' the generated data floods into this 'data lake'. Data sources can be students' mobile phones, third-party partners or even plagiarism prevention service providers like SafeAssign (also offered by Anthology). All this data pouring into the data lake is then translated into 'canonical' data that is a standardized, 'authoritative' representation of data. Put otherwise, data becomes authority in and of itself. Once that transformation is done and all the data is made available from different silos, it is turned into a canonical data model; algorithmic 'magic' can be developed and deployed. Meanwhile, the platform provides dashboards, operational or integrated reporting, visualizations and direct access to data – all sold as students' and teachers' 'benefit'. Now this layered digital mechanism can offer 'answers' to institutional questions such as what kinds of alternative programs and activities or materials should be provided to students depending on where they are at their learning. What kinds of alternative assessment methods could be developed for individual students? And how can the correlations between offline access and students' attainment levels be utilized as 'intelligence' to influence decision-making?

NetSupport School and Anthology are two examples of the wide variety of data-extractive systems available on the market and already integrating into public educational systems. Many others demonstrate similar functions and ambitions. Such products enable data collection, aggregation and processing for tracking, analytics and predicting not only academic outcomes but also behaviour. With these two examples, the digitized classroom is becoming a new playing field with new actors and decision-makers.

However, there are two main problems with digitizing the classroom with products like these. First, they have accelerated the digitization and datafication of education, but these are only an initial stratum of a larger socio-technical *stacking* upon which algorithmic capabilities are layered with promises for *prediction* with *precision*. This larger digital infrastructure *captures* education and therefore holds a powerful instrument that can shape and influence societies. Chapter 3 delves into this more deeply. And second, this larger digital infrastructure presents substantial implications for children's fundamental human rights, autonomy and futures. Succinctly put, this reconfiguration of education can impoverish children's education.

The bigger problems with digitizing the classroom

In *Education and Technology* Neil Selwyn[11] introduces the wide variety of definitions of the word 'technology'. From its simplest form – tools that aim to enhance or improve our lives in some way – to the more advanced where technology is more than just machinery and material artefacts. As with the internet, Selwyn argues, people do not discuss it as the 'copper wires, fibre-optic cables, wireless connections, servers and processors that constitute the material networks that support the internet'.[12] They are typically referring to the activities they participate in, the social cultures and values associated with them. Similarly, conversations about EdTech tend to focus primarily on their pedagogic contribution and its value creation in education. This prevalent attention on the pedagogic 'what works' aspects obscures the significant infrastructural reorganization and reconfiguration happening behind the scenes.

Digitizing education resembles an iceberg. The visible part includes interfaces and features what students and teachers see and interact with.

Beneath this lies a vast and complex structure whose magnitude is hard to determine. These infrastructures express new forms of power, which research defines as 'platformization'.[13] Platformization signifies the integration of digital platforms into various economic sectors and aspects of life, along with the reshaping of cultural practices and perceptions around these structures.[14] However, as Gulson, Sellar and Webb[15] argue, these digital infrastructures also create new modes of governance.[16] They enable larger data assemblages which derive from the capabilities of digital products to come together under a common denominator through data *interoperability* and common data standards or common languages of understanding among different data systems. Larger data assemblages from various applications have the capability to generate 'data lakes', the same ones Anthology aims at, and 'super-platforms' with ever greater computing power layered on top (Figure 2.1).

EdTech and data infrastructures such as in Figure 2.1 have the potential for larger data assembling and powerful computing capabilities. The data flow is asymmetrical. Some actors in the network have more access to the data and control over how it can be used than others. Such data assemblages and processing can reach well beyond education. This is why the acquisition of tech companies by entities like Veritas Capital, Google, Amazon and Microsoft raises significant concerns regarding the knowledge and power they amass. Such infrastructures do not merely enhance or supplement educational processes. They change entirely how education is delivered, governed, imagined and controlled. It is anyone's guess what any of that would look like. They impose new norms and prospects for children.

Gulson, Sellar and Webb define these infrastructures as 'the active form that combines people, networks, algorithms, and computational capacities that provides the material and non-material support for synthetic

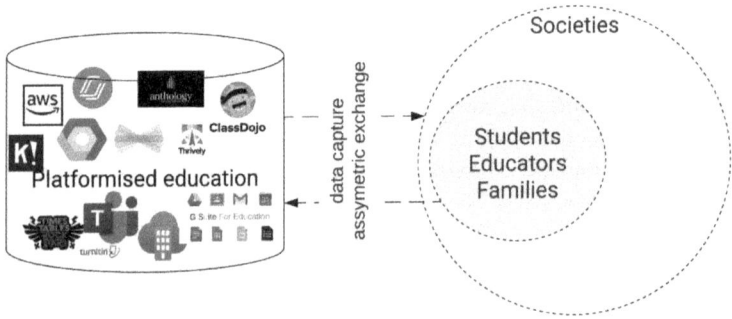

Figure 2.1 Digitized education becomes part of larger digital infrastructures.

governance'.[17] That is, this is a new form of governance that combines both the human and the digital to the extent that 'new modalities of digital governance overlap with network governance, which increasingly relies on new linkages between, and movements and analyses of, data'.[18] These new forms of education governance invite a wider range of participants including from industry, which shows how they 'become new governance players and part of decision-making processes in education, often in quite opaque ways'.[19]

The objective with Figure 2.1 is not to dive into purely technical specifications of the digitized education. However, references are helpful to visualize the 'iceberg' structures. Broader examples of software stacking and data interoperability enable the development of data pipelines and software-as-a-service mechanisms whereby a 'digital identity' is being replicated, copying the original entity and its structures (be that a factory, a business enterprise or a school).

These structures already exist. As mentioned earlier, CRMs and similar software have been serving businesses for a long time now. While these enterprise resource planning and management products are much more sophisticated today, they largely have what looks like data factory-logic designs. Take Palantir Technologies. The American big data intelligence company,[20] and its Foundry software-as-a-service (SaaS) platform, is an example of data factory logic. Foundry is an end-to-end solution for data-driven decision-making. The reasoning behind this is that the detailed data output will enable the advancement of AI, analytics and predictive capabilities, which in turn will inform decision-making, even at a preemptive level.[21]

Palantir Foundry integrates a suite of data and technological solutions to analyse, predict, develop and train ML and AI and enable real-time alerting and dynamic decision-making. In one design, Palantir Foundry demonstrates the development of a digital twin of a factory[22] whose data pipelines make up the massive data system with its AI and ML capabilities. Digital twins, the logic goes, can be created for schools as well as students and from there models for predictive analytics can be developed to provide sufficient insight to guide dynamic curriculum development. These logics are detailed in Chapter 3.

Frické[23] argues that it is inherently wrong to assume that data 'can serve as the bedrock of all else'[24] such as of information or even of wisdom. Within this data factory logic design, the derived information can be just about anything. Who says which information has any value? How will such insight be used? These capabilities quickly gain them special pedagogic roles in the classroom. However, there are concerns with these systems and their claims. I name some of them next.

Privacy loss

One of the concerns that has preoccupied child's rights advocates, legal scholars and others has been on the loss of privacy in the digital realm which children also want to enjoy. In School (capitalized since I use it as a common understanding of a place where children are brought to be educated), the growing data collection has intensified and with that the risks of privacy loss through surveillance or 'dataveillance',[25] enabling control, diminishing personal freedoms and rights and creating information asymmetries. More broadly, datafication is also seen as a form of colonizing populations as the captured personal information can enable their control.[26]

While the narratives of personal data anonymization and deidentification continue to hold false promises,[27] these are far from able to safeguard individual privacy.[28] Meanwhile, such risks have had little effect over the decision-making of governments globally[29, 30] as they let industries that enable datafication into public education without regulatory or licensing regimes and clear procurement standards.[31]

Against some of these risks emanating from datafication, growing scholarship has come to propose data and privacy literacy curricula, to support self-data protection and self-determination, personal data literacies and models for social data and privacy.[32] Still others have suggested that schools should teach data and privacy literacy as a skill.[33] Yet a sort of 'teach but not practice' hypocrisy emanates from these proposals when, in reality, schools and policymakers allow constant student data exchanges with thousands of EdTech businesses, authorities and other third parties. Moreover, such proposals can only be rendered ineffective as sophisticated digital systems advance further into education.

Here I wish to refer to two theoretical frames to support my arguments about the emanating issues with private digital systems gripping public education. The first one is Pierre Bourdieu's (re)production in education,[34] which can explain digital systems as ones beginning to occupy a certain *pedagogic power* through their products, which mediate educational processes. This pedagogic power accumulates through *pedagogic action* and *pedagogic work*. These are expressed by the ability of digital systems to extract student data for algorithmic decision-making. The pedagogic action and pedagogic work legitimize the datafication processes and raise EdTech as *pedagogic authority*. As such, digital systems can have the capacity to legitimize their own pedagogic dominance and therefore influence what will be (re)produced in education. Crucially, it is on schools' grounds that this new pedagogic authority emerges. As such, educational systems broadly do not recognize or do not present an honest account of the power dynamics at play.

Bourdieu's theory of symbolic violence lends itself to parallel that the EdTech data-dependent products become

> the delegation which establish[es] the pedagogic action, in addition to a delimitation of the content inculcated, a definition of the mode of inculcation (the legitimate mode of inculcation) and of the length of inculcation (the legitimate training period), which define the degree of completion of pedagogic work considered necessary and sufficient to produce the accomplished form of the habitus, i.e., the degree of cultural attainment (the degree of legitimate competence) by which a group or class recognizes the accomplished man.[35]

Moreover, with their advancement into education, digital systems begin to emerge as the pedagogic power with technomonopolistic tendencies.[36] That is, they can grow from a mediator of education to an influencer in the (re)production of education to a monopolist through the 'expansion of [data] extraction, positioning as a gatekeeper, convergence of markets, and enclosure of ecosystems'.[37]

To this end, I adopt a second concept from which my arguments originate. This one directly addresses the disillusion and even hypocrisy that emerges as digital products conflate with schools' functions. Bringing Freire's critical pedagogy, I argue that digital systems present a hidden *pedagogy of oppression*, which 'begins with the egoistic interests of the oppressors (an egoism cloaked in the false generosity of paternalism) and makes of the oppressed the objects of its humanitarianism'.[38] A sort of oppressive structure begets from such arrangements when privacy loss as the 'new normal' of a datafied school conflates with digital technologies' commercial project for it. Losing one's privacy on privately owned data structures can lead to children's dispossession of their own rights and freedoms in a supposedly sacred space for development of free thought that are meant to be the educational institutions. The privacy loss in itself cannot automatically cause oppressiveness, losing privacy to data systems with their opaque capacity to nudge, steer and control the student can.

Much ink is spilled about data privacy[39] and the risks of harms from data privacy loss.[40, 41, 42] Here I do not intend to make an exhaustive account of why it is important and to whom. Within the context of educational institutions, the intention is to emphasize privacy as a deterministic *condition* for a growing child who is learning basic freedoms and rights within a *milieu* – that are public schools – where these freedoms and rights are practised.

Privacy plays a critical role in the development of feelings, ideas and identity.[43] Privacy is also an incubator to development of thought, speech and association. Neil Richards[44] calls this intellectual privacy a 'zone of protection that guards our ability to make up our minds freely'.[45] As schools become wrapped by datafication systems, they lose this zone of protection. The loss of privacy then leads to a wide range of risk[46] whose sheer volume begs the question: In what kind of new classroom climate do children learn?

As a condition, privacy also enhances individual autonomy. Informational and decisional privacy safeguard this autonomy by ensuring that one can control who has access to their personal information and to what extent[47] and one has the right against unwanted interference with their own decisions and actions.[48] Without the condition of privacy, an individual cannot enjoy self-exploration and self-determination.

Data collection from a child's assignment, a drawing or conduct by an EdTech application not only risks pinning the child into a data-derived category but also shifts the agentic power from the child to the data systems and their inferencing and surveillance. The data inferencing and surveillance capabilities present a form of oppression that is both at individual (how one practises self-expression and interprets what is learned) and structural levels (inferences derived from data influence curriculum decisions and what one should learn). Adopting these forms of education by schools acknowledges them as legitimate power.

Then there are other more complex aspects following the data utilization such as nudging capabilities. Digital nudging[49] and hyper-nudging[50] become the modes of regulating behaviour by design without a child's ability to control, resist or refuse it. Such techniques entail small changes in the environment, steering individuals to specific behaviours. It is 'a choice architecture that influences people's behaviour 'in the designers' preferred way without eliminating any options'.[51] For instance, Google does not remove certain content from the search results but rather nudges some (sponsored) further up the list. Fruit is not removed from the shelves, only placed further behind the cookies and junk food which are at a hand's reach and so on. Nudging theory comprises concepts like the social proof heuristics – individuals copy the actions of others – and default options – wherein users are made to pick the default option (the junk food at a hand's distance) for doing nothing. In the digital environments, say, how a child is nudged to work on specific tasks or view particular content, such techniques are opaque: it is not known how they work, who designed them and how they may impact not only one's learning trajectory and experience but also their privacy. For example, Tahaei and colleagues[52] discovered that it is often up to the software developers to consider data privacy settings in ways that benefit profit over users' privacy.

While EdTech products are not in and of themselves automatically leading to privacy loss in the classroom, their goal for massification across a market sector can lead to a form of *domestication* and their *legitimation*. They propose a new standard of 'this is how things are done', which also domesticates one's critical faculties by a 'situation in which [a student] is massified and has only the illusion of choice'.[53] Examples of this illusion include the requirement for proctoring software during exams and the restriction that homework must be submitted solely through a virtual learning environment.

Bourdieu's theory of symbolic violence and Freire's critical theory on oppression are mainly also brought for two reasons. First, education is a highly political instrument that continues to be used not only to shape societies and individuals. In and of itself, Schools, as a collection of individuals with their own values and goals, have their own agentic power to *create* societies and individuals. As such, School is a valuable instrument that many would want to have a stake in.

Second, School holds both a current and future market audience. While the new pedagogic authority emerges on School's grounds, it can be argued that the new digital technologies are merely instruments of policymakers to regulate education systems – as Stephen J. Ball says, from a *distance*. The influence and exertion of control is not as direct and bureaucratic but from the outside and covertly – through the means of data and digital products. Nevertheless, this is only short-lived.

Learning models and intelligent tutoring systems

Intelligent tutoring systems (ITS) are computer-based learning environments that claim to personalize instruction and provide 'intelligent' feedback to students via 'peer' avatars – digital representations of teachers. There is much to unpack in this one sentence, but before that, it is essential to discuss learning models albeit briefly and put into context how digital systems reflect and are modelled on – and re-enforce – some learning theories more than others.

Theoretical learning models are shrouded in history, but some conceptualizations endure with practical implications to education today. The intention here is not to walk through the history of learning theories exhaustively but to draw attention to those that many EdTech products are embedding in their designs. The behaviourist model of learning sees learning as changes in individuals' observable behaviours. The focus of behaviourists is on the behaviour rather than on thoughts, desires and possibilities. According to behaviourism, a person can be steered towards a particular behaviour through various forms of conditioning.[54] The psychological constructivist model of learning, on the other hand, looks at a person's way of thinking, positing that a person learns by mentally organizing and reorganizing new experiences and knowledge.[55]

To John Dewey, for instance, students' prior knowledge should be recognized in the classroom and teachers should adjust the curriculum accordingly. Relatedly, drawing from Pierre Bourdieu's[56] model around cultural capital, children have their own, which must be recognized within the process of learning to avoid potential 'symbolic violence' to occur.

The different learning theories give different value to the role of the learner, the educator and the social environment to the learning process. Behaviourists see learners as reactive – responding to the external environment. The educator assumes the active role of the one that modifies the conditions, which shape the learner's behaviour. Dewey has put emphasis on learners' own initiatives: 'Since learning is something that the pupil has to do himself (or herself) and for himself (or herself), the initiative lies with the learner.'[57]

Constructionist and socio-cultural theorists emphasize the importance of individual learner agency further and acknowledge the personal views that can act as guidance towards valuable learning outcomes. Education data fits both the behaviourist and the constructionist models in ways that on one hand data is collected with the intention to capture these views and, through the means of algorithms, condition both the experience and behaviour during the learning process. The focus is more on the process and technique and less on the educator or social environment since data only captures performance, not intimate nuanced contexts.

If it is accepted that education data conceptualizes learning as the function by which what is taught, how it is taught and what is learned is quantified through numbers; form follows function. The learning process therefore can become a uniform pattern that is formulaically predetermined since everything, no matter what, has to amount to a quantifiable number – data. Education data feeds two important sources: a domain or knowledge model (a range of knowledge domains such as math or grammar) and a learner model (the learner's knowledge quantified against the knowledge domain). Expressed quantitatively, these two models are the form that maintains the function (which enables data generation that feeds and allows adjustments to be made in the domain model and helps examine the learner model in the adjusted conditions).

EdTech becomes the means through which this new form strives to achieve the desired function by identifying what is being modelled, how it is modelled and how such models are maintained. While the methods for modelling vary, in basic terms, their common goal is to create a stimuli-response mechanism with an 'expert' standard template against which each response is measured.[58] The template adjusts as the data feeds each source; the stimuli-response mechanism remains the same. In this learning model, data is the main driver of the teaching and learning processes. Data feeds the stimuli that is the domain model, the stimuli demand response from the learner model; the response generates data, which adjusts the stimuli; the loop is closed. As such, an adaptive or intelligent tutoring technology can provide teaching functions by, for example, selecting assignments, giving hints, evaluating student responses and adapting those functions by modelling students' cognitive or emotional responses and behaviour.

While the objective is to achieve positive learning outcomes, the system leads the learning process. Something is done *on behalf of* the educator through the education data that fuels the stimuli that is the domain or knowledge model, and something is done *to* the learner, who has to react.

Education data in this sense serves the interest of the technology as a learning system. Importantly, education data leaves the learner out of the social structure and context of the learning process in a passive – reactive – role. In short, education data drives towards a behaviourist view of learning. It not only compromises the role of the learner but also reduces the learner's basic rights to choose or indeed to object to it.

An important point must be added here on the part of evidence gathering to prove if such models are effective. As briefly pointed in Chapter 1, much attention and funding from industry and philanthropic organizations have supported research to answer the question 'what works' with EdTech in education. It is precisely this notion of seeing what has been done (the input or intervention) and what has been achieved (the result or the output) that has implications for how public education has been changing and what role EdTech begins to occupy in the schools that adopt them. Such form of enquiry provides us 'with information about ... possible relations between actions and consequences'.[59] We learn only about what was done and what came out of it, not, as Biesta argues, what is actually possible. We only obtain a past understanding of what might work in education but cannot guarantee that we would have adequately understood the problem. As Biesta elaborates, what worked is 'old' knowledge which can 'guide us first in our attempts to understand what the problem might be and then in the intelligent selection of possible lines of action ... yet the proof of the pudding always lies in the action that follows', which will '"verify" both the adequacy of our understanding of the problem and, in one and the same process, the adequacy of the proposed solution'.[60] As such, stimuli-response and behaviourist EdTechs only provide a retrospect – we never know if digitizing education benefits all children until it is done.

What this leaves us with is a learning model that drives performativity – both demonstrating the intervention and demonstrating the outcomes of it through the means of data. For it is the measurement of what is effective – what the data says – that becomes relevant to policy and governance. This 'technocratic model', as Biesta argues, 'assume[s] that the only relevant research questions are questions about the effectiveness of educational means and techniques, forgetting, among other things, that what counts as "effective" crucially depends on judgements about what is educationally desirable'.[61] Consequently, anything that does not align with this paradigm is excluded, thereby reducing the opportunities for unexpected learning experiences and creative gestalt. It is the technocratic model that becomes the dominant system that exerts a form of oppression – symbolic violence, reflected in the evolving landscape of education governance. It is a model that wields the 'expertise' of data systems and algorithmic manipulation.

Digital technologies for conviviality or oppression?

Just as the ITSs generate the adaptive stimuli-response mechanism as a form of learning and thus impose their pedagogic action and work, there are other digital systems that impose a more operational authority and action. These are system-level applications that schools may use at institutional level. For example, in the UK the Office for Standards in Education, Children's Services and Skills (Ofsted) uses supervised machine learning techniques to identify schools that need full inspection. These system-level applications can also use aggregated learner analytics and performance to detect patterns in educational attendance and best teaching practices. The machine learning techniques are deployed once data is made available for the systems to work with.

In 2023, the UK Department for Education initiated a program to gather 'live' attendance data from schools, causing public concern due to its 'high-risk' nature.[62] This data, collected and processed by a third-party provider (Wonde, an EdTech), includes sensitive information like demographics, unique pupil numbers and indicators for vulnerable children. While the program aims to promote a 'zero tolerance approach to absenteeism',[63] the UK Information Commissioner's Office (ICO) quickly raised additional issues, including doubts about the legal basis of processing the data and the intention to retain it for sixty-six years. This 'live' data collection undoubtedly sets the stage for analytics and from there for prediction to pre-empt problems. In fact, such examples already exist elsewhere such as with predictive policing.[64] Profiling can become a central instrument to police students. Government's 'zero tolerance' approach pre-empts events before they occur. This not only describes the centrality and authoritative position of data and digital systems but the market potential for the tech industry. EdTech emerges not only as the market supplier of these technologies and their futuristic promises but one with the appetite to capture an important market of future loyal customers that can be moulded and controlled.

Similarly, authorities in the United States are also requesting the collection of sensitive data in schools. The US National Centre for Education Statistics (NCES) has the congressional mandate to gather, analyse and disseminate education statistics and serve as the primary data source for policymakers and decision-makers.[65] NCES's initiatives encompass administrative data collection and various surveys (cross-sectional, longitudinal and assessment), providing insights into early childhood, K-12 and postsecondary education on both national and international scales.

Managing populations through measuring performance and accountability has thus fuelled governments' firm conviction to incentivize and support the establishment of centralized data systems for educational data. And the need for such data fuelled the need for digital technologies that could gather it. The problems schools are left with as a result are that the digital technologies are not neutral physical property items but can be seen as 'borrowed' commercial services with other people's ideas and solutions of how things should be done. Put simply, governments are inadvertently relinquishing their own interest to measure accountability and control of education into the hands of unknown other, private actors – the strangers. From one rule over another with the difference that businesses are not scrutinized and held accountable. Behind them are often an owner and a software engineer with an interest for a quick market entry and just as quick a market exit.

One example of the market ambitions of software entrepreneurs is Nearpod, an EdTech platform for making interactive slides and videos, which was recently acquired by Renaissance Learning, the behemoth EdTech for assessment in reading and maths for $650 million.[66] But so are the hundreds of other such companies that are often acquired and changing ownerships[67] often without students' or teachers' awareness and knowledge – without governments' knowledge of what happens to children's data in such business transactions and acquisitions. Such other unknown private actors may also be large for-profits with armies of lawyers, designers, software developers, marketing teams, data analysts, engineers and shareholders with great appetite for monopolizing whole markets. But so are the risks for financial, scalability, economic, technological and environmental insecurities. The question that emerges is whether schools recognize this new 'authority' in the classroom and the short- and long-term issues it comes with.

It is only logical that education policymakers tend to lean back away from measures to *tame* or control this new 'authority' since they themselves are demanding data collection for accountability measures. This depicts a complex power dynamic in which policymakers demand data to measure schools and EdTech respond to this demand. At the same time, aiming to satisfy this need, EdTech businesses are presented with a business opportunity.

Within this dynamic, we can see the symbolic violence advancing the neoliberalist push to commercialize public education and treat schools as businesses. If schools perform poorly, no parent would 'buy' into them. Therefore, they fail and shut down. Symbolic violence is expressed through the EdTech data-dependent products as they become

> the delegation which establish[es] the pedagogic action, in addition to a delimitation of the content inculcated, a definition of the mode of inculcation (the legitimate mode of inculcation) and of the length of inculcation (the legitimate training period), which define the degree of completion of pedagogic work considered necessary and sufficient to produce the accomplished form of the habitus, i.e., the degree of cultural attainment (the degree of legitimate competence) by which a group or class recognizes the accomplished man.[68]

Said otherwise, EdTech legitimates its position in schools through the promise to provide the 'necessary' education for the 'necessary' time to become what is 'best' for each learner – all driven by and informed through data. Or what American policy has pushed for the past few years: *cradle-to-career* data collection for the development of *talent pipelines*.[69, 70]

Symbolic violence can also be expressed in 'the consequence of a dominant class imposing its own cultural values and interests on a dominated group, who then accept this situation without question'.[71]

Technologies hail from computer science and mathematical and often procedural thinking, an *if-then* logic, which has increasingly been presented as a sort of superior way of doing things and solving social problems. This technocratic model has also been reflected in how education governance has evolved.[72] Governing by numbers and through the power of numbers is seen as reducing 'complex processes to simple numerical indicators and rankings for purposes of management and control'.[73] To convert people, processes, practices and places into numbers allows for their measurement and ultimately influence and control. This technocratic model impels student and teacher performativity. Like in a game, it allows them to obtain accreditation and compile scores, badges, ranking and a 'position' on a spectrum starting from, as in the earlier example with NetSupport, the 'red box' (problematic) to a 'green box' (doing well) on a digital dashboard, in report cards and ultimately in state systems and longitudinal databases with unknown future impact on students' futures.

Long-term, green box and digital badges become priorities at the expense of any other activity or even responding to serendipitous contexts. Any serendipitous context or deviation away from what is programmed – and programmable – becomes irrelevant since it does not contribute to or fit the requirements for badge collection and data needed to change the colour of the ranking box. Chasing points and improving positions on the leaderboards diminish the attention towards other aspects of the learning experience, such as nurturing strong human connections or diving into an unplanned situation. Slowly we see more acquiescence to the 'if-then' logics of the digital systems and less to the convivial and spontaneous.

The symbolic violence is also expressed in how the digital systems can impose their own ontologies and methodologies in the classroom. Nudging and hyper-nudging are examples of such methodologies. These are psychological strategies or tricks that subtly and unobtrusively steer students to perform a (supposedly) desired positive behaviour. They suggest a form of choice and autonomy; as mentioned earlier, this is only illusionary. Nudging can be for engagement by sending a notification or reminder or click somewhere to watch or explore further information. Nudging can be through personalized recommendations or by setting up specific goals or compare and compete with others.

Digital leaderboards or rankings that compare students' achievements in comparison to the whole class are all means of nudging. Nudging to play more in order to collect more points, to score better. Class Dojo is a popular app for classroom behaviour management offering such techniques. The company claims that over 50 million teachers and families use it. Its leaderboards and rewards are a nudging technique for social comparison and competition even though these functionalities are at the discretion of the teachers. It is the illusionary sense of choice the teacher has.

When a dominant class imposes its own values and interests, it can establish a hidden pedagogy of oppression, as Freire examines from critical pedagogical perspective. It 'begins with the egoistic interests of the oppressors (an egoism cloaked in the false generosity of paternalism) and makes of the oppressed the objects of its humanitarianism'.[74] The digital systems' ontologies and methods of influencing educational processes are the examples of such dominant 'class' rising in the classroom. Within it, an individual loses the ability to enjoy self-exploration and self-determination because data-driven systems would have the capacity to act upon the performance or behaviour at any point in order to steer the student in the 'desired' direction. Thus, nudging and hyper-nudging become the modes of regulating behaviour by design without a child's ability or choice to control, resist or refuse it.

The data inferencing and surveillance capabilities of these products further present a form of oppression that is both at individual (how one practices self-expression and interprets what is learned) and at structural levels (inferences derived from data influence curriculum decisions and what one should learn).

Adopting these forms of education by schools acknowledges them as a legitimate power that imposes itself both symbolically (taking pedagogic superiority) and structurally (by mediating and nudging all operations of an educational system). This power derives as the hidden pedagogy of oppression because it leaves few choices for the individual. One is to submit – perhaps remain fearful. Another option is to adopt and adapt to it. As Freire argues, the oppressed suffer duality:

> They discover that without freedom they cannot exist authentically. Yet, although they desire authentic existence, they fear it … The conflict lies in the choice between being wholly themselves or being divided; between ejecting the oppressor within or not ejecting them; between human solidarity or alienation; between following prescriptions or having choices; between being spectators or actors; between acting or having the illusion of acting through the action of the oppressors; between speaking out or being silent, castrated in their power to create and re-create, in their power to transform the world.[75]

The new oppressors watching over as individuals become ever more aware that the new reality will lead the oppressed to suffer this duality – either perform or hide, pretend or remain silent and lose their ability and right to self-expression. What choices are there for students in these *if-then* pre-defined logics? Such environments destroy privacy, which suggests that the only option is to opt out. Alternatively, one is to contest this new oppressive power – to question it as a bottom-up resistance. What alternatives to datafication do schools have to offer children? Another route is for a top-down effort to *tame* and regulate the industries mediating educational processes, control how education data is used, and children's privacy preserved.

A critic is called upon to expose the fraudulent

In *Frontiers of Criticism* T.S. Elliot begins with his thesis that there are 'limits, exceeding which in one direction literary criticism ceases to be literary, and exceeding which in another it ceases to be criticism'.[76] The beauty of this thesis is in that it can address almost anything. In the context of this book, it applies to two aspects: both the excessive adoption of digital technologies and technological evangelism on one hand, and the growing criticism towards both ends – digital and non-digital schooling – on the other. In essence, Elliot alerts us to the existence of critical boundaries. Crossing them cancels all constructive efforts and brings in futile hostility. To be clear, critiquing digital technologies has not been without schools being critiqued (and often condemned) in the first place. And since schools have got their fair share of audits for quality control, so should the EdTech claiming an influential position among them.

Reproaching the negative impact of schools on students' learning success has indeed been a big selling point for the EdTech industry. The critique towards schools has been evident in much of the literature around computers' power to transform lives and level up education for all. Yet one can only wonder how these authors and scientists came to critique so much and discern what is valuable for others if they themselves have gone through often known and traditional schooling path? In the *Second Machine Age: Work, Progress, and Prosperity in a Time of Brilliant Technologies*,[77] Erik Brynjolfsson and Andrew McAfee, two distinguished technology scientists, with particular interest in the digital economy, express optimism regarding the potential for prosperity and progress. The computer appears as the solution to various challenges. Yet it is worth noting that McAfee dedicates the book to his own parents 'who prepared [him] for the second machine age by giving [him] *every* advantage a person could have'.[78] One would doubt if he was referring to the computer as the 'every advantage'. Arguments around how schools fail children's education have often come in excess and by ignoring other contributing factors to a child's learning ecology, even the broader social milieu.

Often, critique has come from the very proponents of computer interaction and computers as a constructivist, self-driven learning. Some have long argued that school is killing children's creativity and maintaining a status quo that is counter-productive to innovation and intellectual growth (see the late Sir Ken Robinson's TED talk).[79] However, it is those proponents of the computer who, ironically, also inspired much of today's intrusive data extractive mechanisms. One of them is Seymour Papert, often called the father of educational computing. Papert, more than once, has expressed his condemnation of schools as the uncompromising institutions, while their instruction only likely suppresses children from letting them thrive through the use of the computer. Or so is the sense his book, *The Children's Machines: Rethinking School in the Age of the Computer*, leaves the reader with. In it, Papert dedicates a chapter on schools' resistance to change. He argues that there is little change, not only due to not enough computers but also due to how schools *assimilate* or appropriate them to fit their own status quo. Schools resist change, Papert laments.

The narrative is simple, almost romantic, when he describes how his life has been entirely changed by the computer (supposedly for the better). He says: 'I know what it is like to have had my intellectual life change, and more than once, through using computers.'[80] When he programmed a 'a soft simulation of economic competition' Papert recalls, it 'clarified' his thinking about the economic reform in Russia. This, Papert assures, 'can happen because I have a computer, in fact several computers, within reach at most times'. Surely it is not merely because of having computers, just as it is not simply by staring in a library full of books for one to say how well they understand the economic reform in Russia. Papert has had intensive years of studies and the privilege to interact with the likes of Jean Piaget, the renowned Swiss psychologist who pioneered contributions to developmental psychology and cognitive theory. These experiences should be acknowledged because they hold relevance when asserting the transformative potential of computers. In this story school indeed is in the way of making a point. For it has never been about access to the internet or the computers. At least not solely that.

Today education is imbued with screens, applications and coding syllabi. But, contrary to Papert's logic, this has no guarantee that everyone will be an expert of the Russian economy, coding or anything else. That school administration, even at state level, intervened and began to dictate and mandate how computers should be used, as Papert bemoaned (creating separate computer labs and curriculum and slowly eroding 'the subversive features' of the computer), is true. Digital technologies are now mandated to be used whether teachers and students want them or need them. But the computers mandated today are far from the computers Papert thanked for knowing about Russian economic reform. Rather, they are systems that infiltrate *despite* what schools might want to protect as status quo, such as children's privacy and safety, for instance.

In a comment, the School Library Journal cautioned about Papert's book that 'educators with a vested interest in the status quo will hate [t]his book' because 'it is about their demise'. To begin with, any separation about *them* and *us*, *good* and *bad*, creates a divisional discord. We see this division consistently in market and even policy discourse in which digital technologies are seen as superior to anything previously occupying the classroom. Datafication and personalization of education through digital products, are a superior *us*, juxtaposed with the 'pre-datafication model of education [which is seen as] unethical, incompetent, or beyond improvement',[81] the inferior *them*. However, supposing the status quo is the instructional approach to teaching in the classroom is not necessarily detrimental and neither is unstructured or co-designed learning (the constructivist approach[82]) always beneficial to students. As is the case, for the enthusiast to learn to play a fine tune, it takes hard and oftentimes dull repetition, while in co-designing, say dinner, any child would go for the tub of ice cream. In the first case, instruction is perhaps boring but necessary. In the second, it is 'self-driven' but unhealthy.

Papert is often associated with his campaign for freeing children to use the computer machine as they know best because, he believes, they do. However, he also belonged to a team whose views align well with today's drive for data-driven designs of one's future. Together with his MIT Media Lab colleagues, he pursued ambitions to create the ultimate intelligent tutoring system.

The legacy of Papert remains with focus on children's freedoms to self-navigate their learning against the prescribed conditions of School. To Papert, School was an institution that imposed unfair limitations on children with regard to how or what they learn and especially when interacting with computers. Yet little debate exists about the bigger ambition Papert and his Media Lab team had, one that was clearly articulated in their co-authored work *Affective Learning – a Manifesto*.[83] In it, the MIT authors state:

> We also value integrating new affect sensing, recognition, and reflection technologies into efforts to build intelligent tutoring systems and other automated systems where there is potential to adapt the learning experience based on signs of interest, frustration, and any other affect-related cues.[84]

Throughout his academic work, Papert insisted that children construct their learning by sharing projects, ideas and creative artefacts. He formalized the theory of *constructionism*, having built on it from his mentor, Piaget, whose theory of constructivism posited that children learn in stages.

Nearly ten years ago, inspired by Papert's views that children self-navigate and construct knowledge, I explored for my doctoral research how technologies can ensure that children's voices 'count' in a formal educational context, having worked with children of all backgrounds – from those more affluent and studying in private schools with all kinds of extra-curricular activities and social clubs, to children from disadvantaged, immigrant communities or living without parents and all kinds of other hard conditions. Indeed, they are all fascinated by the internet and the computer and rightfully so. It is marvellous to see what children can come up with once they have a computer. They create stories, design characters, compose songs, make collages, connect with others, learn about the world and are curious what is outside it. However, today, more often than not self-driven learning, voicing ideas and making mistakes can take a student to a negative pathway in their educational journey because of datafication – all this information can be turned into data and algorithmically manipulated. How the market of digital computing that targets children has evolved begs to ask how Papert's campaign has played its part.

Today children do not solely create or explore ideas or subjects through the use of computers. And Papert and his colleagues at the Media Lab did not entirely think of it only in those terms of interaction that benefits children the most. In fact, Papert did see far into the point where digital data can be extracted from children's interactions with a computer and from children as they simply sat in a classroom to learn. The goals were often not just to reproach School for what it did not do well but something entirely different to the ideals described in Papert's *Children's Machine*. Through various published work and innovations, it was becoming more evident that Papert and team were often enveloped to investigate how children learn by capturing as much data as possible such as from their pulse rate, skin hair, body and eye movements[85] to identify not only what happens at an *affective* level, when a child supposedly learns or engages in an educational activity, but in order to design better machines – computers, which can eschew this captured granular data, compute inferences, predict possible outcomes and immediately attend to these bodily cues to steer the learning child towards a (supposedly) desired behaviour (e.g., improved attention and better learning). What Papert leaned towards was leaving children to unobtrusively engage in a learning process so long as they can be monitored by sensory technology to *measure, assess and advance machine learning technology*, which in turn would (potentially) be able to tutor intelligently in the future classroom.

Papert maintained that the computer is *Children's Machine*, and School must leave them to learn with it. Fair enough. But he, and his team,[86] also argued that machine learning and self-reinforced computation – what today is coming into the classroom – are needed to begin to emulate human beings to understand, predict and be able to teach. That is how, for example, a colleague of Papert, Rosalind W. Picard, also from the Media Lab, co-designed the *Galvactivator*, a skin-conductivity sensing glove which aimed to monitor children's skin to detect any emotion that may be emitted during their learning (skin conductivity measures psychological arousal, which is considered a predictor for attention and memory). Picard believed that the glove device could encourage students to self-reflect around their personal learning style[87] (although it escapes a simpler logic, why not simply reflect on what is being studied). The Media Lab researchers also experimented with a chair wired with *Tekscan* pressure mapping arrays to gather granular and sensitive data from children's behaviour, movement, body temperature and so on to capture what happens to them as they learn.

It is unclear whether this notion stems from an extension of Papert's or Picard's or a collective computer scientists' advocacy for self-learning or if it was his overarching goal all along – to quietly observe and influence children's behaviour through the development of the ultimate machine.

Consequently, these very aspirations have now made their way into contemporary classrooms through a multitude of EdTech. The desires to intrude into the physical and mental realms of children, similar to what Papert and Picard envisioned, are no longer confined to a laboratory setting; instead, they are unfolding in today's classrooms. The digitized classroom includes products that surveil children the moment they 'engage' with a digital device to the moment they need to take a bathroom trip. Products like NetSupport and Blackboard described earlier provide 'classroom management', an euphemism for surveillance and control. A teacher can see every student's screen in real time and control what they do. NetSupport states that 'it provides a great way for teachers to capture how students *feel*, their confidence with a topic and whether they need extra support'[88] so that the teacher can provide timely intervention. There is no Galvactivator monitoring children's feelings but predetermined menu of emojis that gauge feedback.

Today, social scientists, pedagogues and legal scholars address this kind of monitoring by describing it as datafication and data-driven manipulation of human behaviour. Papert's theory posited that the optimal way in which children learned was by actively constructing something shareable and meaningful to them. Yet his research extended to training machines that could become the intelligent tutors of the future.

And so, we have the computer scientist vision to thinking with a computer, to digital systems that impose a techno-logic, determined by data and algorithmic computation. It is almost as though children are there insofar as data is needed to instruct the computer what needs doing, to whom, and advance at it until it becomes the ultimate super-intelligent agent or the ultimate intelligent tutor and so on. A whole generation of technologies have sprouted that reflects Papert's and Picard's and similar thinking and technological production. From the adoption of the advanced computing machines, we witness the capturing of granular data used to train algorithms that promise to analyse, infer, predict, provide efficiency in the classroom, enable adaptive and inclusive learning, assess students with greater precision and steer them to bountiful futures.

Moving beyond the ongoing criticism of the traditional education system, we have entered a digital domain characterized by diverse opinions and varying levels of evidence, emphasizing the need not only for critique, echoing T.S. Eliot's perspective, but also for concrete action. Within the context of digitization and data-driven transformation of education, it is crucial to blend critical evaluation and equally acknowledge the digital achievements with tangible steps regarding the capabilities and limitations of technology. Relying solely on words alone may not suffice, the way guidelines for good practice and standards sometimes fall short on ensuring compliance with data privacy and ethical practices. We need tangible action due to the potential risks and harm that data-intensive systems can inflict on societies. And risks there are aplenty when it comes to data extraction.

The 'gospel' of data

As policies increasingly adopt techno-solutionism through data in countries such as the United States, the UK, the EU and Australia, data collection has spiked immeasurably in parallel with the growing digitization of all educational processes and practices. The availability of data has empowered other capabilities relating to data extraction, something that has already been witnessed across major sectors like agriculture, health care, transportation and urban infrastructure. Data markets are a massively funded European strategy. This gives data adjudicative power.

Partly the drive for data generation across societal sectors has been for promise of *precision* or *exactitude*.[89] These concepts are not new. They are the very foundation of industrial societies and capitalism. Exactitude is the very essence of nascent capitalist society; its legacy is societies being conditioned in this technological sense that time management is the means of labour production and exploitation. In this same way, children are now being conditioned through the means of data and the exactitude extracted from it. On the one hand, this creates a familiarity to what awaits – children are introduced to the world of work because data measures performance on which salaries and job security would one day depend. The performativity in education will later seem familiar, as they are en route to other socio-technical systems and market contexts especially in the job market where performativity and monitoring have similarly been data driven and intensified through digital surveillance.[90] As such, education data reshapes the social structure within the learning process and changes the very purpose of education. On the other hand, data's centrality and arbitrary 'voice' also change the meaning of education. In its simplicity, schools provide certain functions which can vary – from defining education to measuring it.

Here, difference must be made between *School* and *Education*, which problematically conflate. Education is a lifelong process in which an individual learns to deal with the world; this can literally mean anything – from accepting to rejecting it, from manipulating to leading it, from understanding to explaining it. One can argue that educating one's self is one's own responsibility. The alternative is to get School's assistance. In this sense, School is accepted as something that provides an individual with assistance in getting educated. The quality in which School does it leads to judging whether it was done poorly or well. The former is likely to yield individuals who will gain no qualifications worth employability, learn no literacy, no value in inclusivity and justice, and may even drop out midway, unconvinced about School's purpose. A School doing a 'good job' should expect the opposite.

School, as an institution that assists one's education is like any other – church or prison, for instance. Just as church cannot guarantee a true believer, neither can School guarantee well-educated individuals. As an institution, School invests resources and provides a system and a structure. It makes an investment, a sort of 'banking'.[91] Children go to School, which in turn banks on their futures.

One assumes that EdTech businesses similarly bank on children's futures and promise a job well done when children use their products. These logics suggest that both School and EdTech treat children as 'receiving objects'.[92] A pedagogy that initiates such asymmetry only makes way for the world to allow for its fortification and ultimately the disenfranchising of students as ones who are not part of the world but ones who will eventually enter it. This notion explains the broader project of EdTech with their interests to navigate students through a learning-to-earning framework of schooling.[93] Here, data is the primary source that can make this framework possible.

Whom education data benefit is contentious. If education data benefits the technology as the learning system, it can also structurally change the role of educators, the pedagogy, learner choice, voice and ability (or even will) to challenge educational processes.[94] On the foreground, where learning and teaching happens, these systems' functionalities and capabilities are also becoming central pedagogic authority in education.

Similar control over the distribution of knowledge and information emerges in media and communication sectors. News organizations and publishers have been steadily adapting to the growing dominance of large online platforms such as Facebook and Google and their impact on the distribution and consumption of news.

In their book *The Power of Platforms: Shaping Media and Society* Rasmus Kleis Nielsen and Sarah Anne Ganter[95] argue that the power digital platforms possess is based on the relationship with their audiences and the capacity to attract end-users and partners like publishers. This relationship becomes highly asymmetrical as publishers become entirely dependent on the platforms for audience reach. This asymmetry defines *platform power*. But this power cannot be understood clearly without also understanding the publishers' gains, reservations, behaviour, the technology itself and the reason why publishers embrace platforms regardless. In the same way it becomes critical to unpack the infrastructure capture that is enabled in education, and much like the media example, public education (and the authorities behind it) have certain understanding and gains with the platforms.

Similarly, data extraction through the digitization of processes and practices is evidenced in the health care and agricultural sectors.[96] Data becomes in and of itself a source of 'knowledge' and precision. Data comes to be seen as the gospel that the more of it and the more sensitive it is, the greater the claim to 'increase the certainty of knowledge and decision-making.'[97] Therefore, precision is not merely integrated into the practices and processes of health care and agriculture; precision through datafication promises new forms of knowledge but also equally commercial opportunities. Such is the use of data collection from pharmaceutical companies, consumer purchasing data, diagnoses, medications, procedures insurance and other information to create market value of the data for research but also for commercial – advertising – purposes.[98] These two promises drive policy-making and with that the drive for data collection and digitization of education.

During the Covid-19 pandemic, governments globally signed contracts with some of the most powerful platforms, namely Google and Microsoft, to provide connectivity and services to education. Yet those families and children who did not have any internet connection and technologies at home were deprived of access to online schooling entirely.[99] That asymmetry is the result of deep-rooted inequalities. Such conditions are not ideal, and providing digital technologies for all is not the solution either. Any electrical power cut can affect the classroom if all learning and teaching are entirely digitally dependent. The right to education should not equate to the right to digital technologies. Therefore, one must ask what is the main drive to relinquish control over education. Moreover, while governments' responsibility lies with the citizen and the sovereignty of democratic societies' education, corporate capture of public education means that sovereignty also shifts away from governments into private hands.

The most important resources platforms influence, Nielsen and Ganter argue, are *attention*. They add, 'But attention is also a central part of other parts of our societies, and other institutions than just publishers will have to contend with the power of platforms.'[100] The nudging and hyper-nudging underpin the capability to capture audience's attention. A click-bait ability that, some media scholars argue, corrupts the entire process of news making and media quality. The number of users attracted to a story becomes the end in itself, which conflicts with the role and responsibility of journalistic profession. By the same token, one can argue how and towards what is the attention of children in the digitized classroom pulled? Is there a bigger picture that goes beyond the motivation to monitor children's attendance, learning outcomes and the effectiveness of various pedagogic interventions? The 'gospel' of data therefore serves not only the desire to transform education to a process of exactitude but because of its commercial opportunities and the power to capture and steer attention.

The commercial value of data

The problem with data in education is expressed in its intangibility to cross over to other domains, pollinate with other data and inflict its impact in very tangible ways. The aspect of *big data* plays crucial role here. For instance, critical data studies[101] explore the cultural, ethical and critical challenges that big data can affect. Big data is not as scientifically empirical or a neutral thing reserved for mathematics and hard sciences but as something that is part of the 'wider data assemblages'.[102] Such assemblages, as described in Figure 2.1, are already intricately connected with societies and interact with their organization, relationships and functions. As such, big data also impacts on these societies, their organization, relationships and functions.

There is misconception that big data is simply objective information and is a powerful and influential factor in society. Data indeed represents a form of power, as organizations possess vast amounts of user information, and it serves as valuable capital.[103] Adding algorithms and data processing on top of big data can influence emotions and culture[104] and serve commercial interests and agendas.[105]

Once data is extracted, it is never neutral but always active and influencing – part of the information geography.[106] And yet big data is only part of the whole story. To this end, big data and algorithmic capabilities and data-processing tools present a powerful dynamic that Iliadis and Russo argue[107] must be exposed to critical, ethical and cultural perspectives.

Data capture through datafication has opened doors for further risks relating to security, the loss of privacy and exploitation of often personal, sensitive and granular data. Datafication has enabled hyper-tracking and surveillance – hyper-visibility of students, which can be particularly harmful for children with different educational needs and contexts. Hyper-visibility through the normalization of digital surveillance in School has also led to concerns around nurturing trust and confidence[108, 109] of children about the surrounding world. While a certain level of coercion exists within School's bounds, such coercion is now reinforced by private digital systems with control, external to the teaching staff. Seen from critical data studies, these changes assume a rather oppressive learning environment as already said. Moreover, the systems enabling this environment are neither formally hired nor held accountable for any learning or pedagogic failure.

Legal scholars and more recently a growing number of governments[110] are increasingly reacting to these new dynamics and the risks of monopolizing content and specifically over abusive data practices.[111] That said, these risks are addressed through forthcoming European legislature. There are also more frequent fines and greater scrutiny of the so-called very large online platforms or VLOPs. On the other hand, others are sceptical[112] about the pace of change and the effectiveness of these efforts. Then also – what about the multitude of smaller players and their products? As gleaned from the introductory chapter, bootstrapping an application does not take much to achieve, not even any significant financing. Little to nothing is known about the administrative desktops, hosting and management or indeed the coding scripts used while these puzzle pieces are put together. Put simply, there is a great need to look under the 'hood' of these products and assesses their state of security, algorithmic fairness, data management and even organizational ethos, values and practices as they integrate into the daily routines of schools, teachers and students.

Those who have peaked under the hood have been greatly concerned. For example, the Human Rights Watch (HRW) reviewed 165 EdTech products of which 89 per cent engaged in data practices that put children's rights at risk, undermined or actively violated them. Many of them used dangerous permissions online and allowed advertising companies (adtech) to access children's data many of which belong to whole supply chains owned by the most powerful companies such as Microsoft, Google, Amazon and Facebook.[113] The EdTech products investigated were endorsed by forty-nine governments worldwide and deployed in schools and colleges during the Covid-19 lockdowns. Once shared or accessed, this data is processed by advancing algorithms, capable to profile children, piece together more data from other public or private sources to create detailed profiles that are sold to advertisers, data brokers and anyone else who may be interested to target groups of people with similar characteristics online. Such inferred profiles of children can then be used to enable behavioural manipulation over long periods of time.

According to the HRW report, some EdTech products directly sent or granted access to children's personal data to 199 advertising technology (adtech) companies. The number of adtech receiving children's data exceeded the number of EdTech companies transmitting such data to them.

Some EdTech products sent children's data to adtech companies whose algorithms manipulate behaviour and what children can see online. These are small pieces of code, embedded in the script of an application, that allow the transfer of the data collected when a person uses that application. Here is an example of what that looks like with Microsoft Teams, which is used globally across educational systems. The product is not child-specific. It has been recommended by governments including in the United States, the UK, Australia and many European countries. Microsoft claims to have over a hundred million installs. While it has full access to a user's camera and microphone, the HRW also found that the company had installed the following 'dangerous permissions':[114]

READ_EXTERNAL_STORAGE
WRITE_EXTERNAL_STORAGE
ACCESS_COARSE_LOCATION
ACCESS_FINE_LOCATION
CALL_PHONE
CAMERA
GET_ACCOUNTS
READ_CONTACTS
WRITE_CONTACTS
SYSTEM_ALERT_WINDOW
USE_FINGERPRINT
RECORD_AUDIO

In its privacy policy, Microsoft states that it collects users' demographic, behavioural, location and biometric data (voice data) and that it uses users' data for advertising, behavioural advertising as well as user profiling. Its privacy policy also states:

> We also obtain data from third parties. ... These third-party sources vary over time and include: Data brokers from which we purchase demographic data to supplement the data we collect. Service providers

that help us determine your device's location. Partners with which we offer co-branded services or engage in joint marketing activities.[115]

While it also states that the company first requires to obtain parental consent to collect and process children's data,[116] this is not to say that data will not be collected as the recent fine in June 2023, the FTC demonstrated.[117] Even more recently, the Austrian privacy advocacy organisation NOYB found that Microsoft violates children's privacy 'but blames your local school'.[118]

This underscores the financial motivations that assign economic worth to children's data, fuelling highly invasive surveillance and significant encroachments on their privacy.[119] Most tech platforms, deliberately or perhaps unwittingly, installed tracking technologies that surveilled children outside of their virtual classrooms and on the internet persistently. Yet others fingerprinted and tagged children covertly in ways that are unavoidable, even if the user becomes aware.

Technochauvinist machines are not children's machines

The digitized classroom today is full of EdTech that capture and work with granular and sensitive data about children and deliver all kinds of measurements (besides how one feels), much of which Meredith Broussard[120] says in *More Than a Glitch: Confronting Race, Gender, and Ability Bias in Tech* may be statistically valid but senseless. Broussard investigates the bias and injustice already baked into algorithmic systems. She differentiates between social fairness and mathematical fairness, between mathematical truth and social truth. Yet, she contends, many people, including those in education, believe that using more and advanced technologies will lead to societal improvements. The fallacy in such beliefs, Broussard says, is in the *technochauvinism*: which is 'a kind of bias that considers computational solutions to be superior to all other solutions'. The bias baked into this is 'an a priori assumption that computers are better than humans – which is actually a claim that *the people who make and program computers are better than other humans*'.[121]

Technochauvinism has led to substantial financial waste of all kinds of technologies in education. The Global Education Evidence Advisory Panel of the World Bank estimates that there are great buys, good buys, promising but limited evidence, effective but relatively expensive and *bad* buys.[122] Some clearly provide cost-effectiveness, while others clearly do not.

In the United States there is an estimated 2 billion dollars spending (for 2020 alone according to one estimation[123]) on EdTech of which 67 per cent goes unused.[124] According to EdTech Evidence Exchange, a non-profit organization in Virginia, the total EdTech expenditure is between $26 and $41 billion a year, getting little substantial evidence of the *potential* and claims of the real returns.[125] The expenditure is compounded further when other costs are added: training of staff on how to use the technologies; new statutory requirements around literacy; competencies and skills relating to data privacy; cybersecurity and safeguarding; costs relating to hardware, software updates, battery charging, broken screens, meeting different educational needs and more. This expenditure has not even included the cost to the environment.[126]

Sustainable technology or whether technologies need regular repair or replacement affects the total cost of ownership, which is difficult to estimate. The true cost of digitizing the classroom is part of the same iceberg digital technologies built for education. Not only because of the cost of connection in its literal sense (metals, plastic, wires, electricity and software) but also in its socio-structural sense, too. As Nick Couldry and Ulises A. Mejias[127] elaborate in *The Costs of Connection: How Data Is Colonising Human Life and Appropriating It for Capitalism*, our lives become entangled by digital platforms and digital connection in ways that the price we pay extends far beyond the financial transactions and into the very fabric of our social, political and cultural existence.

The bigger cost of digitizing the classroom, the focus of the next chapter, is in the socio-structural capture of educational institutions by proprietary algorithmic systems. And the social structure is the very backbone of School and its people, processes, and practices. This social structure may be imperceptible to the public eye, except for media-worthy stories such as crumbling school walls, teacher shortage, rising costs or mental health crisis. However, its vital role is in protecting, nurturing and maintaining sovereignty against the appetite of corporation seeking market expansion. This backbone is vital to the existence of educational institutions – their well-being, autonomy and how effectively they create thinking and tolerant societies.

These are unprecedented proposals for education. The only parallel that can be made is ironically with factory production line. As the next chapter will delve further, examples of this factory-type thinking are envisioned in education in the United States, Australia and the EU. Digital infrastructures are being implemented with the pretext that they will enable credentialing ecosystems whereby students can demonstrate even out-of-school or any kind of small experience and skill acquisition as part of their employability arsenal.

Additionally digital ecosystems can predict, steer and identify what students will be capable of best and which direction they should take.

Certainly, one of the goals for educational institutions is to train and equip children with skills and competencies that will see them through the future and ensure they have more chances to fulfil their full potential. But should education be seen in the same data factory model whereby such direct link is made between what industry demands as current skills, qualifications and dynamic curriculum modification? The promises of such systems are prediction with precision. But they can easily lead to locking students in narrowly pre-defined roles, which can limit their future life chances. As we will see in the next chapter, digitizing education is part of a much bigger picture, one in which the labour market can directly influence education through the use of data.

The digitized classroom presents two interconnecting concerns. First, the classroom becomes integrated, and its functions exported into proprietary digital products. These, as Kerssens and van Dijck argue, 'contest the institutional pedagogical autonomy of schools and how the integration of digital platforms with educational practices in classrooms challenges the professional pedagogical autonomy of teachers'.[128] Second, more than that, the classroom is now attended to, controlled by and re-conditioned by a new pedagogic authority that is neither held accountable for its actions nor governed in any stringent ways.

Conclusion

In *Hegemony Now: How Big Tech and Wall Street Won the World (and How We Win It Back)*, Jeremy Gilbert and Alex Williams ask: 'How does power leave lasting traces on the landscapes of the social?'[129] The authors argue that modern hegemonic politics involves forming alliances among various interest groups to steer socio-political change, instilling a particular trajectory within a social system.

In neoliberal societies, this entailed an ongoing shift towards market-oriented mechanisms, often enforced by state power. In its extreme form, this can be characterized as 'constituting a kind of *platform power* – the crystallization of the direction of political travel within the infrastructures of technology, the economy, energy, transport, management practices and everyday life' including in public education. Once these infrastructures are established, they 'reinforce a process of transformation, automatic hegemonic influence into the very fabric of the social and technological world'.[130]

As a result, they become a significant focal point of 'political contention, albeit a contention which is often hidden from view'.[131] The authors make the important point that what these elites – financial, governmental leaders and the Silicon Valley tech behemoths – go 'beyond many of the typical ways in which we understand politics' in a conventional way; what 'these groups of people have in common, beyond certain particular interests, is their ability to design, influence, and control some of the key infrastructures which work to structure our contemporary world, from the economy, to social and cultural systems, and even to conventional politics itself'.[132]

Essentially, platform power becomes 'the ability to use infrastructures to exert influence, directly or indirectly, intentionally or unintentionally, to secure goals related to a group's interests. This kind of power becomes so deeply embedded that its 'cunning ... rests in its obfuscation and erasure of itself, its secretion into the future of everyday existence that we merely take "as natural"'.[133] This is akin to Weiser's vision over thirty years ago, where he foresaw technology turning invisible as it becomes 'so embedded, so fitting, so natural'.[134] They are hard to revoke or remove 'through vote or even a revolution'. Initiatives like the Australian Online Formative Assessment, US Chamber of Commerce Foundation's strategy 'cradle-to-career' pipelines, and the European skill intelligence strategy illustrate a growing hidden power emerging and shaping education systems. This broader perspective is discussed in the next chapter.

3

Infrastructure Capture: What Is the 'Big Picture' of Digitizing Education?

The crisis factor

T.S. Elliot lends a hand to describe why a digitized school can be a problem, in the absence of a simple answer as to why it is not. The primary use of poetry, Elliot said, was 'to satisfy one habit of the reader, to keep his mind diverted and quiet, while the poem does its work upon him: much as the imaginary burglar is always provided with a bit of nice meat for the housedog'.[1] Policymakers and often school districts and administrators focus so much on the solutions for education's 'ills' and so little on defining what those are; they are like the dog chewing on the meat while the house is being burgled. The 'ills' have often been described as forms of crises with constant policies being thrown at them, trial-and-error efforts that have often involved revisions, tinkering and refinements. These have been further modulated through and often as a result of processes of influence and re-interpretation.[2]

Martha Nussbaum[3] cautioned that a serious education crisis threatens the future of liberal education and the essential qualities of empathy and critical thinking crucial for democracy's survival. Towards the end of nineteenth to the early twentieth century, the UK education system was also described to be in profound crisis.[4] The neoliberalist project can be seen as Western politics' response to the crises impacted by fascism and communism and subsequently by 'the crisis of Keynesian welfarism'[5] in the 1970s. A similar narrative of crisis was articulated through the report *A Nation at Risk: The Imperative for an Educational Reform* in the 1980s in the United States, depicting the American education as failing to meet the needs of the country for a competitive workforce. As Stuart Hall argues, these crises are a form of disruption, which he labels as 'the long march of the Neoliberal Revolution'.[6] While chewing on the crisis, neoliberalism was born. This march has led to neoliberalism to repurpose the state to empower private capital and expand markets into all aspects of social life, including education.

Some have argued how crises have been the formula deployed by free-market advocates to establish a *corporatocracy* together with national politics.[7] Corporatocracy is everywhere today although it comes in various articulation – globalization, innovation, digitization. Corporate partnerships and business influence have become 'an effective framework for mobilising all available resources for the transition to the knowledge-based economy'[8] in the European Union for some time now. Big Tech firms such as IBM, Cisco and Microsoft have played a significant role in shaping the European education landscape, creating conditions for their investments in the profitable education sector 'without the impediments of existing institutional arrangements'.[9]

More recently, amid the Covid-19 crisis, we witnessed influential networks involving Big Tech firms like Google, Microsoft and Facebook, along with supranational organizations like the Organisation for Economic Cooperation and Development (OECD) and the United Nations Educational, Scientific and Cultural Organisation (UNESCO), venture capitalists and smaller EdTech providers, responding to the crisis.

However, the prevailing policy solutions and corporate voices have not been solely centred on interim provisions to address the mass school lockdowns and children missing on education. Instead, they used the opportunity to call for a long-term digital transformation of education globally – a digital future as a 'natural' next step the world and its children need to take.

The economic crises in Sub-Saharan Africa and Latin America during the 1980s, coupled with reduced bilateral educational aid, enabled the World Bank to gain influence through structural adjustment programs and loan conditions. As Mariana Mazzuccato and Rosie Collington argue[10] in *The Big Con: How the Consulting Industry Weakens Our Businesses, Infantilizes Our Governments and Warps Our Economies*, the demand for multinational management consulting services has not solely stemmed from domestic sources but has also been instigated by intergovernmental entities such as the World Bank and the International Monetary Fund. These organizations have been pushing indebted governments to engage consultants in executing market-oriented economic changes linked to their loan agreements. However, such use, the authors emphasize, 'is not accounted for in national management consulting statistics'.[11] This has allowed, among others, Big Tech players to flood with offers from undersea internet cables (e.g. Meta) to discarding their e-waste in Africa.[12] In the final chapter, I revisit this subject, drawing on Mazzuccato's and Collington's arguments to highlight how consulting firms, while offering both auditing and consulting, have been winning lucrative contracts but ultimately leading to governments' reliance on external expertise and thus undermining public competence and meaningful oversight of their work and influence.

Within the context here, the authors' argument becomes especially relevant in times of crises when powerful actors like Big Tech, working through large consultancy firms, assert dominance with their corporate agendas.

Corporate and supranational voice has been especially vocal in crises, including during the 2008 global economic crash. As Means[13] points out, international organizations like the World Bank and the World Economic Forum have consistently portrayed the structural challenges of capitalism, including stagnation, unemployment, poverty and inequality, as educational problems[14] – often perceived as deficiencies in human capital, related to skills and training. The concept of compete-to-survive and the view of education as a market have introduced new and legitimate voices, particularly from the private sector, to drive reforms. These reforms are often framed as 'necessary' for globalization, innovation and the knowledge economy.

Globalization, innovation and knowledge economy are all words of contention, yet they have been taking and continue to occupy large space in popular discourse, national policies and media globally. The 'knowledge economy', today the 'digital economy', has led to the radical shift especially in education policy.

While lacking clear definition, these concepts have often come to be expressed as necessities – that certain preparations, literacies, skills and therefore changes must take place in education to ensure that if societies commit to these changes, they have only to 'gain' in these new economies. However, within these newly conceptualized economies, the very understanding of knowledge and skills are 'commodified'.[15] In other words, we begin to disregard the fundamental importance of human connections in the generation of value, essentially leading to the impoverishment of the social aspect of education.

Common perceptions of the physical world undergo a transformation from being shaped by social values to a perspective where everything is interpreted, based on quantifiable measures.[16] The commodification of knowledge is prevalent in higher education in the Anglo-American contexts but so is in K-12 education with regard to the rapid digitization. Which school incorporates more digital technologies and how, what credentials students bank, what professional development and ambassadorships teachers take on to demonstrate professionalism and tech expertise[17] and how much further ahead one school is from another one down the road have been driving the marketization of schools within the 'knowledge economy' paradigm.

The commodification and quantification of knowledge have led to its further 'subordination of the purposes of education to economics'.[18] Learning is now transferable as credentials and made '"readable" ... between institutions and countries', as a process of 'exteriorisation', which has moved the purpose of education further away from whether what is learned is a matter of 'truth' in its entirety to a matter of whether it is 'useful, saleable, efficient'; whether it is a matter of obtaining skills and competencies rather than 'ideals'.[19] As French philosopher Michel Foucault debates, the increased focus on students' performance and teachers' 'professionalism' were the 'apparatus of uninterrupted examination'[20] since the nineteenth century. This examination is expressed through comparison (ranking) and judgement (grading and assessments) and 'woven into [schools] through a constantly repeated ritual of power'.[21] Students and teachers are put on the spotlight and made publicly visible through observation, grading and evaluation. But the power that put them in the spotlight in the first place becomes invisible through the digital infrastructures that motion it.

Combined with the neoliberal priorities for free markets and market well-being, the digital infrastructures gripping educational systems present a bigger picture that begins to position schools as 'factories' for labour production (Figure 3.1) and propose that to governments. Policies, data collection, technologies and goals unify to work with the same objective: identify labour market needs and achieve equilibrium of labour (re)production.

Critical work has already looked at such mechanisms for organizing higher education as a function of market well-being.[22] Hall[23] argues that the higher education institution is 'repurposed' so that 'its activities, social relationships, cultures, supply chains and so on enable the production of commodities that can be exchanged'.[24] Similar organizational structures are emerging in the earlier years of compulsory education through the affordances of digital infrastructures. With the digitization of schools, data becomes the means to monitor, predict and, at least in principle, influence

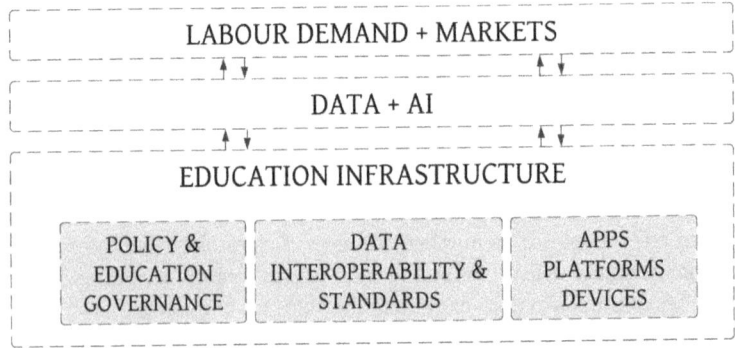

Figure 3.1 Labour (re)production through the means of digital infrastructures integrated in public education.

what needs to be learned in ways that it aligns with what industry needs as skills and competencies. Given similar critique of how higher education is transforming to a mere servant of economic needs,[25] schools are viewed as the means to power the market economy by producing cheap (because the cost of schooling and student training is on taxpayers' backs) and adequately skilled labour. 'Adequately' is promised by data extractive algorithmic systems for prediction and precision. 'Adequately' skilled labour will then be expected to look after the well-being of the market.

Whether health, political, economic or socio-cultural (such as the post-war counter-culture, civil rights and anti-war movements of the 1960s), crises have been instrumental in instigating reforms, which have often been used as levers for corporate advancement. In education, two particular reforms laid the foundation for its digitization and datafication. Within the Anglo-American contexts, these are the teacher reform and the drive for school accountability. As highlighted by Ball,

> not least in the sense that the construction within policy and public discourses of the 'untrustworthy teacher' creates the basis for the assertion of more accountability and more control over their education and their certification and performance … and legitimates the withdrawal of aspects of their professional autonomies.[26]

A brief genealogy of these policies follows next.

Technologies of policymaking: Paving the way for a datafied education

The technologies of policymaking around the time globalization began to enter the political lexicon in the UK and across Europe involved a well-calculated deployment of organization, procedures, articulation, disciplines and specialized bodies of knowledge all of which were aimed, as Ball[27] maintains, towards the 'transformation' and 'modernization' of public sector bodies and systems. Put simply, these technologies aimed to create the education as a market under the assumption that, to work, it can be run, managed and operationalized like one. To achieve this, 'the use of new language is important, the new public management organizations are now "peopled" by human resources that need to be managed; learning is re-rendered as a "cost-effective policy outcome" and achievement is a set of "productivity targets"'.[28]

The new language introduces new ways of thinking, manifested in the demands for accountability, standards, performance monitoring, ranking, national criteria, addressing schools of underachievement and so on.

These reforms were evident predominantly in the Anglo-American contexts, as a point of departure for education, marking the starting point for its transformation within the growing influence of neoliberal orthodoxy. The strategies of accountability and performance monitoring have long been assumed to unburden schools of bureaucracy and centralization, of too much government interference and therefore of an assumed slow process of innovation.

However, as Ball notes, 'it is a mis-recognition to see these reform processes as simply a strategy of devolution and deregulation – they are processes of re-regulation, not the abandonment by the state of its controls over public services but the establishment of a new form of control'.[29] This entails the delegation and independence of 'devolution and autonomy of "freedoms" while still operating within the confines and demands of "performance" and "profitability"'.[30]

Within this re-regulation, the new technologies of policy are not merely instruments that governments can harness and possess. Rather, they are services lent to public education by private commercial enterprises.

An important point must be added here about these rented services. They are not solely used to identify what works in education or how educational institutions perform. Their data-extractive and computational capacities become the conduit for information flow between education, governments and industry (as depicted in Figure 3.1). But equally, it can be between education and industry directly. Such relationships can bypass governments' governance (whether they want it or not) and render them inadequate and incompetent to control or respond to any decisions and directions of influence. Just as EdTech are not mere neutral 'tools' in the classroom, they are also not mere tools in the hands of governments. They are independent dynamic entities of their own standing (the stranger) and should be treated as such.

The principles of education as a market infuse the principles of competition typical of business into public sector frameworks. This results in their fragmentation into distinct 'business' entities, which manifest as rivalry among the schools. Their aim now is to attract students and ensure that their 'income' is maximized at individual student level and top competition at institutional level. The efficacy of competition becomes part of the overall education governance mechanism. It also becomes part of the 'purpose' of education. Market 'failure' directly impacts the continued existence or success of individual institutions. Additionally, parent choice maintains the competitive dynamic of schools. Education as a market loses government bureaucratic control, but simultaneously the meaning of education also changes. It now becomes a matter of competition and survival. Within the neoliberalist orthodoxy, assuming that schools would be run like businesses led to the assumption that their value output and contribution to national economies should be measured, ranked and monitored just like businesses. From there, the need to collect more data that will evidence how well the newly defined goals are achieved, what ranking the school or the student has reached and what interventions were the most or least effective. Logically, this drive for data collection has moved education for *learning* towards education for *performing*.

Performativity is enabled through actions that are demonstrable through data. Data is analysed and allows to draw out trends, create charts, identify correlations and make predictions. Performativity is demonstrated through data, which is then translated as how students perform or where the school ranks among regional, national and international orders. Here focus on performativity is not only on its impact on knowledge and value creation but also on how performativity invited more digitization and datafication as the 'norm' and 'meaning' of education.

To have learned something well means to have performed well that shows on a (digital) dashboard. School performance further becomes a useful framework of thinking about a country's national economy and how it would situate within an international context. School performance could easily be seen to measure the 'population-wealth problem',[31] trapping along the way student and teacher populations within matrices of numbers and rank orders, and now digital dashboards with data visualizations are the normative and legitimate instruments of measuring knowledge and competency. These, in turn, further influence decision-making around education. However, performativity becomes not only 'a technology of oppressions' as Ball argues; 'it is also one of satisfactions and rewards, at least for some'.[32] It becomes a zero-sum game and so is education turned into *gamification* whereby the power of the digital technologies that turn education into a performative act becomes an invisible power and one that can control but cannot be itself controlled.

Ball contends that much of the late nineteenth-century obsession and policymaking was through the prism of eugenics and the 'psy-sciences', which subsequently became more invisible yet still a powerful player in education policymaking as instruments to control populations. In the twenty-first century, we can argue that digital technologies become these same 'virtually invisible and their classifications neutral' psy-sciences, while they still wield power by contributing to the 'displacements, locating patterns of distribution in the intellect, the home, community or the inefficiencies of the school'.[33] Lowe[34] suggests that there is a discernible eugenicist element in today's fixation with testing, which is employed to categorize individuals into various levels of 'abilities'. School, by default, reinforces ablism. Students are classified and categorized according to abilities, 'meeting expectations', 'good progress', green box and so on. Grouping and banding according to aptitude are popular practices. With EdTech interventions their 'diagnostics' treat students literally as patients.

Digitized classrooms facilitate the measurement of various student aspects for 'personalized' learning but risk a pedagogy focused on measurement, which only drives the adoption of more sophisticated digital technologies promising such measurement. To achieve this 'better' measurement, however, the digitization has been followed by problematizing standardization and data interoperability.

Standards and interoperability problematization

To understand the radical shift of digitizing education, a starting point is to map the technical make-up and the greater long-term capabilities the combined technologies offer. Here we are no longer seeing just apps in the classroom but their assemblages and capabilities with cloud computing, platforms and data management systems as a larger unified capable apparatus. Such integrated data systems promise to enhance learner support, cloud-based interoperable platforms to aid school management and guide teaching through data. Key components of a digital infrastructure are standards and interoperability, which increasingly become the governing tools in education.

Contemporary education governance focuses on harnessing educational data and computational potential. The account that follows does not dive into technical aspects but examines the implications of these structures for education and the necessary oversight for the key players involved. For this, I draw on literature that cautions about the opacity of algorithms and AI and the limitations of techno-deterministic views and performativity datafication instils as a dominant form of providing education for children.

The move to digital education has fostered the move towards centralizing discourse and action around data. To realize data's potential requires agreed-upon data interoperability standards. Globally, education policy increasingly emphasizes data interoperability and standardization. Many studies emphasize open data standards to drive enterprise cloud adoption, transitioning from traditional on-site infrastructure to cloud-based solutions managed by providers over the internet.[35] What we have seen as a result of lack of standards is ensuing challenges like vendor lock-ins, which have made it difficult to switch providers due to various costs and constraints.[36]

There has been a growing need for different systems and products to communicate seamlessly and enable data flow, which in turn supposedly unlocks the promised potential of data.

These infrastructures have been advancing in how they are built and operate in some parts of the world. Their advancement expressed in that they have propelled a new form of governance, one that is based on an automation and prediction. A case in point is in Australia. There, Gulson, Sellar and Webb argue that the new infrastructure of governance with the centralization of digital and AI-embedded systems, streamlining of data across levels of education thanks to data interoperability standards, have led to a 'synthetic governance'.[37] In their book *Algorithms of Education: How Datafication and Artificial Intelligence Shape Policy*, the authors take on Foucault's notion of problematization as the approach to analyse the processes through which digital infrastructures with data and AI-capable products have become primary objects of thought and subjects of focus and examination.

Problematizations examine how specific practices or phenomena are brought into focus and considered worthy of intellectual exploration and investigation. When something becomes the subject of problematization, it enters the realm of debates and discussions about what is true or false concerning that particular issue. Problematizations, the authors contend, typically occur within established institutions, where certain claims to truth are recognized and accepted as authoritative.[38] Problematizations create the conditions and frameworks within which different potential responses to a problem such as education data governance and digital infrastructures can be formulated and evaluated. The process of problematization involves defining the key elements that will shape and constitute the various solutions proposed for the issues stemming from the digitization of education. As such, one can observe the priorities digital infrastructures and questions around education data standards and interoperability have taken globally.

National data infrastructures have become a top priority for many Western governments, serving as a means to hold schools accountable, as already noted earlier, and rationalize substantial digital investments in education.

However, for their optimal functionality, data interoperability standards have been the focus of attention by governments (e.g., in the UK), interested to establish a shared data language that enables diverse digital systems to exchange information seamlessly and effectively. The expectation of such interoperability is that it will streamline data exchange across applications and platforms and unlock the potential for activities like analytics, prediction, product development and the advancement of digital systems within the digital infrastructure itself.

Over the past two decades, as the EdTech market has expanded, various initiatives to standardize education data have arisen. Notable examples include the Schools Interoperability Framework (SIF), IMS Global's (now renamed 1Edtech) Learning Tools Interoperability standards (LTI) and others. These standards or frameworks define common data models, ensuring seamless data exchange across different platforms, resulting in more efficient transactions and maximizing the usefulness of the data. Standardization offers significant benefits to school systems in principle as it enables the integration of generic applications into existing systems at reduced development costs and lower risks.

In the United States, the Common Education Data Standard (CEDS) provides a data interoperability template for districts and states to adopt and implement, facilitating 'common language'[39] that contains hundreds of data elements and to cover all educational levels and institutions[40] from the early years. SIF also offers common data formats, promoting data transfers and exchanges between student information management systems and various school applications. In 2006, the UK created a SIF Association, and in 2009, Australian Education ministers chose to adopt and develop an Australian SIF specification. In 2015, the Access 4 Learning (A4L) Community was founded, uniting SIF associations from North America, the UK and Australia. Although the UK moved away from the SIF standard due to challenges with local authorities, inter-regional issues and privacy and security concerns,[41] the UK government in 2023 engaged roundtables with industry, experts and school representatives to re-evaluate interoperability standards and data capabilities.

It is important to note that the SIF standard was launched by Bill Gates, the Microsoft co-founder, back in 1999 who has been an avid proponent of standardizing education data and driving data-driven policies. He was also the co-designer of CEDS, investing over $20 million[42] in research and data systems and has poured even more to support bi-partisan initiatives around data-driven decision-making. Data collection and assessing the value of education data at a global level have been a prime goal for Bill Gates through his eponymic foundation.[43] The commercial opportunities in education through digital technologies and the capabilities stemming from data collection there have been well reported by the Parthenon Group (an EY global consultancy strategy branch) back in 2007 for the Gates Foundation. The report recommended that for data to be utilized, districts must 'recognise the need and ability to drive behaviour change', have the necessary technology that can support analytics, 'identify, implement and train on necessary systems', and 'pay for the system'.⁴⁴ The problematization here is expressed in the solution given first – data utilization for better decisions and ultimately education – from which stems the need for 'essential tools', requisite data for the development of AI analytics.

In Australia, the National Student Interoperability Program or NSIP aimed to implement the SIF standards. However, today the SIF community known as A4L has focused beyond mere data management to include the use of data as 'true learning information for parents, practitioners and learners themselves'.⁴⁵ As Gulson, Sellar and Web describe, NSIP supports various projects related to system integration, data sharing, infrastructure reuse and data synchronization. The national curriculum, National Assessment Program – Literacy and Numeracy (NAPLAN), and national teacher standards are implemented to facilitate students' seamless transitions between schools across the Australian states and territories, enabling attendance tracking and achievement monitoring while preventing learning gaps. This centralization however, the authors argue, also benefits the industry by reducing development costs through common data standard. Additionally, digital governance methods 'overlap with network governance which ... is characterised by increasing numbers of "backroom"'⁴⁶ policy actors, including technical staff working on digital infrastructure development. Lastly, the authors contend, NSIP shows how technical infrastructure issues, like the SIF standard, involve more people in education governance, change it as a result of these new digital modalities and enable the businesses providing the digital infrastructures and products to enter decision-making processes in 'quite opaque ways'.⁴⁷

Standards for education data interoperability settle as the new language that influences governance, meaning and decision-making. It also lowers the entry to market, and therefore it provides an opportunity for it to grow. While standards may not be proprietary within the context of education, they can still lead to lock-in scenarios. As Shapiro and Varian explain over twenty years ago: 'technologies subject to strong network effects tend to exhibit long lead times followed by explosive growth. The pattern results from *positive feedback*: as the installed base of users grows, more and more users find adoption worthwhile'.⁴⁸ Once the product achieves critical mass, it takes hold of the entire market. Moreover, it becomes more expensive to keep outside it than join it. Once commonly agreed standards and interoperability are adopted, the market can swiftly integrate into the education system at scale, which is what has happened in Australia. Not only vendors can directly deal with schools and avoid bureaucratic procurement process, but they can also control the price of their products.

Additionally, NSIP has introduced a Hub Integration Testing Service (HITS) that allows software companies to test their products using fictitious data for school integration. Similar data spaces exist in the EU through public funding. Although dummy data does not pose immediate harm to data subjects, it can be argued that its first benefit is by aiding industry with product development and then speedier integration into education and other sectors, potentially overlooking students' needs and best interests. As Gulson, Sellar and Webb analyse, the standardization has reduced the resources for product development but also the transition to more generic products and solutions.[49] This pro-market approach lets the market shape users' needs and influence what students and teachers use in schools. It not only increases industry influence on pedagogy but also leads to profit and further product development, fundamentally changing education around market needs.

The common language of data for interoperability raises several concerns. First it defines what needs to be collected, how it should be organized, what counts and how to count things in education. However, it may not necessarily serve the best interests of students. The language of data alone requires pedagogical and curriculum expertise to assess its impact on education, as it can oversimplify complex activities.[50]

Second, the language of data interlocks an expanding network of third parties that adopt it. The US CEDS Data Warehouse, mentioned earlier, 'has the capacity to support the full P-20W data pipeline'.[51] It partners with learning agencies, public and private higher education institutions, the US Department of Education, the US Health and Human Services and the US Department of Labour; education data standards organizations, as well as powerful members of the private sector.[52] Some are directly related to education; others are not.[53] Again, with the Bill Gates's foundation support a project called InBloom for collecting student data in a single concentrated warehouse was created. However, it failed following parental outcry against the development of a centralized warehouse of children's education data.[54] Nevertheless, two others that are striving for 'pathways data'[55] – the Data Quality Campaign[56] and Chiefs for Change (CFC), a bipartisan lobby group[57] – carry on. Among many others,[58] especially with much industry representation, DQC and CFC push aggressively for data alignment and student tracking.[59]

Third, the language of data for interoperability has led to data pipeline development across districts and states in the United States specifically and a new way of thinking about education. Some states are introducing 'data lakes', an euphemism for a warehouse or a repository, 'capable of ingesting, storing, and providing data from a large number of sources and for a wide range of users and uses'.[60] Others are promoting data 'backpacks' or electronic student records that contain all sorts of academic and personal student data – test scores, behavioural patterns, 'non-cognitive variables that impact achievements, as well as an "early warning system", self-management skills, behaviour/character education, and a record of community service'.[61] In the UK, too, data interoperability, learner and workforce data alignment have been envisioned.[62] In other words, the language of data and the capacities stemming from data interoperability have enabled for a direct link to be made between education and industry (the labour market). For example, education policies have proposed[63] education and training according to how clustering into industrial zones has been implemented, such as in Washington[64] and Virginia.[65] I return to this point later in the chapter.

Lastly, data's influence on education narrows learning to quantifiable numbers, potentially limiting students' agency and benefiting systems over individuals. Centralizing data's role in education amplifies the emphasis on measurement, raising concerns about educational autonomy,[66] originally governments' prerogative. In turn, the ever-growing influence of the private sector into public education is advancing with tech industry's sway in areas like STEM development, undermining other subjects. As data and tech permeate public education, the lines between education and business become less clear, prompting questions about whom these changes truly benefit. This also sparks concerns about education's quality, scope, depth, purpose and the value of schools.

If the value of schools is increasingly measured by what future workforce they produce, thanks to the granular insight data promises, what sort of education do we promise children and young people today? Undoubtedly, schools' connection to industry is of value. Schools prepare future citizens, consumers and workers. Still, a shift toward corporate influence and away from social investment neglects important human aspects, which can hurt individuals and the collective well-being. How exactly such link is made – the bigger picture of digital infrastructuring of education with corporate influence[67] is discussed next.

Talent pipeline management – workforce production

What exactly happens in education today? Who decides what (digital or other) systems and instruments operate there? What do these institutions (are meant to) produce? What becomes undone as a result? The digital technology sector with a concentration of US-born Big Tech providers at the bottom layers of the stack (to use engineering jargon) is becoming the main infrastructures – the 'arteries' transporting, storing, managing, controlling, enabling and governing educational processes.

Policymakers are seeing the abilities of digital technology systems as an opportunity to enable tracking of students' learning pathway from the cradle to the workforce. From computers and apps in the classroom to whole digital infrastructures that capture future loyal customers and future 'useful and docile workforce'.[68]

Those who have control over these infrastructures can and have the power to set the rules. They become significant power with regulatory and normative authority (Figure 3.2).

The stacking of student information systems, software applications, digital credential programs, courses, surveys about students' well-being and opinions and so on enable data collection for profiling and exchange across systems with the purpose to support better decision-making, better allocation of resources from educational resources to student loans, better ways of steering students to the 'right' learning or career pathways, to better informing industries about the kind of workforce schools are producing. But within this platformized education, data exchange and how decisions are arrived at create information asymmetries in which students and teachers know less about the machinations, the data used and the way in which decisions are made. This leads to unequal power distribution and ultimately monopolies of knowledge.

Here is what I mean. Industrial societies brought about the factory-like schooling that many tech evangelists condemn today. Learning happens anywhere at any time. Industry changed that by introducing compulsory education. Education is different from learning. Education is the product of the industrial society – knowledge is packaged into marketable skills, into a commodity that is necessary later in one's life to exchange for other commodities such as food, shelter, clean air and traveling – ironically, as Ivan Illich contends, all necessities that today are luxuries demanding significant financial wealth.[69] This industrial organization manifesting in educational

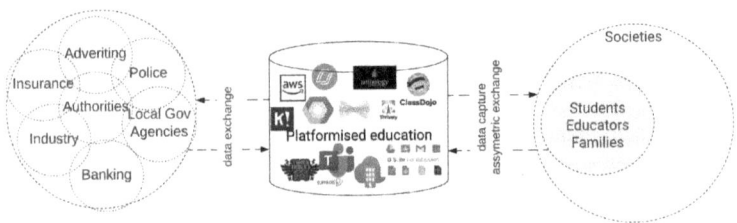

Figure 3.2 Interoperability enables data-driven decisions that transcend sectors. Those with control of such data interoperable systems can influence decisions and influence populations.

institutions is imposed on most societies today. Digital systems not only reinforce and sustain this organization; they claim possession of it. They design, dictate and promise to produce outputs (workforce) or outcomes (grades, degrees), which they simultaneously also begin to decide which will qualify as 'necessary' or 'valid'. Becoming dependent on such structures can disable societies and impoverish individuals. People can become, in Ivan Illich's words:

> helpless to recognise evidence unless it has been certified by a professional – be he a television weather commentator or an educator; organic discomfort becomes intolerably threatening unless it has been medicalised into dependence on a therapist; neighbours and friends are lost unless vehicles bridge the separating distance (created by the vehicles in the first place). In short, most of the time we find ourselves out of touch with our world, out of sight with those for whom we work, out of tune with what we feel.[70]

In mercantile societies, Illich and Verne write:[71]

> [T]he idea of education underwent a first transformation, as it came to mean the manipulation of one individual of another ... Industrial societies transformed the idea of education a second time; by education they meant the manipulation of children by adults using a programmed instrument called the school.

In compulsory education, 'we are no doubt witnessing a further reduction of the idea of education, this time for the exclusive benefit of the capitalists of knowledge and the professionals licensed to distribute it'. Today, the capitalists of knowledge are the owners of data-driven systems. They are not licensed to participate in education in any pedagogic sense. Yet they monopolize the purpose of educational institutions. Their systems can be programmed to shape the kind of workforce or social tiers societies should have.

We see this happening in the United States through vocational or career and technical education (CTE), programs that are offered in nearly all public education. Policy and federal funding are driving student tracking and clustering from as early as K-12, and through the support of corporations like Amazon, IBM, Cisco and others, those mediating the flow and knowledge distribution (Figure 3.2), curriculum is increasingly watered down and hyper-narrowed predominantly for those more disadvantaged and children of immigrants who are more likely to take on CTE programs. In research

I conducted with colleague and journalist Jeff Bryant in the United States, we found from families about how education is increasingly narrowed down while corporations encroach on public curriculum with their own programs, luring students to warehouse trips, credentialed courses and promise for future job placements.[72] Students are taught not computer science but Cisco systems. They do not study engineering but Amazon Future Engineer.[73]

Narrowing down of curriculum and subject breadth has also been witnessed in the UK.[74] This has been the result of the drive for performativity measures and the focus on 'core' subjects since at least the 1990s, leading to an emphasis on science, technology, engineering and mathematics (STEM) education similar to its American counterparts. This drive has increasingly restricted curriculum flexibility, limiting arts and culture education opportunities due to funding cuts and performance measurements – redirection of funds on EdTech.

However, hyper-specialization and narrowing down education have repercussions for the future opportunities of individuals once they go out of school into the world of work. Hyper-specialized or narrowed education has shown to lead to long-term job insecurity.[75] It is one thing to study computer science with subjects that span from philosophy to history to ethics; it is quite another to be trained on Amazon systems, which can and do change unpredictably.

When individuals become hyper-specialized, they remain highly vulnerable to the changes of the market. To this end, with the accelerating technologies the dominant corporate interests follow an unpredictable path, generating for the dominated an even greater sense of insecurity.

The predictive and prescriptive initiatives propelled in schools through data systems are highly experimental. Ultimately, technologies change fast. There is little substantial evidence to suggest what the best skills to acquire in primary education today will have value in ten years.

Ensuring school skills lead to secure jobs is certainly needed but challenging, probably impossible because of many factors. Algorithmic systems increasingly shape labour markets, and public education's embrace of private companies for digitization, automation and platformization can further limit curriculum flexibility. Algorithmic management systems are already used to coordinate, manage and even select labour within organizations.[76] However, an important difference is that public education is welcoming private companies to shape and influence all its processes, practices and people. The guarantors become the algorithmic systems and their unknown developers and owners who not only enable to track and predict labour supply and demand, but they also claim future labour markets by providing their own needs for skilling and reskilling. Algorithmic systems are fed data about children in order to inform educational processes, manage credentialing programs, track and steer students – what the US Chamber of Commerce Foundation (of the US Chamber of Commerce, the largest lobbying group in the United States) says the 'manage talent pipelines'.[77] Similarly, in the EU, by harvesting skills intelligence through the development of a 'permanent online tool for real-time information' for 'all interested stakeholders', careers can be tailored and education policy informed based on industry demands.[78]

Educational technologies and platforms play the role of digital host for educational systems globally.[79] Their components – from hardware to software – make up the new 'technologies' of policy-making. They receive little resistance from either the education community or policymakers. On the contrary, as previously stated, often it is national policymakers and supranational organizations on the global stage that advance the discussion around digital infrastructures as a solution to achieving global educational (and economic) goals. Many EdTech companies themselves often occupy the same policy tables where global visions and strategies are drafted. See for example an relatively unknown DXtera Institute, which prides itself to be 'an investment in the future of higher education'.[80] It has crawled into policy ranks at European level by growing networks of AI and EdTech alliances (typically with expensive membership plans), by providing input to global organizations like UNESCO (the Broadband Commission's 'Data for Learning'[81]), and by establishing for the European Commission 'a Community of Practice to support a new Digital Education Hub'.[82] One surely can enquire further into the effectiveness of these initiatives; nonetheless, long term they can count as small drops of gospel preaching around the capabilities of AI and the digitization of education. See also UNESCO's Global Education Coalition[83], which was launched following the Covid-19 pandemic as a 'multi-sector partnership to provide appropriate distance education for all learners'[84] – all 'admirable and ambitious aims', as Williamson argues. These coalitions put forward the tech-driven agendas, and together with the multilateral organizations, they also partner with the private sector (starting with Facebook, now Meta, Google and many others), with little clarity as to their contribution, let alone expertise on pedagogy and learning.

The commonality among all these initiatives is that the digital is the way forward and that data will pave the way to educational success, economic prosperity, achieved sustainability goals and so on – ultimately a particularly powerful story that many policymakers endorse.[85]

This new data-intensive digital governance replaces the old technologies of policymaking and governance of education. Digital systems promise to remove bureaucratic inefficiency, yet integrating them seems like solving one problem and letting new ones surface – from data privacy and security risks to more complex ones stemming from their algorithmic capabilities. Digital infrastructures indeed promise efficiencies, but essential critical questions should be asked about the implications for submitting to their new principles. They propose new governance, but who is governing them?

The earlier sections of this chapter examined how policies played a role in the growing trend of data collection for assessing performance, subsequently paving the way for the digital transformation of education. Specifically, crises have presented opportunities for both policymakers and businesses to align their agendas into a common one of embracing digital futures.

The upcoming sections in this chapter are dedicated to elucidating the digital reconfiguration of education through platformization. This features a dual input-output model and is considered the means to generate economic value and streaming of economically viable output from schools – with the promise for precision.

Datafication, platformization and credentialing education

From siloed data and disparate use of apps, platforms and digital resources, the digitization of education has been both a proposal and a gradual process of building an architectural unified system that can work as one, inspired by the data factory logic (see Figure 3.3). Architectural designs such as Figure 3.3 have already been evident in other sectors, as pointed out in Chapter 2. In education, proposals for such singular systems have been in the making in the United States and elsewhere for well over a decade. Such a seamless vision of data → analysis → prediction can be seen both at the level of schools/educational institutions but also at regional and national levels.

Such tailoring has consistently come with the problematization around data privacy and security risks for children's data. Undoubtedly, the digitization of education has led to increased cyber insecurities and privacy concerns. While many proposed solutions have been made recently to tackle these, it has been more so that a bridge is built to greater data utilization than solely for clarifying the purpose of data collection about children in schools.

Today, this type of discourse persists, much like the argument related to crises of cyber insecurity and privacy loss. In the context of the latter, industry representatives and policymakers have formed intricate relationships and 'networks' with shared objectives and opportunities, whose finances, management and ownership are hard to follow. The aims emerging are not only to offer 'solutions' for the classroom with students or school management but also to enhance and solidify specific forms of

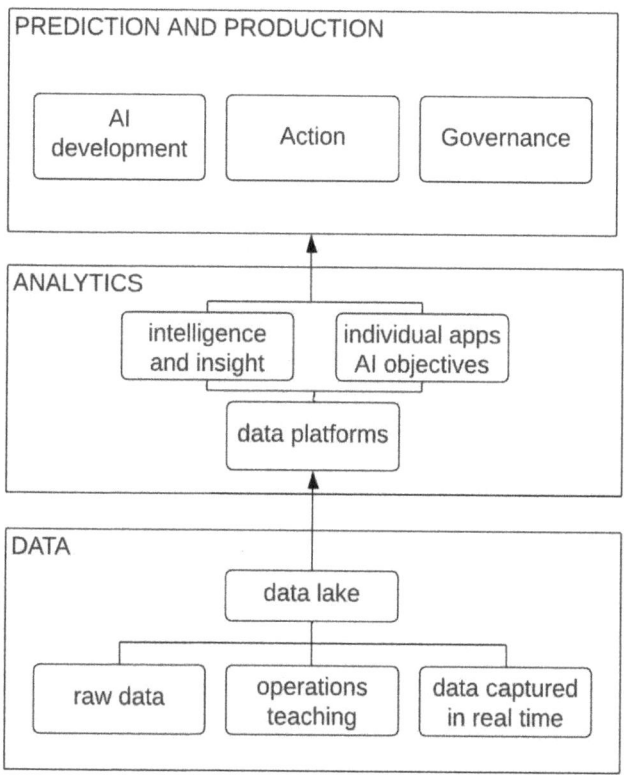

Figure 3.3 Platformization of education: From digitization to datafication to automation to prediction. This model depicts a factory structure through the means of data. The structure promises intelligence, prediction and production.

governance and control. In other words, the opportunities have been emerging not solely around data. At a higher level, the prospects have extended beyond even education – to encompass managing markets and controlling populations, too. Such systems for control and management with market imperatives already undergird Western societies. However, they are now augmenting sophisticated digital systems whose commercial owners are becoming central mediating power player and are also extending to schools and children at an ever younger age.

For instance, the education data landscape in the United States has paved the way for the development of Interoperable Learning Records (ILR) (see Figure 3.4) as proposed by this American Workforce Policy Paper.[86] It

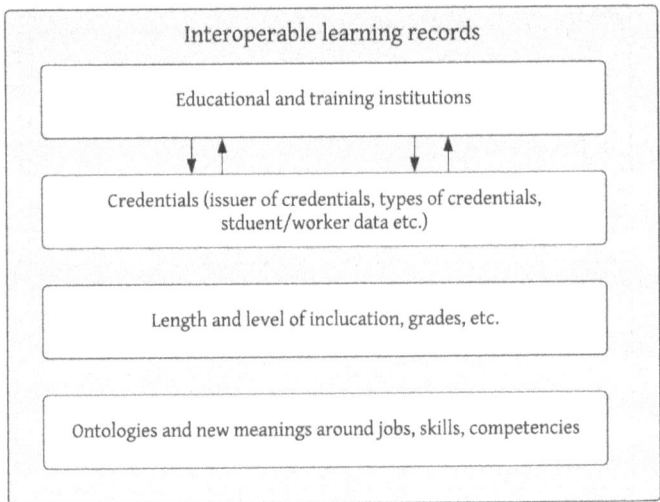

Figure 3.4 Interoperable learning record protocol, simplified concept from the original.[87]

proclaimed that American workers committed to lifelong learning need a way to convert their education, training and work experience into transferable skills records for better job opportunities. Former president Donald Trump addressed this issue with an executive order, establishing the National Council for the American Worker (NCAW) and the American Workforce Policy Advisory Board (AWPAB).

These initiatives set on course to improve data transparency, enhance recruitment and training practices and boost employer-led training investments. What followed is the development of data pipelines set-up and 'talent pipeline management'[88] through the use of data. The white paper explains ILR protocols using a 'file cabinet' metaphor, which serves as a framework for transforming education into a precise conduit for workforce production.

The file cabinet manages and shares learner credentials, ensuring their integrity using blockchain and similar advanced experimental technologies for extra security and legitimation. The vision includes 'an envelope' for data verification and a 'letter' with specific credential details.

Lastly, an 'ontology represents common language and schemas for occupations, jobs, competencies/skills and credential types etc.'[89] Interoperability, data ontology, data lake, canonical data and so on form part of the common new language as already introduced earlier. They are carved into education and becoming the language of governing and transforming education.

I analyse the extent of policy, white papers, agendas and technical documentation elsewhere.[90] Here I only detail with an example of how education is envisioned – and what is decided upon children and learners generally – through the complex machinations, interests and ambitions of policymakers and industry members.

The layers of this protocol are mainly four broad ones: data standards, ontologies and frameworks, products and services, and obviously uptake with pilots.

Standards

On assessment, interoperability, data and standards, there are several large entities that also have direct market involvement, challenging the notion of an independent non-commercial educational system. On the one hand, there are entities like IMS Global Learning Consortium, now called 1Edtech, which play a powerful role in capturing not only infrastructure but the market and educational institutions and staff. IMS Global was founded in 1995 and is a non-profit organization focused on creating technical standards for digital education materials, especially in assessment and curriculum. Their key initiatives include OneRoster®,[91] a standard that assists secure sharing of class rosters and data between a student information system and various systems like McGraw Hill digital tools. Adopting this standard, IMS Global assures and streamlines user account, content assignment, and class roster management:

> [W]hen districts and their partners adopt OneRoster® standards, it simplifies the management of user accounts, content assignments, and class rosters. McGraw Hill's Single Sign-On (SSO) and Auto-Rostering Access Service utilizes the OneRoster® standard.[92]

Other products include Question & Test Interoperability (QTI) and Accessible Portable Item Protocol (APIP) specifications, which promote interoperability in assessment systems.

Interestingly, IMS Global renamed itself in 2022[93] – unbeknownst to the public. It is now called 1Edtech and does a lot more than standards. IMS TrustEd Apps Seal also is a certifier that 'an application satisfactorily completes the rigorous and trusted TrustEd Apps veto process and its ratings on the TrustEd Apps Rubric are fully disclosed and meet a specified level of expectation.'[94] Not only do they certify products but also schools, encouraging them to then '[s]eek out suppliers with the IMS Data Privacy Seal'. This program is thrusting schools to buy specific products whose vendors in turn have to be serviced by IMS Global to get certified. The loop is closed with IMS Global, enticing educational institutions to become IMS 'contributing members', an 'affiliate' or a 'TrustEd Apps Alliance member' to endorse this whole structure of the commercial 1Edtech.

There are other standards of course. In a similar fashion, they create markets for both educational institutions and educational technologies. This business model of offering 'a plug-and-play architecture and ecosystem that provides a foundation on which innovative products can be rapidly deployed and work together seamlessly'[95] are lowering the cost of product development and deployment but at the same time are increasing the dependency of schools and their populations on their structures and suite of products.

Schools' dependency increases on this particular provider and its own market capture of EdTechs and also gives it more advantage for market expansion and product development. To re-enforce the dependency, 1Edtech also offers assessment and certification of EdTech products and memberships that cost anywhere between $5,000 and $61,000 and for schools and districts anywhere between $1,000 and $5,000.[96] In a word, this is a whole ecosystem within which educational institutions are increasingly locked in and paying for.

Products and services

For instance, Burning Glass Technologies provides data analytics for the labour market, helping job seekers, employers and educators bridge skill gaps, 'reshaping how the labour market works with data that identify the skill gaps that keep job seekers and employers apart and tools that enable both sides to bridge that gap and connect more easily'. According to their profile:

> This real-time strategic intelligence offers insights, such as which jobs are most in demand, the specific skills employers need, and the career directions that offer the highest potential for workers. According to their profile they are used across the job market: by educators in aligning programs with the market, by employers and recruiters in filling positions more effectively, and by policy makers in shaping strategic workforce decisions.[97]

Concentric Sky offers a product called Badgr for verifiable credentials to 'allow institutions to design stackable, cross-disciplinary learning pathways that build off prior learning assessments, industry certifications, and other external credentials'.[98] Core Learning Exchange (CLX) aims to 'enhance' competency-based learning. National Student Clearinghouse (NSC) aids in reporting and data exchange.

All these initiatives are encroaching nationwide. Indiana, for example, is aligning education with workforce needs. They have received significant funding, such as a $1.5 million grant for ACE Learner Success Lab and Strada Education Network to 'develop and pilot a Learner Success Lab that will provide opportunities for postsecondary institutions to strategize and implement effective policies and practices that help students meet the demands of today's workforce'.[99] Indiana's scale-up of Credential Engine is by listing all public institutions' programs and their fees, with future plans for graduate earnings and other data to be collected and made available. The state emphasizes the alignment of skills from education and training with what employers are looking for in terms of labour. This priority is reflected in various statewide programs, including NextLevel Jobs, Skillfull Indiana and partnerships with the US Chamber of Commerce Foundation, all aimed at understanding employers' worker needs (Figure 3.5) and translating that into how education and curriculum should be restructured.

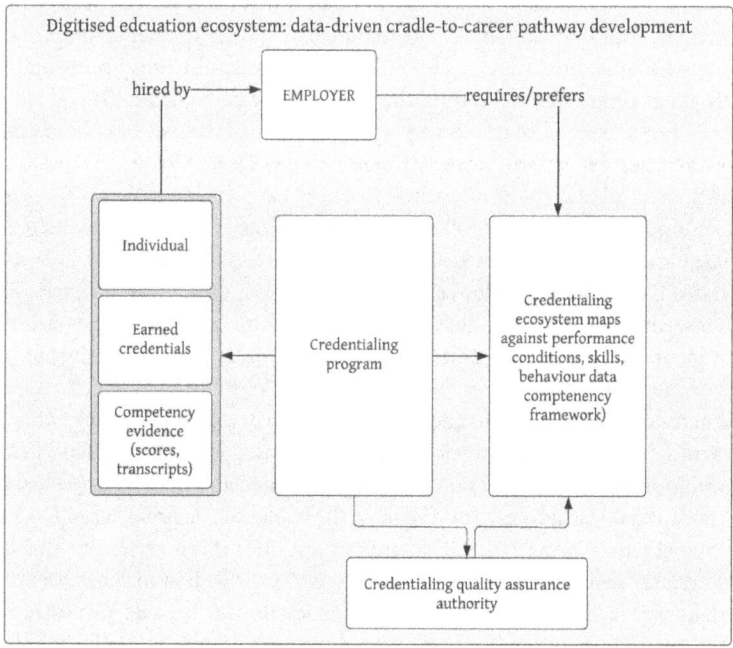

Figure 3.5 Data-driven, cradle-to-career pathway development; interoperable learning records for streamlining what industry needs[100] in terms of skills and competencies and what education should 'produce'.

Similar efforts are emerging in Europe through Prometheus-X Education & Skills.[101] The French non-profit association comprises a substantial international community to create digital commons for data sharing, focusing on education and employment. Their goal is to 'build a technical infrastructure for education and skills data exchange and interoperability'.[102]

A vision for technical infrastructure, technical delivery of governance and technical orchestration allows various commercial and policy actors to enhance and tailor their services through data sharing for the purpose of aligning education output with workforce demand. Part of the project's architecture is to develop 'universal plugin SDKs', software development kits, as an open-source tool for creating EdTech plugins that work with various educational software, reducing development costs and promoting data integration.

Many software platforms, such as Moodle, Blackboard and Microsoft Teams for Education, support enhancing their features through special tools and connections (e.g. plugins and APIs or Application Programming Interfaces, which act like bridges that allow different software programs to talk to each other and share information). However, each of these platforms needs custom development work, often in different language-specific data models. This individualized integration and plugin development process imposes substantial expenses on EdTech businesses, ultimately contributing to data centralization within the main software systems. The goal is therefore to provide a universal plugin development framework compatible with major education software, similar to how React Native, a framework that streamlines multi-operating systems like Apple's iOS or Google's Android, allows for app development – what 1Edtech is also doing with their standard, as described earlier. In Lawrence Lessig's words, 'code is law'.[103] Indeed, these standards foster innovation and reduce the cost of developing software applications, but they also embed their own laws and can constrain student and teacher freedoms and behaviour. This presents the vision of standardizing architectures (similar to iOS or Android) onto which anyone can create their own apps and put them into the new Prometheus or 1Edtech 'stores'. This also means schools are rethought not as markets but as clients within markets, changing how education is treated and what it is expected of educational institutions. The vision of these markets is procedural. On the Prometheus-X project site, it describes how, once this architecture enables seamless plugin of apps and AI is deployed to provide best matches between skills and labour market demands, individuals will be able to utilize all the available app providers to create their profiles around skills, hobbies, personality and preferences. By sharing data from these multiple sources, 'app providers can determine ideal career paths and skill deficiencies. Some of the visions include the following:

- They can share this data from multiple sources with app providers to help them identify the best career move (next title, job, sector) and the skills gap.
- They can identify which career move is best for them and share their skills gap with AI providers that match them with training catalogues, content providers to get the right learning recommendations.
- Recommendations of career moves and job/training offers can be easily integrated into any interface of the ecosystem, showing the relevant information to people where they are.
- People can share their full profile and plan with the relevant stakeholders to put it into place (coaches, managers, training providers, etc.).
- All the while they have full control over their data and who can access what.[104]

These logics emanate procedurally from the logics of digital architectures. The architecture described in the quote suggests that individuals are empowered to create profiles based on skills and preferences, share data for career guidance and maintain control over their information. The described architecture further promises to facilitate the management of supply and demand, such as workforce and skilled workers, through data input and artificial intelligence. This implies that data pipelines and software can handle these dynamics effectively. The proposed architecture foresees infrastructures with components dedicated to manage data privacy and security and enables interoperability; broadly speaking, they present a blueprint for how data will be governed. From there, they promise to govern education and the distribution of populations according to credentials, skills and tailored career pathways into the labour market.

Cradle-to-career architectures

Furthermore, the described digital infrastructures like 1Edtech and Prometheus-X are altering the purpose of education, steering the collective and policy thinking towards the idea of an algorithmic precision that would produce ideal alignments between what is taught and trained in education and what is needed in the world of work. These data and digital infrastructures are reshaping education governance into a singular, automated, networked system, with new participants, with complex and obscure policy structures.[105]

Education has often been seen as the instrument to fixing the problems of industry. Most of industry's problems relate to (re)training and retaining valuable resources, human capital. As education is transformed through digital means, the data pipelines supply the information needed to analyse, predict, infer and control the production of human capital. As Ball notes:

> Education is now regarded primarily from an economic point of view. That is, the role of education as a producer of labour and skills and of values, like enterprise and entrepreneurship and of commercial 'knowledge', as a response to international competition. The social and economic purposes of education have been collapsed into a single, overriding emphasis on policy making and economic competitiveness and an increasing sidelining (other than in rhetoric) of the social purposes of education ... This is evident across a whole variety of policy texts in virtually every nation on the planet.[106]

There is a growing body of scholarship around the theory of human capital education (HCE). It manifests through and is propelled by neoliberalist politics – ones that focus on the well-being of the market first and foremost as condition of well-being of societies. This book does not aim to delve into much detail around the HCE theory more than refer to it occasionally as an investment made in education. As Alexander J. Means argues, the evidence about the success of such investment is historically contradictory. What it settles as a legitimate force to policymaking is that it 'reifies labour as capital "stocks" and education as enterprise'.[107] Within the angle of HCE, individuals are seen as resources of capital that can be moulded and (re)produced. Human labour becomes the necessary ingredients for neoliberalist markets, which requires constant accumulation and growth, competition, but also maintaining 'a fine balance between expanded accumulation and a relative level of unemployment and precarious employment'. This precariousness 'is the basis for a neoliberal society'.[108] It is one of several states of being[109] upon which neoliberalism exists. Inequality, insecurity, depoliticization, and financialization are factors contributing to 'a mode of domination', as described by Bourdieu. This mode induces a state of perpetual insecurity to coerce workers 'into submission'[110] and accept exploitation, ultimately subjecting them to *flexploitation*. Examples of that are the casual – task-oriented – and the gig – on-demand – worker.[111]

Policies enable this transformation where education becomes the enterprise, the resource where one is moulded to fit the industry needs. The data systems promise dynamic curriculum adjustment, matchmaking of skills, courses and employment, albeit without any substantial evidence that adopting such logics would ever work. They promise to map who is who; who would be good in what; what niche or skill in the labour market is needed. The data infrastructures propose to make a direct link and a dynamic loop between the demand for labour and the supply for needed workforce. If Amazon demands X amount of web administrators for its new headquarters in Virginia, the state lends its education system to fulfil the anticipated labour demand.[112] This model, however, leads to the symbolic and structural violence, as Bourdieu has argued, which subjugates individuals to the dictates of the industry (and the digital infrastructures). The structural violence bears on workers' 'unremitting commitment [which] is obtained by sweeping away all temporal guarantees'.[113]

The problem is that both the gig and casual workers might be earning something but might equally need retraining at any moment. And so, they are left to 'hang on an arbitrary decision of a power responsible for the "continued creation" of their existence – as is shown and confirmed by the threat of plant closure, disinvestment and relocation'[114] – indeed, as the data infrastructures dictate. As Falk notes, these conditions of policy and digital infrastructures working for the well-being and demands of the neoliberalist market are 'sentencing learners to life'.[115]

Theodore Roszak argued that much apparatus can be distracting and that 'free human dialogue, wandering wherever the agility of the mind allows, lies at the heart of education. If teachers do not have the time, the incentive, or the wit to provide that; if students are too demoralized, bored or distracted to muster the attention their teachers need of them, then *that* is the educational problem which has to be solved – and solved from inside the experience of the teachers and the students'.[116] This is a trouble that does not depend on an app. Apps, in fact, may only exacerbate or prevent agile dialogue to unfold. As the digitized classroom and master cradle-to-career architectures drive for more measurement and performativity, it is concerning how much time teacher and student have left to practise agility of the mind with social dialogue whose end is not a predictive diagnostic or to train a better algorithm which will reciprocate later with better analytics.

Instead, as Biesta says, we live in an *age of measurement*, in which the problem becomes acute when the drive for measuring and evidence gathering begins to define education. This focus on measuring 'what works' is raising questions about education's quality, breadth, depth and purpose. Biesta's response is that this is a bit extreme sort of a new global consensus that ... education is about effective production which are already problematic terms of measurable learning outcomes, but we should do evidence based interventions that if we know how the brain works then we will all be saved forever ... that the main ambition is to position a school system or a country high in particular rankings which means that there is a need to control the whole educational endeavour but also the mindset is one of competition.[117]

Referring to a speech held by the minister of education in Australia in which he says that the main ambition for all Australian education is to make sure they are the top five best performing countries in the world, Biesta muses: 'I cannot understand how a teacher would go to work in the morning and think "my job is to push Australia in the international ranking".[118] So, Biesta says, '[T]here is a huge disconnect between that kind of policy speak'[119], and what happens in the classroom and the purpose of education.

Conclusion

This chapter examined how digital means and private actors have seamlessly integrated into pre-existing systems of control and management of populations but also have gained further domination in educational infrastructures, mainly with their undisclosed intentions and business motives. The purpose of education has shifted from managing human movement during urbanization to a focus on data collection, prediction and workforce development – in a way, to manage and control the (re)production of populations with even greater precision. Concerns centre on the role of education in addressing societal and economic issues and the opacity of technologies and business interests, leaving uncertainties about their intentions and the outcomes of their designs.

From digitization to cradle-to-career, digital infrastructuring of education seems to offer policymakers new policy tools that can align labour market needs with educational paths within a neoliberal economy. These tools involve measuring not only current students but also potentially future workers, which raises concerns for what is left for children to exercise their rights and agency in such gripping structures where labour market demands can align with educational pathways for students. Measurement is not only of students today but arguably and disconcertingly of future workers.

This chapter illustrated a perspective on how education is changing following its digitization and a long-pursued business-oriented model. Schools are increasingly turning and often steered to digital technologies for teaching and learning, simultaneously submitting to aligning with the labour market's needs to guide students towards specific careers with data-infused products promising for precision. In this context, students are also increasingly pressured to keep up with evolving technologies and acquire specific skills that tend to be technically narrow. Students increasingly are put in a subordinate role, with technology holding specific powers to shape the direction of their progress.

The notion of perpetually playing catch-up with new skills can inadvertently place students in a competition that they did not necessarily sign up for. It suggests that students are in direct competition with computers, and the objective is to ensure that humans remain relevant in the digital age of automation. This poses the question, is the primary goal of education to prepare individuals to compete with machines, or should education have a broader purpose that encompasses personal growth and finding purpose? When educational institutions focus solely on producing workers who can keep pace with advancing technological systems, they stand on the losing side in a game whose rules are written by the opposing player – the computing system (and its owner) with its language, rules of data, etc. Playing by someone else's rules assumes that, in this case, technology has an advantage. This not only positions individuals and the collective on the side of the losers; it neglects their unique strengths such as empathy, creativity, excellence and originality. With automation, discussed in the next chapter, it can even override their ability to decide on the terms and rules entirely.

4

Automation: What Are the Risks of Automating Children's Education?

Vorsprung durch technik

It is 2 June 1993, in a hospitality room in Dublin's *Factory* (a secret recording place, apparently), where U2, the Irish rock band, is working on their upcoming album. Bono, the lead singer, asks a journalist who is writing a piece on their forthcoming album, if he has read anything at all by cyberpunk writer, Gibson. 'It's a sort of fucked-up sci-fi', he says, 'and this track [with the song *Zooropa*] shows you what I mean when I say the textures on this record were very much influenced by what he writes about the future'[1] especially because, as it goes in the song, no one truly knows the limits of what humans have created.[2] Especially true for digital technologies.

Vorsprung durch technik[3] – progress through technology. This preposition *through* creates a particular meaning for this marketing slogan. It assumes that one undergoes progress through the optic of (digital) technologies. As I pointed in Chapter 2, this suggests an imposition to see the world as becoming better only through some things and not others, in this case through digital technologies. As Meredith Broussard put it, it is an 'a priori assumption that computers are better than humans' and therefore 'the people who make and program computers are better than other humans'.[4] However, within this technochauvinism lies 'very human factors like self-delusion, racism, bias privilege, and greed'.[5] Notions that computers are impartial and algorithms – fair – are not only misconstrued but limiting and dangerous.

Computers cannot make social and ethical decisions; anything they *can* do comes from the people that design them. Today, it is not just a handful of technology experts creating niche innovative products; it is a rapidly expanding and complex industry becoming mainstream in every societal domain that is challenging to track, oversee and held accountable. Commercial technology companies have entered public education and normalized automated student data collection for measurement, assessment, management, prescription and prediction. They are influencing and outpacing policy and regulation. Progress *through* technologies is being drawn out by those same product developers and owners, and everyone else is committing to their way of seeing the future.

I open this chapter by referring to several lines from U2's Zooropa song to highlight three points which tend to create contention in education. First, generally no one knows *what we've got* in terms of digital technologies in education and what their limit might be. At least there is no universal list of all the EdTechs that are good and all those that are just bad and should be binned. Even those that make the technologies would not know what they have created until their product goes to market.

Recently, Facebook's engineers, for example, admitted that they have no idea how their algorithms work exactly, where their users' data goes and what the company does with it.[6] As technologies advance, it becomes harder to get a clear answer as to what their limits and potentials are.

In 2016, an unconventional self-driving car surfaced in Monmouth County, New Jersey, developed by Nvidia. What set it apart from models by Google or Tesla was its ability to learn to drive by observing a human driver rather than relying on traditional programming. This learning process is akin to how DeepMind's AlphaGo grasps the rules of the ancient game *Go* through the so-called 'self-reinforcement learning'. DeepMind's managing director Demis Hassabis described it, 'free to learn the game for itself, unconstrained by orthodox thinking'.[7] Software will write and create other software and then the responsibility or the logic behind it becomes impossible to track, control or hold accountable. While such achievements are indeed *vorsprung*, they raise questions about their limits. Not knowing their limits can be disconcerting. The disconcerting bit is that, in education, we should ask whether there is already an invisible student observing and learning from children in the classroom, whether that is fair and ethical; that it is done on the backs of children and what it would lead to.

Philosopher Daniel Dennett emphasizes the importance of understanding how and why AI provides answers, suggesting caution in trusting AI explanations. 'If it can't do better than us at explaining what it's doing', Dennett says, 'then don't trust it'.[8] That no one knows how these technologies work exactly should require that everyone is lined at the same starting position, developers/sellers and buyers/users of technologies before progressing any further. For, even though a small representative of our societies creates, designs and controls these products, that does not mean that they are experts in everything else in education or that everything else in education that does not need their expertise is less important.

Second, there is this conflicting argument about how knowledgeable software developers and AI experts actually are. On one hand, we hear that Facebook's people do not have a clue about how algorithms deal with data.

Others are not sure of where AI can take us. And when there is no certainty or they get caught in exploitative practices, companies quickly shut down and change names, or their leftovers get acquired and they simply carry on. On the other hand, they also show immense confidence in their solutionist[9] capacities. All of EdTech's vernacular is about how they will solve one problem after another in education. How can all these thousands of businesses be experts of education?

And third, these very contentions highlight the necessity of taming our overall hopes and dependencies as well as taming businesses' common sales pitch. The success of one technological project, say, DeepMind in its own narrow domain, does not mean we should immediately drive digital experimentation across all social domains. Winning games of chess does not make a master of all board games.

Taming expectations in education means to leave room for educators to be able to find direction, when there is *no compass and no map* (as U2's song goes); maintain the objective to have purpose that is not conditioned by digital automation when none is needed; and as a result, collectively insist on education systems globally to create environments in which children have the options for alternatives that uphold their right to education. Put simply, the capacities of technologies and what about them is actually desirable in education should be laid out more transparently – progress *mit* – *with* – technology, not through its point of view.

Great expectations for AI and task automation, including in education, have persisted for a long time. As I delved into the *New York Times* digital archive recently, some reports from as far back as the 1950s highlight this. In one article the reporter proclaims: 'Computer develops capacity to think', adding:

> Evidence has been found that modern electronic computers may be able to 'learn' from experience and get things done without being told exactly how.[10]

That much of the 'evidence' we have today is still not known and exactly how it is achieved has not changed. And neither has the rhetoric. Lina Rahm created a genealogical mapping of these 'educational imaginaries of technology'[11] to understand how education has influenced our vision of the future involving technology. The author examines educational policies and related data to understand how they outline perceived challenges and solutions for the envisioned automated future while simultaneously actively shaping it. As education increasingly progresses *through* the technological viewpoint, education's role has also been reshaped.

As discussed in the previous chapter, there is a growing policy drive for digital and data skills thus prioritizing the needs of the digital and data economy. As Rahm argues, these needs are not inevitable progressions but a response to political and economic factors. Certainly, there is much to celebrate about digital technologies. But they are also highly experimental and as businesses – speculative in nature. To examine the breadth and depth of integrating automation in education, this chapter looks at two levels. On a micro-level, daily school activities reveal how automated decision-making is articulated and works. On a macro-level, AI is seen as part of the process of reconfiguring authority in educational governance, as noted by Gulson and Witzenberger.[12] The former is discussed first.

What is AI automation in education?

In *Education and Technology: Issues and Debates*, Neil Selwyn defines AI as computer systems that use data and past experiences to make human-like decisions and predictions, which can also automate various tasks without any direct human input. Terms like 'algorithmic data processing' and 'automated decision-making',[13] Selwyn notes, are often used to describe AI due to its ability to process vast amounts of data quickly, highlighting its computerized decision-making based on extensive data analysis.

The automation of processing data and the subsequent output such as analytics and prediction have often been touted as computers' opportunity to enhance and automate decision-making and therefore educational effectiveness. The term 'AI', however, is also the most widely misunderstood, as Meredith Broussard argues. The 'real AI', she explains, is 'narrow AI. It's math. Lots of people have and use every day'.[14] AI also has sub-fields, such as machine learning, expert systems, natural language generation or processing. She writes:

> When you use machine learning, you take a bunch of historical data and instruct a computer to make a model. The model is a mathematical construct that allows us to predict patterns in the data based on what already exists. Because the model describes the mathematical patterns in the data, patterns that humans can't easily see, you can use that model to predict or recommend something similar. This is machine learning. The 'learning' part happens when the machine derives the mathematical patterns.[15]

The model improves as more data is input, resulting in more accurate predictions or recommendations. And as education systems are increasingly entangled with digital technologies, the data generation also grows. As the present discussion has advanced into the subfield of machine learning in education, the clear definition Broussard provides braces this chapter greatly.

A second definition is also helpful here. In *Fairness and Machine Learning: Limitations and Opportunities*, Barocas, Hardt and Narayanan[16] identify three types of automation: rule-based, where already existing decision-making rules have been developed and are translated into software. The application of something already set up is now automated into specific cases such as eligibility determinations for government benefits, job qualifications or college admissions. The second type is ML-based automation. This approach replicates human judgements that are primarily based on informal judgement rather than specific sets of rules. Machine learning is used to learn decision-making schemes from historical human decisions. These schemes are then implemented again into software to replace human decision-makers. And the third type is data-driven automation. This form learns decision-making rules from data by identifying patterns in data sets that predict an outcome or policy of interest. The computer uncovers these patterns, which can be applied either manually or automatically. Machine learning plays a crucial role in developing these rules. What the authors emphasize is that the relevance of automation 'is in the process of developing the rules, not necessarily applying them'.[17] For example, these could be rules that suggest certain intervention strategies for students at risk of falling behind in their coursework, based on predictive models that analyse historical student performance data. Each of these types presents both opportunities and risks. Here are a couple of examples. These are both based on real products.

1. A student is recommended a learning path based on what an adaptive software tells him he should focus on next as per the diagnostic assessment the software has done on him. As the student advances through the questions, he is prompted to ask the following question:[18]

$$\boxed{\text{What is 300,000 more than 576,763?}}$$

If the student answers, 'I don't know', the system responds with the next query, which is:

$$\boxed{-8 + 10 =}$$

When the student answers correctly, the next question is:

> What number does CDXVI represent?

2. An algorithm assesses a high-achieving, low-income student in her Spanish test scores much lower than she expects since the algorithm predicts her result based on historical performance data for her school which is predominantly of low-income households and performing far below the state average in key measures for college readiness.[19]

What these (and other)[20] examples have in common is that they both represent automated decision-making systems that can easily be called unfair.[21] In the first case, the adaptive learning platform conducts diagnostic assessment of a student. It is not clear how the system comes about with such questions and whether it treats all mathematical operations equally. First, what is the logic, for example, from a wrong reply to the question relating to six-digit numbers for the system to switch to operations with single digits? Second, the system also does not provide any meaningful feedback to the student as to how it arrives at these decisions or why the student gave a wrong answer. For learning, feedback is crucial. Third, the student is in a solitary experience with the screen and the platform without necessarily having any social interaction with a teacher or students. The socialization, as I return to in greater detail in Chapter 6, is an important domain to *good* education.[22]

The second case involves Isabel Castañeda, a student from a high school in Colorado in the United States, who discovered that an algorithm unfairly graded her International Baccalaureate Spanish exam, as it was based on historical student data, teacher estimates and past student performance data, not the student's actual knowledge.[23] This is clearly unfair. As Barocas, Hardt and Narayanan contend, such unfairness, as evidenced in the two examples, is not about how specific individuals or groups are treated but the '*legitimacy* – whether it is fair to deploy such systems at all in a given scenario'.[24] This further implicates the 'legitimacy of the organisation deploying it' and the very institutions that adopt these systems, to which I will return in the conclusion of this chapter. For now, without producing an exhaustive list, I would like to explore some of the systems that are already integrated into educational environments, where, in many cases, they go unnoticed.

Automation requires big data. Today's available digital technologies enable the collection of personal data in and around the classroom, moving beyond mere observation. Big data consists of detailed interaction data, captured in seconds, from potentially millions of students during their interactions with learning environments like intelligent tutoring systems, simulations, apps and games.

Micro-automations are common in education, such as automatic plagiarism checks, grammar corrections and auto-suggestions in writing software. The aim of ongoing data collection and processing regarding students' educational performance includes the use of in-classroom apps like SeeSaw, ClassDojo, Thrively and others to track behaviour over time.

This, in turn, reinforces the idea that corporations naturally appropriate and process data to create value. Like NetSupport School, described previously, these technologies enable tracking and reporting analytics over digital dashboards in ways that give concrete, legitimate and authoritative notion (through their visual and interactive presentation of data). Their visualizations make a convincing case that teachers might not question or even understand the methods these systems use to arrive at these results. From there, the systems assess students' performance and offer highly personalized learning experience.

Those most avid supporters demand further data collection from children like wearable technology to monitor children's 'mood and stress level' by tracking heart rate and other 'biological forms of data, neural data, behavioural data' so that 'at any point in time, the student themselves or their carer would have an incredibly accurate picture of how that student is feeling, as well as how they're performing in school', although 'it's very intrusive'.[25] Thus, through data, not only is digital automation enabled but automation of surveillance, prediction and decision-making, too.

Growing discourse has surrounded the opportunities stemming from big data mining which has propelled the AI development – and use – further. Some see such work at micro, meso and macro levels[26] such as using clickstream data, text data and institutional data. Capturing clickstream data, such as students' interactions and actions within an online learning environment like time spent, clicks and scrolls, search queries, navigation paths and so on, promises to help personalize instruction and learning. Student writing, or text data, such as textual information or content generated or used by students like essays, student feedback, forum discussions, and so on, can be examined with natural language processing (NLP) again for deeper insights that may otherwise escape the human eye. And, institutional data, such as admissions, enrolment, graduation and retention numbers, and so on, promises to aid in decision-making via course guidance and early-warning systems.

Now that all this data is available, computational capabilities like NLP are capable of automating the analytical processes required to process it and make sense of it. As economist W. Brian Arthur puts it, 'the overall collection of technologies bootstraps itself upward from the few to the many and from the simple to the complex'.[27] Linguistic tools can be utilized for multiple purposes in the analysis of student writing. These tools promise to reveal patterns in lexical, syntactic or morphological features. They offer to help to better understand collaborative writing among groups of students and assess the quality of student writing compared to essays scored by human graders. For example, Coh-Metrix, a program that uses NLP,[28] focuses on text complexity by evaluating various components of text quality and readability.[29] Similarly, the Linguistic Inquiry and Word Count tool measures psychological attributes like confidence, leadership, authenticity and emotional tone.[30] Additional methods involve social network analysis for inferring relational positions and grouping techniques.

Some studies have demonstrated how automating systems can enhance the cognitive performance of students by supporting them with automated feedback, by automating homework and essay grading, and by automating the evaluations of student learning. As data availability expands, such tools are able to sift through thousands of students' interactions, coursework and their reading comprehension data sets. The evaluation of student writing is now possible to be automated, which is often the key selling point that such automation will significantly reduce teacher workload in grading essays and free teachers to focus on more important aspects such as engaging with their students and creative work.

Lan and colleagues,[31] for example, examined automatic grading of open-response questions in mathematics in STEM courses. Open-response problems were converted into numerical features which were then clustered into incorrect, partially correct, and correct solutions. Based on instructor grade assignments for each cluster, the student responses were then automatically graded.

Research has also explored intelligent tutoring systems and their use of automatic context-specific hints, especially in computer programming courses.[32] These studies consistently show that such systems boost student performance, surpassing the outcomes of students receiving traditional instruction. Price et al.[33] utilized the Hint Factory, an algorithm, trained on historical data, that gives students hints for programming assignments, helping them find the right answers easily.

Research on behavioural engagement has also investigated student participation and resource-seeking behaviour, often analysing large data sets from tens of thousands of students. For instance, Demmans Epp et al.[34] studied communication in online discussions, highlighting student pronoun use. The researchers found differences in engagement between instructor-facilitated and peer-facilitated courses.

Peralta et al.[35] created a metadata-based recommendation system for teachers exploring learning resources online. Building student demand models based on their online behaviour is the subject of a growing research[36] for the development of AI-based recommendation systems.

Studies on emotional aspects have explored learners' self-perception, feelings and motivation during their learning experiences, often involving hundreds or thousands of students. For example, Crossley and authors[37] used NLP tools to uncover how students' language skills related to their maths-related self-perception, such as maths value, interest and self-concept.

Similarly, Allen et al.[38] used NLP to analyse essay writing characteristics and their connection to emotional states like engagement and boredom. Research looking into automating the assessment of text data has shown to offer insights into students' comprehension, opinions and even emotions. It can also reveal community relationships. Studies using text analysis have shown to aid instructors in enhancing engagement and peer-to-peer learning. The downfall is that none of these studies consider the wider contextual factors within which students engage and learn.

Automation is evident everywhere in education today. Analysing vast student data such as records and behaviour through the use of AI promises detailed insights into learning processes and then further potentials for automating intervention, personalizing instruction, assessment, monitoring and even more analytics. As Raso et al.[39] point out, writing is increasingly assessed by automated systems. Education systems typically prioritize the nurtures of strong writing skills in students, which are a prerequisite for their academic success and later when they go into the world of work for their employment and for self-expression. Automated essay grading can affect student progress and their future opportunities not only by how students have been graded but also the feedback they would receive as a result. While automated grading can indeed support teachers by streamlining and offloading some of the workload, the systems enabling automated grading often fall short in assessing content quality and validity, which can potentially lead to imbalanced focus on form over substance. However, Raso et al. express optimism regarding automated grading systems in the context of human rights. These systems, the authors argue, have the potential to improve the right to education by offering broader feedback, particularly benefiting underserved students. Enhanced writing skills can empower individuals to exercise their civil and political rights more fully, such as free expression and social participation. Nevertheless, the influence on free expression is multifaceted due to extensive data collection, which might deter some from written self-expression.

Having mentioned some of the existing research, consensus around the impact and contribution to such systems is far from unanimous. Research has also shown how automated grading systems are unreliable creating further issues. First, students may not receive fair scores due to misclassifications. This is particularly pertinent to students with developmental language difficulties.[40] Second, unreliable features can be exploited by students for cheating. Cheating would involve using various keywords or even subtle input modifications, both of which have proven effective and received significant research attention ('Don't take "nswvtnvakgxpm" for an answer').[41] Social media provides amusing accounts of students, some as young as primary school level, on how to hack AI apps if 'you hate learning games on [sic] school on DreamBox or stuff'.[42]

AI-infused automation is also becoming increasingly prevalent with attendance tracking, grading and intelligent tutoring systems such as the example glimpsed from Century Tech's diagnostic test earlier. Diverse and sophisticated applications of AI are used including advanced interfaces that employ technologies like NLP, speech interfaces, avatars and so on.

As concerns continue to grow around the explainability, risks to data privacy, bias, security and inadequacies, explainable AI (xAI) has more recently been proposed to build into the AI environments including in education. Simply described, it is an AI on top of AI which aims to explain any AI output in ways that is human-understandable.

xAI in education, some argue,[43] has the potential to assist and create a more trusted environment by making AI's decision-making transparent and interpretable. xAI promises to support students' metacognitive processes, provide detailed feedback on grading and explain recommendations for resources and activities. xAI has also been deployed in systems providing content recommendations. Digital libraries and online platforms have xAI functionalities implemented which aim to give explanations about why specific content or course material is recommended to students based on their interests or past interactions. However, issues of accountability arise as decisions are increasingly delegated to AI systems entirely, including the explanations – now *explAInations*. While the objective of xAI functionalities has been to give more transparency – explainability – about how an AI system works and how it arrives at certain decisions, it also naturalizes and centralizes the very systems as legitimate decision-makers. In other words, the promise of xAI has also been seen to promote and 'enable human users to understand, appropriately trust, and effectively manage the emerging generation of artificially intelligent partners'.[44] Besides this proposal that AI will explain other AI functions and build some kind of human-computer trust, developing, testing and providing these functionalities are also expensive and require expertise and a continuous iterative process of gauging end-user response and satisfaction.

Some experts argue that AI systems can become 'black boxes' for various reasons where xAI can still fail to deliver the necessary transparency.[45]

There is a relatively subtle integration of digital automation in education about which no longer suffices to mull over what is bad or good; rather, as some scholars propose,[46] we should focus on practical negotiations around regulating, governing or even resisting these technologies because of their wide potential and mixed evidence.

What are the risks of automating education?

Adaptive learning and automating systems indeed can shift, as some argue, 'in the timings and spaces of education'[47] in unprecedented ways. Automation brings an altered and pre-emptive sense of timing to education. Automation prioritizes the idea of anticipation, prediction and dealing with future risks. This is prompted by comprehensive monitoring, continuous measurement and real-time feedback. Collectively, these functionalities of automation, anticipation and prediction turn into something from *Minority Report* or a *Black Mirror* scenario – humans are led to act upon something before it has happened. But who is to be held accountable if these systems make a mistake and lead to the wrong action? In the classroom, the responsibility remains with the teacher, yet classroom decisions are increasingly externalized to AI systems, which are also prone to error, bias and inaccuracies.

One of the risks emanates from the 'invisible student' in the classroom: the AI with agentic powers that are yet to be understood and figure out how to govern. While this invisible student is steadily learning on the backs of students, it is simultaneously steering them. It can be argued that schools have continuously been used as lab grounds for testing products, programs, interventions, methods and sophisticated software systems. In a way, innovative pedagogic methodologies may be considered that, too, but this is nothing like AI systems which are commercially driven and with layers of complex unknowns. Often, descriptions around their functionalities are also intentionally insufficient.[48]

There is nothing necessarily nefarious if systems improve with human interaction, but when commercial companies own these algorithms, this necessitates proper scrutiny not only of the technologies but of their businesses models. Moreover, those on whose time this development happens (students and teachers) should be made aware and build greater collective consciousness around the long-term implications of such interactions and dependencies with AI-infused systems.

The use of algorithmic technology for diagnosis, inferencing and prediction carries risks due to flawed data models which can lead to bias, injustice and various other harm. Some legal scholars have been concerned about the limitations of the EU General Data Protection Regulation when it comes to foundation models. Although this term has entered the public lexicon relatively recently,[49] these types of algorithmic models have been 'trained on broad data at scale' and are 'fine-tuned' or modified for 'specific downstream tasks'.[50]

For example, some argue that the General Data Protection Regulation (GDPR), the data protection law enacted by the European Union, does not explicitly provide for the 'right to an explanation'[51] while others assert that even if such right existed, xAI may still be unhelpful because of their opaqueness.[52] Additionally, the GDPR provisions may be bypassed when humans are involved in the decision-making process when a fully automated system can no longer be challenged. While the regulatory provisions and guidelines[53] assume that individuals should get an explanation around how AI works, students specifically may find it difficult to challenge decisions that have been generated by automating systems both because of their complexity and also because it may also be in combination with a human decision.

Overreliance on AI insight about students can further lead to decisions that overlook important contextual aspects. Say, if a student is unwell and affects his performance during assessment. Overreliance on such systems to steer the learning, practice and assessment can lead to loss of human autonomy and judgement, which is essential in class (ultimately humans are responsible, not the algorithm).

A teacher has immediate insight into socially significant cues that are highly sensitive and unique to human perception. Such ability enables her to instantly identify if a student is experiencing personal difficulties. Algorithms lack such awareness when providing diagnostics. Moreover, algorithmic diagnosis may lead to the creation of information 'bubbles' and a form of social stratification which can exacerbate social inequality. Take for example an EdTech platform which uses algorithms to recommend educational content to students based on their characteristics and some past data about their learning outcomes. Content is adapted, and also specific content is generated and recommended according to the input characteristics. If this system relies entirely on the student's past preferences and performance data to generate or recommend specific content it may inadvertently reinforce students' existing knowledge limiting them to exposure across diverse perspectives or serendipitous learning that otherwise a student may stumble upon just as what happens in human-to-human conversation. As such, adaptive learning, while allowing for individuals to take learning at their own pace, also leads to isolating pupils from each other by keeping each one at their own individual bubble or recommended 'railway track' and diverting them to destinations pre-empted by obscure algorithmic work.

Direct human-to-human interaction and collaboration may be reduced and lead to dehumanizing a highly social process, and socialization is fundamental part of learning. In Chapter 2, I described two EdTech products, one for classroom management, the other for navigating coursework and providing 'intelligent insight' about students among other functions. To be effective, even to exist as a value proposition to education, such products require consistent use and widespread adoption. Before then, nothing happens, of course. But when they are fully integrated into everyday practices, the typical teaching and learning activities transform with the expected human dynamics changing entirely. Instead of the teacher asking how a child feels, she does so via the digital platform. The student then has to select from predefined emoji options or respond to a survey. The very opportunity to enter in conversation and practise such skill is removed because there is an app to use instead. In reality, a teacher would know so much more about a student's context on any given day. Digital mediation of teaching and learning can erase crucial social contexts and hinder the development of essential social connections. Some scholars emphasize this by calling it a 'desocialization' whereby automation is able to 'recast and reduce the act of education into an individualised and nonsocial activity'.[54]

Recommender systems also exert 'soft' power as they can subliminally interfere with individual autonomy and thus may infringe on it, impacting on individuals' ability for self-determination, human rights and freedoms. To this end, academics argue for regulations addressing the power imbalances these systems create, including algorithm design, data protection rights, and transparency and oversight.[55]

At the same time, automating classroom processes also present an option for a rather frictionless teaching and learning, something that may well be described as 'robotic'. Automating technologies thus promise to 'manage the "messiness" of relationships by reducing them to transactions' and 'create an environment where interactions can happen without people having to make any effort to understand or know each other'.[56]

Automation can also lead to losing authenticity and personalization; procedural models are created based on finite data points collected from students' interaction with digital systems for automation and adapting learning.

Automated systems may fail to personalize the learning experience for individual students as they still lack the ability to assess cultural nuances, contexts and children's continuously changing minds and interests as they grow and develop.

Without strict oversight and governance, digitizing education has no concrete breaks on what aspects of education should be left untouched because they are simply already functioning well, which I will return to in the next chapter. Ultimately, digital opportunities should not remove *all* opportunities. Therefore, as Michael Veale puts it: 'The focus should be on taking off the "tech goggles" to identify problems, challenges and needs, and to not be afraid to discover that other policy options are superior to a technology investment.'[57]

Systems can enable and exacerbate bias, racism, gender inequality and be exclusionary. There is no easy way of knowing which EdTech products adhere to accessibility standards, for instance. Globally, the number of children with disabilities is estimated at almost 240 million according to UNICEF.[58] As an example, about 20 per cent of the world's population experiences hearing loss.[59] Those EdTech products that fail to offer quality captioning or transcription services significantly limit everyone's opportunities equally.

Regulatory authorities worldwide are rapidly updating policies to enhance accessibility. For instance, in the United States, the Federal Communications Commission (FCC) modernized accessibility laws with the twenty-first-century Communication and Video Accessibility Act (CVAA) to encompass modern technologies.[60] Marking the first enforcement action, in 2021, the FCC fined ViacomCBS, the US media conglomerate, for accessibility rules violations.[61]

Similarly, the European Accessibility Act in the EU aims to improve accessibility in the market with the act expected to enforce nationally by July 2025.[62] Who will oversee that EdTech products adhere to minimum appropriate requirements and web accessibility standards[63] and ensure inclusivity? These regulations make accessibility a legal requirement for both public and private organizations. The story of Isabel Castañeda demonstrated in the earlier example I gave at the start of this chapter shows how algorithms can be deeply unjust. As Broussard states, they will 'just take in historical data and predict that Black and Brown students will do worse than white students'.[64] I write more about the full spectrum of assessment and governance frameworks, guidelines and requirements in Chapter 7.

Automating the transformation of learning

Automation of learning processes in education can be expressed through systems that develop personalized learning pathways, collect data and generate analytics, recommend likely content and automate its delivery, adapt assessments and scale each of these functionalities. Thus, it can be argued that automation changes how the process of learning is conceptualized and proceeds.

Learning has traditionally been theorized as a process, in which greater learner agency and experience should be facilitated.[65] It is also seen as a social process of activity within the socio-historical and as a socio-cultural condition.[66] To Vygotsky, for instance, 'the word is a direct expression of the historical nature of human consciousness'.[67] It follows that conceptualizing learning begins in an individual's mind, partially because it is also socio-historically conceived and therefore contextually disseminated through other learners' interpretations and artefacts.[68]

With adaptive learning technologies, learning begins with what is in a learner's mind followed by an interaction with what the software proposes. Or even before that, the student is invited to wait until the system provides diagnosis and an adapted learning pathway. Data is needed all along for any of this adaptive learning to take place.

Data drives what is conceptualized as learned or unlearned based upon which the algorithms direct the learning process. On the one hand, data can be a source of information for timely pedagogic interventions. On the other, it can also reduce personal agency in how, why or what should be learned. Made central to the learning experience, it becomes crucial to understand how data-enabled automating and adaptive technologies may diminish the role, choice and voice of the learner – what conceptually is considered important to a successful learning process.

There are three considerations that follow from these changes of the learning process. To begin with, breakthroughs with adaptive learning remain unproven.[69] The second consideration is more complex because it is *conceptual*. The collected education data that powers the systems to enable automation for adapting, recommending, assessing and so on is already perceived as the 'necessary' and sufficient 'knowledge' to provide education. But data is just a fragment of the broader narrative, whether it pertains to individuals, processes, practices or places. Consider what a machine knows about a student, akin to what Google knows about you for search results. Is that the entirety of who you are – what Google displays as results? Similarly, when for example Google Maps prioritizes efficacy and speed in providing a route to a desired destination, it might limit our exposure to unique experiences and encounters, just as classrooms, heavily reliant on adaptive technologies, can potentially hinder the serendipitous learning, thought-provoking experiences, critical thinking and the element of surprise – all prerequisites that drive discovery and diverse skill practice.

As much as an adaptive software looks enticing and interactive, it is still prescribed and procedural. Learning becomes, as Sherry Turkle describes, a transactional process. 'Tutored by technology', Turkle says, 'we become reactive and transactional in our exchanges because this is what technology makes easy'.⁷⁰ Technologies may excel in various ways compared to humans, yet they only excel in a very narrow domain – what they are trained for.

When Garry Kasparov played a chess match against the Bulgarian grandmaster Veselin Topalov, during which they were both allowed to consult a computer, Kasparov realized: 'since we both had equal access to the same database, the advantage still came down to creating a new idea at some point'.[71] In other words, technologies exercise excellence in the domain they are built to. But they cannot innovate or be truly creative. Programs can produce prose, if programmed, yet cannot decide what to write next.[72]

Algorithms can process data and mimic life with impressive accuracy, yet genuine innovation remains a distinct human capability, which is borne out of much more than can be vested in a software to provide including experience, memory development, socialization, ideation and so on. While combining human and machine abilities, as in the case with the chess game, offers advantages to human players, arguments favouring human-machine collaboration often overlook the substantial human effort needed to demonstrate expertise before engaging with machines, the story that takes one to play – even fall in love with – chess, experience, experiment, socialize and generate original insight. To foster that kind of learning, is it safe to make adaptive digital systems central to it? What conditions are a prerequisite to guarantee success?

Automation for efficiency

Perhaps one of the popular arguments for AI in education has been that it will triumph with efficiency. Cambridge dictionary[73] defines 'efficiency' thus:

- The quality of achieving the largest amount of useful work using as little energy, fuel, effort, etc., as possible.
- The quality of working well in an organized way, without wasting time or energy.
- Something that is done to avoid wasting time, energy or money.
- The relationship between the amount of energy put into a machine or process and the amount of useful work that it produces.

Now imagine applying these definitions to the following activities:

Reading a book
Dancing hip-hop
Building with Lego

Playing table tennis
Writing a sonnet
Composing music for cat memes
Learning about Dutch history, in Dutch
Swimming
Knitting
Hula hooping
Yodelling
Imagining a mythical creature
Organising a Japanese tea ceremony
Doing aerial silks
Playing didgeridoo

Of course, 'efficiency' can be plugged into all of those. ChatGPT-like language models can now summarize any text and write poems (ignoring the quality). Computer programs allow music 'composition' without the need for much musical background. But for neither of those activities efficiency is ever the goal.

With more granular and diverse data collection, there has been an even greater emphasis on and promise for efficiency such as by automating grading. Teachers [are promised to] see crunched data and diagnostic results about a student behaviour, attendance or academic performance on an interactive dashboard. Content platforms, like DreamBox Learning, offer thousands of interactive lessons for pre kindergarten to eight-grade students along with continuous assessments to personalize learning pathways and lessons. Yet the program may encounter a long list of errors and issues.[74]

The promise is that data collection and processing would lead to automation and to increased efficiency and along the way – to effective learning. The assumption is that teachers will have more freedom and students will receive more tailored support due to the data collected about them.

To achieve this efficiency and lubricate the system of data collection and processing, schools have undergone another significant change – the standardization of how students should be assessed, how data should be collected and organized, and what attributes and titles every bit of data should be called. When all the components are thus standardized and the expected 'whole' is concretely drawn out, there is no wiggle room for anything out of the ordinary, which does not have a name or does not fit into a data schema. Therefore, what is not counted no longer counts.

Efficiency benefits businesses. As Astra Taylor puts it: 'Somewhere, right now, a manager is intoning to a broke, exhausted underling that someone is willing to do the same job for less – or, that some *thing* is willing to do it for free.'[75] Automation, however, Taylor argues, is oversold as the big futuristic game-changer that makes human workers obsolete. Instead, she calls this 'fauxtomation' which is a marketing trick that aims to disqualify the value of human labour – be that at the fast-food restaurant or in school. It is the everyday reality and interaction with digital technologies that often underscore fauxtomation.

Many teachers would attest to the daily challenges with sophisticated technologies in the classroom from the more straightforward ones such as uncharged or broken devices and lag time, to more complex issues such as software glitches, limitations in meeting the needs of culturally and linguistically diverse students[76] or lack of alignment with curriculum.[77] Even more challenging is becoming the growing cyberattacks and plain tech fatigue.[78]

Efficiency does not benefit learning. Cutting corners where business needs to survive is not the same as shortcutting on learning. ChatGPT can summarize a book, but this robs one of opportunities and experiences: from practising late gratification to concentration and then the pleasure of going in-depth through a story, immersing in the history and contexts, learning different literary voices, imagining characters – depicting the worlds in individual and unique ways, developing empathy, calming and more. Much scholarship has been dedicated to describing the benefits of reading – from concentration and enriching imagination to building intelligence. Are these practices enhanced or removed when students are placed with self-paced automating systems? It is unclear.

Once efficiency becomes the starting point and purpose in doing something, the process and outcome of the experience change. And not always for the better. There is nothing wrong with being inefficient in education. All great achievers (geniuses) from Mozart to Newton and Einstein had the tenacity to persevere and drive into deep flow of work. Darwin was assumed an aimless young man, and yet his 'inefficiency' led him to deep dive into science and discovery.

Csikszentmihalyi spent much of his professional concentration on studying creativity following on many such prominent figures, creative artists and thinkers. I return to this discussion in greater detail in the next chapter with attention to everyday creativity, with less interest in the geniuses. This everyday creativity forms part of learning and children's self-expression, discovery, development of character and personhood – all part of their basic human rights, part of what education should be about, not about efficiency.

In recent years, education policies, global consultancies and international coalitions have increasingly emphasized the potential of data and AI in education, subtly overlooking discussions about cultures, educational content, individuals and collective efforts in local communities. The economic imperative for efficiency outpaces other needs. and technologies proclaiming efficient scalability have spread far and wide from the rich-income countries to low- and middle-income (LMIC) regions. Often these 'other' communities and 'the rest' of the world are said to need devices, data, automation and so on for the efficient provision of education in order to level up with the richer world; their education will be enhanced; their populations empowered; their economies improved. They will be transformed if they are equipped with the advanced technologies of the Western world. Certainly, automation can offer efficiencies by scaling educational provisions across socio-economic disparities. But who attests to the qualities of these scalable systems? And while the focus of this book has remained on the digital infrastructure integrating into the Western, Anglo-American educational systems, more critical questions should be raised about the digital proposals being made to LMIC regions with urgency.

Disparities in narratives

Marketing discourse is powerful, and businesses tend to be loud about their value proposition. Research has shown that factors like home environment, parental educational background, school environment, student-teacher relationships significantly influence academic outcomes, particularly in subjects like mathematics. Despite claims by EdTech companies about their positive impact on academic performance, a closer examination of some of their evidence can tell a different story. Consider Sparx Maths, a personalized learning platform. It claims that the time spent on the platform improves students' performance. A study commissioned by the company showed that where use is total time spent on the platform, watching its videos and doing the tasks are associated with higher scores on progress in understanding mathematics assessment (PUMA) 'albeit with a relatively small effect size'. For every hour spent using the platform, there was an associated 0.03 points increase in score.[79]

However, this suggests that the more a child spends on the platform the more likely their score will increase. But such conditions conflict with more important factors such as a child's well-being. How long should a child spend on the screen, even if it contributes to improving the final score? Moreover, there are other essential factors that influence a child's academic outcomes such as teachers' attitudes and emotional assistance in the learning process. And what sets this platform apart from others that offer similar features and objectives? Most importantly, the study did not find significant evidence that such a product benefits underprivileged children.[80] The study's findings highlighted that mere access to the technology makes no difference to children's learning outcomes. Indeed. Moreover, gaps in learning attainment between groups of students remain 'persistent and difficult to shift'[81] even where access to such platforms exists.

There is no denying that products like Sparx and many like them offer support in maths. Also, some children do enjoy them while others clearly do not (like the example of how to hack DreamBox, or similar attitudes about the 'talking heads' of EdTech content providers are many). But there is a need to tame the tone that they are the panacea to successful learning, the new 'natural' learning environment[82] as this also 'denaturalizes' older forms of education, which are not all bad (more of which in the next chapter). Naturalization of AI 'others' older forms of education.

As mentioned previously, this 'othering' expels any previous notions of schooling as plausible and beneficial to children's learning. 'Othering' entails subtle, conceptual assumptions and processes that shape how we perceive and interpret the world. In its manifest 'othering' becomes the symbolic violence on all those who do not fall within a specific category. The 'othering' approach is not new, and while beyond the book's scope, it is essential to briefly note its historical impact. Rooted in colonialism's epistemology and the Western effort to mould knowledge and identities for control over non-Western regions for domination,[83] this epistemic regime excludes alternative ways of thinking and living. This epistemic othering can be traced through the use of institutions, language, imagery, scholarship and even colonial bureaucracies to see how they 'organize and regulate social practices, influence our conduct' and 'consequently have real, practical effects'.[84] Similarly, Western (and its market) discourse surrounding the digitization of education exhibits comparable structures and principles of othering the old ways of teaching and learning against the new way which is through sophisticated technologies the markets are offering.

Back to the example with Sparx Maths, it also demonstrates that even a slight distinction in its search for evidence of positive impact often turns the notion of *potential* into pseudo-scientific *fact*. This is the scholarship discourse that works towards othering the non-digital alternatives of improving maths attainment. Not that they are worse; they just do not sell products.

Similarly, Century Tech claims to detect autism with 96 per cent accuracy.[85] While on the market for nearly a decade, there is little concrete proof of the product's assertions. Additionally, questions about handling sensitive children's data, or how 'learning paths' are suggested and what their creation process is, remain obscure. And yet policy reports and media outlets continue to circulate favourable portrays of such products as scientifically proven and 'the future'. For instance, the white paper authored by former Prime Minister Tony Blair and Lord William Hague, titled *A New National Purpose: Innovation Can Power the Future of Britain*,[86] endorses Century Tech, claiming how it reduces teacher workloads without any supportive reference.

On the other hand, disparities in discourse exist in other critical aspects of the businesses of tech. As an EdTech investor once pointed out to me,[87] it is crucial to know an EdTech business's financial viability. What they should be showing and audited for; 'if a company has run at a loss for a while now it should be a red flag'. Who does the due diligence around the financial health of these businesses before they are allowed in School?

Many automation, adaptive learning and intelligent tutoring systems are in early development stages and have business risks; if the product does not sell, the business may shut down. Some, however, get acquired and continue. Educational institutions use all kinds of products, some given to them to try for free, others at hefty fees. This makes it difficult to understand procurement processes and the evaluation criteria used.

For example, Knewton, an adaptive learning platform, once criticized as 'snake oil'[88], was acquired by publisher Wiley & Sons continues to sell as Alta.[89] It is unclear why but like many other EdTech products, Knewton was 'free' in its early days and therefore mainly used by under-resourced schools. The original visions were to

> create individual, psychometric profiles that would presume to say, with statistical authority, what students know and how they learn. Such records could theoretically follow those students into the job market, profoundly affecting how they are viewed by graduate school admissions committees and potential employers.[90]

Knewton's initial business attempt failed, however, following the new acquisition; it is unknown what happened with the collected student data, how its software today diverges from the original intent of creating invasive psychometric profiles of students and how the new version is different or better.

In another example, PowerSchool Holdings is an EdTech company which offers end-to-end solutions connecting school data from central offices to classrooms and homes, supporting student management, communication and improving student outcomes for over 50 million students across over 90 countries and 16,000 US customers. Its net worth as of October 2023 is $3.36 billion.[91] PowerSchool was once owned by Apple Inc.[92] and then sold to

Pearson[93] which sold it to Vista Equity Partners,[94] a private equity company with a substantial portfolio of businesses spanning across various sectors – from marketing to healthcare to security to retail.[95] PowerSchool itself is a powerhouse of multitude of subsidiaries including Naviance, Schoology, Chalkable, Teacher Match, eSchool Solutions and many others[96] including 'career readiness solutions',[97] making it a pipeline of connected EdTech products and a substantial conduit to data generation. This raises questions about businesses' financial insights (risks and ambitions), control over and interest in educational data, trust in their evolving products, and schools' and policymakers' awareness of these dynamics.

Lastly, we also need to look at automation and the price we pay for it. At what cost do children (are made to) give away their data? The notion that data collection is an inherent – and more so central – part of learning can lead to the idea of data-driven social change without recognizing the full cost of connection – from the physical wires and cables and the computational energy required to the cost of data extraction and how it influences decisions and individuals' futures. The value of data increases because data can be re-purposed and re-used, and a positive feedback loop can be created which promotes the flow of data and the interconnected nature of information systems.[98]

The cost of data and computation to the environment is also a growing concern that cannot be ignored. At the same time, the cost of investing in the digital economy (mobile technology, the internet and cloud) has created a paradox – no visible improvement of productivity growth.[99] Economists explain this with the general scarcity of 'exceptional talent, which – unlike labour and capital – isn't subject to digitisation' creating a sort of 'production bottleneck'.[100] The scarcity of 'superstar workers' ironically highlights a failure in education and the unfulfilled promise of digitization to enhance learning.

The wider potentials of data are seen as a point of connecting industry labour demands that can inform educational curriculum development and outputs. In the United States this is clearly observed through policy and various initiatives whereby cradle-to-career is driven through the promise of data, as described in the previous chapter.

How do EdTech produce 'insights' and suggested career pathways, grades and even labels about students' current well-being or what they are likely to do next? As Broussard asserts,

> just because we use the term 'black box', it's not that it's impossible to describe what happens inside the model. The ability to explain it is limited by the descriptive abilities of the people in the conversation, the context of the conversation, the mathematical background of the people

in the conversation, and the imaginative ability of the people in the conversation.

This might turn out to be a very small group of people who understand how EdTech generate results and the subsequent potential biases and injustices baked into them. It is not due to a lack of expertise but rather the absence of a mandate for companies to comply and prioritize transparency in their algorithms. As advocated by Broussard and others[101], 'we need to audit all of our technology to find out how it is racist, gender-biased, or ableist. Auditing doesn't have to be complicated'.[102] Instead, it can involve both public and government initiatives to ensure the EdTech industry addresses bias and injustice promptly.

As I argued in Chapter 3, data and digital systems are also transforming education governance into a complex, automated network in which private actors have greater influence and say, and there is little understanding about how they are held accountable for public education and children.

Conclusion

The problems with automation lie on so many levels, and they are impossible to cover exhaustively not solely because of their complexity but because of the many unknowns around them. AI models raise concerns about data quality, accuracy and adequacy.

Treating data as all the information – all the 'right' or all the 'needed' one – for education is flawed.[103] This notion conceals the superficial and decontextualized method of data generation and collection from individuals.

Data also raises problems when it is made central while rapid changes can befall the education environment. As Broussard highlights, machine models lack the agility to adapt quickly, unlike human experts, underscoring their inflexibility, for example, the sudden shift to remote learning due to a crisis like a natural disaster or a global pandemic. When students and teachers transition to online education, the data patterns and behaviours change significantly. ML models, which rely on historical data, may struggle to adapt to this new environment. For instance, the models might not account for the challenges students face in digital learning, such as limited access to technology or distractions at home. They may not understand the sudden changes in assessment methods, participation or engagement. As a result, the models might inaccurately predict student performance or needs, potentially leading to biased recommendations or interventions. These models lack the ability to quickly adjust their reference frames to the rapidly evolving educational landscape just as in the case with the Covid-19 response through lockdowns.

Or consider the implementation of a new teaching methodology or curriculum in a school system. If schools transitioned to more innovative and experimental teaching and assessment approaches, ML models that rely on historical data might not adequately adapt to this change. For instance, if new curricula emphasize project-based learning or alternative assessment methods, the models might continue to favour traditional metrics like standardized test scores. As a result, such models could inaccurately assess student progress or teacher performance, leading to biased outcomes. ML models may not quickly recognize and incorporate the nuances of the new teaching methodology, highlighting their inflexibility when it comes to adapting to changing educational practices.

This is why scholars like Meredith Broussard, Kathy O'Neil and others have proposed algorithmic auditing. Algorithmic auditing stems from the proposal for the envelopment of public interest technologies. As the final chapter delves in greater detail, it helps to offer a brief segue to it here. Public interest technology, in the context of education, would refer to the development and use of technology and related practices with a primary focus on addressing societal needs and promoting the well-being of students, educators and the public at large.

But public interest technology can also be policies that can drive in either direction – towards the development and set-up of systems of oversight that only ethical and equitable designs and technologies make their way to the classroom or the market of a 'wild west'. Public interest technologies prioritize the needs, fundamental human rights and well-being of individuals and the collective. What that means is the subject of the next chapter.

5

Voice: What Do Children Say about the Digitized Classroom?

A fine balance

Children are not the people of tomorrow, but people today. They are entitled to be taken seriously. They have a right to be treated by adults with tenderness and respect, as equals. They should be allowed to grow into whoever they were meant to be – the unknown person inside each of them is our hope for the future.[1]

Janusz Korczak was a Polish educator, paediatrician, writer and a child rights campaigner who chose to march along with Jewish orphaned children into the Treblinka death camp during the Second World War. His words quoted above adorn this chapter to emphasize the significance of children's voices, rights and freedoms in a world that we leave to them to have and repair (because of what we leave behind). Korczak's words serve as a reminder for adults reading these pages of our responsibilities towards children. Children should not be seen as 'people of tomorrow'. Childhood is not a universally recognized concept, and its treatment varies significantly across the globe. Cultural, social and economic factors impact the experiences and rights of children.

Today we still witness the exploitation of child labour with millions of children engaged in hazardous or exploitative work rather than enjoying their right to education and a safe upbringing. In conflict zones, we still hear about children being forcefully recruited as child soldiers, experiencing a complete denial of their rights to safety and development. Access to healthcare, nutrition and education can be extremely unequal among children from different socio-economic backgrounds and parts of the world. However, child abuse and violations of their human rights exist even in richer economic regions of the world. Disparities are well documented in reports and studies by organizations like UNICEF, Save the Children and Human Rights Watch, which highlights the necessity for global efforts to ensure that there is a global consensus and priorities especially from industry that children's rights are upheld, and their well-being is prioritized.

Voice as 'value'

Before I move to voice in the digitized classroom, I would like to provide some rationale. In his book *Why Voice Matters: Culture and Politics after Neoliberalism*, Nick Couldry argues avidly about the role of voice in societies. He sees voice as a unique *value* to have and a *process* that takes societies to a tolerant and convivial cohabitation with democratic and social principles. Voice becomes 'an act of valuing, and choosing to value, those frameworks for organizing human life and resources that *themselves* value voice'.[2] He addresses the point of having a voice not in the way that everyone has 'voice' to the risk of triviality but as a process in which voice is not undermined or discriminated against. He challenges the dominance of neoliberalism and its devaluation of voice in society paying attention to the neoliberalist discourse that has been entrenched in Western politics, culture, media and technological innovations.

As Couldry asserts, the neoliberalist discourse is rooted in an economic perspective that disregards the importance of voice and forces a specific economic outlook onto politics 'via a reductive view of politics as the implementing of market functioning'.[3] Couldry's emphasis on why voice matters serves as a connecting term to challenge neoliberal economic views, fostering an alternative perspective on politics that values the processes of voice and acknowledges people's capacity for social cooperation, based on voice. In the digitized classroom, it is critical to understand not only how children are provided the space to give voice and value it as a process of developing it but also to uncover any processes or digital architectures that may obstruct their voice and the ability to develop it.

Devoting this chapter to children's voice is also important to contrast it against that other voice of data and algorithmic decision-making. In this context, I anchor the discussion regarding children's voices in their basic rights. Bringing evidence from existing scholarship, I look at children's experiences, perceptions, thoughts and ideas in their own words. Doing that I aim to highlight the significance of their voices, not only in regulating technology but also in fostering their self-development, character and social responsibility.

However, according to Laura Lundy, gauging children's voices is not as straightforward.[4] Lundy argues that the increasing recognition of children's voice, which is underpinned by the United Nations Convention on the Rights of the Child (UNCRC) Article 12 has stirred debate due to its concerns about challenging adult authority. Terms such as 'pupil voice', 'the voice of the child', 'the right to be heard' and 'the right to participate' are commonly used terms which, Lundy argues, can ultimately water down the full extent of this right when it is used individually. One contention is that adults often express concerns about children's capacity to contribute meaningfully to decision-making and how giving children a greater say may undermine school authority. Conversely, research has also shown how children can grow weary of 'consultation fatigue' due to the growing effort from government to engage them in consultations, while at the same time such efforts can often yield minimal benefits in their daily lives. This means that as we view their voices, we also must make room for understanding of these contentions and find the right means to integrate children's contribution in ways that neither authorities nor children become undermined.

To achieve this fine balance, Lundy suggests a framework where space, voice, audience and influence are essential elements in understanding, policymaking and practice of respecting children's rights to voice. In this model, children should have the space to express their views, be facilitated to do so, have their views listened to, and, when appropriate, see their voice lead to action. Easier said than done especially in the digitized classroom.

Children today are growing up with data-driven technologies embedded in their lives with their data used for profiling, analysing their behaviour, inferencing and predicting. Their online behaviour and footprint are not only captured and tracked but can also be subjected to commercial exploitation. Despite the legal constraints especially when it comes to children's data collected by EdTech applications, loopholes, data sales and repurposing continue.[5]

Unethical and unlawful data practices can be challenging to comprehend, even for adults, let alone for children. What are their voices, rights and freedoms in this complex digitized world?

As unique members of our societies children grow up and develop in diverse environments and cultures and experience different things, enjoy different opportunities but are also subject to many limitations and hardships. While child development is a universal concept, children mature at different ages. It is said that children today have different *evolving capacities*.[6] This is important when we think about education, the use of EdTech or the future children will take as young adults.

Children's voices should not only be seen from human rights perspective alone but also as a dimension of emancipation and participation in their own lives. For example, when we conduct educational research around questions relating to 'what works' in digitized education, does this research seek to identify useful answers about the capacities of children in these scenarios? Or is something done *about* them, and they are positioned as the recipients of an intervention (as with the randomised controlled trials)? On the other hand, when we ask children to participate in designing EdTech, when do we cross over into a space that may not lead to anything beneficial to children at all? For example, some scholars[7] are vocal about drawing children in co-designing technologies. This allows children to exercise their rights to participation in their lives. But how will this be implemented in ways that is beneficial to children? To co-design a game, children would love to have free 'skins' and 'gems' – virtual items and currencies in video and online games. Their game time could increase, but these designs, as a middle-school teacher in the United States tells me, 'are merely reinforcing the token economy'. As an aside, the token economy is a behavioural management system that uses tokens (or points) as rewards to reinforce desired behaviours. In the context of online games that children play, the token economy is indeed reinforced through such in-game currencies like gems and skins.

Badges and digital credentials related to what children and young people have learned or acquired as skills create intricate, technology-driven profiles that define individuals' worth but can also restrict their freedoms. A quest for tokens will reinforce the digital dependence. In one study conducted in Ireland,[8] students shared mixed feedback on the token economy steering behaviour. While motivational in the early school years, its value diminishes over time. While competition adds some enjoyment, frustration also arises due to difficulties in earning rewards – the focus around studying is also aligned with focusing on what will earn one a token. Crucially, respondents argued that as student-teacher relationships develop, the token system loses its value.

Every right

The UNCRC defines a 'child' as 'every human being below the age of eighteen years unless under the law applicable to the child, majority is attained earlier' (Article 1).[9] The understanding of one's human rights is evolving.[10] The age of majority is typically the point at which a person is legally considered an adult.

Laws typically consider a child based on their chronological age with varying degrees and purposes for example for sexual consent, alcohol consumption, leaving school and so on. Historically, child development theories guided age-based restrictions on media access. For instance, the Child Online Privacy and Protection Act (COPPA) in the United States sets the minimum age for social media use at thirteen. However, the evidence supporting such age-based restrictions for digital services is often ambiguous or outdated.[11] Some have argued that the lack of such clarity is problematic regarding the impact on children's rights to freedom of expression and association.[12] Their proposal has therefore been that 'the imposition of age limits should be justified, evidence-based, and rooted in scientific theory'.[13] As a result, the focus has become more on children's *capacity* than age as the determinant in the exercise of their human rights. In other words, the UNCRC regards the 'evolving capacities' of a child not only as an interpretative and policy principle but also as an enabling one. That is, as children grow and mature, they gain the ability to exercise more agency over their rights.[14]

Yet how does one determine such evolving capacity accurately? If the state devolves responsibility from the parent, who is responsible – the state, the teachers, the schools? Where does it follow that the state is capable of discerning what the child needs? And where do teachers' responsibilities towards their pupils end? Will more monitoring and data be needed to assess each child's evolving capacities and parents' commitment to respecting children's rights and freedoms?

For instance, in acknowledging a child's growing autonomy and the need to respect their evolving capacity to exercise their rights independently, the Committee on the Rights of the Child requires information (data) on minimum legal ages for things like seeking legal or medical advice or undergoing medical treatment without parental consent. Furthermore, undermining parental autonomy can lead to conflicts between parents, children and state. Will family bonds weaken as a result of these new dynamics and what are the implications of that for the growing child?

Imposing state control over the protection of these rights can further infringe on families' and individuals' privacy and civil liberties. It is also important to consider long-term how young people will understand, be prepared for and participate in their societies.[15] In other words, children need the time and the opportunities to effectively transition to adulthood and develop decision-making skills independently of their parents or guardians.[16] All this describes a complex, delicate and uneven terrain in which highly experimental and fast-transforming technologies become deeply engrained. EdTech's fast-paced nature does not allow to properly monitor their impact on such important issues such as children's evolving capacities and rights.

The UNCRC came in 1989 and for the first time a global effort was made for governments to agree to recognize the rights of children. The Convention incorporates fifty-four rights which are interlinked. Articles 41 and 54 address adults and governments' responsibilities to ensure that children and young people enjoy these rights.

At their core, they stipulate that every child has the right to live and develop, to equality and non-discrimination, to be heard and to participate in society. Additionally, every child is entitled to an education to support their development and achieve their full potential; to play; to freedom of thought; to voice and peaceful protest; to protection from harm; to equality and non-discrimination; to participation; to identity; to enjoy their own cultures and practise their religion and use their own languages if they belong to an indigenous or minority group. However, the UNCRC states:

> In all actions concerning children, whether undertaken by public or private social welfare institutions, courts of law, administrative authorities or legislative bodies, the best interests of the child shall be a primary consideration.[17]

As Van Der Hof et al. point out, this statement argues for *a*, not *the* primary consideration, which means they include those of commercial entities, which in practice may 'be weighed against the interests of powerful companies that may very well be the direct opposite to those of children'.[18] In 2021 a General Comment No 25 was published on children's rights in relation to the digital environment.[19] Over 130 submissions were received, including more than 700 children, and young people from twenty-eight countries were consulted which confirmed that their fundamental human rights must be respected in the digital environment too. These fundamental rights are a useful lens to guide the *taming* of *EdTech*.

For that, this chapter looks at and reflects on children's own voices, perceptions and experiences around the digitization of education.

As I have tried to articulate up to this point of the book, the digitization of education can be described as experimental, speculative, disruptive, commercial, uncertain, instant, at times makeshift, but also transmorphic – it does not change only some things; it changes everything. For example, some scholars maintain[20] that the provision to support children's rights to education and prepare them to become responsible and independent adults within a 'free society' has yet to acknowledge the impact of digital inferencing systems used in education, which have the capacity to steer individuals without their awareness. As I will delve further in this chapter, mandated technologies leave little freedom of choice for students but to sign into classroom technologies and prevent behavioural tracking by third parties.[21]

That said, there is still a significant gap in how much we understand and know what children think, feel and what their role is in the changing digitized classroom; globally, too. Tech businesses continue to articulate often convincing imaginative narratives about academic success across the board and a bountiful future. They have also influenced policies that are constantly driving for a re-evaluation of what is taught and prioritized in schools. In relation to new technologies, it has been a constant moving target: from media literacies to digital skills, from data understanding to computational and algorithmic thinking, to generative AI.

Global educational policies, especially in the wake of the pandemic, have pushed EdTech centre stage. With that, they have also ushered in the growing problems around data privacy, autonomy and surveillance.

A growing concern has been the digital profiling of children online for targeted advertising, whether they are using EdTech or digital technologies generally. This has drawn considerable attention and prompted governments to act, albeit not equally, not always in a timely manner and mainly in retrospect when harm has surfaced.

Commercialization and digital profiling have also crept into education, masquerading as a way to offer personalized learning experiences. The lines continue to blur between why it is 'creepy' because it personalizes an advert and why it is not when it personalizes the learning subject – or career pathway. The commercialization of education, particularly noticeable in American schools, has been an ongoing problem, gaining further momentum with EdTech companies permeating public schools. While the ensuing data use as a means to manage the talent pipeline as described in Chapter 4 is contentious, we should not overlook the other growing problems of data privacy and cyber threats.

Yet children and young people are naturally inclined to explore and try out new things and risky ones too, make meaningful connections, express their creativity, explore identity, and so on. Digital technologies give immense opportunities for all that. Before delving into a critical analysis of the business models of EdTechs, this chapter begins on a positive note by showcasing children's voices expressed through digital technologies. I begin with creativity.

Meaning making, making ideas

Making things is our way of self-expression, discovery and communication. It is the everyday creativity that children love to immerse themselves in. Creativity, seen as the act of generating innovative ideas and uncovering new insights as a form of personal accomplishment, represents a potent process, a condition and an inherent state of being.

I begin with creativity not only because it is considered a necessary twenty-first-century skill but also because it is a unique human trait. As an inherent value present in all humans, creativity depends on social, cultural and situational contexts.[22] It is a prelude to and also an outcome of learning.

Much literature on children and learning has revolved around creativity. Creativity has been researched not only as an acquisition of social or language skills[23] but an action – a demonstration of applied imagination. The creative output from the interconnectedness of play and learning[24] should be of interest when EdTech come into the classroom insofar as the creation has meaning and value to the creator and is not just a manifestation of mechanical production.[25] As such, substantial scholarship has also examined and developed frameworks, curricula and policy around digital literacies and skills as a matter of importance in the classroom, one that is becoming highly digitized.

Digital technologies have been seen as great tools to nurture this most basic but very commanding desire – to make creative things as a form of self-expression and meaning making. Making creative things also reflect agency and autonomy – the agency to see the broomstick as a horse and the autonomy to make the rules of a game.

Creativity, as an everyday self-expression, also reflects children's fundamental rights to play; the freedom to form an independent thought and personhood; the freedom to authentic existence. In Freire's words, only in true freedom can one 'exist authentically'.[26] Within the discourse on fundamental rights, children's expressions and their freedoms, we should ask: Does the digitized classroom enable freedom and the right to exist authentically?

Communicating creatively – creative ideation – represents a form of flexible mind that, faced with changes (such as cultural, technological, ecological and so on) can act upon, solve a problem, adjust and adapt to changing environments.[27]

I speak of creativity with a small c here to focus on children's daily expressions,[28] which are so important in their development. Oftentimes adults in a child's life have certain expectations in which children should articulate knowledge and thought, and 'failing' to meet those expectations may result in judgements through particular grades, clustering in specific bands and levels of progression and abilities from where long-term implications may stem not only for children's futures but also for how children perceive and internalize these judgements.

And yet all children are creative and view things in their own unique way. As the joke goes: to a child, 1 + 1 does not always equal 2; it equals 1 if you chew two pieces of gum together. How children articulate their ideas and what they see matters in the effort to ensure that digital technologies respect their unique views to which they have every right.

Creative expression plays a significant role in the process of identity development, which is central to young people's lives. Digital technologies offer powerful tools for exploring and shaping one's identity, becoming increasingly important at an ever-younger age.[29, 30] The need to communicate and make meaningful connections is what makes social platforms such as Instagram, Snapchat and YouTube thrive. Play and learning interlink with creativity[31, 32] and for that many applications deployed for educational purposes are designed with play in mind. Education is often presented as gamified experience because of all the promises of learning through play.

But gamification has also taken one particular model often adopted in platform and app designs targeting children. Many of those adopted in classrooms today, as described in Chapter 2, are based on the behaviourist model of steering towards an expected performance with award mechanisms praising whenever a child demonstrates an expected desired behaviour. A child does not disrupt the classroom by talking when not invited to talk – Class Dojo allows teachers to issue a badge and an award. On the other hand, extrinsic motivations, such as evaluation or rewards, have shown to inhibit creativity.[33]

But creativity can also be less personal and more of a process of social interaction with expert others within a domain.[34] Through such intelligent interactions, judgements of individual performances in society are made. The context in which children engage creatively as a function of learning matters greatly in how their creative potential will be unleashed or suppressed.[35] What is the impact of children's creativity and motivations in the datafied classrooms where automation steers the educational process and standardized test scores produce digital dashboards articulating insight as coloured boxes?

There has been sufficient body of literature in support that creativity and learning can be fostered through the use of certain digital technologies.[36, 37, 38] They allow self-paced learning and facilitate safe exploration that physical environments do not or cannot necessarily provide. Software products can provide safe and rich environment. Learning through concrete objects and experiences within the safe confinements of the rich audio-visual and virtual reality environments of apps can engage in learning and creative activities just as real physical objects can. There are fine apps that provide for creative explorations.

Children can discover the outer space. The NASA app,[39] for example, features a vast collection of the latest NASA content, including over 19,000 images, videos, Solar System Exploration and stories. Albeit at a cost, Star Walk 2, an augmented reality (AR) app allows star-gazers to point-and-display the sky and use a digital compass to navigate and learn the stars and constellations.

Merlin Bird ID,[40] created by the Cornell Lab, gives young naturalists (and anyone curious) the opportunity to learn about different species of birds allocating them either by their sound or a picture a child can take with a device. Similarly, with Seek, the app developed by iNaturalist,[41] I spend many a time with my young naturalist son (a proud member of the British Naturalist Society) exploring plants, animals and all sorts of creepy crawlies that cross our path. That is learning enabled through digital technologies beyond the classroom.

World Atlas for exploring countries and cultures, Scratch for coding and Google Earth Tour Guide where children can learn about life in the deep ocean, world heritage sites and more – there are great digital tools for learning and enjoying beyond the classroom. Indeed, when the notion of datafication and surveillance creep is not in the background, and when there is purpose, these applications can be truly beneficial.

Scratch, a block-based visual programming language created by MIT Media Lab for ages eight to sixteen, is freely available to all children and coding enthusiasts, offering a user-friendly introduction to the world of computers. These examples showcase the marvel of technologies for education. In the realm of education, particularly in relation to play and creativity, the concept of 'creative teaching' has frequently garnered attention within academic circles and policymaking.

The creativity discourse has extensively examined the possibilities of technologies and the extent to which teachers creatively integrate them, serving as a prerequisite for effective technology utilization and, subsequently, student benefits. Often, however, the responsibility for this has fallen squarely on the shoulders of teachers.[42] But focusing on utilization or creative use has led to overshadowing the deepening concerns around the opaque machinations and capabilities of digital infrastructures and the constant generation of data in the classroom and when children are thrust to use digital systems for 'educational purposes'. These are niche products, and often their price, in combination with the wider technological cost, is not scaled equally across all children. Instead, what is entering the classroom is often deceptive, promising benefits but with unclear, often hidden, intentions and evidence of meaningful impact.

Instead, commercial platforms attract users with instant benefits such as a free service, subsidized devices, access to information, skill acquisition or credentials. Such is for instance the Chromebooks given cheap or for free to hundreds of thousands of students, who at the same time become loyal Google customers. Students are also locked in to use pre-installed applications that have further commercial intent or purposefully are placed to monitor and surveil. Of the latter kind is Gaggle – a surveillance technology – students would be asked to let it monitor them; otherwise they may not have access to their classroom materials which are all stored on their Chromebooks. This seemingly advantageous initiation masks the underlying deceptive intention of ensnaring users into exploitative and dependent long-term benefits for the platform owner.

As these tools begin to integrate into a more intricate digital infrastructure, the compounded data generation and interoperability fuel the development of ML, deep learning, reinforcement learning and other AI, whose impact on education and humanity remain disconcertingly unknown, as discussed in Chapter 4.

In this chapter, my effort has been to demonstrate how children and young individuals are naturally attracted to these technologies due to their curiosity and creativity. However, they are also unwittingly drawn into the less transparent realm of AI development through their data and behaviour simply by going to school. The preceding chapters primarily delved into the top-down technological stacking and simultaneously the computational capabilities arising from data interoperability and from there – the acceleration of AI. The emphasis now shifts with an emphasis towards the individual and collective voices concerning these overarching architectural advancements and the various products and services that are shaping students' daily educational experience.

However, an essential point to emphasize is also the overstrain of calling for children's voices in digital education debates. Yet again, this need has been upturned, as students are increasingly subjected to extensive surveys and assessments of their emotions and experiences. They are asked to self-report on various aspects, including lessons, teachers, attitudes and more. This information, combined with background data and socio-economic factors, can build detailed profiles about children with predictive capabilities. Collecting their voice is ironically taking a less desirable shift with the pressing question: What kinds of creative expressions and freedoms are indeed enabled in the digital classroom if a child is constantly monitored and surveilled about their opinion, thoughts and feelings? And so, I thread on this topic of voice on the side of caution.

Here is an example, for which the 'walkthrough' methodology[43] was used again. Thrively is a popular platform used in US classrooms which assesses 'strengths' and 'multiple intelligences'.[44] It is imbued with positivity around 'thriving', 'hope', 'well-being' and 'building agency'. Every positive buzzword one can imagine has been crammed into its content. 'Discover your superpower strengths', a tutorial chimes, with 'our proprietary inventory', which was researched and developed by 'two leading paediatric neuropsychologists'. It pertains to twenty-three strengths and 80 questions, swapping between 'feeling' questions and 'functioning' ones. Multiple choices navigate respondents through the 'interest inventory with personality types' to create 'portfolios based on the profiles of the students'[45] – their voices. And 'once completed, the strengths profile becomes the basis for the rest of your students' Thrively experience'.

A question from its inventory asks, 'I'm pretty easy-going person, and when plans change, I don't really have a problem with that'. The child is now asked to select 'true', 'depends on the situation' or 'I have a hard time when plans change'. It is essentially a glorified personality survey assessment through often derisory and as disconnected questions such as these: 'I am able to put someone else's needs and wants before my own.' With one of three options as one choice for answers. Or '[i]f a genie granted me a wish … ' one would have to pick one of these:

- I would wish to be the most successful person in my career.
- I would wish for world peace.
- I would wish for more friends.
- I would wish to be the president of the United States.

Besides the bizarre videos asking to rub belly while tapping your head and swinging your leg to test how hard it feels doing it, other questions are just as inappropriate underscoring ablism. Asking whether a student feels like the sporty type, one possible answer is:

> I am one of the two fastest runners in my grade. That means without a shred of doubt, I know that only one other person in my entire grade could beat me in a thirty second sprint.

What good comes out of it even if a child agrees to such a statement? Why lead them to think about such things? What about children with disabilities? Or different cultures where bragging is frowned upon? The platform also allows teachers to set goals for their students and watch them track progress. Children as young as eight are asked to voice if they agree: 'I know myself', with an action plan such as this:

1. I will do each phase of the identity project with my learning community.
2. I will reflect on my new learnings in each phase of the project.
3. I will post a highlight from my Thrively folder that I am most proud of.
4. I will post my Self Portrait and my 'What I Wish Everyone Knew About Me' writing.
5. Top of form.
6. Bottom of form.

On the platform's *Sparks* functionality, children can simply spend days without leaving their device. There are 'widgets' organized by topics which then can let them exit to external websites (with their unknown data privacy rules[46]). There are the *Sparks* library items such as *news feed, history and geography, practical life skills, coding, games, social studies, what's happening* – more content and more engagement. So much for the two neuropsychologists developing the cognitive tests who also run private practice in treating, among other conditions, child internet addiction! The demo video explains that all this is a 'short 35-minute multimedia assessment that reveals [children's] top five strengths'.[47] For thirty-five minutes children are glued to the device, answering Thrively's tactless questions. Having tested the product, the question arises: is the digital classroom, having products like this, allowing true freedom for authenticity? Does collection of green emojis for 'happy' count as children's voice being heard? Does it count when we are asking them whether they feel lonely or whether they would prefer to excel in their career or have more friends?

Educators and policymakers have the responsibility to critically examine how EdTech influence these conditions so indispensable to children's healthy development and to uphold their fundamental rights. Educators should be able to resist them while governments must consider stricter scrutiny. Before diving into critical debate, the next section explores children's and young people's thoughts on the broad use of digital technologies in education, remaining within the Anglo-American contexts. This review aims to capture children's voices and perspectives on their experiences, rights and freedoms and on their perceptions when it comes to EdTech's designs and business practices, though it is far from exhaustive.

It has the potential …

Digital media's presence in children's lives has grown as these technologies become integrated into daily routines. More recent research efforts are drawn not only *about* children but also doing research *with* them.[48] While scholarship on children and young people's perceptions and use of digital media and the internet broadly continues to grow, children's voices around EdTech and the digital classroom have been propelled more recently following Covid-19. As the pandemic drove the digitization of education further, with that, there is more interest in understanding the implications for children's education and well-being.

The Office of Communications (OFCOM), the regulatory authority for broadcasting and telecommunications in the UK, had recently investigated media use, attitudes and understanding among children and young people aged 3 to 17 establishing that while a small minority still lacked proper access to adequate technologies for educational needs at home, the majority of children have increasingly become 'relatively passive consumers of content'.[49] On the other hand, while the majority are entertained by funny videos, 39 per cent of them would still watch 'how-to' videos or tutorials about hobbies or things they are interested in, indicating their desire to learn and be creative. When it comes to education, more than three-quarters of children aged 12 to 17 find being online helpful for school homework (77 per cent), and half believe it is useful for acquiring new skills. Approximately 43 per cent feel it can enhance their creative abilities and helps in improving reading and numeracy skills. Another study[50] in the United States explored children's views on EdTech use and well-being, with most expressing positivity, while others acknowledged frustration around their use.

Children and young people can be resourceful in how they deploy EdTech, and frustration may sometimes stem from intergenerational differences. Yet other scholars have highlighted that many children's responses from using EdTech in the classroom can be 'passionless'. In a recent study conducted with Australian youth aged between eleven and eighteen, students bluntly define EdTech as 'the usual shit'.[51] Yet other students perceived them as beneficial for various aspects of their schooling, such as information seeking, writing and composition, accessing, preparing and submitting homework.

Students overwhelmingly relied on their schools' learning management systems (LMS) as a centralized hub for all their academic needs, describing it as the 'one place for all my work and information I need'.

Their interaction with these systems has been primarily one way and directive, with the LMS guiding and informing students about their tasks and schedules. The researchers conclude that educators should temper their enthusiasm for digital technologies, as their primary use in education is for logistical and teacher-led purposes, such as for mundane tasks like taking notes and essay writing. Instead, educators should focus on understanding how students instrumentally use these technologies in their learning experiences, rather than expecting them to fundamentally transform the nature of education.[52]

Oher studies have noted that students sometimes utilize these EdTech tools beyond the required use in the classroom. The same Australian study showed that students utilized EdTech to access supplementary materials and alternative educational sources. Some sought additional explanations and deeper understanding of subjects by using non-approved resources such as online tutorials and summary videos like CrashCourse and SparkNotes for English. Students appreciated these applications for providing clarification on challenging topics and offering better-explained examples when classroom instruction was unclear. Similarly, others have followed how students' agency was expressed by utilizing online platforms and digital resources beyond the classroom boundaries and expectations.

Technology-enhanced experience in the classroom has also demonstrated support for embodied interactions within the context of embodied learning (EL) within the context of embodied cognition (EC) theory, which explores the connection between the brain, body and one's surrounding environment. Technology-enhanced embodied learning environments, like Kinect-based educational games, Wii, exergames, leap motion, and VR devices, have gained popularity in research. Studies have examined the effectiveness of these environments in enhancing students' learning outcomes across various subjects, including math, language learning, history and memory performance. In one such four-year investigation within a K-12 classroom setting, researchers used Kinems, a commercial suite of movement-based interactive educational games Unboxit and Lexis games for vocabulary and linguistic development. The results showed 'significant gains'[53] in students' cognitive performance, motor skills and academic performance in language. However, as the investigators note, these conclusions are preliminary; their broader applicability to other educational domains remains uncertain. The study involved diverse samples, including mainstream elementary students and those with special educational needs (SEN); however, the experiments lasted only five months, which restricted the ability to assess the interventions' long-term effects.

Yet, when it comes to their privacy, safety, rights and freedoms in the digital realm there is growing evidence around children's concerned voices. Some researchers[54] have highlighted that while children enjoy and value their digital experiences, they also become frustrated when digital design, provision and regulation fall short of meeting their needs. Children are becoming more informed about privacy risks and the potential collection of their private information. An eight-year-old's perspective underscores their expectation of responsible businesses and comply with laws, emphasizing it this way:

> When you download a game, it says, can this game access your files? Then it's, why do you want to see what my files are? That's in my bad interest because I don't want it going through my files, thank you very much.[55]

Even though the study introduced children to the concept of digital rights as a starting point of the research, it highlighted that children quickly learned those and even took initiative to suggest improvements around aspects of privacy and security. An eight-year-old suggested to the researchers that

> age restrictions should become harder to bypass as I see many young children below the age of 12. You also should look into higher censorship

as there have been many events in the past of extremely gruesome clips: a guy shooting himself, a guy getting hit ... and children playing with guns.[56]

The concerns around datafication of children have also been brought to their attention with greater effort from the research community, schools and policymakers. Some literature has shown that not only do children increasingly care about the various implications of datafication on their lives, selves and others, but they demand a chance to take action. Through ten co-designed sessions with fifty-three children, researchers in the UK[57] examined how children, aged between seven and fourteen, want to be supported to cope with the datafication practices providing insight about creating age-appropriate support for algorithmic literacy development, emphasizing the importance of tailored approaches. Children expressed their vision for a more humane and autonomy-supportive digital future. A ten-year-old put it this way:

> If the platforms were humane, which I think they are, which I hope they are. They would know they are dealing with actual people, we are not just statistics in their database or whatever.[58]

Children have openly shared their concerns around data collection and profiling not only of them, but of their loved ones, as expressed by one twelve-year-old:

> How my data, my friends data, my parents data, and everyone's data is combined and merged by them [platforms] and how it [datafication] would have effect on every single one of us.[59]

The same study concluded that children, aged seven to fourteen, would like to be supported in understanding datafication and what future data-driven digital experiences should be like for them; that they demand a shift of the current data ecosystem towards a more humane-by-design and autonomy-supportive future. Children further identified what enabled or limited their freedoms to practise and enjoy their rights in the digital environment with regard to specific design considerations.

Ongoing debates in the field remain between those expressing concern and others highlighting potential benefits. These debates should undoubtedly consider the increased digital technology use in the classroom, compounding overall daily interaction with the screen, implications for children's well-being including cognitive strain, sleep issues and physical health, the influence and impact of algorithmic systems, data capture and the emanating computational capacities.

Growing concerns about children's well-being and digital technology stem from the potential substitution of play, family time and in-person interactions by technology. This shift can have adverse effects on children's emotional, physical and social well-being. Increased digital technology use can lead to issues like cognitive strain, aggressive behaviours and sleeping problems. There are also health concerns about children's likely reduced physical activities and the influence of commercial exposure on childhood obesity. The increased technology use has been associated with eye problems, headaches, eating disorders and fatigue, sometimes occurring after just thirty minutes of use.[60]

While EdTechs are often celebrated for promising inclusivity, greater opportunities for learning, levelling up and equity, the evidence for that is mixed and often insufficient. For example, the belief that technology is a great equalizer often overlooks how culture, law, policy and technology itself can reinforce disparities especially for children with disabilities.

Some research looking at how the fundamental human rights of children with disabilities are met[61] notes that technological advancements have enabled children with disabilities to access information, communicate, socialize, learn and play in ways that were previously inaccessible or limited. Video-calling has improved communication for those with hearing impairments.

Learning beyond the classroom, some children describe, is an incentive, while those with visual impairment would sometimes find automatic spell checks frustrating as these features could alter the intended meaning without them being able to verify accuracy.

On the other hand, in her exploration of digital technologies use among children with disabilities, Meryl Alper underscores the fact that merely giving a child a talking tablet does not ensure their ability to express themselves. As she puts it: 'at their core, these incomplete remedies are based on a seductive belief in the easy technological fix as well as a view of individuals with disabilities as most in need of fixing – whereby technology repairs or elevates impairment'.[62] Alper provides alternative perspectives on 'voice' in various contexts and argues that many digital platforms fail to accommodate individuals with disabilities, creating a new form of exclusion.[63] The reliance on technology to 'fix' disabilities is a techno-deterministic perspective that does not consider the more complex reality revealing a 'participation gap' for children with disabilities. Not to mention that those caring for them also have to learn to navigate and use the technologies. It is simply not just 'grab and go'.

Concerns about data collection and privacy in assistive technologies should also consider children's distinct perspectives, ensuring they have an equal presence in discussions about the governance of these technologies.

Likewise, only in recent years disabled individuals have gained recognition for their ability to make decisions about their own assistive technologies which has further gained legal influence in regulating these technologies. This argument aligns with Neil Selwyn's[64] that encouraging a more diverse range of people to share their perspectives on education and technology would lead to a more accurate representation of both the shortcomings and less-than-ideal histories in the field. Meeting at the centre – between the gloomy views and tech evangelists – is a hopeful way forward to building better governance of these technologies and protecting children's basic rights and attending to their diverse needs.

Children are always excited to grab the latest technology and dive right in. They enjoy digital technologies, but they are generally sceptical about the companies that provide them. They accept the digitized classroom. However, it is not just because of the 'educational purpose' or the entertainment but rather *when* and *if* they feel the emotional support in the classroom, when they perceive usefulness and trust.

Additionally, students also seek emotional and educational support – all of which condition their acceptance of digital learning experience. Emotional support relates to the provision of tangible assistance such as one provided by a teacher in helping students to accomplish specific tasks, course material sharing from peer students – aiming to address learning issues. When students perceive a sense of educational support, such as a teacher explaining a problem, they are more likely to engage in the course study and value them, making them self-regulated. Such educational support is positively related to technologies perceived usefulness in that regard.

Similarly, when students receive emotional support, the provision of empathy, encouragement, love and care,[65] which does not necessarily deal with purely educational support but rather deal with stress or other uncomfortable experience during digital learning, effective emotional support can attenuate the mental effort needed to cope with the negative, resulting in fewer difficulties in adapting to digital technologies as the mode to learning. Cognitive offloading through such emotional support helps alleviate stress and allow students to find more mental effort to adapt to the digital learning.[66]

As advancements like virtual reality (VR), augmented reality (AR) and mixed reality (MR) technologies become more available in the classroom, there is promising potential to enhance students' learning and experiences. Virtual worlds are computer-based, three-dimensional environments allowing users to create persistent virtual identities. There, users engage through 'avatars', a term borrowed from Hinduism which signifies a deity's earthly form;[67] in the virtual world, these are user-controlled characters.

Several research projects have shown the positive response from students of utilizing such products with education in mind. For example, one study investigated how advanced applications support tertiary students' studies in physiology and anatomy through three-dimensional applications for human organ systems and structures.[68]

From a comprehensive review of research scholars examined the use of VR, AR and MR technologies to teach elementary, middle and high school students. The common themes identified included collaboration, communication and critical thinking, also considered twenty-first-century skills.[69] Along with the 'metaverse' technologies like VR, AR and MR, considered the Web3 media (Web1 and Web2 being the worldwide web and social media respectfully), are promising to enable immersive experiences and practices. In the metaverse individuals are immersed actively in the creation of virtual worlds.

Creating and participating in video games and fantasy worlds are evolving into 3D virtual environments in combination with innovative technologies that provide an immersive experience. Virtual worlds are still not in the mainstream classroom; however, research and recent marketing rhetoric continue to drive the attention in that direction. Some educators are encouraged to use virtual worlds for their promise to allow students to practise tasks that are otherwise unsafe or costly in real life.

The gamified designs in virtual worlds promise to enhance user immersion into a specific field and facilitate authentic learning in a discipline or profession through role-playing and realistic scenarios.[70, 71] Some research has found that gamification enhances student motivation and engagement,[72] challenging them to apply novel knowledge and skills at a higher cognitive level than traditional didactic methods.[73]

Metaverse-like experiences are offering virtual classrooms through apps like the NearPod VR Lessons. One K-12 student of the product's website says how he likes to use it as it gives him a 'chance to go there' to the virtual place he has never visited. Says another student, '[I]t's like you're there, it looks real.'[74] Yet the context of the video is important. NearPod promotes its product among students from highly disadvantaged backgrounds. Most of the children interviewed in the video are non-white, coming from Aspire Palo Alto Phoenix Academy, a charter school with 93 per cent Hispanic students, 63 per cent of whom are eligible to free lunch while 10 per cent are eligible to reduced lunches.[75] Is this saying that students who have been used to praise the product after experiencing it are likely to not be able to afford to travel to those far-flung corners of the world that the app is offering them to visit virtually? And while NearPod VR Lessons provide the alternative opportunity, who takes on the bill for these technologies and their required infrastructure? Furthermore, analysing the actual experience, one can argue that students remain with a limited sensory engagement, social interaction when they are immersed in these digital visits and can even miss on the richer cultural contexts that can never be supplanted by the virtual experience. There is a lack of authenticity as much as Paris or the Taj Mahal may look 'realistic' – the applications provide an idealized version of these places and not the reality. Ultimately, the dependency on digital technologies also grows.

Looking at these technologies in the current context is relevant as they are intricately connected to the playful experience that children can be easily attracted to. The businesses of digital and immersive games have crossed over to education – what literature refers to the 'gamification of education'.[76] The lines between gaming and education are blurring but so are the lines with commercialization and the exploitation of children as a primary target audience.

Meta, for example, entices young people that in their Horizon Worlds, the company's Roblox-like digital playground, 'you and your friends can collaborate and bring your wildest ideas to life – without ever leaving VR'.[77] While children's perspectives and experiences with these are yet to be studied in greater depth, something more concerning can also be flagged. Children, for instance, are exposed to aggressive targeted marketing in these virtual worlds. Such games are now partnering with fashion brands, initially offering free virtual products – often otherwise expensive items in the physical world – such as Louis Vuitton, Lacoste, Nike and others for children to engage with in a sort of innocent and playful manner, such as playing dress-up. Lacoste and Minecraft World, as it says in a YouTube video, offer players to:

> take a trip to Croco Island for a stylish adventure in this free map created by Blockception! Design your own tennis court and mingle with Mr. Crocodile in the Lacoste theme park.[78]

Users are invited to replicate their avatars' favourite outfits in game and change their look based on their mood.

With over 2.6 billion gamers globally, gaming is now the largest entertainment sector. Minecraft, one of the best-selling games, is played worldwide; Minecraft's unique position allows it to connect the digital and physical worlds through commercial products. Minecraft, however, is also a product that has carved its way into schools[79] (with a free version which was reportedly available at some point in more than fifty countries[80]), where its owner – Microsoft – also has significant presence! This raises serious questions about what if any monitoring and assessment are done around these commercial product placements, the companies accessing, collecting, managing and using the data collected about children as they engage with the games and products.

Similarly, PacSun, an American retail clothing brand, has expanded partnership with Roblox due to its young user base. Over half of Roblox's 50 million daily users are under thirteen; the 17–24 age group is also growing rapidly. PacSun have seen significant purchases after users engaged with augmented reality feature on Snapchat[81] with the aim to translate to online and in-store sales. These companies aim for and measure the intent for purchase. The freebies they provide to their target customers – an ever younger future loyal client base – enable tracking of behaviour and engagement with the products. However, little is known what data is collected, who has access to it and for what purposes. Zepeto, a social media platform, and Roblox have already featured Ralph Lauren, a clothes retailer, aiding the company in attracting a younger audience and boosting digital channel sales.[82]

These are targets outside of the education realm. However, they impact children in immense ways. First, these practices demonstrate how businesses optimize on the digital through data collection to their own advantage, which is a tale of caution for those same tech businesses in partnerships with other industry players now entering the classroom. The cases in point are Minecraft, Roblox and the already widely present in educational institutions Microsoft. And second, educating children about these practices bounces back as a responsibility of schools and families. This is a one-sided requirement; instead, it should be shared with the business sector itself that is crossing over to education under the guise of play and learn.

'Don't make assumptions about me'

Children's insights into the digital classroom should extend beyond surface-level experiences to encompass their understanding of technology design, data practices and business intent around these. While children are becoming better informed and aware about the inner workings of digital applications and the wider digital realm of digital media beyond the classroom, there is a knowledge gap about their perspectives around the business practices and motivations of those technologies that are encroaching on education. Also, while growing research sheds light on children's voices with regard to their diverse and unique experiences, yet they can also be unified when it comes to justice and fairness.

One study, for example, analysed how seven- to thirteen-year-olds perceived data collection practices and its potential impact on them.[83] The findings revealed three key areas where children lacked understanding: they did not recognize the individuals involved in data processing and how data was transferred between platforms and their own data ownership. These results suggest the importance of improving transparency, fostering autonomy in design and re-evaluating the existing data governance structures to better support children in increasingly data-driven environments.

Children are more trustful of technologies used in schools although still a proportion of eight- to seventeen-year-olds (21 per cent) think only some things are true that they access in school.[84] Children are becoming more familiar with the outcomes of profiling but are also generally unaware of how that works.

Most children especially older ones can have experiences with the outcomes of profiling. In one study, children talked about a range of outcomes, including videos that were recommended to them on YouTube and search engine suggestions. Nevertheless, few understood the process of profiling and the various mechanisms involved. To a great extent, this can be attributed to the fact that children can be less aware of data that platforms and websites collect indirectly. This proves especially apparent in discussions about cookies – one of the mechanisms that could be used to profile users. While many have heard of cookies, few children know how they could be used to build up a profile of them and how that may be harmful.

Using common methodology that blends research and consultation with children across different locations including Austria, Belgium, the UK, the United States, Malaysia, Cambodia, Thailand and Indonesia, research[85] sought to gauge their voices and experiences concerning privacy and the utilization of their personal data in the digital realm. When it came to data privacy in the digital classroom, the researchers noted how children generally expressed trust in their schools' decisions about their data, assuming 'good faith'.

Children generally recognized the necessity of extensive data processing for their education, often relying on third-party platforms integrated into their school interactions. They trusted that only teachers would access their data and expected the school to keep it secure, believing the school would not engage in anything 'creepy' because 'they're my school, they're going to keep my data safe', according to an eleven-year-old respondent from UK. In the United States, a child using Google products for school assumed that Google would not sell their data or use it beyond 'target advertising or impersonal data collection'. However, the authors conclude, children have limited understanding of their personal data being collected and processed by commercial actors. They would generally be aware that Google 'sees'[86] their personal data and that 'Google knows everything about us'.[87] Some children in the UK, the authors highlight, were aware of issues like the Cambridge Analytica scandal and doubted the trustworthiness of big companies. Yet they often questioned the value of their own data, wondering why anyone would want to track them.

More recently other scholars have found that children's perceptions around data collection are not 'life and death' when it comes to data from their social media use even though they also acknowledged that some digital companies could be motivated by 'malicious intent'.[88] In some ways, there seems to be no urgency around the subliminal ways of data extraction and automating decision-making in young people's eyes. Yet, when they were made aware of the practices of data tracking, as in the study, the participants seemed more reluctant, as one of them told the researchers, 'Because I know you were tracking me it felt different ... it put me off using [his mobile phone].'[89]

Conclusion

I wish to conclude with an important caveat at the end of this chapter. Student voice is and should be addressed within the context of a space where the conditions and instruments (e.g., surveillance through digital technology systems) are mandated top-down.

More often than not, children cannot opt out of any aspect of the digital classroom. A student has limited or no choice but to sign into the classroom technologies and prevent behavioural tracking by third parties.[90] Assignments cannot be submitted without going via a digital platform. Exams cannot be passed. Well-being is monitored and so are attendance, school behaviour and movements – be that when a student goes to the canteen, library or restroom. Additionally, as some academics maintain,[91] any provisions to support children's rights to education have yet to acknowledge the impact of advancing digital systems and their capacity to influence individuals without their awareness or consent.[92] We still know little about how children would feel about adaptive systems influencing their learning daily. There is little that we know about children with special educational needs and disabilities and their interpretation and perspectives on the digital classroom, datafication, digital surveillance and adaptive systems for learning.

Many EdTech products in class today will be entirely useless not only if they are not mandated but also if there is no perceived need or usefulness by the 'users' themselves. Following the Covid-19 pandemic, research has looked into the factors that influence adoption of EdTech. During the pandemic, EdTech companies seized the chance to streamline online education, offering enticing options to both governments and directly to schools, families and students. During lockdown, numerous learning apps were provided free to children, resulting in a significant increase in their use.[93]

Since most schools globally went online overnight, there was little to no choice for students, families and schools to figure out how to carry on with schooling. On the one hand, the conditions to adopt EdTech depend on the availability of the technology but also on whether students are willing to embrace them. Some studies[94] have looked at how technology acceptance depends on variables such as subjective social influence, enjoyment and computer anxiety.

Others[95] have emphasized how the educational function of digital learning is connected to students' acceptance of it and students' abilities to cope with negative emotions. As precursors, the influence of students' emotions on their acceptance of EdTech mediating education cannot be ignored.

Like social media, digital learning can foster an important conduit for exchanging social support. Students can collaborate, share course-related knowledge and material, but also socialize and share feelings, empathy, support and care. This perceived support that is both educational and emotional is crucial to whether students adopt and accept EdTech but also whether they are happy in school and therefore motivated to learn, be creative and get the best experience of being in it. A big condition of that is the very environment, the teachers and students and how they all come together to organize, socialize and work in a social common way. Again, the mandated technologies are changing this environment to which both teachers and students are now learning to adapt without choice while they know little about the functions, objectives and even the influence exerted on them by these products.

In the wake of the health pandemic, digital technologies have undeniably also caused significant difficulties. As screen time and concerns from the use of social media increased, the EU, for instance, has been funding various projects aimed at assessing and protecting the well-being of students and teachers in digital education. One in particular is a project in collaboration with the EU's Joint Research Council, in which I have been involved and have been mapping literature and gauging children's, parents' and teachers' voices to develop a framework for assessing their well-being. It is ironic that in pursuit of solving one problem, another one is created. The question is just how worse this other one becomes.

A growing body of research has concentrated on examining the adverse effects of digital technologies on children's physical health. Nevertheless, the industry has often been swift in addressing these concerns before any substantial regulatory limitation has been able to slap their advance into children's lives. For example, to correlations between screen time and childhood obesity, there has been a surge in the availability of technologies that promote physical activity.[96] Things like fitness-tracking devices have been introduced not only as trendy gadgets but have also found applications in school settings under the guise as monitoring the physical well-being of children.

Some digital technologies have been reported to enhance motor skills and handwriting in primary school students, while others have been linked to issues like disrupted sleep and negative physiological outcomes like high blood pressure.[97] Yet, while not an exhaustive list, these are impacts in relation to screen time. They do not encompass considerations regarding the content or types of digital technologies being used.

Furthermore, these studies have often failed to distinguish between findings based on different educational levels, socio-economic backgrounds, languages, cultures and other important factors around children as individual subjects.

Digital technologies have been reported to exert mixed impact on the well-being not only of students but also of teachers. While the focus of this book is on children, teacher well-being and their role in the classroom and on children's education should not be disregarded. Yet research on the impact of digitization on teachers is scarce and seldom reaches the wider publics and media. As I delved into the policy and politics of education in the earlier chapters, historically, teachers have tended to be part of the system failure whenever failure in the system has been named. Teacher distrust has been growing in societies like the UK and the United States while at the same time teachers have their own experiences and views to what happens inside their classrooms.

Teachers and schools deal with discipline, behaviour, safety and all kinds of socio-emotional issues that students go through – issues that come from outside and have nothing to do with school. There is just so much besides teaching; the digitized classroom has added to the social, emotional, political, financial, structural and pedagogic challenges further.

The digitized classroom has the potential to inadvertently impact teachers' sense of identity by encroaching upon their traditional roles. This has further exacerbated their sense of deprofessionalization or, as they themselves have called it, demoralization![98] The digital surveillance has affected teachers as much as children – putting them under constant assessment. This matters because teachers contribute greatly to the whole spirit of the classroom. Teachers are often tethered to devices themselves. As I explored NetSupport in Chapter 2, the platform expects the teacher to view her class through the platform; see her students as miniature digital screens, with their feelings as red or green emojis or 'thumbs'. What teacher, and for that matter parent, is fine with that; importantly, why?

Digital technology companies have the privilege to sell a product to children – and schools. As this chapter explored, children are generally excited about these products, while the businesses behind them have essentially low barrier to entry. They are however profit-driven and will often cut corners to get to the financial success as soon as possible. This means compromising on many aspects that require time, cost and resources. At the same time, their market entry experiences little friction and resistance.

All children have the right to education. It is also their right to have full participation in it. Yet children have relatively no sense of control or say over what products they use in class and even less so – what data is being collected about them or how such businesses use this data. However, their concerns are there and growing. What remains to be seen is how to make their voices count.

The debate surrounding the granularity of data and algorithmic prediction for behavioural modification about individuals leads to at least two general assumptions, neither of which can leave room for more novel thinking (with regard to identifying the possible scenarios of negative impact and with regard to ameliorating or preventing such impact).

On one hand, there is concern that presenting young people with a 'black mirror' views of how their personal data is used for extracting deep knowledge could lead to unnecessary moral panics. As pointed out in this chapter, some have found that many young people do not necessarily consider their personal data collection by third parties a 'life and death' situation.[99] While students may generally remain unaware of personal data misuse by third parties, data literacy, as research often concludes with as the next logical step, can, to some degree, help them become more informed and even lead to more proactive attitude towards their privacy (e.g., fixing own device privacy settings).

The problem with data literacy proposals is that they do not scale up and consider implementation on multilevels, as part of a greater and concerted effort of governance where businesses and everyone in the life of children are aware of and participate in the common goal. Data literacy curricula or practices make little impact for change in the data extraction and behaviour modification industry more broadly.

The very sense of inevitabilism that dominates government circles and often school leaders[100] that schools should keep up with technological progress and provide the necessary digital skills of the future assumes an already narrowed and pre-determined way forward. This can taper individual agency. Importantly, as one senior platform engineer told me 'if the product is done to deceive there is almost nothing one can do to stop it'.

Even if data literacy promises to lead to individual perseverance and skills to navigate the digital maze and opt out from tracking and surveillance, the subordination of institutions – the education sector as its own pillar in society – to predictive systems defeats the purpose of any data literacy efforts to begin with. By the same token, where legal efforts have paved the way for data ownership and portability (the ability for individuals to request all their data from tech companies that collect it), for transparency and accountability, the effort remains an isolated case. For example, Mahieu et al.[101] found that even in jurisdictions where individuals have the right to access and own their data, the majority of individuals still do not do much about it due to lack of transparency about data processing and because people 'don't care'. In the meantime, the business of data extraction for behaviour modification carries on.[102]

The normalization of data-driven systems permeating a child's ecology (be that school or the home) is presenting a new 'normal' where people shrug off as one school director in England said to me, '[P]rivacy is gone, what privacy, we've all got this [pointing to her iPhone]. What's there to hide? They know everything about us.'

For those who think of surrender, Daniel J. Solove makes a poignant argument about the misconceived: 'I've got nothing to hide.' This is a flawed argument, Solve says, assuming that, as security expert Bruce Schneier argues, 'privacy is about hiding a wrong'.[103] Nothing to hide, as Solove contends, 'denies even the existence of a problem'[104] related to data collection and use. However, data collection, aggregated over time, structural surveillance, datafication and the invasive nature of such practices position individuals and the collective in a long-term disadvantage because someone on the 'outside', beyond one's control – be that the business harvesting the data or governments, or third-party malicious actors who have come in possession of such data – leaves individuals in the mercy of those who hold their data as a sort of hostage.

Law professor Anne Bartow contends that arguments around privacy do not 'have enough dead bodies' and lack 'blood and death, or at least … broken bones and buckets of money'.[105]

Research capturing children's and young people's voices, perceptions and equally misconceptions around digital technologies often includes proposals for improving or providing for digital and data literacies and education as already noted. Efforts have continuously emphasized the need for improved data privacy literacy through special curricula for data protection and self-determination,[106] personal data literacies frameworks,[107] models for social data and privacy[108] and advocating for schools to teach data and privacy literacy as unique skills.[109] However, a contradiction arises as schools and policymakers permit constant and ever-growing student data extraction with constantly changing EdTech products and services, which can undermine these proposals or render them inadequate and ineffective. To prevent this, EdTech businesses have a role to play, and that is, they need to undergo strict scrutiny, monitoring and evaluation to ensure that they respect children's voices, observe their rights and be tamed.

6

The Good Intentions of School: Why School Matters?

Master of my fate[1]

School is meant to provide a safe space for children and young people to learn, acquire important new skills and become the subject of their own lives – master of their fate; find purpose, contribute to society. With these and other such objectives in mind, School plays an important role in societies.

Yet, if we consider one of its objectives to deliver education, it is safe to say that this alone does not solve all societal problems. For many problems stem from very well-educated individuals. Just walk through human history for examples. To paraphrase Ricky Gervais's character Derek, from the eponymous TV series, perhaps one need not be clever or good looking but kind. Therefore, School has – or at least should have – a purpose that is beyond merely providing some kind of education. The problem with answering what more it should provide then is that it cannot be done in isolation of the contexts of our existence: Global economic precarity, international conflicts, growing uncertainties for global peace and climate stability, and accelerating AI, with corporate appetite behind it. On the one hand, education can equip individuals with the knowledge and skills necessary to navigate and potentially attend with care to these complex and interconnected challenges. On the other hand, education alone cannot address the root causes of all of these problems alone.

To begin with, every school, and I speak of mainstream public educational institutions, strives to have high standards (even if their audits do not rate them as such). Audits and ranking aside, it would be surprising to find a school whose staff would greet you at their gates with words about how theirs is incredibly unsafe, poor academically or lacking values. Schools pursue excellence within their constraints, committing to deliver public good. Today, having digital technologies is seen as a path to achieving high standards in schools. However, just as school rankings from audits can create mixed perceptions of school performance, digitization also produces mixed results. These range from the overhyping and underutilization of technologies[2] to the global inequalities exposed by the shift to online learning during the Covid-19 pandemic.[3]

Additionally, the embrace of technological innovations in the classroom as a form of striving for high standards in School has brought about the rise of digital surveillance, datafication and automation of educational processes as discussed in Chapter 4. In our turbulent political landscape, surveillance is further propelled[4] as a means of 'protection' in public places, including schools.

The previous chapters described how educational systems like that in the United States and the UK have long been pushed to perform and act like businesses which have brought about a culture of constant performance assessment and auditing.[5] Digital technologies and data have come to promise a seamless system that not only maintains this culture efficiently but growing into a deeper and wider socio-technical infrastructure that is more and more seen to serve the interests of Western markets through the alignment of education with workforce needs. These systems have further encroached on schools with their data-driven and diagnostic proposals for education and positioned a generation of schools between 'manoeuvring themselves to survive in an auditing culture'[6] and EdTech cluttering the education landscape.

All of the preceding chapters have illustrated an evolving educational environment as a result of mass digitization. Within this context, however, children are gradually exposed to a world where the concept of privacy increasingly holds conflicting meanings. Excessive screen time, once a concern, has now become commonplace even in the classroom. Additionally, the curriculum increasingly resembles narrowed pathways aiming towards the world of work and an ever-growing urgency to acquire important skills needed in the age of AI, which ironically some say is likely to wipe out most of work as we know it.

What can be gleaned from numerous policies and a minefield of standards, audit processes and continuously evolving statutory requirements, School's duties are many. School must provide a learning environment and prioritize various aspects such as academic quality, address individual pupils' needs, foster personal growth, provide safeguarding, enrich student opportunities and experiences, stay current with global issues and much more. But for all those things, schools are the result of human endeavour.

Invariably, governments, international communities, parents, commercial and non-commercial entities highlight these aspects and acknowledge the importance of School. Indeed, policy may address it as the 'ugly and unendurable'[7] problem that needs fixing, others swiftly following the same narrative. On the other hand, it is in this constant policy-making aimed at 'fixing' the 'ugly' bits that highlight School's very value.

The Covid-19 pandemic underscored School's significance, too. Before the pandemic, the proportion of children in 'Learning Poverty' was 57 per cent.[8] Due to extended school closures and limited access to digital resources, it was estimated to have risen to 70 per cent in 2022. These closures and inadequate remote learning resulted in significant learning losses, with students forgetting roughly thirty-two days of learning for every thirty days of school closures.[9] School certainly has value.

Many visions and opinions on reimagining School have come from various corners including global supranational organizations and industry alike long before as well as after the pandemic. The OECD, in its *Future of Education and Skills 2030* report, outlined a framework, recognizing the crucial role of School and human efforts behind it. Having collaborated with schools worldwide to foster ideas, share best practices and shape a new learning environment, the OECD emphasized skills like compassion, critical thinking, creativity and empathy.[10] Nevertheless, these reports and agendas frequently emphasize the digital realm, too, the necessity for new skills in response to technological advancement, and the urgency for all children and schools to keep pace.

Other international organizations similarly have consistently emphasized innovation and globalism as paramount in education, potentially diverting focus from the everyday realities in classrooms and what is actually suitable and needed. One example is with the World Economic Forum (WEF) and their vision of the *Schools of the Future: Defining New Models of Education for the Fourth Industrial Revolution*. This report illustrates a form of distraction by heavily promoting innovation, globalism and technological skills as the foundation of the future School, potentially neglecting the needs and challenges that children face at a basic level, such as access to food, parental support in a highly uncertain economic and political environment or stable housing. While there is often an assumption that School will address these problems, how can we prioritize the most critical life-dependent needs in ways that even powerful organizations and industry attend to them first before spotlighting technological globalism and innovation? Teaching children about globalism, innovation and other such 'essential' skills for navigating advancing technologies sounds great. However, tilting the balance towards them often also diverts budgets away from where they are needed most.

Amid these visions and the increasing prevalence of public-private partnerships and agendas for the future of education, there is a consistent focus on developing new education frameworks and assessment tools – mostly, more digital integration. It is within these changing discourses that a crucial aspect often gets neglected: An important responsibility of School to *preserve* childhood, not just *prepare* students for adulthood.

School and childhood

Childhood is important to acknowledge here because School's existence is directly linked to it. Early kindergartens were established in the nineteenth century to protect children who were left unsupervised when their parents worked long hours in factories,[11] also highlighting that there is some dependence of childhood on School – therefore, the dependence of societies on progressing by educating their young.

In Medieval times, where the concept of childhood did not exist, education was also absent, as Neil Postman points out in *The Disappearance of Childhood*. Postman brings Ariés's remarks that 'everything was permitted in [children's] presence: coarse language, scabrous actions and situations; they had heard everything and seen everything'.[12] Childhood, Postman maintains, was the construct that separated the world of adults with all 'its mysteries, its contradictions, its violence, its tragedies – that are not considered suitable for children to know; that are, indeed, shameful to reveal to them indiscriminately'.[13]

Childhood acts as a bulwark, allowing certain truths and knowledge to be gradually revealed and understood well, while others are reserved for adulthood. School predominantly operates within these bounds. In the Middle Ages, children were exposed to adult content and experiences without restraint. According to Ariés, 'the practice of playing with children's privy parts formed part of a widespread tradition', a tradition that today, Postman adds, 'will get you up to thirty years in prison'.[14] The absence of literacy, education and the concept of shame in the medieval world contributed to the lack of a distinct idea of childhood. As a result, there was no need for an intermediate stage between infancy and adulthood. There was no need for School.

During that time, there was no specific children's literature, paediatrics or differentiation in language between adults and children either. Schools were unnecessary because there was little deemed crucial to teach children, many of whom were engaged in labour or apprenticeships. Certainly, the concept of childhood, as well as the understanding of the lifespan, was drastically different, with a high child mortality rate. Parents often gave multiple children the same name (no need to remember different ones), hoping that a few would at least survive to adulthood. This preconditioned the emotional attachment to them as well.

The emergence of the printing press subsequently led to a clear distinction between adults who could read and those who could not, separating the secrets of adulthood from children based on literacy. With that, School emerged as the middle ground where children would experience childhood and would be prepared to transition to adulthood.

In today's Western thinking, the focus extends beyond childhood rights, as discussed earlier, to consider children's 'evolving capacities'. This concept acknowledges that children develop differently worldwide and have varying levels of understanding regarding their rights. However, their increased exposure to the adult world through digital access infused with rich audio-visual content raises questions about the changing nature of childhood, what is genuinely beneficial and desirable for children to see and learn.

Additionally, the prevailing idea of everyone's voice has also caused what Alen Prout argues as the 'destabilizing'[15] of childhood through various changing conditions and experiences, which are 'often contradictory, not necessarily beneficial for children'.[16] As soon as childhood had turned into society's 'project', Prout says, the efforts to provide services aimed at improving children's lives and well-being simultaneously 'rendered children objects of knowledge brought into the adult gaze, to be kept under surveillance, studied and understood'.[17]

Although the initial enthusiasm for safeguarding childhood has waned, Prout asserts, and despite significant investments aimed at improving children's lives and well-being, there is still a lack of concrete evidence for these improvements, mainly because often the purpose and intentions behind these efforts remain unclear. Additionally, the ambiguity surrounding childhood is partly due to the portrayal of children as either *at risk* or *a risk* to self and society. The former depicts them as vulnerable, dependent and in need of protection, which has led to increased adult supervision and surveillance. The latter portrays them as a potential danger to themselves and others, resulting in efforts to control such children, again through prevention, surveillance and intervention policies, further deepening these existing divides.

As Richard Freeman posits,[18] the tension between protection and prevention has created an ongoing cycle where failures lead to renewed efforts in either direction. This, as Prout concludes, is 'one in which children, as a primary target of prevention, seem caught in a system that can respond to its own failure only by ratcheting up control'.[19] As a result neither of these portrayals of childhood fully grasps the position of children today. What is needed is a more comprehensive way of representing childhood, a 'seed', which Prout suggests, can be 'found in the idea of children as social persons'. However, this brings us to the question of how the digitized and datafied classroom affects these notions of childhood.

Childhood and the digitized classroom

The push to digitize the classroom, as outlined in many government policies, reports and visions from global organizations, international convenings, forums and expos, tends to neglect these contentions around childhood. In the *Schools of the Future*, for example, WEF briefly mentions childhood three times, with the emphasis not on why it matters or what it is for but rather seen as part of education with its significant impact 'later in life and earnings outcomes'.[20] Prominent consultancies, including McKinsey, EY, PriceWaterhouseCoopers and others, promote digitizing education with little regard for the impact or importance of childhood. Their emphasis is on the importance of digitization, data and AI skills, aligning with the belief that these are crucial for everyone's future.

In a similar tone are the marketing communications of EdTech businesses. They primarily emphasize education as a means for individuals to emerge as more prosperous, well-rounded adults with confident employment prospects. Their view of School is often described in ways that make no room for either childhood or their rights to develop themselves as unique subjects.

We observe children's prolonged screen time, and concerns about their innocence and safety grow from threats emanating from social media, dis- and mis-information, cyberbullying, online radicalization, issues related to health and so on. For that, some argue that childhood is disappearing[21] because children see it all.[22] Some of the concerns expressed include that digital media would replace other childhood activities.

On the other hand, there has also been enthusiasm about the digital world for its unprecedented opportunities for democratic participation, for mastering diverse skills and for creative expression, exceeding any previous generations' expectations.[23] However, such optimism often omits to explain how all this comes into being. There is *a* period necessary to provide the opportunity for intelligence and critical thinking development to begin with. As OECD articulate, the current challenges students are faced with are 'the lack of sufficient time to master key disciplinary concepts or, in the interests of a balanced life, to nurture friendships, to sleep and to exercise'.[24]

True, children make meaningful connections with friends considering the legal and various other constraints and lack of time for play in a more traditional sense. But those discourses need update in light of the prevailing data collection and exploitation through the digitization of every aspect of childhood and education.

How childhood is viewed is related to how School is viewed. Childhood experiences in contemporary Europe for example have changed due to factors like welfare-state policies, family structures and economics. Notably, children and young people make up a smaller proportion of the EU population compared to the global average, with declining birth rates and increased emigration contributing to slower population growth.[25, 26] A contemporary climate of uncertainty and economic precarity has supplanted the rigid notions of identity, authority and morality prevalent of the early twentieth century. Late modernity has introduced novel family, marriage and work dynamics, along with heightened recognition of complexity and overall diminished trust in the social institutions.[27] When discussing childhood, children are frequently portrayed as either angels or devils, as Prout points out. What is essentially needed, he suggests, are 'ways of thinking about the real, lived experiences of children and the complex character of childhood in a changing world'.[28] As Christensen notes:

> what may be challenged are those traditional perspectives … (in which) … children have little or no influence over their own social representation … This focus leaves more or less unaddressed the child as a social person in their own right, to be understood through his or her perceptions and actions in the social and cultural world.[29]

In the digitized and data-driven classroom, where children's profiles and rankings are determined by artificial models and algorithms, the individual's social identity can be completely taken over. Dominant educational forces, including school audits, summative assessments and teachers' judgements shape how children are assessed and perceived.

In contrast to these conventional tools, digital systems, like Thrively and PowerSchool described earlier, lack transparency about how they affect the perceptions of children and childhood. This points to the reciprocal relationship between not only political representation of children through citizenship and social and cultural discourse but the possibility that digital systems are further excluding and separating children from public life by embedding the routine but unhelpful stereotypes of children that dominate public discourse. In other words, we should ask: What social stereotypes are likely to be embedded within the EdTechs' models?

This is not an exhaustive view of childhood and its complexities. However, drawing attention to it was done as it links to other important purposes of School. The next section looks at what else School is for.

Good school/*bad* school

Schools have been a topic of ongoing debate, critiqued for their effectiveness and even relevance. School is expected to provide a structured environment for intellectual growth, foster social and character development and serve as a sovereign dedicated space for children to grow and develop into subjects of their own lives, not objects of market needs. As we have seen, it is important for childhood.

Indeed, some sociologists of education have seen School as a place where division can be (re)created and social inequalities (re)produced. Previously I have drawn from Bourdieu's discourse around the very notion of *Reproduction of education* to draw attention to the dominant pedagogic authorities that can impose symbolic and structural violence on a dominated few. Bourdieu explained these structures through *habitus* which is a sociological concept that refers to the norms and values or the principles that structure one's culture.

The *habitus* is thus a system of 'durable dispositions inculcated by objective structural conditions even when the conditions that gave rise to it have long disappeared'.[30] Bourdieu believed that culture is not a fixed and predetermined cycle but rather a dynamic process. The *habitus* was seen as a kind of grammar, which can enable the creation of new expressions that might even change the grammar itself, similar to how language can transform its own rules over time or digital data and automating systems and their capacity to transform what we value as information. The principles of the *habitus* underpin the structure of culture itself.

Bourdieu looked at School partly as a central force where reproduction of culture and reproduction of society can certify a dominant cultural code and through that 'secure a monopoly of legitimate symbolic violence'[31] since this dominant cultural code begins to be imposed onto everyone else. His theory of symbolic violence is particularly important as a departure point to what is construed as *good* or *bad* School, and within the broader arguments in this book – what is good and bad with the digitization of education.

He viewed School as an institution that adheres to a culturally arbitrary code associated with social class, which also indicates readiness to acquire knowledge. As such, School tends to favour those ready to conform to a particular class culture, therefore excluding others. Bourdieu examined how it is on school grounds where a dominant culture can act as the legitimate authority imposing itself on dominated others.

The very School then is seen as the dominant legitimate authority which establishes pedagogic action by demarcating what content will be inculcated, how one will be inculcated and the legitimate training period of one's inculcation, 'which define the degree of completion of pedagogic work considered necessary and sufficient to produce … the degree of cultural attainment (the degree of legitimate competence) by which a group or class recognizes the accomplished man'.[32]

Bourdieu also saw an opportunity for a 'universal curriculum',[33] one that is culturally specific, takes nothing for granted and is able to succeed with every pupil, not just some. He believed that this could change by promoting the progress of students from diverse backgrounds to match those from the dominant culture and middle class. Conversely, he contested that schools fail by refusing to develop such universal pedagogy. As Nash elaborates:

> A school system controlled by the socially and culturally dominant classes, it is supposed, will perceive students who possess the *habitus* of the dominant classes as evidence of 'readiness' for school knowledge, and perceive students who possess the *habitus* of the dominated classes as evidence of a deficit of the child or the home, as cultural deprivation, rather than as an indication of a deficiency on the part of the school to develop pedagogic practices responsive to the mental formation and behavioural dispositions such children bring to school.[34]

Ultimately, Bourdieu did not see *Reproduction* as the final conclusion but as part of an ongoing research process.[35] More recently, there is no denying that diverse needs are widely recognized due to growing scholarship, citizen activism and the amplification of marginalized voices through digital media. Policymakers have also been active in driving change and ensure inclusivity in various ways in School. Evidence exists of educational institutions' efforts to combat injustice, level up disadvantages, promote inclusivity and provide equal opportunities. While these efforts are far from perfect, they represent progress towards common public goals. They also challenge *Reproduction*. That said, it is imperative to observe how data-driven algorithmic systems inherit School's limitations while proposing their own approach to universal and inclusive education. For they can equally be seen from the *Reproduction* perspective to imposing their own language and biases through data.

Technologies change

I shift slightly to enquire here by taking Shapiro's and Hal Varian's insight[36] that while technologies change economic principles endure: Are there lasting features of School (that also often parents ask about) and what are they? Among the many things that change, some do not; they just take different form and articulation. For one, how education is perceived broadly is through the accreditations, assessments, accountability measures and reports – most of which has not changed dramatically. There is no magic bullet (so far) about how we learn either. And even the most advanced AI is not going to give us a short-cut. Additionally, the questions parents and guardians ask about School have also remained relatively consistent for its 'users' – parents and guardians.

Typically, it all begins with the question 'is it a *good* school'? Then there are others. Where is the school and is it easy to get to it? Who else goes there? Is it close to a busy road, pubs, offices, train/buss stations, or is it in an unpopulated area? What is the exterior like? What are the classrooms like? Who has graduated there? Did they get to 'good' universities from there? Do other parents say it is a 'good school'? What kinds of extra activities does it offer? What facilities does it have? Is there specialized teaching staff to attend to students with special educational needs? Are there arts, drama, and sports facilities? Does it offer trips and other enrichment programs? How are students motivated and supported to learn? What pedagogies are used in the classroom? Is it just teacher talking and pupils taking notes? Are pupils encouraged to speak, co-partner in learning and participate in co-teaching? What methods are used for assessment? Daily evaluations? Weekly assessments? End-of-term exams? Teacher observations? Written assignments? Making projects? Oral presentations? Some of this or all of this put together? For some of the subjects? Which ones? What subjects are taught? What subjects are not taught? Are their medical facilities – school nurse, dentist, social worker, psychologist? Is there a police officer on site? If yes, why? If no, why not? Does the school require a uniform? Does it provide lunches? How much does it cost? How much do lunches cost? Does it cater for allergies? What are its safeguarding policies? What are its measures to assess their successful implementation? What are the policies for mobile phones and social media? How does it monitor and prevent (cyber) bullying, racism, violence and misconduct?

Maybe parents and care-givers would also ask other questions: What are the school's values and guiding principles? Who decided them? How does it introduce and instil them in their pupils? How does it deal with problems relating to parents or difficult home situations? For how long has its principal been working there? How often does its teaching staff change? Does it have enough teachers? Do teachers know what the school's values are? How are teachers supported in their professional development? Who provides this professional development and according to what criteria? What kinds of traditions and cultures are being performed, observed and taught in the school? What kinds of education and other support are provided for parents, pupils and even for the wider community to which the school belongs? Are its facilities rented out to external businesses or local communities? Who are they? For what reasons are its facilities rented out? Who makes sure the facilities remain safe and intact? Has the school and/or its pupils been awarded anything? For what and why? What is its relationship with the local community, businesses, neighbours? Does it meet all current and evolving statutory requirements for safety? Is there easy information about news updates? Where and who makes these updates? Does it have its own media channels, social media, magazine? Who organizes and contributes to them? Are students encouraged to take part? If yes, how? If no, why not? Who forms part of its leadership and governance? How were they selected and according to what criteria? How is their contribution evaluated?

The *good* intention of School is to answer these and more[37] questions positively. They aim to shed light on the world of work needed to make school a school. To achieve positive response, there are many constraints, dependencies, conditions and unforeseen challenges which mainly attend to the effects of human relationships – the most unpredictable of conditions. Merely adding EdTech to the ecosystem of School as it grapples with such questions requires careful examination in what ways that is done, how and why. EdTech changes and cannot answer all these questions.

The purpose of *School*

In the start of the book, I highlighted my dual role as both a teacher and a student of pedagogy,[38] education policy, sociology of education and education governance. As I delve deeper into these massive fields, I encounter compelling arguments, theories and philosophies about the purpose of education. This has prompted me to reflect, and I extend the same invitation to you (practitioners, future teachers, students, policymakers): to consider how these meaningful discussions can play a more integral part in the conversations about digitizing education, rather than observing further dislocation of truly meaningful philosophical discourse around the purpose of education from industry-inspired global visions of digital innovation.

For example, Gert Biesta speaks of teacher judgement and its link to *good* education. Biesta identifies three dimensions of education's purpose: qualification which comprises knowledge, skills, qualifications; socialization, which as noted earlier on the reproduction of education has the potential to reinforce and equally challenge various established societal structures; and subjectification, the ability for individuals to become responsible agents and subjects of their own lives, rather than 'objects of the actions of others'.[39] At its core are relationships, the ability of one individual to connect and understand another.

Education is thus a human endeavour. As such, education centres on human relationships and the nurturing of individual potential while fostering a sense of self, community and belonging. In fact, the sense of belonging greatly influences a child's success in school, as true education involves socialization and genuine human interaction every day. Human interactions are unpredictable unlike the editable behaviour online or following app instructions.

Take, for example, a primary preparation for end-of-year school play. The extensive organization, teamwork, teaching, learning and creativity involved are unmatched. Even on a typical day so much happens in the classroom. The image of passive children silently listening to a teacher's monotonous lesson is only a popular caricature. In reality, it is rare to see thirty children sitting quietly through every lesson. However, before criticizing the lack of discipline in learning, consider the contrast of thirty digital devices added to thirty children in a classroom. It can be a mess.

Studies have shown that when students engage in computer multitasking, it negatively affects the learning not only for them but also for those around them.[40, 41] This is to say that human interaction is a precious resource in education, one that everyone with vested interest in School must acknowledge, nurture and value.

Digital technologies should not be underestimated, certainly. They should neither be considered a single, generous item that merely delivers access to education or educational support. I have previously discussed the different aspects of these technologies, including their business nature, objectives, somewhat mysterious machinations and their much larger prospects. Their function in education is not supplementary; their potential to predict, guide, adapt and personalize is distinct from one's choice to just use them optionally. They are not simply added. Their adoption transforms entirely the purpose of School, the learning choices available to children, and even the content they learn, all without a clear understanding of the outcomes. This transformation starts not only with the new language of data but with one that renames everything about School to achieve its full transformation.

The changing language in education

As participation from the EdTech industry continues to grow in public education, the language used to describe the problems, needs and even the purpose of education begins to change. The normative, technical and even regulatory language about education shifts the focus away from the purpose and desirability of what is being taught in School. Education is increasingly expressed as twenty-first-century credentials and skills that can form part of a digital 'backpack' for a student as described in earlier chapters. School and education are not only expressed as 'transcript data', 'demographic information' and 'national testing data', but also other data that is organized into schemas, data elements and multitude of categories that still suppose to 'represent a more holistic picture of student achievement – such as a gradebook of standards-based performance data and a portfolio of personal bests – and better capture the student's progression at any moment in time'.[42]

The language of 'enhanced data would provide a context for attendance and behaviour patterns, supplementary support services, grades, and other performance information such as proficiency scores and learning gains'.[43] 'Since this data would follow students to each new learning experience, learning could be tailored to meet their individual needs from the first lesson rather than requiring the extra time teachers must spend diagnosing student needs and abilities'.

All of this leads to changing School as a premise similar to a hospital where 'vitals' and measures are taken as check in, interventions are prescribed based on diagnosis (assuming there is an 'illness' or something that needs 'fixing') and intervention waiting to take effect. A 'learner profile' is created and builds an 'official transcript' of data backpacks to provide additional clues to unlock learner needs, preferences and potential. But such data also 'feeds' into larger data 'lakes' that allow for more potion to be concocted and tailoring to one's education.

Firstly, the language in education is influenced directly by the computer language – data analytics, digital diagnostics, algorithmic prediction, data-driven automation, lakes, digital credentials and so on. What is remarkable about this kind of language is the concentration of a narrow circle of topics, needs, problems and expectations for, about and from School. This narrow semantic view of education further creates a sort of 'common sense', which policy, international organizations and schools themselves are adopting fast. These words are combined with children's rights to education, agency, inclusivity and opportunities. But all of them go hand in hand with EdTech's value propositions to satisfy all needs. This is a new default conversation that prevents any possibility of considering whether any part of digitizing education is even desirable. We have discussions around utilizing education data 'for good', infringing on children's rights to education if they are deprived access to technologies and similar conjectures.

The second point is to do with the legitimation that this language gives to digital technologies. Their language is considerably expansive, sometimes new, but also becoming familiar, concrete and therefore convincing, and thus legitimizes them but also gives them leeway to interfere with the reality of others and their environment. With their concreteness, EdTech are not merely added to the learning and teaching process; they are ecologically integrated creating ecological dependencies. A school day does not go by without a teacher or a student not interacting with a device, a platform, or a software application. The language fosters and is further embedding through continuous use and dependency.

Through this language they cultivate a certain kind of normative power. Platforms and EdTech apps can impose their own interpretation of academic success, problematic behaviour and so on. Ye, they do not have individual responsibility for students or for teachers. If a student fails an exam, the platform is not chased to explain why or be fired. This responsibility is still reserved for the only other stakeholder in schools who is regulated and scrutinised – the teacher.

Third, they also cultivate a certain amount of 'regulatory' power. Through it, they impose unique vertical contracts of consent, which have the capacity to override any existing laws or societally accepted values.[44] Microsoft and Google override standard privacy agreements, granting themselves authority to access, modify or delete user data such as emails, calendars and other content, disregarding privacy laws and consent agreements, under the guise of product improvement. I return to this in Chapter 7.

Digital systems and their language also change the understanding of reality. They depict it, describe it, visualize it, measure it and classify what is important and what is not before one has a chance to do so on their own. Biesta brings attention to the conflict between the representational view of knowledge and an experimental approach to describing knowledge. While representational knowledge is seen as a passive observation, what John Dewey calls 'spectator view' of knowledge, experimental methods involve active intervention in the world. Biesta contends that from a representational perspective, these interventions may be seen as distorting reality, potentially 'pos[ing] a threat to the possibility to gain true knowledge'. In that sense, how are EdTech products distorting reality?

One can recall French sociologist and philosopher Jean Baudrillard[45] who argued that contemporary society has entered a stage of *hyperreality* in which the distinction between reality and simulation becomes blurred. He claimed that modern life is dominated by a proliferation of signs and symbols, and that our experiences are increasingly mediated by images and simulations rather than direct, unmediated encounters with the world. Baudrillard used the example of the rear-view mirror to illustrate his ideas about hyperreality. He suggested that when we look in a car's rear-view mirror, we see a reflection of the road behind us, but it is a representation of the past rather than the actual present. This mirror creates a sense of continuity and connection to what is behind us, even though it is only a mediated representation. An example of this representation is Disneyland or video games but also the classroom which is represented on a teacher's device with the students as miniature computers or emojis on it.

As Biesta points out, there is no effort to undermine representation or the very experimentation with knowledge, which is how knowledge is created in the first place. Instead, we should aim to understand how such processes alter knowledge and our interpretation of it, what we value and what we neglect (or even forget). In that regard, an EdTech app or platform may pose a challenge by pre-determining the learning path, mediating between the student and the knowledge to be explored, questioned, resisted, experimented with. Consequently, digital technologies influence the relationships between them and set expectations, judging whether students have 'succeeded' or 'failed' to grasp knowledge, even determining which knowledge should be acquired. All of this is done in unknowable way because the student is unaware of how this mediating relationship happens. Combined with the wider social, political and economic context, such mediation can change School in significant ways.

Up to this point, I proposed some more primary discussions about education's purpose, childhood and School's vital role in it but also the transformation of education through the language of EdTech. The next sections of this chapter turn to the changing notions of the digitized classroom as an economic value.

The economic value of School

Over a century ago Stanford University professor Ellwood Cubberley described the link between American businesses and public schools this way:

> Our schools are, in a sense, factories in which the raw products (children) are to be shaped and fashioned into products to meet the various demands of life. The specifications for manufacturing come from the demands of twentieth-century civilization, and it is the business of the school to build its pupils according to the specifications laid down.

Ironically, the perception of schools as factories 'fashioning' finely-tailored 'products' to cater to corporate needs has been a permanent criticism of many tech evangelists today. Yet, the very same data-driven conveyer belt for decision-making is now being orchestrated through the products of those same critics as this section describes. Because schools ultimately produce the future citizens, consumers and workers, the interconnection between school and business is inevitable.

Looking at the skills, qualification and competencies needed in a market are a valid aspect that helps to shape schooling. And considering the diverse roles and purposes expected from (taxpayer-funded) public schools and the various stakeholders they aim to satisfy, it is only reasonable to anticipate the use of a range of criteria needed to assess educational institutions' success.

Seeing education through the framework as noted earlier in the book of human capital has been seen as a way of enhancing the efficiency of human labour necessary to drive technological innovation and economic well-being.[46] However, the restructuring of education to 'reflect market rationalities and corporate imperatives' while 'abandon[ing] prior forms of social investment' and coming to 'conceive the *purpose and value* of education primarily as a human-capital vehicle' has come to mean the rejection of crucial human aspects and necessities to the detriment of individual and the collective well-being. As Lingard and Rizvi observe, 'governments have increasingly preached a minimalist role for the state in education, with greater reliance on market mechanisms'.[47] Simultaneously, there has been a narrowing of the objectives of education down to 'human capital development' whereby 'the role of education must play to meet the needs of the global economy and to ensure the competitiveness of the national economy'.[48]

American education can be seen as having undergone three major waves of reforms. The first one can be observed around post-First World War when heavily influenced by the concepts of John Dewey; pedagogical progressives emphasized the 'whole child' and student-led learning as a way of changing the education system. They shifted focus from viewing education as a science, driven by managerialism and test-based assessment towards embracing teachers' methods and hands-on learning as the preferred pedagogy, departing from Cubberley-like principles of measuring school outputs akin to businesses and assessing students based on their abilities in order to determine the efficacy of taxpayer spending.

Learning by doing was a way of departing from the age grades and separating students based on abilities. The focus was more on bringing up emotional, social and physical preparedness and tackling poverty, crime and unemployment. However, the learning by doing was quickly embraced by corporate leaders eager to bridge the industrial skills gap among American workers and boost international trade competitiveness.

Consequently, learning by doing became vocational education, a 'permanent fixture'[49] of today's high schools, whose curricula and tests aimed to distinguish college-bound students from those suited for industrial or commercial pathways. Furthermore, this shifted priorities towards preparing workers over nurturing civic-minded citizenship. Yet there was a lack of solid evidence that vocational graduates earned significantly more than those without such training. Nevertheless, enthusiasm for work-oriented education persisted among businesses. Cuban articulates:

> Even when evidence surfaced that school guidance officials and administrators were assigning students who failed academic courses to vocational tracks or separate vocational schools – a process called 'dumping' – the practice drew little public criticism. Preparing students for the labour market was so important that legislators dismissed data challenging the effectiveness of vocational curricula and cheerfully endorsed more funds for vocational education.[50]

By the 1920s, these core assumptions had permeated public school goals, governance, organization and curricula. Not even during the Great Depression, when the reputation of business leaders suffered, were serious objections raised against the schooling model influenced by the private sector. Instead, by mid-1970s business leaders, along with other education critics, focused on addressing school shortcomings such as the declining test scores and inadequate job preparation by assuming that what schools needed to fix their failure are the adoption of standards, testing accountability and increasing efficiency. These marked a second wave of reforms.

The English educational system followed a similar path to the American to arrive at measurement, accountability and datafication of education as the 'natural' way forward. Within the English context, however, much of the 'fear' that stirred educational reform towards corporatization, managerialism and accountability was from the problems associated with the growing urbanization. Migration from the countryside into cities created massive social problems around housing, health and political instability. Education was seen as one of the instruments to control, educate and also to mould an obedient workforce.[51]

Technologies of education policy varied; a key one was the '"state professionalism" with its "expert" and esoteric knowledges ranging from social statistics to forms of psychology and eugenics'. These instruments deepened class and gender separation until the neoliberalist New Right education views from late 1970s disqualified the welfare state and collectivism by promoting individualism and the value of free market. The aim was to reduce

> the 'influence' of the state and eliminate its 'institutional inefficiencies' produced by its bureaucracies in their place introducing market forces as

an antidote to regulation and intervention both within the public sector and in relation to the management of the economy.

This enabled free choice and competitive market dynamics but also transformed the education system and its institutions into competitive markets for survival. Going through the history of English education policy, Ball describes how the Conservative economic and social policy ultimately rejected heavy state regulation by aiming at 'deregulation, liberalization, and privatization'[52] and reducing public inefficiencies by introducing measures for accountability and performativity.

Similar transformations were evident in New Zealand and Australia. New Zealand was an early adopter of market-driven reforms in education. In 1988, a Labour Party government, influenced by the Chicago School neoliberalist economists,[53] enacted reforms which restructured the education system by reducing the central bureaucracy, eliminating regional education boards and granting self-governance to educational institutions. This model empowered institutions with budget, staffing and decision-making autonomy. Here an important caveat must be made that state authority control did not disappear. It was a 'strategy of devolution' – a process of "*reregulation*", not the abandonment by the state of its controls over public services but the establishment of a new form of control'[54]; the liberties and limits 'are set within the boundaries of requirements of "performance" and "profitability"'[55]

These transformations of public education systems across the English-speaking nations and how they have come to value schools have had global implications. Much to the tune of the wealthiest nations, we see how supranational organizations are 'exploring alternatives to direct public provision', guiding and influencing through frameworks, best practices and policies that stimulate the transition towards privatization and corporatization deemed 'important' policy options. For the past twenty years, OECD has been pushing, guiding and driving privatization and commercialization of state-owned enterprises for its member-states. The localization of governance and management of public sectors has been the new paradigm promoted across the developing world.[56]

The goal has been, on the one hand, promoting independence and localized governance, and on the other, increased expectation for measurement and meeting tight performance targets. Such frameworks typically articulate autonomy to be conditioned by the achievement of stringent performance goals, which are also part of the broader concepts of globalization and innovation. A sort of prescribed 'formula' is provided for developing nations to bridge the gap with more developed ones. This same model has reflected in education with performativity drives from OECD and similar other supranational organizations. With OECD, the Program for International Student Assessment (PISA) standardized test used to compare fifteen-year-old students' reading, math and science performance is an example of this performativity drive. Supranational organizations and their policy instruments (often achieved with business participation) are now shaping the global education narrative around digitization (further enabling large scale investments and scaling of cheap technologies in low- and middle-income regions through what some scholars call 'philanthrocapitalism').[57]

Despite the implementation of various accountability measures since the 1970s, and particularly with the integration of computers into classrooms, we are now witnessing a third wave of reform – one that is centred around the granular data extraction for the automation of futures. The digitization of education has inspired desires to see schools, as Cubberley saw it, the factories that shape children as the 'raw material' into the future workforce economic competitiveness requires. This, policymakers and the tech industry see, can be implemented through the means of digital infrastructures and their advancing algorithmic capabilities. Today, corporate involvement is not only evident at the level of these digital infrastructures but also through their own training, ambassadorships and programs (for example, see Amazon Future Engineer[58] and Google accreditation programs,[59] among others, which promise such employability and future security without much accountability around the possible outcomes from taking such courses and training).

Changing what is valued

If education, seen as a social structure of what is taught, how it is taught, and what is learned, aims to serve the interests of the child, does education data serve the same interests?

Theoretical learning models are shrouded in history, but some conceptualizations endure with practical implications to education today. The behaviourist model of learning, for instance, sees learning as changes in individuals' observable behaviours.[60] The focus of behaviourists is on the behaviour rather than on thoughts, desires and possibilities. Through various forms of conditioning one can be steered towards a particular behaviour. The constructivist model of learning, on the other hand, looks at a person's way of thinking, positing that a person learns by mentally organizing and reorganizing new experiences and knowledge.[61] To Dewey,[62] students' prior knowledge should be recognized in the classroom and teachers should adjust the curriculum accordingly. Relatedly, drawing from Bourdieu's model of cultural capital, children's cultural capital must be recognized within the process of learning in order to avoid potential 'symbolic violence' to occur. A symbolic violence is 'the consequence of a dominant class imposing its own cultural values and interests on a dominated group, who then accept this situation without question'.[63] Cognitive constructivist and social-cultural models of learning at different points in time expand on the development of mental representations through assimilation and accommodation, for the former,[64] and the role of relationships and the social milieu that can lead the learner to their greater potential, according to the latter.[65]

Importantly, each theory gives different value to the role of the learner, the educator and the social environment to the learning process. Behaviourists see learners as reactive – responding to the external environment; the educator assumes the active role of the one that modifies the conditions, which shape the learner's behaviour. Dewey, on the other hand, put emphasis on learners' own initiatives: 'Since learning is something that the pupil has to do himself (or herself) and for himself (or herself), the initiative lies with the learner.'[66] To Dewey, education is neither 'pouring out' nor 'pouring in' but rather 'taking a hold' on a child's interests and instincts, which should be used as the direction towards a valuable learning outcome. Constructivists and social-cultural theorists emphasize the importance of individual learner agency further and acknowledge the personal views and perspectives that can act as guidance towards valuable learning outcomes. What follows is to see where education data fits in these models and what kind of learning process and social organization education data fosters.

If it is accepted that education data conceptualizes learning as the function by which what is taught, how it is taught and what is learned is quantified through numbers, form follows function. The learning process therefore can become an if-then uniform pattern that is formulaically predetermined since everything, no matter what, has to amount to a quantifiable number – data. This is evident in the digital dashboards that learning applications and platforms provide for teacher and learner. The digital dashboards not only demonstrate where a learner is on a particular spectrum (as defined by the collected data and metadata) but also make suggestions as to what kind of content and how much of it the learner should practise.

Education data feeds two important sources: a domain model (a range of knowledge domains such as mathematics or grammar) and a learner model (the learner's knowledge quantified against the knowledge domain). Expressed quantitatively, these two models are the form that maintains the function (which enables data generation that feeds and enables adjustments to be made in the domain model and helps examine the learner model in the adjusted conditions). The EdTech application is the means through which this new form strives to achieve the desired function by identifying what is being modelled, how it is modelled, and how such models are maintained. While the methods for modelling vary, in basic terms, their common goal is to create a stimuli-response mechanism with an 'expert' standard template against which each response is measured.[67]

Data is the main means of communication in this mechanism. Data feeds the stimuli that is the domain model. The stimuli demand response from the learner model. The response generates data, which adjusts the stimuli; the loop is closed. As such, an adaptive technology can provide teaching functions by, for example, selecting assignments, giving hints and evaluating student responses and adapt those functions by modelling students' cognitive or emotional responses and behaviour. In this, while the objective is to achieve positive learning outcomes, the system leads the learning process. Something is done *on behalf of* the educator through the education data that fuels the stimuli that is the domain model, and something is done *to* the learner, who has to react. Education data in this sense then serves the interest of the technology as a learning system (and its developer). Importantly, education data leaves the learner out of the social structure of the learning process in a passive – reactive – role. In short, education data drives towards a behaviourist view of learning, which not only compromises the role of the learner but also reduces their basic rights.

How does education data change the social order in the learning process? If education data benefits the technology as the learning system, they can also structurally change the role of educators, the pedagogy, learner choice, voice and ability (or even will) to challenge educational processes.[68] Through the cognitive modelling system that is able to track and assess student behavioural patterns, data can dominate in the content infrastructure (what should be taught and learned), the method of instruction (how something should be taught) and the assessment (the frequency and nature of how to assess learning). While adapting the teaching method is not new (teachers do that all the time in the classroom), growing availability and granularity of education data and greater computational capacity has increased the desire to develop algorithmic methods of such adaptive teaching at scale and with greater promise triggering hyperbole.

For instance, the Bill and Melinda Gates Foundation hailed for a new Adaptive Learning Market Acceleration Program (ALMAP) and mass-marketed its use.[69] The resulting experiment with several higher educational institutions and commercial entities for course material and EdTech applications to mixed student perceptions showed no discernible results. The ALMAP outlined crucial drawbacks to adaptive learning such as discrimination and labelling of students. Lastly, ALMAP demonstrated that data-driven systems can have a narrow view of what is considered as knowing and learning. Making such systems central to the learning experience risks positioning learners as passive recipients, leading to the need to re-think education data governance with greater urgency.

Conclusion

Given that School is of significant value to both governments and the economy but also to childhood and societies, it should preserve its worth and value its value. School is primarily a public creation, meant to empower individuals to be subjects with the agency to generate novel ideas and in their own right. This point of view centres on School as a unique environment children attend where teachers teach and guide them through various processes of discovery, negotiation, socialization and co-partnership. Schools are important to education, personal development and societal progress. Educators, researchers and policymakers must defend and emphasize School's role as a place where children can gain qualifications, social skills and self-empowerment.

Carl Shapiro and Hal R. Varian tell businesses (and policymakers) that 'technology changes' but 'economic laws do not'.[70] The authors say, 'we're not sure exactly how software for viewing web pages will evolve' but one thing is certain that software is 'fundamentally vulnerable because' a big competitor like, say, 'Microsoft, controls the operating environment of which a Web browser is but one component'. In a framework of lock-in, applications are faced with 'a classic problem of interconnection'. That is, an app needs to work in conjunction with the major operating system – Microsoft, Apple, Google and so on. This lock-in is not new. Back in 1900 local telephone companies faced similar dependency with Bell Company. The same is with the railroad, the airline and the computer industries, among many others. In that sense, all these companies experience tremendous vulnerability.[71]

What are the dependencies the technologies and business owners impose on School and turning it in servitude to their business success? What should safeguard the purpose of education and the human endeavour that prevents these dependencies and risks putting children as the main losers in this business arrangement? The vulnerabilities of EdTech must be made transparent to educators, policymakers, teachers and students. These are the questions this chapter aimed to pose.

Criticism of School persists, questioning its relevance. Yet their continued existence suggests they serve a purpose. These institutions have produced world leaders, inventors, professionals and teachers. While schools have evolved, many of their core objectives have remained consistent and mostly transparent. The belief in the power of education and educational institutions' capabilities is recognized even in oppressive regimes where individuals may be denied access to school. School matters greatly as much as it is condemned for its outdated nature. But there is no guarantee in the hands of digital systems it will be used in children's best interests. In their defence, efforts are underway, which are the focus of the next chapter.

7

Governance by Distraction: What Guarantees the Benefits of Digitizing Education?

Governance by distraction

Up to this point in the book, I described the ways in which educational systems in the Anglo-American and Western contexts are evolving as digital technologies are progressively present and made central to the teaching and learning processes and practices. Versatile applications but also larger and more complex AI-infused automating systems are interfering with the traditional governance of education. The acceleration of technologies and data analytics taking central stage in decision making have opened doors for far-reaching imaginaries for reconfiguring education. Entrenched in neoliberal and globalist traditions, these imaginaries present a bigger picture for the reproduction of societies.

The remaining chapters address those more apprehensive views about what these imaginaries might mean for children's and, broadly for societies', futures. There are many proposals – such as frameworks of assessing EdTech products, guiding principles and so on – that reflect these more concerning views. Some of them are described in this chapter. However, they should be seen more as a symptom of a larger problem than scalable solutions. For that, this chapter generally labels all this effort as a sort of distraction (the meat that the housedog chews on), an instrument of neoliberalist hegemonic processes.

To begin with, our modern world is driven by the pursuit of attention. Capturing it is a lucrative market. Deriving from the world of advertising and coupled with the power of data to profile and predict, the likeliness of one's attention to be captured is worth investing in if it leads to the accumulation of hegemonic power[1] and equally maintaining such power.

Hegemonic power is understood as a 'form of leadership where particular groups acquire the ability to determine the general direction of travel of a given social formation, while other groups must only be fully recruited to the views and outlooks of the hegemonic when it is strategically necessary'.[2] There is a certain pervasiveness of a complex 'structure of feeling', which enables this hegemonic process. According to theorist Raymond Williams,[3] the 'structure of feeling' is the gap between policy and regulations. It combines 'a cynical resignation at the lack of political agency enjoyed by most citizens with a conscious but ineffectual critique of capitalist selfishness and an embrace of the everyday pleasures of an advanced consumer society'. Put simply, hegemonic powers structure societal feelings in which individualism is encouraged with a sense of freedom of choice, self-expression, resistance etc. Both consent and dissent are available to societies and individuals, yet they act upon neither of them but rather settle with 'varieties of passive consent'.[4] As such, the structure of feeling is transformed into *believing* and *accepting* that 'things are the way they are', without questioning them, a feeling imposed without authoritarian rule, making it particularly insidious.

This chapter brings both points of governance *by distraction* and the *hegemonic* imperatives of how societies should be ruled and what should be expected of their education systems to explain why the existing governance structures fall short on ensuring that EdTech benefit all children equally.

As such, there are two contentions to unpack. The first one relates to the governance by distraction – the sense of choice and abundance of work that policymakers and various active members of industry and specialized publics create to demonstrate that something is done to govern the digitization of education. The second is to do with the prevailing *feeling* that bolsters the distraction away from questioning the very idea of *what* needs digitization, *why* and by *whom*. The hegemonic rule creating this 'feeling' about the need to digitize education suggests that societies no longer have to question that (*why* is this desirable, which aspects of digitization, for whom will this be done and who says who will do it?) but rather think only in terms of *how* this should be done. This is accepting the hegemonic belief and the inevitability of digitizing education, as when various decision-makers including in policy and education say, 'the Genie [AI] is out of the bottle'.

The first contention addresses education governance and the technologies of policymaking which generally cause substantial distraction (and therefore suppress any form of resistance) away from important work that essentially needs to be done (instead of getting distracted) with regard to the digitization of education. As articulated in Chapter 3, policymaking is often a moving target – many things are proposed, at times, for the sake of showing that something *is* happening. For instance, the current focus on digitizing education in the UK and the United States reflects a highly dynamic policymaking landscape addressing ongoing and often changing issues from cyberbullying, cyber insecurities, data collection, protection of biometric data and more recently to use or not to use generative AI in schools. Within education governance, more attention has been given to governing education data which has led to substantial development of tools, guidelines and frameworks. But more than anything, these, too, have mostly steered the collective attention away from action and concrete results. The action necessitated requires that we collectively shift the thinking away from the inevitabilism about digitizing education and identify what exactly is negotiated and accepted in this transformation. As far as the second contention goes, there is a need for a different 'structure of feelings' and belief that nothing is inevitable. There is no better way to start restructuring this belief from education itself.

The chapter therefore explores mainly these two concepts – *governance* and *distraction* – put together, to argue that the explosion of frameworks, guidelines, toolkits and resources addressing the concerns emerging with the digitization of education have created a hodgepodge of designs, adding to the collective 'feeling' that something *is* happening, yet no concrete system of accountability holds the sector that is transforming education. This feeling ultimately distracts from meaningful and hard work around developing more meaningful governance. First, it is relevant to provide introductory background to the concept of education governance.

Education governance

Education governance is a complex and evolving concept, serving as a 'heuristic device, discourse and technology of government'.[5] It marks a departure from the limitations of state and welfare planning. As such, education governance is also a 'self-transmuting moulding' that is 'continually changing from one moment to the next'.[6]

While state monopoly is avoided, effective governance becomes increasingly debated in the presence of advancing data-driven algorithms mediating both governance and educational processes. While it is seen as an intervention,[7] education governance also involves the challenge of maintaining control amid contestations across subjects, roles, constraints and conflicting needs.

As Wilkins and Olmedo argue,[8] regulation becomes difficult to implement due to its elusive nature. Instead, education governance primarily seeks to superficially stabilize complexity within interconnected systems, aiming for navigable and calculable sites of comparability and performance.[9] This, in turn, opens doors for data systems and from there a drive for deducing education to calculable and prescribed elements. Policies are the technologies or 'mechanisms of change'.[10] As Ball defines them, policies are 'ramshackle, compromise, hit-and-miss affairs, that are reworked, tinkered with, nuanced and infected through complex processes of influence, text production, dissemination and ultimately recreation in diverse contexts of practice'.[11]

Added to this, we have the notion of 'governing by numbers' which explains why digital technologies can make sense in education. Chapter 2 briefly touched upon the ubiquitous use of customer relationship management (CRM) and project management tools (PMT) in education. Here I follow the depth with which governing by numbers is historically embedded. Carmona and Ezzamel[12] discuss how ancient accounting systems were deployed to handle individual-state, state-individual and individual-individual relations. These systems focused on controlling money and resources, managing work by setting concrete numerical targets, assigning tasks, measuring performance and reporting actions taken. The initial effort was to control finance and property.

In medieval England, accounting systems ensured stewards' accountability on noble estates to protect the landowner's capital and financial integrity. From the mid-thirteenth to the fourteenth centuries in Northern Italy, for example, merchants combined capital for trading activities, which led to the adoption of bookkeeping – the foundation of modern accounting. As industrialization spread in Europe, accounting became crucial for recording profits[13] to further facilitate the development of capitalist structure. Thus, accounting became embedded in commercial life.

The modern state further relied on accounting to ensure proper management of state funds. These forms of 'governance by numbers' gradually spilled over into social affairs, where numbers gained importance. In the eighteenth-century German estates with the emergence of statistics, demographic data began to be collected in order to improve governance and the collection of population censuses.[14] Accounting became so integrated into everyday life that the modern state increasingly became reliant on it. Quantitative techniques emerged deeper into businesses for the purpose of achieving efficiency and utilizing scarce resources. Ironically, neoliberalist practices – pursuing economic growth and perpetual production – have led to the total depletion of resources. Yet it was with Taylor's principles of scientific management, known as Taylorism, which launched the principle of industrial production. Today, this sort of management is deeply embedded into major societal domains – from healthcare and agriculture to education. This new form of public management through accounting systems and the power of numbers expanded to all societal corners. Moreover, as neoliberalism further broke down the barriers between social and economic spheres, allowing the latter to profit from the former.[15]

As Piattoeva and Boden argue, 'this is legitimised via the language of economy and efficiency'.[16] In other words, success is measured by the profit the market makes, which in turn is measured by how well resources such as labour and capital are utilized. Yet 'the social sphere is not amenable to such measures as it is not-for-profit'.[17] As public services such as in the UK were increasingly opening to private providers as part of the liberalization of the political economy, private contracts managed various public services from laboratories to prisons.

To monitor and hold accountable, these contracts increasingly required performance measures based on numbers. The result was numbers and performance measures further extended into the social realm to determine the effectiveness of public service delivery. They fostered ruthless competition even among public providers, aiming to push down costs and improve efficiency. As the private sector is encroaching on public education, measurement and performance indicators are impacting entirely how educational institutions are governed and work. Such competitive environment is already evident in the UK, US and Australian schools, where league tables and performance measure encourage competition among schools and influence parental choice for their children's education.

A derivative of the accountability regime is the audit explosion in education. 'The audit explosion' in education of the 1990s, as Michael Power puts it,[18] has been the result of devolving of direct state involvement in education governance and, ironically, for the purpose of filling up a regulatory gap which was formerly occupied by government authorities. Today, the same devolvement reflects the lack of clear criteria for measurement and a universally accepted minimum standard for EdTech products, which makes audits hard to convince with their effectiveness.

Instead, we have an added involvement through consultations with white papers, toolkits, guidelines and reports by various international and national digital strategy teams, industry alliances, associations and consultancies. While many of them offer sophisticated ways forward, their models and auxiliary frameworks, to discuss in a moment, also add to the general complexity – distracting away from answering questions about what is actually necessary and suitable in education.

Some scholars have argued that 'audits and similar accountability frameworks dependent on third-party evaluation play directly into the tech company playbook by positioning responsibility for identifying and addressing harms outside of the company'.[19] Others have also seen the 'audit culture' having counter-effects by exacerbating overall distrust in education.[20] When it comes to AI, a report by *AI Now Institute* maintains that any claims generated from 'a burgeoning audit economy' where audit-as-a-service is offered will provide *no* impactful change simply because there is 'no clarity on the standards and methodologies for algorithmic auditing, nor consensus on their definitions of risk and harm'.[21] The same can be said about the mounting frameworks for assessment of EdTech products. They have also opened opportunities for industry to take a leading role in its development.[22]

The proposals are also often with a sense of urgency and veer towards digitizing education and equipping children with the 'right' digital skills as the 'natural' way forward. A sort of naturalness arises from such work and defines what is deemed as 'good' education through what Bowker and Star[23] call 'trajectory of naturalization'.[24] This process involves intentionally 'forgetting' more traditional elements of education and allowing new categories like data, digitization, automation and AI to become *naturally* and unquestionably the standard over time.

For example, the principles set forth by the European Commission (EC) following the Covid-19 pandemic highlight this distraction. While it said its findings were based on over 2,700 contributions from its open consultation, it is the very question it asked that can be construed as a lead-on. Much more happened than unequal digital access during Covid-19. More families fell into poverty while major risk factors such as domestic violence and abuse and other such ongoing and serious issues heightened.[25] Instead of looking at these as symptoms of the challenges and needs in education, these reports are concentrating their enquiries around digital disparities in education. Such concentration narrows the possible answers and leads towards an expected solution which centres around the digital, distracting away from other meaningful discussions relevant to education or children's well-being. As a result, the principles that emerged from this consultation and boosted further the drive for digitization concentrated around adding more technologies. They included:

- High quality and inclusive digital education …
- Transforming education for the digital age … include an enhanced dialogue and stronger partnerships between educators, the private sector, researchers, municipalities, and public authorities.
- Appropriate investment in connectivity, equipment and organizational capacity and skills …
- Digital education should play a pivotal role in increasing equality and inclusiveness. Digital skills are essential …
- Digital competence should be a core skill for all educators and training staff.[26]

This techno-driven view calls an urgency for skills, 'inclusive' technologies and more skills to enjoy the inclusive technologies. It provides a narrow understanding of what is realistically needed for families, children and their education. 'Access to digital education' alone guarantees no quality learning, teaching or future life chances. The notion that digital education will increase these chances is conceptualized as a possibility, not a guarantee. As the chapter on *Voice* exemplified, social relationships, bonding, meaning and purpose, belonging and a social support system matter above and beyond access to digital technologies.

Should the question have considered the essential needs in education for children in the aftermath of the pandemic, entirely different principles may have emerged from those consulted by the EC. For instance, imagine the question was posed this way: define the problems that were heightened during the pandemic and draw priority needs that require urgent attention. Other principles could be drawn that would require funding not in more technologies as 'inclusive' as highly needed but on things such as:

- Ensure fair access to essential needs and assistance, including nutritious meals, mental health services and a secure learning environment regardless of digital availability for all children and young people.
- Establish human support systems that address the well-being of children, considering their physical, emotional and social requirements.
- Foster local community and neighbourhood engagement and strong partnerships with the private sector to tackle unique challenges faced by at-risk children, building a robust network of support, to include things such as providing transportation, basic necessities and facilities like bookstores, libraries and recreational spaces for enrichment activities and community building.
- Implement measures to integrate educational initiatives that alleviate and break cycles of poverty, such as offering economic support to families, access to healthcare, housing, nutrition and transportation.
- Embrace culturally responsive education that respects the diverse backgrounds of all children and at-risk children by involving extra funding and specialized training for teachers and social workers and collaboration with community members and organizations to shape curriculum design and extra activities that prioritize cultural diversity and inclusivity.

Focusing solely on technology access and skill development in education neglects critical societal needs and undermines impact when essential priorities are ignored or isolated, even if one argues that these problems are reserved for other institutions to handle. Instead, the EC attributes the exacerbation of poverty and disadvantage to the lack of digital access and digital skills.[27] The belief is being instilled that something good will almost automatically happen to education once EdTech becomes available. Still, time and again evidence shows[28] that some marginal improvement exists; the technologies favour the already well-off, less so the most disadvantaged and displaced populations.

Even if more digital skills help with breaking the cycle of poverty, the created urgency and implied warning that poverty awaits for those with no digital skills have led to reallocation of funding straight into the hands of the few private actors. In other words, relying on digital solutions to address education disparities has resulted in outsourcing solutions to consultations, public-private partnerships – primarily the industry.

Mariana Mazzucato and Rosie Collington argue that externalizing IT consultancy to the private sector ultimately infantilizes governments, placing research, development, governance and monitoring of the digitization process in the hands of private entities, leaving governments vulnerable to their influence.[29] Outsourcing digitization reforms to the private sector results in countries gradually losing their own IT capabilities due to the incremental nature of "'systemic retrenchment" that results; a loss in state capacity'.[30] This slow erosion of state capacity occurs 'when consultancies are contracted over many years'.[31] Similarly, in education, expertise is gradually concentrated in the hands of a few who understand data systems and required technologies, leaving governments and educational institutions struggling to catch up. This transfer not only affects the management of technological systems but also the governance of education.

On the flip side, an international effort has recently proposed the creation of new roles in education.[32] Such roles include at state, regional and local – school – levels such as chief data officers, learning technologies specialists, data analysts, regional data officers, school IT and cybersecurity officers and others. For example, the regional data officer would supervise education data processes and implementation of data governance policies, incorporating advanced technologies like machine learning and generative AI.

Suppose this indeed prevents state infantilization once such data, ML, AI and IT specialists at all levels of education take position. Are we still talking about and providing education or something fundamentally new? Suppose that such roles should also ideally be occupied by candidates who have some expertise in education, pedagogy, children, child development, adolescence and other subjects relating to children, pedagogy and learning. Indeed, this implies substantial breadth of requirements from individuals who should work in education under the new conditions of digitization and datafication, a challenge to find a pool of such experts in itself.

But this is not just about adding new roles. The whole education ecosystem is flooded with outpouring requirements, guidelines and sophisticated digital products that are integrating into education *now*, measuring and impacting children *today*. These new roles and requirements are coming hand in hand with industry, and they are hard to understand what they aim to achieve and whom they are truly benefiting. Rightfully so, mediating brokers including data privacy consultants, officers, research experts in data, AI, pedagogy, cybersecurity, children's rights and so have been flooding the scene with guidelines, 'blueprints' and proposals for governing the digitization of education and governing education data.

A hodgepodge of frameworks for governing EdTech

More recently, concerns are brought to the fore around what can be done to ensure trust, transparency and accountability, given that these EdTech tend to be offered by private companies with business interests and little substantial scrutiny and evidence of their lab-to-market initiatives. Simultaneously, there are greater critical end-user views towards EdTech products[33] while schools are also increasingly seeking evidence[34] about EdTech products' value to education.

A parallel can be drawn with the emergence of environmental, social and governance (ESG) auditing in response to climate change, where companies use standards to demonstrate their positive impact on the environment, relationships with employees and communities and effective governance structures. The expectation is that companies disclosing their performance on ESG criteria will receive a 'higher value', benefiting both 'their bottom line and shareholders'.[35] Consequently, the demand for corporate ESG frameworks and financial ESG investing metrics has surged more recently. The consulting industry, as Mazzucato and Collington point out, is a major provider of ESG frameworks and related services, promoting their adoption en masse.

Similarly, in education there has been an explosion of frameworks of assessing EdTech, certifications coupled with vetting programs and 'evidence-based' assessments. By the time this book is published, there sure will be more coming up. So the list below is not exhaustive, and some mentions may become irrelevant. The objective, however, is to point to the impact of this work in terms of distraction away from asking the critical question of what societies are consenting to, how it benefits children and whether alternatives for education are still provided as part of the collective responsibility to uphold children's well-being and right to education.

The frameworks, solutions for governance and EdTech benchmarking can be categorized into national and international legal requirements and standards and industry-led principles and guidelines characterized by complex associations and partnerships. It is within this other layer surrounding the digitized education in which the decision-makers and influencers as well as the specific criteria for quality and standards often remain unclear.

Privacy-by-design measures, for instance, have gained importance as solutions offered to provide visualization labels on the end users' side and guidelines on the software development side. On both ends such efforts are in abundance.[36] Such guidelines and labels following vetting intend to help end users to better understand the data collection process and related implications of using digital technologies.

For example, global institutions have put forward their frameworks, giving directions to both governments and education stakeholders internationally. The World Bank's Systems Approach for Better Education Results (SABER-ICT) *Framework*[37] is aimed at policymakers and governments to help them in their process of designing and assessing key policies linked to information and communication technologies in education. The *UNESCO ICT Competency Framework for Teachers*[38] (for which UNESCO partnered with Microsoft, CISCO, Intel and International Society for Technology in Education's) is similarly provided for policymakers intended to help them reform teacher capacity and professional development, while another one aims to map the 'new directions of hybrid education systems'.[39]

The *PISA ICT Framework*[40] aims to assess the integration of digital technologies into teaching and learning. Then there are the *Framework for Stakeholder Inclusion,*[41] *Technological, Pedagogical, and Content Knowledge* (TPAC)[42] and related to it the so-called T3 Framework (elevating the influence of EdTech into 'transnational, transformational, and transcendental'[43] domains), the International Society for Technology in Education's (ISTE) *Standards for Educators,*[44] the ISTE *Edtech Product Evaluation Guide for Teachers*[45] and its *Five Pillars for Edtech Procurement,*[46] and many more. Former IMS Global, 1Edtech (described earlier in the book) provides its own 'standards' and vetting of EdTech products, certifying and training educators and similar commercialization of all kinds of services.

Added to these frameworks and direction, associations and public-private partnerships have also been defending the market of EdTech in various ways that make the market of EdTech particularly potent. ISTE standards, for instance, 'gather actionable feedback and insights from the field that inform go-to-market strategies'.[47] Some use buzzword mash-ups like the '7-step AI readiness framework' for 'educators or for businesses'[48] to express enthusiasm about AI, but these guidelines often lack consideration for social needs, contextual values, organizational dependencies, basic student needs or children's rights and freedoms in education.

Moreover, these private associations offer more than standards. First, they are based on paid memberships which allow 'special access' to things such as professional development, market insight and support at a cost. For premium memberships such as those of ISTE for instance (prices vary around $295 annually), members such as teachers can get digital subscription to their 'two peer-reviewed journals ($198 value)' and things such as 'early access to book your hotel for ISTELive', VIP events, and access to 'two ISTE U courses – one on learning styles and one on digital citizenship ($274 value)'.[49] 1Edtech and DXtera operate on paid memberships, limiting any chance of influence of teachers or students in markets that increasingly control the procurement, vetting and development of EdTech and digital systems.

Understanding the funding sources and the extent of influence of organizations like ISTE and 1Edtech is perplexing. The proliferation of such entities contributes to market-driven activities from teacher training in EdTech products to establishing affiliations and ambassadorships where teachers promote these products rather than question, critique and even resist them. These organizations also engage in high-level commitments with districts and schools by providing training and technical support. This demonstrates the lucrative business around the digitization in which educational and training programs as well as activities such as participating in trade shows along with exciting trips (see the glamorous ASU+GSV Summit) are generated to centralize the position of EdTech. There are also the ISTE standards for educators, for students, for administrators, for computer science teachers, for EdTechs.

There are standards around quality online teaching,[50] matrices on how to integrate technologies,[51] for quality assurance of e-assessment,[52] an age-appropriate digital services framework,[53] technological, pedagogical and content knowledge (TPACK) framework,[54,55] the EdTech Digital Promise framework,[56] education Services Australia's Safer Technologies 4 Schools (ST4S) initiative used by both Australia and New Zealand[57] and many more across the globe.

There are the legal frameworks such as the EU's General Data Protection Regulation and the new EU legislative suite addressing AI, digital and data markets, the California Consumer Privacy Act, the US' Children's Online Privacy Protection Act and the Family Educational Rights and Privacy Act and frameworks relating to cybersecurity such as the European NIS2 Directive,[58] the UK Cyber Essentials and NIST in the United States among many others.[59] There are also frameworks relating to child rights Impact assessment (see UNICEF's)[60]; the European age-appropriate digital services framework,[61] child cantered designs[62] (albeit generally, not targeting EdTech specifically); guiding kits for developers[63] and design principles with children's rights in mind,[64] and many more offerings and ideas Undoubtedly more will emerge.

For EdTech companies and broadly digital service providers targeting children the confusion is no different. Recent research[65] identified that most start-ups struggle to comply with the General Data Protection Regulation's (GDPR's), the European Union's data protection law, basic principles. What to say about the mounting other guidelines, frameworks, blueprints and prerequisites some of which are listed above? While some enforce and successfully apply standards and frameworks through a top-down approach, such as the age-appropriate design code[66] with its idealistic principles, evaluating the alignment of each digital company with these standards is a separate challenge. How many companies will meet these? How will they do so? What is the evidence we are expecting to gather to demonstrate that they meet them? What happens in the meantime? Additionally, much of the attention surrounding data privacy-by-design, age-appropriate principles, security standards and so on tend to target large companies rather than start-ups. In the EdTech domain the majority of the market are small-to-medium, early stage and start-ups, yet with sufficient power to spearhead development, commercialization and disruption. How do all of them meet these expanding requirements?

The resulting confusion about compliance creates a chaotic environment that can be overwhelming and distracting from what matters in education. It makes it even more challenging to identify meaningful solutions for navigating the impact of technologies on public schooling. In the Western neoliberal context, the role of law and institutions emphasizes prioritizing market progress for societal well-being; as the market and businesses thrive, the benefits will eventually reach the broader population, so the promise goes – less government interference, more running of businesses because they know best how things are done. In essence, what matters is how the market performs first and foremost. Yet reality bites. Presently, the wealthiest 10 per cent of the world's population claims 52 per cent of global income, while the bottom half earns only 8.5 per cent.[67] Despite billions experiencing the challenges of escalating food prices and hunger, the number of billionaires has doubled in the past decade.

That said, regulatory measures targeting the most powerful in the digital sector are certainly growing although we are yet to see how they will play out. The EU has addressed the digital age with a suite of legislature encompassing digital services, data markets and AI. In the United States, the Federal Trade Commission has also sought to tackle digital surveillance more sternly.[68] Varied proposals for decentralization and digital services as utilities have also been debated.[69] However, it is unclear how these can be realized, and how such alternative forms of governance can trickle down to the EdTech sector. Meanwhile, the value that EdTech businesses extract from amassing education data can be considered excessive and exploitative[70] especially when many of the services are provided for free (meaning, somewhere, somehow, they must be trying to make ends meet). Regardless of the laws, we see how the market assimilates every sector, including education, as I have described up to now, incorporating it as a component within its own machinery. In turn, education is imagined to help it sustain itself. As a result, we observe the decline of education as it diminishes into a data schema tailored for algorithmic recitation.

The second reason stems from the first. While legal frameworks, guidelines, directives, toolkits, etc., offer some governance to address data privacy and security concerns in a digitized education, they only divert attention from recognizing fundamental risks associated with the digitization. The book up to now has consistently revisited the question of the purpose of education and has emphasized the significance of preserving the sociality of education as the main means to generating ideas, fostering empathy and nurturing children to become subjects of their own lives, rather than mere objects of a market narrative and interests. Even if laws and guidelines are met, digitizing education still has to be seen from the socio-ethical considerations in digitizing education. That is, there is still a bigger need to look beyond the immediate technological benefits but assess how these changes affect the broader social fabric of School and societies.

Third, there is a strong focus on innovation and the transformative potential of technology in education, with a nearly obsessive pursuit of technological solutions for societal issues, as exemplified by the vision of Salesforce, an American cloud-based software company spreading into education, 'so that everyone is an Einstein'.[71] In contrasting reality, educational institutions grapple with various challenges, including teacher shortages[72] and demoralization[73], crumbling school buildings[74] and difficulties meeting basic necessities for students.[75] One might argue that this reality takes a backseat when governments' allegiance falls on the well-being of market expansion and technological innovation. Privacy guidelines, blueprints, and frameworks confine the understanding of broader societal risks associated with digitizing education or human existence. They primarily establish boundaries and ensure compliance without addressing whether these products genuinely contribute to fundamental human needs and interests. In reality, claiming to cater to all basic human needs is an overstatement, as such needs are as many as humans are and possibly cannot be universally fulfilled. If someone aspires to do so, then we are really in for a dystopian world of engineering alphas and epsilons.

Ironically, narratives around freedom, interests and rights are often used to parade digital technologies as harbingers of good as they enable education or improve the human experience. But these narratives can also be viewed as an obscure weapon to regulatory immunity – i.e., one must not interfere with or control the companies whose products underpin one's basic human rights.

A recent UNESCO Global Education Monitoring (GEM) report[76] questioned on whose terms are the EdTech 'tools' and revealed that regulations from outside the education sector may not adequately cater to education's requirements. Some key questions the report focused on included:

- Can EdTech help solve important issues in education?
- How to know if EdTech 'works' in education?
- What do countries prioritize when they buy EdTech?

Not everything has simple answers. To begin with, whose education and what is considered an issue to their education? Additionally, maintaining education connectivity in poor countries would cost $ 1 billion per day.[77] Additionally, it is harder to track to what end this cost is 'worth' and for whom. Among other important aspects, the report also addressed headlong the question of governance.

Excessive focus on technology in education can be costly, diverting resources away from essential elements like classrooms, teachers and textbooks, particularly in low- and lower-middle-income countries. This detour might impede progress in reaching the education goal set by the United Nations – goal No 4. Considering that affluent nations have mostly achieved universal secondary education and basic learning skills for their people without heavy reliance on digital technology, it raises questions about why such universal goals are envisioned through EdTech for the rest of the world.

Some of the GEM Report's[78] most avid findings highlighted that only 16 per cent of countries have laws that ensure data privacy in education. In ten of these countries, children's rights remain unguarded despite such legislation. Data regulations for educational data are scarce, except in the EU where public schools follow the GDPR. Only 16 per cent of countries globally have laws addressing cyberbullying in education, and 38 per cent of them enacted such laws during the Covid-19 pandemic. Meanwhile, as digitization grows and the hodgepodge of frameworks jumbles EdTech companies, cyber *in*security grows and with that risks for children, their privacy and basic human rights.

Cyber uncertainties

Increasingly, government policies are including the role of EdTech in compulsory education. At the same time, however, there is no government intervention in regulating the expanding industry. Market forces alone do not incentivize the sector to satisfy the security demands of end-users. The level of cybersecurity EdTech vendors implement can be an indication that the concept of protecting the user (students and teachers) should be understood and addressed at a basic level. However, it would be a mistake to assume that quality security and privacy measures are designed by default in the world of business. Oftentimes, it is a matter of cutting corners, marketing, scaling, making a profit, and satisfying shareholders and investors – even merging with or selling to a bigger company (and leaving the fate of student data into someone else's hands) as I already gave some examples earlier in the book.

From information security economics, security failures in the digital domain can be seen as poor security investments and practices because of poor market decisions, the lack of policy incentives to prioritize cybersecurity, little cost-benefits (since cybersecurity measures are preventive, not motivated by profit), and overall lack of regulation. The economics of information security helps to understand the factors that influence companies' decisions around cybersecurity measures and investments. In one study, I aimed to understand the present state of the EdTech sector and the optimal cybersecurity investments for EdTech companies. Several concerns emerged from the research. As some[79] have argued, spending more on a mandatory standard can increase the cost of EdTech products, which schools would ultimately have to bear. Sifting through complex frameworks with hundreds of requirements, implementing controls and getting external validation incur substantial costs to start-ups. However, as one vendor had told me, 'cybersecurity frameworks benefit the development of one's product and even start-ups can attend to these guidelines'.[80]

In many cases, the EdTech products and digital platforms are imposed on schools – they often cannot resist or refuse them. The post-pandemic reality can be seen as a surrender of schools to the institutionalization of digital platforms and EdTechs. This institutionalization is demanding of the education community to adapt quickly and navigate through often highly technical challenges. For that, much of the government policies tend to address the education community and the cybersecurity awareness and skills they need. School priorities are shifting from what one should be taught to how one should be taught with the range of EdTech products and technical risks they come with.

Schools generally do not have the expertise and cannot always afford to build the capacity to discern from the different EdTech products across the ever-growing lists of criteria. At this point it is also unclear how teachers and educational institutions use EdTech systems and education data. For example, do they just know how an EdTech app or platform works? How does one use the diagnostics presented by an app? Is there an accepted school policy with regard to the use of EdTech data and diagnostics? Are there agreed codes of practice and expectations from all teachers within an educational institution when it comes to the use of EdTech products? Is a teacher at risk of losing his job if he chooses not to use a certain application and does not know how to or even opts to rely on the product most of the time with some of his students (what are the criteria to decide on that and who decides it)? To such questions, one EdTech consultant told me:[81]

> [E]ducation is a big part [of the issues]; from the schools' point of view a big part of the data protection is just learning the tech. A big challenge for schools is teachers even being able to use the technology, let alone to be able to pick it apart and figure [it] out.

Indeed, data privacy officers, one line of defence for schools and students, as well as entities like the Student Data Privacy Consortium in the United States, through the Global Education Privacy and Security Standard (GEPS/GESS)[82] have set up specifically for EdTech vetting and procurement and provide as much support to schools as possible – through training, information and EdTech procurement. But the lack of coherence (when schools buy into a product that has not had its impact assessment yet or a teacher simply decides to choose a new and exciting application in class one day), and the added responsibility to schools to understand the risks emanating from data and technologies (while such knowledge also takes time to build) calls for rethinking meaningful and coherent solutions in procurement. As one data privacy officer has told me: 'we know we need a standard ... something needs to be put together'.

Similarly, within the Australian context, the NSIP carry out technology assessments across cybersecurity guidelines through the ST4S, mentioned earlier.[83] Yet again because of the voluntary basis on which this auditing across cybersecurity requirements is conducted, some of the biggest players in the sector refuse to go under the microscope.

Government intervention for adequate measures of oversight is highly needed for the sake of protecting the environment of compulsory education. The neoliberal tendency to let the market sort itself out should be taken with caution. Some policymakers I have met have argued against government intervention because the EdTech sector is a relatively young and fast evolving.[84] However, evidence has shown that self-regulation does not work. The rise of platform power that has been seen in other sectors such as (social) media increases the risks for individuals due to government inaction and outdated or slow action on the side of regulation. Platforms such as Facebook and Google have grown powerful due to a combination of factors including the 'inaction' from governments, 'safe harbour provisions' protecting platforms from the 'consequences of their users' actions ("intermediary liability exemptions")', data protection and privacy frameworks that fall behind technological innovations, and lack of authorities' attention over the potential of long-term harm from large scale-data collection.[85]

Self-regulation is created to deflect statutory control. Crucially, in the context of EdTech and the sector's duty to meet minimum standards that guarantee safety, self-regulation, government inaction and inadequate regulatory frameworks should not be considered the norm.

Cybersecurity frameworks are guidelines; substantial maturity is required to navigate through them and deploy the right ones. Besides organizational and individual (e.g., developers) maturity, cultural ethos and duty of care are also required from EdTech companies. Without incentives and appropriate level of scrutiny by governments, there is little guarantee for School that EdTech companies would be aligned with appropriate cybersecurity benchmarks. Technological challenges must be tackled first by those in the business of EdTech, the way pharmacologists and chemists have the know-how of what goes inside pill.

EdTech providers acknowledge that schools have become more aware and demand to see companies meet adequate measures of data privacy protection and cybersecurity controls. That said, it is far from clear what questions should be asked and even how to request evidence that the right controls are implemented. The known frameworks contain hundreds of questions, many of which overlap. Written in highly technical language, not all of these are relevant to compulsory educational settings. If many EdTech companies find it hard to navigate around these, how can one expect of schools to be able to?

Further, the GEM report,[86] for example, evidenced that many governments had conflicting alignment of their goals with those of EdTech businesses. Governments also find it challenging to govern EdTech. Similarly, I asked questions around EdTech procurement at a more regional and national levels (in the UK and the EU).[87]

- Who decides what EdTech products will be adopted in schools?
- What benchmark is used to make such decisions?
- Who assesses what EdTech vendors deliver against their claims?

- Are there any criteria used to recognize when an EdTech product fails and who decides what those are?
- Who is held responsible if/when EdTech products fail?

These questions highlight that it is not just data privacy and security by principle and design that should mitigate these concerns, but everything that digital products and devices can do and *un*do to the learning experience for a child. Many societies *do* have 'ideal' principles and canons to follow, yet how many individuals do so wholeheartedly? On the other hand, civilized societies have created enforcement mechanisms when some of these commandments are broken. Said otherwise, beyond the guidelines, the businesses pervading education with their digital products need to be regulated and rules enforced.

Education data governance

Existing governance of EdTech companies along with privacy-by-design guidelines, privacy compliance and impacts assessments fail to address the power accumulation of private businesses through infrastructure and human capture through data. There is also a risk of convoluting the notion that digital systems mediating educational processes are automatically do-gooders once they display privacy-by-design or 'health check' labels of compliance. Many of these guidelines also overlap, yet holes remain such as their pedagogic contribution, or their societal, even ecological, socio-ethical or well-being impact.

This is not to deny their importance; however, privacy-by-design guidelines risk distracting policy and stakeholder attention away from the actual accumulation of data collection and the centralization of private power as described in Chapter 3. We see higher education infrastructures being captured by Big Tech[88] with the same modelling being proposed in compulsory education.

What follows is from research I have worked on over the past few years regarding EdTech procurement and governance. The simple question I first began working with is, who decides what products should be used in class and according to what criteria? Having discussed until now the rights of children, their voices and the purpose of education, my premise behind this ongoing research has been on thinking about something even simpler as a statement: *Unlicensed bus drivers will never drive the school bus; why should unlicensed EdTech products mediate educational processes*? Licensing involves established regulations, conditions, standards and systematic independent oversight. This can be compared to a system akin to traffic signs and wardens whereby everyone who occupies the public space, where children are crossing or a playpark may be nearby, know clearly what the rules are. A system of signs, wardens, fines and monitoring are introduced to ensure that the rules are observed. And so, just as drivers (irrespective of their vehicle) may unknowingly violate the road rules, businesses in education technology must adhere to guidelines ensuring children's right to education is protected. The landscape of EdTech procurement lacks such a unified framework and system. Negotiating this minefield, schools must navigate diverse offerings, ensuring products meet safety standards, security requirements as well as justify budget allocations. A task easier said than done.

The UK respects the General Data Protection Regulation (GDPR) while, at the time of writing, the Data Protection and Digital Information Bill is being reviewed,[89] which aims to make provision for the regulation of processing data relating to individuals.[90] As such, schools and EdTech providers must also follow the principles of the GDPR. In practice, things can get more complicated. The GDPR principles include aspects such as lawfulness, fairness and transparency, purpose limitation, data minimization, accuracy, storage limitation, integrity and confidentiality. The practical application of these principles faces challenges, particularly when schools engage with EdTech products since schools act both as the 'data controllers' and as the mediators between the user (the student) and the EdTech provider. Joint control of data is thus also common, but issues arise when the EdTech vendor contracts lack clarity with regard to the purposes for which they process students' data. As a result, the challenges to clearly identify roles and responsibilities can also hinder school control or allow unanticipated data processing by the providers themselves. The lack of emphasis on the very benefits from all the data that is collected in education in current procurement practices adds yet another layer of complexity. It therefore impedes upon the straightforward task to enforce rules. The lack of clear approach led to a recent case where the UK's regulator, the Information Commissioner's Office (ICO) 'reprimanded' the Department for Education as a result of its prolonged misuse of personal information of around 28 million children[91] which nearly cost millions in fines.[92]

Correcting (one's own) homework

The frameworks, resources and broad enterprise standards are many as mentioned earlier in this chapter. Assessing digital technologies based on children's fundamental human rights (reflected in the code) is also challenging. There is growing attention in recent years that the digitisation of education and broadly digital spaces that children have access to need careful attention. In the UK, the Data Protection Act of 2018[93] required the Information Commissioner to create a code of practice for age-appropriate design standards (the Age-Appropriate Design Code) for relevant Information Society Services (ISS) likely to be accessed by children.

The code aims to ensure compliance with the DPA and UK GDPR, safeguarding children's personal data in information society services.

Additionally, the April 2019 online harms white paper proposed a new regulatory framework for online safety,[94] highlighting the fragmentation of existing regulations. This led to the introduction of the Online Safety Bill, at the time of writing progressing through the UK Parliament. However, the Bill has faced delays due to scrutiny, political uncertainty, and challenges in agreeing on amendments.

According to ICO, the legal and policy context is crucial for understanding the external environment affecting the delivery of the code. The DPA further mandates consideration of the UNCRC, the international human rights treaty which grants comprehensive rights to children (17 and under). The UNCRC, including General Comment No. 25 on children's rights in relation to the digital environment,[95] emphasises protection against privacy interference (Article 16) and protecting children's best interests (Article 3). Take the principle of building digital products in the best interest of the child.

What a product may do in the best interest of one child may be in direct conflict with the best interest of another. The problem becomes even bigger – and so decisions may become more cut-throat or entirely symbolic – when the product offered is by a private entity that is trying to make a profit. Then governing based on principles is like governing people based on the *Ten Commandments*. Perhaps it breathes hope that people will not cheat and do no harm, but how do we know that everyone sticks to these?

In research I conducted in 2021[96] with data privacy officers, EdTech procurement consultants, school administrators and leaders identified this gap and challenge the education sector is facing not only in the UK but everywhere.[97] For example, data privacy officers (in UK and EU contexts), EdTech freelance consultants, procurement departments and district or school leaders (in the case of the United States) aim to support decisions about the choice of EdTech products to buy into and use – be that by vetting, developing contractual agreements or conducting data privacy impact assessments. DPOs in the UK seek to establish whether EdTech vendors adhere to data privacy conditions set forth by the GDPR.[98] In the United States, a school district in Cambridge, Massachusetts, I have done research on[99] forms part of a consortium dedicated to vetting EdTech products by using specially developed data privacy contractual agreements (obliging vendors to adhere to the Family Educational Rights Protection Act[100]).

While vetting and signing contracts sounds like a straightforward task, DPOs and school leaders I have spoken with in the UK say it is not. First, EdTech vendors are not obligated to undergo a wide range of assessments beyond data privacy impact, and more recently the Age-Appropriate Design Code, mentioned earlier, for those vendors considered ISS and where the Code applies.[101] Even though in the cases like that in the UK, the ICO provides a self-assessment checklist for vendors to determine their role (whether they are a data controller, joint controller or processor) this is challenging not only because vendors are not obliged to carry such assessments but also because in educational settings it is challenging in the case that controllers (the school) also serve as the intermediary between the EdTech vendor and the student.

Major corporations such as Google and Adobe are more elusive to such assessments. Their evaluation is further complicated by the diverse terms and conditions and data practices, particularly when users transition between different services, like moving from Google Workspace for Education to YouTube, also a Google product with other terms and conditions.[102]

Second, schools often adopt EdTech products before any such assessments are carried out. As one DPO told me, school and vendor 'have already sealed the deal ... there is no motivation for the vendors to undergo a risk assessment'.[103]

Third, EdTech vendors' understanding of GDPR varies widely. As one officer said, 'some providers have wild terms and conditions and such wacky interpretations of the GDPR, some picking and choosing as to which articles of the GDPR they fancy complying with'. Another officer told me that 'some don't even bother saying anything at all about data protection; they just put "in accordance with GDPR" at the end of every line of the contract and think that that suffices'.

EdTech vendors often label themselves as processors in contracts, even when acting as controllers or joint controllers, creating ambiguity in data-processing purposes and lawful bases. This process creates challenges for vendors who face varying due diligence questionnaires, never a clearly understood set of questions across the sector and never exhaustive that consider a range of requirements – from pedagogic to legal to accessibility to human rights.[104] Simultaneously, it poses difficulties for schools unsure about what compliance expectations to set since vendor responses differ. The constant emergence of new EdTech products and from EdTech providers who operate internationally further complicates risk assessments and introduces cultural challenges for local adoption. In a word, there is still no clear definition of what constitutes 'good' EdTech – and 'good' for whom.

An officer in the UK who has been for over thirty years in education says that his work encompasses many strands: from helping EdTech vendors better communicate with schools to helping the Department for Education with the development of a data protection toolkit for schools. He elaborates further:

> [P]art of that work has been what can be a standard model ... something that would lead to answering the question of what good edtech look like, because that's one of the questions that still hasn't been answered.[105]

As it stands up to now at the time of writing, a possible answer to this question would be, as the same officer suggested, 'something like, there's a bit of this and there's a bit of this and, it's hard to sometimes pin that down'. The bigger problem, however, is that finding a standard model that unifies the various needs of schools, EdTech vendors, DPOs and importantly children and their parents would be a 'low priority' to government departments because the responsibilities of EdTech procurement and selecting the 'good' EdTech products remain in the hands of schools. This leads to the question of liability: who remains responsible when these products fail?

The absence of clear regulatory principles and strong enforcement of rules unique to the education technology sector heightens liability risks for schools, allowing unproven products to enter with unclear pedagogical benefits and uncertainties around the digital systems' bigger potential for mediating and influencing public education. One EdTech consultant noted the lack of focus on data protection and highlighted the challenge of identifying good vendors and products telling me how schools lack the 'full view of who the good vendors and products are' on the market. The absence of a systematic approach for evaluating products beyond legal compliance also contributes to schools' overall confusion and often distrust of technology, making it equally difficult for well-intentioned companies to navigate the landscape.

In the United States, to set clear boundaries for EdTech vendors, as mentioned earlier, some districts have developed standard contractual agreements with the vendors, which subject them to transparent disclosures of what data is collected and processed but also what limitations are given as to the purposes the data is used for. Such vetting and audit are done to ensure that vendors adhere to conditions the schools put forward. This is a 'tactical' way of dealing with student data privacy, as the Cambridge school district's chief information officer and then senior database administrator had told me.[106] Common expectations are outlined clearly across all EdTech vendors and for all school districts participating in such efforts.[107] While conventional in a legal sense, such data privacy contractual agreements demonstrate two urgent needs that must be met in support of educational institutions and ultimately students.

The first one is School's responsibility over the security and privacy protection of children and their data since legal frameworks do not satisfy this fully.[108] Recent evidence has demonstrated that despite the legal impositions, EdTech providers still find loopholes in the existing laws[109, 110] and in the technologies themselves[111] and continue to exploit children's data.

The second is the need to re-think scalable and sustainable governance framework that should be associated at legislative levels, not merely left to isolated and voluntary effort on the side of schools, districts or the EdTech sector itself.

Beyond data privacy

In a digitized classroom, data is generated, often stored and processed in separate systems some of which is beyond the control of educational institutions or students. As one senior database administrator had explained to me: 'students log into applications via their browsers, generally on Chromebooks, so all the application's data remain with the vendor'.[112] Some of the data is crucial for reporting at various levels and also necessary for EdTech products to work. Data is also captured throughout a child's digital journey such as when using Google Classroom and getting to the YouTube video-sharing service.[113] In fact, because of this in 2019 Google was fined $170 million civil penalty as YouTube illegally collected personal information from children without their parents' consent, violating the US Children's Online Privacy Protection Act (COPPA).[114] Microsoft and Google impose their own terms and conditions which bypass any horizontal contracts of privacy and consent – these power players reserve the right to read, monitor, modify, destroy, and control one's email correspondence, calendar, contacts or assignments as a student uses their products. This goes against any privacy understanding and laws even if all Microsoft and Google do that is for their own business development needs. Millions of students across the globe use Microsoft and Google as recommended or directly contracted by governments.

Their terms and conditions are complex, often lack transparency and get even more entangled and illegible for any user when third-party apps are accessed via their platforms. Their contracts have a 'hidden vertical structure',[115] not only through their data privacy conditions but through the unique interface designs, algorithms adapting and nudging individuals, labelling learners and so on. In the absence of regulation and strict scrutiny, these technologies are demonstrating a sort of quasi-legal order and a loose form of 'jurisdiction'.[116]

A social contract, in Rousseauan terms, for a collective will of the people and the general will, as the basis for a just society, refers to the implicit agreement among members of a society to cooperate for mutual benefit, establishing the foundation for organized governance and societal order.[117] Within the vertical arrangements established between users and digital systems through designs and data utilization, users do not have much negotiating power and are often faced with a take-it-or-leave-it situation, where they must accept the terms to access the platform. These terms undermine the collective agreement which would reflect the general will of the users. Individuals are subjected to specific and often unilateral conditions imposed by the digital systems. As such, digital systems cultivate a certain kind of *normative* power as well. Algorithmic systems specifically can impose their own interpretation of academic success, problematic behaviour and so on. This is again *vertical* hegemony imposed on users that escapes the social contract of School or society of which School is a function. Yet these systems do not have individual responsibility for students or for teachers. If a student fails an exam, a digital platform is not chased to explain why that happened or be fired. This responsibility is still reserved for School.

To mitigate this hegemony is for example to scrutinize more strictly these companies and how they use education data. But to have full access and control of the data, as the same school data administrator said to me,

> A lot of rules have to be enforced that vary by vendor. There needs to be a broker between [a school's] student records database and the vendors ... A nicer, easier way of configuring per-application access rules would be great. Not having to do transformations (to accommodate vendors' data formats, Boolean formats, field lengths and such) would be great too. But I would need the broker application to be under my control. I personally would never trust a vendor to have and keep their end configured the way we want, even if they have the best intentions. Once the data are on vendors' systems it's out of our hands, so we limit that data as much as possible. We only want to send the data we choose, for the students and staff we choose.[118]

In other words, rather than relying on personal judgements, at the institutional level there is a need to configure per-application access rules when it comes to governing education data. This highlights that addressing governance is, to a great extent, a technological challenge.

Propositions for technological solutions that can automate the governance of digitization and data have been in the making in the health[119] and the public sector.[120] Although a technological solution would lead to decentralizing and automating data transactions, which are otherwise currently handled manually through data privacy contractual agreements, there is a need for technological provisions that establish an innovative and consistent governance mechanism. This mechanism should adapt to the fast-evolving EdTech products and their enhanced algorithmic capabilities. I describe that in greater detail in the final chapter.

Additionally, addressing data processing from an ethical point of view is unaddressed despite the contractual agreements being set out or any other mechanisms for data privacy protection. Relying on contractual agreements for assessing EdTech products indeed imposes legal terms on data access; however they are highly laborious, costly and not easy to scale. The lack of well-defined ethical review procedures for EdTech companies raises concerns about the ethical handling of data unlike established practices in academia for instance. The ethical grey area persists when it comes to EdTech and the use of education data, requiring further examination and clarification, particularly regarding the repurposing of de-identified data collected in spite of the existing data privacy regulations. The conditions in which ethical go-ahead is given rely on the imposition of the legal frameworks like Children's Online Privacy Act (COPPA)[121] and the Family Educational Rights and Privacy Act (FERPA)[122] in the United States, and the data privacy contractual agreements, mentioned earlier, to which the EdTech provider commits upon signing. However, while FERPA provisions control for what data can be used, once collected, repurposing its use still remains, as the CIO of the Cambridge school district said, 'a grey area'. It also becomes hard to find data misuse. In one case, the vendor of a popular maths product used the collected data to carry out research on student learning and published a paper. The school district CIO told me: 'this use of collected data can be unethical even if there is no harm done; under our data privacy agreements, you can't do that'.[123]

There are no clear ethical review procedures that EdTech providers undergo for their product deployment or data processing and use. Terms of service and data privacy policies make no mention about relevant ethical reviews of the processes by which companies improve their software, conduct internal research or even work on new product development. In any research setting involving human subjects – in this case, they are also minor – would require prior ethical approval. In contrast, EdTech providers usually do not seek any form of prior ethical approval. Research on whether EdTech products undergo ethical data assessments are also meagre. In the UK, for instance, EdTech products are assessed mainly across data privacy regulations as mentioned earlier.[124] In Australia, data governance is expressed through the assessment of EdTech products based on security, privacy, interoperability and online safety.[125]

Thanks to data privacy laws like the GDPR, awareness of the need for impact assessments in technology involving personal data has grown. However, in light of the advancing AI, legal and technology experts have argued that there is a need to think beyond data privacy since the data that has already been made available has been used to train present and future models with power to influence individuals in ways that is hard to control or estimate the risks. Even if individuals have the right to data erasure as part of GDPR's 'right to be forgotten', it is difficult to remove something that has already been used or shared online. As such, ML exacerbates any efforts to protecting individuals' privacy.[126] Once fed into a machine learning model, the data input into it can be retained endlessly, which is bad news for individual as well as collective[127] privacy. Scholars have come to argue that data privacy protection through data privacy impact assessments is not enough, but rather relevant human rights and socio-ethical dimensions should be considered in evaluating the impact of technology.

Alessandro Mantelero thus proposes the Human Rights Ethical and Social Impact Assessment, or HRESIA model,[128] which integrates human rights analysis and ethical and social values, and advocates a human-centred, multi-stakeholder approach with elements of traditional risk management models. Mantelero critiques existing GDPR-based assessment models, asserting that HRESIA provides a more comprehensive assessment, focusing on rights and freedoms relevant to data-intensive systems beyond mere data protection. Such view to assessing EdTech systems for example would interplay between legal and socio-ethical dimensions. That is, technologies do not just change the sociality of education but also the intersection of individuals as groups and their effects on the larger social fabric.

Thousands of teachers globally today use AI-integrated products like PowerSchool's Schoology and SchoolMateAI to automate their work. SchoolMateAI in particular is a good example to show how a product's fast evolution exceeds meaningful efforts for governance and even critical perspective by those who use it. The product evolved from simple EdTech advice blog by a 'teaching and tech expert' Mr P ICT.[129] It now provides automated lesson plans, assessments, reports, emails and so on. This advanced tool, akin to an automated robotic assistant, offers to generate educational content and other services, at a fee. Significant socio-ethical concerns arise short and long term.

For instance, should not a qualified body vet and approve such a product? Are parents and students fine with teachers using a generative tool that spews lesson plans? A question should address teachers themselves: If lesson plans, reporting and grading are automated what becomes of their role? Will they not be needed at all soon?

What perceptions students have about teachers asking bots to design the lessons? Children are introduced to a game in which they are thrust in direct comparison with computer capabilities, and worse, with other humans *with* access to such powerful computer capabilities.

Let us also not forget that these applications come at a cost. Khan Academy recently integrated ChatGPT, called Khanmigo, which is at a subscription fee.[130] This shift not only incurs a financial cost to students and schools, and thus limiting access only to those who can afford it, but it also amplifies societal inequalities in unprecedented ways. A new kind of inequality: between the *have-nots* and the *have-bots*. The latter do not merely access a whole library and computer services, but a whole library with AI capabilities for scalable processing and instant results. It is also quite another problem altogether if any of these divided populations are actually prepared to critically understand and utilize both the tools and the results they spew, which brings us back to the purpose of education.

Conclusion

Moving forward, clearly, the current institutional instruments and toolkits available are inadequate – or at least they are used in ways that depicts an inadequate picture – as it has been the case with regulating Big Tech[131] to assess harm and impact of the rising pedagogic and authoritative powers of digital technologies mediating all educational processes.

A distinction must be made from the start: Are the existing regulatory measures, the multitude of frameworks, standards, principles and the available oversight prioritizing what is best for children or what is best for the market?

While standards clearly have to be achievable and therefore something more levelled with the industry should be tried, top-down efforts should demonstrate clear thinking about where priorities lie, which should be with education and children, regardless of the digital market's preferences. This will come indeed through clear standards, procedures and systematic rigorous scrutiny of the businesses and their EdTech offerings but one that shows industry clear route not one that confuses and is unachievable.

On the other hand, clear thinking also means that the obsession with digital solutions should not blind people to all non-digital and equally valid alternatives – the good intentions of School as the previous chapter discussed. In fact, opportunities for learning and future should not be constantly explained through digital products simply because these will always give uncertainties and many dependencies around them, and education should not be tethered to the conditions of the market and its high unpredictability. Digital opportunities should not replace or eliminate *all* opportunities.

Mandating systematic supervision centred around the industry is a topic I delve into more thoroughly in the final chapter. Here, I wish to conclude with thoughts on what the next steps can be following this chapter's portrayal of a bustling market with endless principles and visions for governance and what 'good' EdTechs should look like.

Simply put, it should be mandated that they are externally *validated*. Mandating external audit and validation will create the necessary pressure for vendors to embark on the journey of growth – one towards meeting minimum appropriate standards and contextual requirements. This, however, can be neither a one-size-fit-all blanket model nor a market of churning certifications.[132] Rather, there is a need for meaningful discussion led by schools, educators and policymakers, proper funding, clear roles, and crucially – consensus on the local priorities and contextual needs practices, and cultures,[133] rather than global(ist) models that risk streamlining standardised educational systems and processes that are only imagined through the digital technologies mediating them.

In reality, schools are increasingly burdened with having to make sound choices as well as fend for themselves when it comes to cyber insecurities, data privacy, pedagogic value, and children's well-being (including and especially safeguarding and screen time, in relation to the cross-over between EdTech, gaming, and social media). The multitude of requirements and niche technical understanding they are expected to exhibit when procuring EdTech products are simply unsustainable. In the attempt to unpack where responsibilities lie when things go wrong with student data, there is an incoherent ad hoc effort which dilutes the responsibility amongst some of the main stakeholders involved in the procurement process including schools, districts, councils, freelance consultants and even teachers and social media (for example, the so-called Mr P ICT or Mr. Chips and 'Just Ian' and their TeachMateAI, mentioned earlier, 'designed to help teachers successfully streamline everyday tasks – from lesson planning to risk assessments – and to create engaging and bespoke curriculum content' which cost 'as little as £6 per month' and as much as '£830 per year' for a large school up to thirty accounts[134]).

There is also a need for the whole EdTech market to adhere to commonly agreed policies, terms and conditions within national contexts. EdTech oversight should be a policy priority where the assumption should not be that regulation will stifle innovation because it is a relatively new sector but that ensuring that standards are met that will drive innovation in a *direction* where children clearly benefit. The concern that the EdTech sector is still too young to regulate emerged from the conversation with the EU Director General for Innovation, Digital Education and International Cooperation when I spoke to their team in 2021.[135] The argument has been that this is a young market and should not be held back by regulation. The market actually consists of a growing mix of startups (immature?), mature organizations, and major tech companies like Google, Microsoft, Pearson, and Amazon. This diversity makes the market challenging to understand, trust, and hold accountable (in fact, the EdTech sector is becoming a field of study in its own right.[136] Yet the entire opposite is witnessed with the unregulated social media. Due to lack of regulation, powerful platforms like Google, Amazon and Facebook have won gatekeeper status,[137] stifling competition, swallowing small businesses or killing them altogether.[138]

Policymakers actively support uninterrupted innovation, engaging the industry in round tables and public initiatives on digitizing education. The involvement of EdTech companies in discussions is acceptable for solving specific problems, but it is contradictory to let businesses dictate educational needs, just like it would be if one were to insist on consulting the pharmaceutical industry for individual health needs. One would assume that it is best to first discuss one's health with a doctor, physio, nutritionist or any other expert of the human body not with the businesses that manufacture pills.

Regulated markets, such as the online gambling industry, for example, have grown fast (especially among small nation states) precisely because of putting regulatory measures, open standards, strict enforcement and licensing regimes. For example, once the laws and directives came into force in Malta[139] the gaming sector has since contributed nearly 12 per cent to the national economy.[140] Similar path has been witnessed in Gibraltar and Cyprus. Online gambling operators require licences, following rigorous and intrusive audits, duty of care towards players, live monitoring of transactions, continuous monitoring and reporting systems that adhere to clear regulatory frameworks.

It is erroneous to believe that the EdTech market is young. It is not. Developing education technologies have existed since pre-digital time.[141] Having been around for 20 years, Meta (née Facebook) is not an embryonic company. Yet no laws or regulations stopped it from manipulating[142] or harming young people.

Besides the minefield of guidelines, this chapter also shed light on the challenges in education brought by the mounting risks of cyber insecurities. Bringing cybersecurity up to standard for an EdTech start-up has no immediate cost benefit and does not seem like an urgent task in comparison to scaling up and more innovation. This presents more challenges for schools to fend for themselves. While much of the risks indeed emanate from schools, they are also conjoined in a risky gamble with companies that generally do not meet cybersecurity standards. This gamble should be at the expense of children's education and privacy. A way forward is to distribute responsibilities more fairly across the different stakeholders, including EdTech companies. Cybersecurity responsibilities should be shared, and governments must ensure their fair allocation. Schools should neither bear the cost of no security nor for *more* security. For any of these initial steps of discussions, propositions and rules, one more thing is needed as the next step forward: a licensing regime.

8

Licensed to Operate: How to Fix a Fragmented Governance of EdTech?

Rule-making Odyssey

When Mithridates VI, the ruler of northern Anatolia between 120 and 63 BC, created[1] the 'mithridatium', a medicine made by over forty ingredients[2], it was considered a cure to all illnesses until 1780s. It was not until 1540 in England when the mithridatium and other medicine were subjected to evaluation under the Apothecaries Wares, Drugs and Stuffs Act. That same act appointed four inspectors of 'Apothecary Wares, Drugs and Stuffs' and established the pharmaceutical inspections that would later lead to the first Pharmacopoeias – official books on drug quality standards and formulas – to which pharmacologists began to comply with. The final standard for the manufacture of mithridatium in England came in 1618.[3] It took nearly a century to work out a standard for medicine-making! Yet rigorous global standardization did not set in until and only after numerous catastrophic events during the nineteenth and twentieth centuries.

In a webinar when I told this story, an attendee asked me, on that scale, what year are we at in arriving at a decision to regulate the education technology sector? The answer is very much dependent on two things. We may be close to the mark of change if something terrible happens and someone is harmed for policymakers to take a heed[4] as has been the case with social media and impose stricter rules and a licensing regime. Or we may be still a long way to go if society continues to accept the digital transformation unquestioning it and with a sense of complacency. Sometimes it feels more like the latter option but sometimes it feels like the former. Here is what I mean. At the time of writing this book (October 2023), a person called Sam Altman, executive director of Open AI, the American AI research company, created his own currency, installed iris scanners on public places and told people to scan their eyes in exchange for $200 in his currency and protection against the coming robots.[5] This is to say that the time it takes to design and implement meaningful regulation may only stretch further (in the mithridatium sense) since the very deployment and evolving capacities of technologies are accelerating at an unprecedented speed.

There is a third option for an answer: that is, pre-emptively impose guardrails through rules by working directly with the EdTech sector from now. This entails action from the ground up until a unified standard regulating the sector is defined *with* industry to ensure they know what is needed to uphold children's rights, prioritize their well-being and support quality education even if it means eliminating some products that are below standard or unnecessary. I work, research and collaborate for this third option with other researchers, experts, schools and policymakers.[6] This last chapter describes this effort and proposes it as a way forward in some small way.

Unlike in medicine, a possible harmful impact of educational and AI-infused technologies in education is not clear-cut. People generally would not assume that something harmful is used daily in children's classrooms. However, assuming that software cannot be harmful overlooks the important detail that these products are business offerings with a financial interest, often built on pure speculation or potential. Money defines priorities. In that regard, 'code is law',[7] as Lessig posits, but so is money!

Indeed, it is not as straightforward to pinpoint to immediate tangible harms from digitizing the classroom. We tend to know what has happened in education only much later. Making algorithmic assumptions about students' performance and, say, clustering them into groups of different abilities as a result of these assumptions makes it difficult to later determine impact. It simply is impossible to isolate all the decisions, factors and software products that have influenced one's life.

Assuming that data-driven AI systems in education can be as harmful as an unregulated drug would likely shock anyone reading this. Governments and many school leaders generally do not assume risks of harm inflicted by EdTech. If they did, one would imagine that stricter measures and control would have been imposed by now on anything that comes into School. For now, adoption is ad hoc while generally the sentiment around EdTech varies widely.

In the previous chapter I drew attention to the proliferation of the environmental, social and governance (ESG) frameworks that the private sector is increasingly pressed to be measured against. However, as Mazzucato and Collington argue,[8] the lack of a universal standard has led to the impossibility to monitor what industries meet. Moreover, the authors contend that the mere presence of ESG frameworks does not guarantee ethical, environmental or socially responsible behaviour from businesses. Instead, the effectiveness of implementing ESG rules relies on accurate comparisons between businesses, with ESG aiming to facilitate market competition whereby companies can actually lose share value and profitability if they do not meet clearly identified ESG criteria. Applying this logic to the EdTech sector, could we argue that those EdTech businesses failing to meet criteria that prioritize children's needs, safety, privacy and quality pedagogy would automatically experience a decline in their share value and profitability? This would logically hinge on widespread commitment to such criteria, which, if prevalent, could lead to greater support for a universal standard.

In reality, even if the EdTech sector is preached to practise such ethical, lawful and safety principles because good things will happen to their finances, we are still left with no clear universal standard. As Mazzucato and Collington assert,[9] the absence of such universal standard and clear metrics renders the entire system flawed.

Having delved into the complex landscape of frameworks in the previous chapter, this section concludes the book with a more pragmatic approach. First, it expresses optimism about the growing awareness and efforts to educate all involved and interested publics surrounding the challenges of digitizing education. The expectation is that there are ample tools in the regulatory toolkit, and the focus should now shift to their application. I find inspiration from two sectors on how such application can happen. These are education itself and online gambling.

On the latter, my experience working in the sector as a cloud service provider to online gambling operators during its early days over two decades ago informs my perspective, particularly regarding its regulatory regime in some parts of the world. While not flawless, there are valuable lessons, especially regarding software and intrusive monitoring systems which can be applied to the EdTech sector. Relying solely on reading terms of service and privacy policies, the current practice,[10] is insufficient for building trust and ensuring EdTech ethical practices. If a company intends to deceive with its software, it will find a way.

On the former, in education, I draw parallel from the 'audit culture' that has portrayed much of what today's American and English education systems have been operating in. This audit culture for school and teacher accountability serves as a good model that can and should be adapted for auditing the EdTech sector. There are certainly gains and losses in instilling an audit culture for the EdTech sector; however at least three gains are certain to help us move towards more support for schools when they are being digitized with products that tend to play fast and loose. I begin with the introduction of what is governance and what (new) should be governed better in education.

Governing what?

Cambridge dictionary defines the word *governance* as 'the way that organisations and countries are managed at the highest level, and the systems for doing this'.[11] Governance requires a structure, a system or a model of sorts. Governance incurs costs and establishes a legacy of practices (good and not so good) and therefore can come in many forms – global, local, political, public and corporate.

The dictionary also provides adjectives that are often used with the word *governance*. These include *good, democratic* and *effective*. Certainly, there may be many more but for the present purpose of education we can stay with these three. These three words alone describe what is wrong with the growing digitization of education and why this book is calling on stricter governance and regulatory measures.

Another good definition of governance in relation to education comes from education policy scholars. Andrew Wilkins and Brad Gobby define it thus:

> Governance refers to the ways in which government and non-government entities intervene, both formally and informally to shape the way organisations and individuals conduct themselves. These interventions are designed to facilitate certain kinds of change (change in individual behaviour or organisational structure) or limit the possibilities for change in order to maintain the status quo. In both cases, governance is designed to improve conditions by which change can be affected or limited to serve different political, economic and environmental aims.[12]

By this logic, educational leadership and managing educational institutions, the authors argue, are a function and condition of governance since they provides a set of important relays for linking the formally autonomous operations of schools with the political ambitions of states and the wider public's interests. In this sense, the authors assert, it is crucial to examine the relationship between governance and educational leadership. Exploring governance can help to better understand the specific rationalities and configurations that impact the direction and success of schools, what forces influence such direction, what interests are involved and how these serve or may be excluded.

Wilkins and Gobby differentiate two types of governance practices: 'Instrumental-rational' and 'agonistic-political'.[13] The first relates to the blueprint for making schools publicly accountable 'audited and monitored, high achieving, financially sustainable, law compliant and non-discriminatory'.[14] This way, the authors assert, governance is seen as apolitical and technical. Leadership and management of schools as organizations are about striving to generate critical mass to meet certain strategic and operational priorities that enhance the quality and standards of schools.

However, this is highly politicized because school leadership must be deemed legitimate, aligning with a prevailing notion of educational leadership and its objectives. As previously described, the purpose of education, as Biesta contends, can be seen to encompass three dimensions: socialization, subjectification and qualification. Achieving a balance or realistically assigning different weights to these dimensions is a challenge. Consequently, leadership and its purpose also become more politically charged, involving decisions on emphasis or maintaining a delicate equilibrium. Yet Wilkins and Gobby ask: 'Who gets to decide the purpose and design of educational leadership?'[15] Furthermore, in light of the digitized classroom, how are decisions influenced when increasingly the EdTech industry plays a part?

Taking all this, we can establish a direct link between what is also needed for those who become part of this leadership and the educational configurations, that is, the EdTech actors themselves. In a word, the governance model applied to schools can be adopted to apply to the EdTech sector to ensure they are 'high achieving, financially sustainable, law compliant, and non-discriminatory',[16] instrumentally and practically.

Wilkins highlights[17] that the transition from government to governance has eased concerns like state monopoly while intensifying others. Paradoxically, governments advocating for decentralized governance have instituted 'hard governance'[18] elements such as accountability measures, performance targets and benchmarks in the aim to foster competition and also ensure collective trust within the system. The same therefore can be asked of the EdTech products and services and those configuring, controlling and owning them, where accountability measures can be introduced to ensure trust but also a 'race to the top' competition, as the example with companies measuring against each other across meeting ESGs. Companies compete across what benchmarks and standards they meet, not just across market capture. In other words, there is a logical need to implement similar 'hard governance' mechanisms to cultivate a positive cycle of trust-building with the private EdTech industry. In the words of the International Organisation for Standardisation (ISO):

> The overall aim of certifying products, processes or services is to give confidence to all interested parties that a product, process or service fulfils specified requirements. The value of certification is the degree of confidence and trust that is established by an impartial and competent demonstration of fulfilment of specified requirements by a third party.[19]

How does this translate for what societies should collectively demand when it comes to protecting the quality and sovereignty of public education? To begin with, the essence of good governance is that states represent their citizens and prioritize their duties to them. How they govern their citizens – and how citizens get on in their lives – can be a measurement of good governance. Since at least the nineteenth century industrial and democratic societies have maintained that education is state sovereignty.

Education is a powerful political tool through which history is interpreted, the organization of society is maintained, and a state's own international position is established. Education has its own sovereign freedom when it comes to enquiry, teaching, the development of thought and creativity. Good governance thus should maintain this independence from corporate influence of any kind because corporate interests are never in the best interests of individuals but in the best interests of their businesses. Yet the increasing dependency on data extractive systems has the capacity to take away this sovereignty. As I have described, digitizing education means allowing almost all forms of state governance for the protection of School's sovereignty to be relinquished into the hands of the private sector or concentrated into the hands of very few who access the systems, control, (re)configure and own them. But while a state's duty remains with its people, that of private actors remains with their business well-being.

Second, democratic governance suggests that governance is run in a trusted, transparent and accountable manner by democratic institutions at national, regional and local level.[20] According to the Council of Europe, democratic governance means that

> democracy and governance reinforce each other and are essential for preventing conflicts, promoting stability, managing crises, facilitating economic and social progress, and creating the conditions conducive to sustainable respect for human rights and the rule of law.[21]

In democracy, while an imperfect form of ruling, citizens participate in choosing the systems, the leaders of the institutions and even the laws that will support the democratic rule and the rule that serves them well. Yet, in School, we see systems that neither students nor teachers tend to choose. Moreover, the very products are often designed and hyperbolized in ways that it prevents for any informed decision and rational choice to be made, for disagreeing, resisting or even rejecting them.

And third, effective governance means that there is evidence and results that demonstrate the kind of governance a community or society has achieved. According to the United Nations Human Rights Office of the High Commissioner (OHCHR),[22] effective governance includes key attributes such as transparency, accountability, responsibility and participation and responsiveness (to people's needs). The effectiveness, however, is expressed in the evidence around each of these. Interestingly, accountability, responsibility and transparency have led to the 'audit culture' in education. Quantifying accountability through reports, assessments, evaluation of teachers, pedagogic practices, school processes and so on can be used as a model to build accountability system that governs EdTech integration, measures and holds accountable EdTech products and their providers.

Here I address *school governance*, which is a narrower term of *education governance*, which, as Wilkins and Olmedo discuss, 'aims at building relations of trust between schools and various stakeholders ... to bring lay and professional judgements to bear upon the actions of those who run schools'[23] such as teachers and school leaders. Schools typically have well-structured governing bodies, including governors and trustees, which undergo strict background checks, continuous training, and maintain clearly defined roles and responsibilities (which lie with the well-being of the students, staff, and the effective functioning of a school). Governing EdTech systems can follow similar principles to ensure that the businesses providing them are held accountable and that their products meet appropriate standards and benefit children and their education.

Here it is also relevant to add that governance is the contestation between decisions and judgements which are often presented as norms and values and as Kooiman and Jentoft describe 'implicitly or explicitly, governance means choosing between'[24] these. But there is also another contestation between theory and practice, empirical and conceptual work and by combining 'plurality of perspectives, analytical strategies and research approaches, thus aligning education governance more closely and rigorously to an interdisciplinary field of critical enquiry and scholarship'.[25] School governance represents power that is shifted away from the state into a group of various actors, networks and community members, but it is within these networks and partnerships that the role of data-driven systems and their automating and predictive capabilities emerge. Maintaining education governance sovereign and govern its transformation into what Gulson, Sellar and Web call synthetic governance[26] requires a similar approach to the 'audit culture' that has aimed to maintain quality and accountable educational institutions. How that can be implemented is the subject of the next section.

License to operate

The second sector to draw inspiration about EdTech governance, as surprising as that may be, is the online gambling industry. Similarly, the financial sector has strict licensing regimes, but because I have had experience and still collaborate with engineers, data security experts, and auditors from the online gambling sector, it is easier for me to describe it as a potential existing practice that we can draw from.

Here are a few important points to make from the start: the online gambling sector, like many EdTech products aim to 'engage' individuals – the more they stick around, the more the business provider benefits. The online gambling sector is also a highly lucrative one with an estimated $131 billion for 2027.[27] The projected revenue for the EdTech market is US$239 billion.[28] According to HolonIQ, a global market intelligence, the whole value of the education sector is estimated at $7.2 trillion.[29] This number combines the total global expenditure from governments, companies and consumers together. This makes education one of the world's single largest industry making more than 6 per cent of GDP,[30] yet in comparison to the online gambling industries its governance is more fragmented and with little concrete measures of oversight. With online gambling companies, one is required to obtain a licence in order to legally operate; with an EdTech platform there is no clear-cut process of licensing.

In online gambling, licensing (where such regimes are set up) strictly governs data and technical requirements and can even require intrusive monitoring of their systems.[31] In Malta for example, the Malta Gaming Authority is the regulatory body responsible for overseeing the regulation of the online gaming sector (as it is known). The authority's goal is to ensure integrity of gaming operators, fair playing and the well-being of players. Online gambling operators must obtain a licence from the authority in order to operate legally. A licence means that the operator's financial standing, business plan and technical set-up are examined and that it adheres to anti-money laundering and duty of care for the players requirements.

Player protection means that the authority emphasizes on the need for the licensed operators to ensure that they implement measures to prevent underage gambling and to promote responsible playing and evidence tools for players that help them set limits on their spending and playing time. Other controlling measures may be included under the condition of licensing such as implementing robust *Know Your Customer* procedures. These are also known in the financial sector. The entire licensing regime includes clear technical standards and compliance measures, with the ultimate goal of ensuring integrity and responsibility among online gambling operators. The licensing regime is supported by a complex organizational structure that includes audit, compliance and enforcement committees; fit and proper committees; a supervisory council and chief officers responsible for various activities, including regulatory, operational, finance and policy functions.[32]

Importantly, the licensing regime comprises systematic audits and compliance checks. These are conducted to validate and verify that operators adhere to all the requirements and standards. Rules and terms that make up the licensing conditions are also subject to updates and reviews. Technologies change and these may demand reviews and modifications of the existing guardrails.

Once an operator obtains a licence, it is not indefinite. These require renewal along with additional audits and verification of their systems. Similar regulation exists in the UK, in some American States and elsewhere. In the UK, the Gambling Commission oversees the online gambling industry. With the implementation of the Gambling Act of 2005, regulation of the online gambling sector was strengthened with the aim to protect children and vulnerable adults.

Operators are further subject to adhere to responsible advertising practices. Their commercial messages must not be misleading and must not target vulnerable individuals. Because of the nature of the business (people gambling money and often losing which also relates to addictions), the regulatory authorities put strong emphasis on the commitment to social responsibility. Licensed operators are expected to demonstrate such commitment, prevent and address whenever there are issues related to problem gambling.

That said, the online gambling sector still inflicts tremendous adverse effects on young people. A recent study identified that around 55,000 children and young people in the UK were facing problems with online gambling. In 2019, a survey reported that 11 per cent of eleven to sixteen-year-olds[33] engaged in online gambling-style games, while 47 per cent of those used mobile apps for such activities.[34]

Similar to online gambling, education is increasingly online and digital. Neither of these online domains however is likely to prohibit or remove any part of the digital. Yet, outside of the education domain, the health sector, child's rights activists and experts, child psychologists and others address screen addiction and the negative impact of digital media on the growing child.[35] There are even industry representatives openly speaking about the addictive models and tactics tech developers and entrepreneurs use that thrive on our human vulnerabilities[36] (see *Hooked: How to Build Habit-Forming Products* by Nir Eyal).[37] EdTech and online gambling differ significantly of course, and comparing them may even be perceived as offensive to some. However, while online gambling is strictly regulated – or, where it is not, it is simply illegal – EdTech, with many of the products' features resembling online gambling (e.g. winning and losing tokens and digital badges), is not regulated in the same strict sense.

For one, public perception and historical context play a crucial role, with gambling historically associated with concerns like fraud and addiction.

EdTech, on the other hand, is often perceived as a positive force for education and innovation – so, the logic goes, no one should touch it. Not licensing EdTech unlike online gambling operators can be seen as unnecessary because the focus is more on the opportunity these technologies provide for education. It is the benefit (or at least the potential) that leaves the door open to these products without much thorough diligence.

Licensing in online gambling aims to protect consumers from fraud, ensure fair play and address addiction. Operators have a clear framework which they need to adhere, standards to meet in order to be licensed to legally run their businesses. In the EdTech sector, while there is more awareness and pressure that they demonstrate data privacy and security requirements are met, the primary focus has often been on ensuring quality education and demonstrating 'what works' and their pedagogic value. Therefore, such perceived need for licensing (with strict scrutiny and intrusive assessments) is not apparent. The EdTech industry is also becoming localized (smaller products and operators while most of their services are hosted on larger US cloud providers) and unless it is seen for the fact that much of the big platforms and digital infrastructures are ultimately a concentrated power on its own, legislation may not face similar to the online gambling level of international coordination.

The two sectors can also be seen at different maturity levels which reflect the level of scrutiny. Unlike the online gambling sector, the EdTech sector is considered less mature which is flawed. Most of the biggest companies providing digital infrastructure and services have been around for over 20 years. A company like Anthology mentioned earlier has been around since 1988 as a campus management and providing administrative functions. Even after a decade in the market, Century Tech still labels itself as 'small' (as an aside, having no significant financial growth is odd after 10 years but also the 'small' status has allowed the company to refrain from disclosing financial accounts, which is also reflective of the common practice among many EdTech companies of keeping their business models and true financial viability in obscurity). The question then becomes: How can we translate the audit culture of education and the licensing regime of the online gambling to address the need for governing the EdTech sector?

From the ground up and inside out

To start with, the likeliness of imposing top-down rules – introduce a standard – is challenging for a sector the majority of which is small companies. We already witness how challenging it is even without much scrutiny and regulation of the EdTech market. I meet many EdTech start-ups who tell me this: 'I don't have the funding to be assessed but can you just send us a to-do list of what we should meet?' Ninety-three per cent of EdTech companies in the UK, according to one estimation,[38] are considered small and medium-sized enterprises and only 7 per cent are considered large companies.

Most of these companies would have products with components bootstrapped off-the-shelf with messy code and gone to market as quick as possible to ensure they show proof of concept and signup customers, or test freely first, soon after selling premium services, only then think of cleaning up the house and figure out what is 'ethically' necessary to add.

Fouad, for instance, argues that the costs of cyber incidents tend to be transferred to the end users, and, due to the lack of state mandates, there is little incentive for EdTech companies to prioritize budgets and efforts to increase the security of their products. This creates a 'culture of acceptance for software and hardware insecurity'.[39] Flawless cybersecurity, and with that 100 per cent individual privacy, the industry may argue, is never achievable. However, this does not mean that liability should be left entirely to the end user. Even if the industry bears the cost of cyber incidents, some argue[40] that the end user (schools) will still pay the final (increased) price. In either scenario – whether industry or end users bear the costs and liabilities of insecurities – the risks of cybercrime remain. An alternative therefore is, as Fouad maintains, for government intervention by incentivizing the sector to prioritize their cybersecurity efforts by legislating security incident reporting and by providing standards or models for security requirements that schools should look for when procuring EdTech products.

Similarly, when the age-appropriate design code came into force in 2020 in the UK, online companies that fall within the scope of the code (i.e., be considered an Information Society Services including 'apps, programs, websites, games or community environments, and devices with or without a screen that process personal data and are likely to be accessed by children in the UK')[41] had a twelve-month transition period to meet it. However, while all eyes have been on Big Tech and how they implement the necessary changes to meet the code and much change indeed has taken place worth celebrating, there are ongoing concerns due to persistent systemic breaches contravening with the code.[42]

EdTech providers must meet cybersecurity, data privacy, age-appropriate designs and accessibility requirements, among other things. They must also provide evidence of their pedagogic value, demonstrate how they prioritize children's rights, ensure their well-being and show algorithmic fairness where relevant. Is it realistic to expect from the whole sector to meet these even if a grace period is provided? Is it realistic to expect all

EdTech companies to meet even half of these criteria? Furthermore, is there a system in place that has the capacity to monitor that the sector complies? The answer to these questions is no. So what can be done and where to begin?

Undeniably, there is a need for both top-down and bottom-up efforts and significant financial, human and other resources to achieve both. In the first case, top-down efforts should demonstrate governments' clear thinking and decision-making about education regardless of the digital market's preferences. Governments should mandate that the EdTech sector meets necessary privacy and security criteria when it comes to their use of children's data. However, this is not to say that meeting privacy and security criteria, data can be automatically utilized. On that point also, standards around data privacy and security already exist. Clear procedures for and systematic scrutiny of the companies however are also necessary.

Outside-in and bottom-up forms of oversight and control should also be encouraged through mandates and welcomed by industry. Data privacy compliance can be helpful to build trust between education stakeholders and the EdTech industry. However, these are limited as assessments have yet to cover many more aspects like data processing and repurposing of data, logic models, values companies put on education and children's well-being and so on. Elsewhere,[43] I suggested adding that governance of EdTech should be seen from technological, ethical, socio-structural and pedagogical lenses. More recently, having been a part of several large working groups, one seeking to develop a cybersecurity framework for K-12 education, and one European project that works on developing a framework to assess the well-being of children in the digital education, has led to expanding the scope of requirements. Added to these are the need to ascertain how businesses uphold children's human rights and how they design their products to cater for children with different learning needs.[44] Updating the criteria of assessments will certainly be work in progress as technologies advance – new requirements may emerge. And so, minimal principles of assessment can look like this (Figure 8.1).

Each of the five broader groups or modules of characteristics already represents existing frameworks and standards that are either catering for the wider technology sector or address specific needs relating to children, education or both. While some of these 'vertical' modules have already been mentioned in the previous chapter, here I will only briefly reference the underpinned standards and literature.

Data privacy and responsibility incorporate not only data privacy requirements as stipulated by the EU (or the UK) GDPR; it queries operators

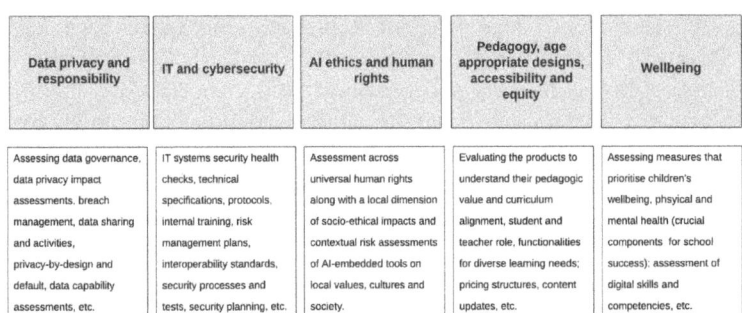

Figure 8.1 Minimum principles and standards that EdTech operators should meet in an ideal 'license-to-operate' scenario.

to provide records of processing, consent and notices and to identify their maturity with regard to data capabilities.[45] This means that EdTech operators should be able to provide insight about the maturity of their organizations and their software capabilities with regard to data processing and utilization (as was the example with the AI capabilities Anthology and other platforms like it deploys).

The cybersecurity requirements reflect existing directives (like the EU NIS2 Directive mentioned in Chapter 7) but also the Global Education Security Standard (GESS),[46] the result of a collective work of international stakeholders. GESS is a 'a matrix/crosswalk of all existing security frameworks along with the core set of controls applicable to PK-20 data' (where PK-20 means pre-kindergarten (PK) through higher education). Aspects of AI and contextual socio-ethical criteria will be challenging since industry has to allow that their code is assessed. Also, socio-ethical aspects will necessitate external expertise to evaluate how the product meets local cultures, values and needs.[47] With regard to the pedagogic assessments, some organizations[48] already make a great effort to assess products pedagogically albeit in isolation of all other important criteria which limits the scope to have a comprehensive understanding of the EdTech sector. And lastly, measuring well-being, frameworks such as the Self-reflection on Effective Learning by Fostering Innovation through Educational Technology (SELFIE)[49] which is based on the DigCompOrg conceptual framework, encompasses some key elements that look at ways to effectively integrate EdTech into school policies, processes and practices. These do not specifically assess the EdTech products themselves; however, the development of measures that do so is critical in order to educate and nudge the EdTech sector to prioritize across well-being factors.

A standardized framework and compliance can create hope for a responsible EdTech sector. For such work to take on, we further need enforcement mechanisms and a standardized comprehensive licensing system. Such system should consider educational values, opportunity costs or risks, usability, accessibility, interoperability, data protection, pedagogy, safety, well-being and security as drawn out in Figure 8.1. Indeed, these are many requirements, and they should not be disregarded for the sake of market advancements. Undeniably, many EdTech companies may not be able to meet them and obtain a licence. But can we be honest that some products are just not worth the cost and time?

Added to such requirements is transparency at the level of the software code itself. Is it possible that within the code are baked dangerous permissions that enable data sharing with third parties for commercial purposes? The Human Rights Watch report in 2022 found out that it is as some were described earlier. The International Data Accountability Council[50] had discovered similar unethical practices only two years before that. Then, what is the way to intrusively monitor companies when impact assessments and reading policies seem unable to prevent such unethical and unfair practices?

There are intrusive monitoring systems used in the case with online gambling. Coin-in and coin-out transactions are monitored in real time to ensure that no malpractice is at play when it comes to people's betting. The 'house always wins' but algorithms playing to that tune can be detected instantly. Such intrusive systems require regulatory provisions. This means that both static and dynamic (real-time) monitoring and audits should be mandated top-down.

Assessments and external validation are already happening ad hoc through research and as the industry players themselves try to do their part and show responsibility. These are good starting points reflecting on the 'outside in' or 'inside out' form of governance – that is, external validation (looking outside into the company), made transparent to the relevant publics and support educational institutions in their procurement. But again, these ad hoc practices such as DPO data privacy impact assessments, data privacy policy assessments or independent consultancies will not transform the industry. Also, such assessments are expensive. They are limited in scope and isolated in terms of impact on the industry's journey to amending their practices.

A case in point is with cybersecurity assessments. From the perspective of information security economics, for instance, security failures in the digital domain can be seen as poor security investments and practices because of poor market decisions, the lack of policy incentives to prioritize cybersecurity, little cost-benefits since cybersecurity measures are preventive, not motivated by profit and overall lack of regulation.

Yet cybersecurity is a crucial prerequisite to the safety of children in a digitized education. Cybersecurity attacks disrupt education, lead to loss of sensitive information about children and teachers and render systems unusable; some schools have even been forced to shut down.[51] Student data breaches, ransomware attacks, social media defacement, online class and school meeting disruptions are some of the incidents that affect education and individuals.[52] In 2021, ransomware attacks cost $3.56 billion to schools in the United States.[53] Between 2021 and 2022 around 41 per cent of primary schools and 70 per cent of secondary schools in the UK experienced cyber breaches.[54] In the United States, Illuminate Education, an educational software, went through an avalanche of cyberattacks affecting the personal information of millions of current and former students.[55]

At a high level, it is important to structure a cycle (Figure 8.2) in which the assessment process of EdTech providers and their products are being reviewed. This cyclical system will enable for the requirements to be regularly updated, inform stakeholders and maintain transparent process of what is being assessed, who is being assessed and what the outcomes are.

A comprehensive governance framework across socio-technical, ethical, critical pedagogic, and human rights imperatives for governing the digitization of education is a systematic iterative process that requires funding, multi-stakeholder effort and consensus. Figure 8.2 is an attempt to draw an applied governance framework and methodology. As mentioned earlier, both the audit culture of education in Western societies like the UK and the United States, and the online gambling licensing models serve well to structure meaningful governance for the EdTech sector. In practice, this takes the following approach (Figure 8.3).

An assessment of EdTech operators would be a systematic check and understanding through a methodology similar to any review process of academic research: having 'hard' and concrete measures of assessment, blind

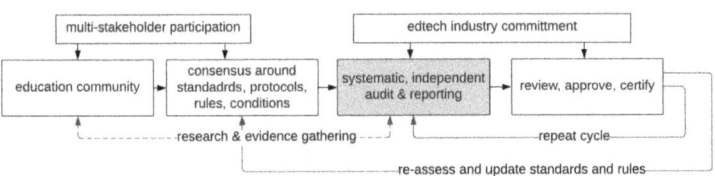

Figure 8.2 How to ensure that EdTech mediate and influence teaching and learning to the benefit of children?

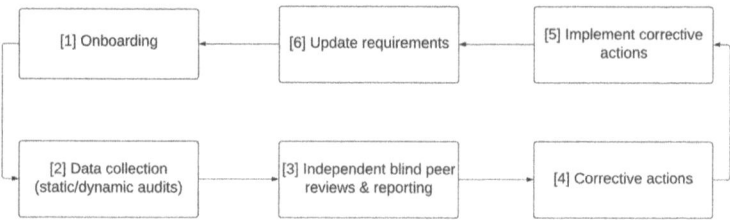

Figure 8.3 Cyclical audit of EdTech operators.

peer reviews, external validation and benchmarking (against other EdTech operators) which will rank them and therefore foster competition through a 'race to the top', corrective actions demanded from the EdTech operator; in some cases – rejection.

An audit would look like this (Figure 8.3):

- Obtaining primitives about the operator – basic data about aspects such as company name and organizational structure, values and teams' education background, financial health check and business model, country of registration.
- Standard or framework against which the operator's product is assessed (security, privacy, ethics, algorithmic fairness, pedagogic or accessibility criteria and so on).
- Report with corrective actions that the operator must meet.
- Audit approach and methodology – enquiry-based interviews; observations; tests around product functionalities; key persons included in the audits; and any tests made to the system.
- Evidence obtained during the audits to substantiate the results – what documents were reviewed, their versions and dates, any walkthroughs that were performed, samples reviewed, policies and terms of services – and their updates and so on.
- Audit results and corrective actions and recommendations made.
- Management plan and deadlines for any pending issues that need to be resolved.
- Repeat audits annually (or quarterly of some aspects of the audit process).

This is one way to concretize action, although this can take different forms. The objective is to begin from somewhere with greater effort driving towards an audit-to-license regime. Certainly, there are assessments done with various EdTech accelerator programs (for example the University College London

Edtech Labs[56]), independent research and through industry-led initiatives (such as the EU Edtech Alliance). However, this work also needs regulatory teeth – greater scrutiny, fines, not just reprimands[57] and even revoking of licences or suspending operations.

In *Between Truth and Power* Julie Cohen argues that 'to be effective, policymakers must devise ways of enabling regulators to evaluate algorithmically embedded controls that may themselves have been designed to detect and evade oversight'.[58] This requires more intrusive monitoring, more teeth. As asserted in the previous chapter, assessing across data privacy is not enough to assure that the socio-ethical issues are addressed where data-intensive applications influence decisions in education. As Mantelero contends, 'it is the sensitive nature of the processing, the size of the data sets, and the knowledge extraction power and complexity of the process that is truly different'[59] and requires deeper and wider scrutiny.

Broussard describes algorithmic auditing as the means to see what an algorithm does and how it may fail or inflict bias. Algorithmic auditing already adds to the complex and long list of criteria to assess EdTech providers in a license-to-operate regime. Cathy O'Neil, the author of *Weapons of Math Destruction*, leads the field of algorithmic auditing with her ORCAA organization, in which auditing begins with two simple questions:

- What does it mean for this algorithm to work?
- How could this algorithm fail, and for whom?[60]

These are not only important questions to start an audit but also important points for both governments to find rationale for stricter scrutiny and for schools to demand to see evidence as part of their procurement processes.

An audit-to-license regime also requires financing because audits are not cheap. But there is good news for several reasons. First, educational institutions are more aware of this need and support it fully. Many schools and Multi Academy Trusts in the UK for instance see this beyond their capacity to deal with assessment as part of their procurement process. A nation-wide vetting program – or licensing regime – will solve an initial big hurdle. Second, international organizations are also becoming more vocal about this need. UNESCO and the World Bank are highlighting the problems around fragmented EdTech procurement and are showing support to identify structures that will facilitate a 'race to the top' for EdTech operators. Third, there is a growing participation by mediating assessment brokers who are investing in time and effort to vet and assess EdTech products and services. While I am a part of one such effort, the challenges in this regard are the expense involved and the general reticence of the sector to be forthcoming and transparent. 'There is a silver lining in the push for a licensing regime. Licensing incurs costs, which are covered by industry representatives in sectors like online gaming. In the case with auditing schools as my second example, both independent and state schools incur compliance costs. If the EdTech industry cannot afford to pay for audits and obtain operational licenses, that itself is information worth knowing.' Governments, particularly the education sector, can financially benefit from the lucrative EdTech market.[61] There is a risk that a licensing regime will not take off which goes on to question the finances underpinning these imagined digital futures[62] In that sense, bad news is still news: we get to know the sector more realistically.[63] That said, more operators are willing to participate, having gained pressure both from the public and schools.

Fourth, alternative calls for public interest technologies have also come to the fore not just in the EdTech realm but for technologies generally and globally. These are exactly what they sound – developing technologies that serve in the public interest. This can mean both, in technological sense, creating products that serve in the public interest or in methodological sense, creating auditing systems that ensure the products work in the public interest.

In their book *Power to the Public*, McGuiness and Schank describe them thus: '[W]e define public interest technology as the application of design, data, and delivery to advance the public interest and promote the public good in the digital age.'[64] Broussard further defines algorithmic auditing and algorithmic accountability reporting as strands of public interest technology that can 'show most promise for remedying algorithmic harms'.[65] As such, auditing should be seen as a 'public interest technology' that needs to be developed from now for the EdTech sector.

Defending their values

In Chapter 6 I discussed the purpose of School and attempted to highlight its good intentions and value. School is also an institution that serves in the public interest and typically has values reflecting that.[66] Here are randomly picked school values: independence, cooperation, generosity, freedom, caring, tolerance, love; compassion, community-minded, cooperation, courage, accountability, appreciation; respect, responsibility, tolerance, thoughtfulness, friendship, love, courage, appreciation, honesty, empathy; respect, honesty, integrity, care, fairness, creativity, collaboration, trustworthiness, responsibility; perseverance, responsibility, honesty (being trustworthy and showing integrity), patience, respect everyone, be kind and helpful, always try your best, never be afraid to make a mistake. Ask any public school, and their values are likely to be a mixture of similar words. However, how do these blend when schools' infrastructures become entangled with digital systems whose often commercial entities have different values that typically start with the word 'market'?

A 'clash of values'[67] arises between educational institutions prioritizing student well-being, diversity, autonomy and privacy, and EdTech businesses that, conversely, prioritize their own commercial interests. That is, commercial digital tools are deployed in public spaces, but both entities would have different values and commitments, thus creating moral, ethical and even legal conflicts.

For example, as Bogaerts, van Dijck and Zuckerman describe,[68] a public broadcaster in the Netherlands, having grown dependence on proprietary digital infrastructures, is left with little room to function independently online. So, to evaluate their audience impact, on which the broadcaster's funding depends, the organization deploys traffic analytics software such as Google and uses commercial products like Microsoft CRM and others. To measure audience engagement and interact with their audience further, the broadcaster also resorts to social media platforms like YouTube, Twitter and Facebook. Nevertheless, all these digital products are built with commercial interest that is to extract data from individuals (the broadcaster's own audience in this case) to monetize and exploit it as their main economic model.[69] In other words, the public broadcaster who serves in the public interest automatically exposes their own audience to the commercial surveillance and privacy loss as a result of its digital dependence. This serves as an example to demonstrate how any institution serving in the public interest, including public education, can become 'trapped in a digital ecosystem driven by commercial and corporate values'[70] and clash with them.

To maintain its core values, the authors describe how the broadcaster has worked through a five-step process, developed by a Dutch PublicSpaces coalition of cultural organizations who defend five specific core values of their organizations specifically openness, transparency, accountability, autonomy and user-centredness (including a user's right to privacy). This approach is flexible enough to apply to any public interest entity, including educational institutions. The steps[71] are as follows:

1. *Inventory*: providing clear values of the organization, the initial work is to make an inventory of all the digital products that it uses organize

them across operations (internal among staff, external with students and other entities).
2. *Spreadsheet*: a yes/no questionnaire encompassing all digital tools utilized by the organization and its affiliated partners, including PublicSpaces' five core values, is employed. This questionnaire prompts the organization to assess each software's compliance and rank its alignment with the core values.
3. *Applying a score*: the organization is asked to provide a score to each software product which can and how well it complies with the organization's public values. The score can range from 0 (no compliance with the five core values at all) to 100 to indicate complete compliance.
4. *Roadmap to improvement*: the scores allow for a more concrete and transparent way of looking at what products the institution is working with and arrive at the possibility of replacing the software that scores the lowest.
5. *Publish roadmap and exchange best practices*: Make these assessments public and share with other educational institutions to create transparency, pressure and build trust from the ground up (starting with educational institutions).

These are undeniably practical ways of auditing in-house and equipping schools to defend their own values. They do not have to do this alone but in coalitions with other schools and even delegate this work to resourceful organizations to support this initiative. Having said that, in-house or collectively, they would still require means and capacity to produce such work at scale. Additionally, many educational institutions also enter contractual agreements and commitments from which there is no straightforward and cheap exit. For example, public school administrations in the Netherlands have joined the PublicSpaces initiative, urging commercial EdTech operators to show ethical practices, enhance privacy settings and offer fairer pricing.[72] Moreover, since clashes in values are not unique to cultural organizations or the education sector only, greater cross-sectoral effort and collaboration can re-shift the balance of power and put more pressure on commercial technology companies. It can also result in the innovation of open-source software products that are otherwise expensive to produce by individual sectors. This kind of bottom-up work also adds to the overall pressure for the development of more ethical and value-based products by industry itself – another push towards a 'race to the top'.

Conclusions

Lack of regulation that requires to see the 'ingredients' of the EdTech software, its objectives and its effects leaves the customer in the dark with a 'medicine' that promises to heal all ills. So far, education stakeholders know little about the ingredients as much as their own engineers do (note, in many cases these are *not* educators). This knowledge asymmetry is not conducive to trust and not a safe way of moving ahead with digitizing education globally. Not knowing how something works or what its ingredients (such as of your computer or a kitchen appliance) are not the cause of distrust, but the symptom of the exploitative and unethical practices digital technology companies have been caught doing.

The premise that digitizing education with data-intensive algorithmic systems will lead to innovation, free teachers of mundane work (such as data analysis, writing reports and preparing lesson plans) to focus on more meaningful one like being with their students is erroneous. In the first case, data extraction and rendering it for automation of processes or behavioural modification of children must not be overlooked in terms of how that influences both processes and individuals daily and long-term in the future. In the second case, technologies have always held the hope to gain us free time, time that can be spent on more meaningful things. Instead, however, with digital mediation we have transferred work outside the classroom or office – and it still leaves us no time to ever finish all tasks. If teachers can automate their lesson planning today, their free time may easily be filled with more work like adding students virtually. If a physical classroom only takes thirty students, the digital classroom can take unlimited avatars, digital versions of students. Essentially, within these imaginaries we should consider the quality of education.

The education community – teachers, students, school leaders and administrators, EdTech procurement and financial departments – should demand that their governments demonstrate clear thinking through their policies when it comes to digitizing education and embedding AI. For one, this means that the obsession with digital solutions should not be blinding to non-digital and equally valid alternatives. Opportunities for learning and future should not be constantly explained through digital projects. Furthermore, it is crucial to acknowledge the cost of digital dependence on both the environment and humanity, particularly its impact on the sovereignty of public education and the prospects for future generations.

Cost versus levelling up

Speaking of cost, to provide education is substantial but so is the digitization. More than twenty years ago, in 2000, during the United Nations Millennial Summit the future Sustainable development Goal #4 was articulated: 'To ensure inclusive and quality education for all and promote lifelong learning'.[73] Delivering high-quality education for all, however, still seems like an impossible task considering the limited resources available per student. What constitutes 'good quality' education also seems like a constantly moving target. Today 'good quality' is often connected with digital presence in schools and how well they prepare students for the digital age and the age of AI according to policymakers and industry usually siting at the same table. But the cost of sovereignty should also be considered and with great urgency. Schools can lose when they submit to the data colonialism, which, as Couldry and Mejias argue,[74] only serves capitalist expansion and enriches the very few (the owners of the digital systems).

It is tempting to know that AI can be the great equalizer. In his book *The Coming Wave*, Mustafa Suleyman, one of the founders of DeepMind, says that AI 'will offer extraordinary new medical advances and clean energy breakthroughs, creating not just new businesses but new industries and quality of life improvements in almost every imaginable area'.[75] That is true at the minimum condition that it does not come with a premium subscription. In the neoliberal market, it always does. We have ChatGPT today, but it only has some 'knowledge' up to 2021. Premium use – assuming better libraries, data and outputs – comes at the minimum of $20 a month. For now. Khan Academy with its Khanmigo and TeachMateAI, described earlier, too, can be the great 'equalizer' tools, only if one is ready to pay for them.

This is less about access and more about the financial shackles that the increasingly essential digital industry can clasp around societies. The disparities therefore will not only worsen, but it can become entirely impossible for any levelling up.

From delivering quality education has derived the delivery of 'lifelong' learning much of which has sparked again the imagination of ed- and Big Tech businesses alike. 'Lifelong' learning has come to mean that one is never good enough. Not that we do not learn because learning happens every day, but a certain lifelong learning is pushed through the need for data collection, banking skills and showing accreditation for them. The frequency and speed with which educational policies and frameworks are proposed to update curricula in the Western context are head-spinning. In Chapter 2 I brought to the fore Bourdieu's argument around *flexploitation*. In his essay *Job Insecurity Is Everywhere Now*, Bourdieu articulates job insecurity as a structural violence that begins from casualization which profoundly affects 'the person who suffers it: by making the whole future uncertain it prevents all rational anticipation and, in particular, the basic belief and hope in the future that one needs in order to rebel, especially collectively, against present conditions, even the most intolerable'.[76] The sense of precarity ensues.

Similarly, Tyler Cowen[77] describes the world in which a zero-sum game awaits those who lack the 'right' education and skills – another crisis is articulated. Precarity sets in – the 'permanent threat of unemployment'.[78] Cowen depicts a dreadful future landscape where automation and computational capabilities will create a 'hyper-meritocracy' in which the 1 per cent will marvel in abundance while the majority will suffer precarity and unemployment. This, Bourdieu argues, is a 'practical instituting of a Darwinian world in which the springs of commitment in the job and the company are found in insecurity' – the 'ultimate basis of this economic order placed under the banner of individual freedom is indeed the structural violence of unemployment'.[79]

The so-called 'middle class' is hollowed out and 'a new global underclass' has risen – 'an opaque world of employment that is "ghost work"'[80] is formed. In that regard, temporary or alternative contract-driven work brought by self-employed workers or those temporarily employed – the so-called casualization of the workforce – has grown from 10 to 16 per cent in the US economy over the past decade.[81] Casualization can be observed as product of digital automation which, as discussed in Chapter 4, seemingly affords efficiencies and comforts that depend on significant human labour. Mary Gray and Siddharth Suri expose this hidden cost, describing a world of work where salaries and job security are replaced by a chaotic line of micropayments and projects, what once was the assembly line of the factory jobs. The flexploitation. But flexploitation is not levelling up.

Digitizing education for designing future workers

The digital gig and casual jobs are everywhere including in the EdTech industry. Products like Gaggle[82] track students' socio-emotional behaviour by scanning their Google files. Behind this scanning are part-time remote workers doing a 'dead-end job'.[83] A parent once told me[84] how Gaggle was installed on her daughter's Chromebook; objecting to it, she would not be able to access Google Classroom. If there was, say, 'any concern detected (for example suicidal thoughts of a student), this would be reported to a call centre in Chicago with a bunch of part-time employees who would have access to our children's private information like where they lived, what grade they were and their student ID number'. Amazon, with its Mechanical Turk, has been at the forefront of driving exactly this kind of 'gig' work.

The expectations begin to hang so intensely onto the shoulders of educational institutions to deliver educated young people, equipped with the 'right' skills. Human capital investment, banking skills – digital micro-credentials – and catching up to the constantly changing demands for competencies and skills become all the prerequisites and educational priorities. The expectations are to stress on innovation – the digital, now data, now synthetic economy – or become inapt, irrelevant, unemployed. Alexander J. Means noted that by addressing highly automated futures, education systems downsize in all areas – such as literature, philosophy, political science, fine arts – that are unrelated to the core 'value-adding' Science Technology Engineering and Mathematics (STEM) fields, 'while also creating new degree programs in areas designed to serve the rich, such as elite spa therapy, plastic surgery rehabilitation and butler etiquette'. Tyler Cowen imagines a future mirroring a digitized neo-feudal version of Downton Abbey.[85]

As Herbert Marcuse wrote in *One-Dimensional Man*, '[i]n the construction of the technological reality there is no such thing as a purely rational scientific order. The process of technological rationality is a political process'.[86] Megan Ericson further puts it bluntly:

For the elite business class, the animating purpose of technology in classrooms is to develop human capital more efficiently, to make some people smarter and faster, and sort out the rest into the discard pile of American capitalism: low-wage labour. Because industrial capitalism makes us all, workers and capitalists alike, dependent on the market for acquisition of the basic necessities of life, we live lives dominated by market imperatives.[87]

To this end, the book also discussed the purpose of education.

The purpose of education

There is a continuity of class division and therefore the purpose of education for some, more than others, is always different. Public education in Anglo-American contexts continues to be largely defined by the neoliberalist imperatives, and digital systems re-enforce this bigger picture, as Chapter 3 described. If Python takes two to six months to learn and any toddler can learn to navigate through a smart phone in a matter of minutes, what is the rush to occupy lessons in any of that? Why not teach children to learn something more complex like languages? That Google can translate is not an automated activity that saves time; it deprives children of the profound knowledge that springs from learning a language and another culture.

EdTech products are also mostly about the technique of how to provide education. In 1970s Neil Postman and Charles Weingartner argued that, at least in much of the Western societies, 99.9 per cent of all the public hollering about education was about the technique.[88] There is plenty of evidence that in 2024 it still is. But technique says nothing about the values or the content it aims to impart. (Do students study history? What history do they study? Who wrote it? How does the teacher teach it? Do students participate with discussions?) The focus has moved so past the individual towards the advancing machinations of efficiency, what digital technologies are at their core, that little to nothing is said about what these produce; even less so – *who* should say what they are expected to produce.

An algorithm dressed in a colourful design promising to teach all children in the world to become excellent coders is an ambitious business (and policy) goal. But this does not answer whether that is what is worth achieving and whether that is what every single child in the world aims for. These become futile philosophical questions that find no use in today's growing market of EdTech products and services. Meanwhile, those of the privileged few, it is said,[89] are studying in schools that prioritize the harder tasks and shun technologies during the formative years – a great irony that those same Silicon Valley supporters for the digitization of education globally keep their own children away from their own tech products.

The debates about the digitization of education should maintain equal space for thinking about and discussing the purpose of education, in spite of technological advancements. This is in part what inspired this book. Media, policy, powerful marketing rhetoric and convincing technical language build up a reality which turns into pseudo-science and turns into history that becomes inevitable and is not questioned.

It is perhaps useful to point what Foucault in his own writings, he says, wanted to do. It was 'to show people that they are much freer than they feel that people accept as truth, as evidence, some themes which have been built up at a certain moment during history, and that this so-called evidence can be criticized and destroyed'.[90] We should conceive of the possibility that we can collectively resist the automatic acceptance of the digital promise because they only have specific techniques and not universal truths. The same way we should question and resist the digital classroom as the truth and science about bringing up individuals as subjects of their own lives, rather than objects in the world of objects.

Education is about learning to read the word and the world, in Paulo Freire's words.[91] That means that even when words are someone else's, it is our own imagination that can build images and worlds through those words we learn to master. Using the rear-view mirrors that are digital devices, whose concrete images and algorithms of exactitude deliver their own wrought worlds, makes it very hard to overcome and imagine our own. It is the true learning when ideation and originality emerge that is not one presented in the digital menu. But that cannot happen without reading and exchanges of stories through the social relations that form part of education. It cannot happen through apps and platforms that convert children as green and red emojis according to their academic performance. School is but one of these milieus where social relations are deliberately provided; the socialization is now interrupted by rear-view devices in the promise that more of them will lay the ground work for the 'inevitable' digital future.

In this book I hoped that whether it is practitioners, undergraduates, early career researchers, policymakers, industry providers, advocates, or parents reading, everyone engaged in the education and well-being of children should have a sense of the spectrum of issues that concern education as it transitions to digital form.

Digitization is not about providing devices and applications connected to the internet although, if that is all it really is, it would have been a rather straightforward discussion. Designing larger systems similar to those in Australia and the United States, as described in Chapter 3, the digital education strategies in the EU and the cradle-to-career data pipelines and AI integration for steering 'talent' from the early years are unprecedented designs, which can only be described as digital *matrices* for the attribution of individuals and populations. While I have remained focused on developments in the Western context, digital futures are also planned for the rest of the world. The Secretary General of the United Nations *Roadmap for Digital Cooperation*[92] has drafted plans for how the world should be digitized. Projects like GIGA aim to wire all schools of the world to the internet. Platform Gateways[93] is building 'digital libraries' of pre-approved (by whom is unclear) EdTech platforms and digital education content for the developing world. Funding outpours for platforms of unknown quality via organizations such as Global Partnership for Education, The Rockefeller Foundation, and others.[94] It is great to think that all schools will be wired to the internet, given that this is what all school children in the world equally need. But these can also be seen as 'metapolicies' drafted by multistakeholder alliances and coalitions driving global digitization[95] and steering educational systems in the direction of the digital matrix because it also makes great commercial sense.[96] The digital matrix is presented through data and algorithms that is imagined solving problems like poverty, hunger, ignorance, ecological disasters and war. But these algorithms are proprietary – someone designs, controls and owns them; they are complex, inaccessible and mostly untested. The bigger picture of this matrix (or matrices) is not known either.

One can argue that such matrix in which education globally is drawn into is the base of the politics of globalism behind which is neoliberalist thinking – the markets depend on growth and hunger for more. Digital matrices have generic designs and promise efficiency, prediction with precision, and access to education and to resources in general. Compare any EdTech product's marketing text; they all sprinkle similar words around them: 'empowerment', 'equity', 'success'. Combined, however, they have very specific hegemonic goals. One can question them as an output of the neoliberal market rules brought onto societies and geographies everywhere. Digitization, just like globalism, is proposed across geographies and populations with an undertaking that this is the better way of living, and bounty awaits for those who adopt it and have the right skills to face it. But just like School is governed through strict accountability rules, so must the digital products and actors that are defining this new matrix School is lured into.

While education is considered a human right, it is a privilege for businesses to sell products in education. Businesses should earn this privilege, while governments must defend children's most basic of rights, the right to be their own subject and design their own future through quality education, not by what they see in the rear-view mirror of the digital system they are bound to.

Notes

Chapter 1

1. Garner, R. (2002), 'School-Gate Drug Dealers Face Longer Jail Sentences', *The Independent*, 22 May. Available online: https://www.independent.co.uk/news/uk/politics/schoolgate-drug-dealers-face-longer-jail-sentences-130162.html (Accessed 30 July 2023).
2. United Nations Office on Drugs and Crime (2017), *Handbook on Children Recruited and Exploited by Terrorist and Violent Extremist Groups: The Role of the Justice System*, Vienna: United Nations Office on Drugs and Crime. Available online: https://www.unodc.org/documents/justice-and-prison-reform/Child-Victims/Handbook_on_Children_Recruited_and_Exploited_by_Terrorist_and_Violent_Extremist_Groups_the_Role_of_the_Justice_System.E.pdf (Accessed 30 July 2023).
3. Zuboff, S. (2019), *The Age of Surveillance Capitalism: The Fight for a Human Future at The New Frontier of Power*, London: Profile Books.
4. Liu, Z., Iqbal, U., and Saxena, N. (2023), 'Opted Out, Yet Tracked: Are Regulations Enough to Protect Your Privacy?' [Online] *arXiv.org*. doi: https://doi.org/10.48550/arXiv.2202.00885.
5. Human Rights Watch (2022), 'Online Learning Products Enabled Surveillance of Children', *HRW*, 12 July. Available online: https://www.hrw.org/news/2022/07/12/online-learning-products-enabled-surveillance-children (Accessed 30 July 2023).
6. Federal Trade Commission (2023), 'FTC Will Require Microsoft to Pay $20 Million over Charges It Illegally Collected Personal Information from Children without Their Parents' Consent', *FTC*, 5 June. Available online: https://www.ftc.gov/news-events/news/press-releases/2023/06/ftc-will-require-microsoft-pay-20-million-over-charges-it-illegally-collected-personal-information (Accessed 30 July 2023).
7. Mollenkamp, D. (2022), 'Popular K-12 Tool Edmodo Shuts Down', *EdSurge*, 16 August. Available online: https://www.edsurge.com/news/2022-08-16-popular-k-12-tool-edmodo-shuts-down (Accessed 30 July 2023).
8. Reuters (2021), 'Daily Mail Owner Sells Its Edtech Business Hobsons for about $410 Million', *Reuters*, 18 February. Available online: www.reuters.com/article/us-dmgt-divestiture-hobsons-idUSKBN2AI2T5 (Accessed 30 July 2023).
9. Sanger, D. E. (1984), 'Computer Makers Pursuing Campus Sales and Research', *The New York Times Archive*, 20 January. Available online: https://timesmachine.nytimes.com/timesmachine/1984/01/20/189700.html?pageNumber=1 (Accessed 21 September 2023).
10. Dougherty, P. H. (1984), 'Advertising: A Family Computer Magazine', *The New York Times archives*, 18 March. Available online: https://timesmachine.

nytimes.com/timesmachine/1983/03/18/041610.html?pageNumber=90 (Accessed 21 September 2023).
11 Boreham, M. (2019), 'Mobile PCs on Track for 18 Per Cent Growth in K-12 Education This Year', *Future Source Consulting*. https://www.futuresource-consulting.com/insights/mobile-pcs-on-track-for-18-growth-in-k-12-education-this-year/ (Accessed 20 September 2023).
12 UK Department for Education (2020), 'Schools to Benefit from Education Partnership with Tech Giants' [Press release], *Gov.uk*, 24 April. Available online: https://www.gov.uk/government/news/schools-to-benefit-from-education-partnership-with-tech-giants (Accessed 20 September 2023).
13 Singer, N. (2021), 'Learning Apps Have Boomed in the Pandemic. Now Comes the Real Test', *The New York Times*, 17 March. Available online: https://www.nytimes.com/2021/03/17/technology/learning-apps-students.html#:~:text=During%20the%20same%20period%2C%20the,market%20research%20company%20in%20Britain (Accessed 12 September 2023).
14 UNICEF (n.d.), 'Giga: Connecting Every School to the Internet'. Available online: https://www.unicef.org/innovation/giga (Accessed 18 September 2023).
15 UNICEF (n.d.), 'Gateways 2 Learning', *UNICEF*. Available online: https://gateways2learning.org (Accessed 18 September 2023), n.p.
16 Sieckelinck, S., Kaulingfreks, F., and De Winter, M. (2015), 'Neither Villains nor Victims: Towards an Educational Perspective on Radicalisation', *British Journal of Educational Studies*, 63: 329–43.
17 Adams, R., and Weale, S. (2022), 'Revealed: UK Children Being Ensnared by "Far Right Ecosystem" Online', *The Guardian*, 3 August. Available online: https://www.theguardian.com/politics/2022/aug/03/revealed-uk-children-ensnared-far-right-ecosystem-online (Accessed 21 September 2023).
18 Great Britain, Home Office (2023), 'Prevent Guidance: For England and Wales: Statutory Guidance', Home Office, 18 October. Available online: https://www.gov.uk/government/publications/prevent-duty-guidance/prevent-duty-guidance-for-england-and-wales-accessible (Accessed 20 October 2023).
19 Rogers, and Larsen (1984), *Silicon Valley Fever*, London: Basic Books, 259.
20 Jones, S. (2015), 'Bill Gates: Digital Learning Will Revolutionise Education in Global South', *The Guardian*, 22 January. Available online: https://www.theguardian.com/global-development/2015/jan/22/bill-gates-digital-learning-revolutionise-education-developing-world (Accessed 18 September 2023).
21 Code.org (2022), '50 Governors Sign the Governors' Compact for Computer Science'. Available online: https://www.ceosforcs.com (Accessed 2 October 2023).
22 National Centre for Educational Statistics (NCES) 2023, 'Back to School Statistics', NCES, viewed 18 May 2024, https://nces.ed.gov/fastfacts/display.asp?id=55 (Accessed 3 October).
23 Nvidia Canvas (2022), 'Nvidia Canvas: New Update: 4x Higher Resolution and 5 New Materials', *Nvidia*. Available online: https://www.youtube.com/watch?v=wKztRskmsig&t=10s (Accessed 2 August 2023).

24 Office of National Statistics (2016), 'How Do Childhood Circumstances Affect Your Chances of Poverty as an Adult?', *Office of National Statistics*, 16 May. Available online: https://www.ons.gov.uk/peoplepopulationandcommunity/educationandchildcare/articles/howdochildhoodcircumstancesaffectyourchancesofpovertyasanadult/2016-05-16 (Accessed 2 October 2023).
25 Dean, E. B., Schilbach, F., and Schofield, H. (2017), 'Poverty and Cognitive Function', in C. B., Barrett, M. R. Carter, and J. P. Chavas (eds.), *The Economics of Poverty Traps*, 57–118, Chicago: University of Chicago Press.
26 Fazackerley, A., and Helm, T. (2023), 'Children without a Bed Aren't Going to Be Interested in School: Can England's North-South Education Divide Be Repaired?', *The Observer*, 27 August, https://www.theguardian.com/education/2023/aug/27/children-without-a-bed-arent-going-to-be-interested-in-school-can-englands-north-south-education-divide-be-repaired (Accessed 12 October 2023).
27 Biesta, G. (2007), 'Why "What Works" Won't Work: Evidence-Based Practice and the Democratic Deficit in Educational Research', *Educational Theory*, 57 (1): 1–22, p. 8.
28 Ibid.
29 Bailey, J. (2022), 'Meet ChatGPT: The AI Chatbot That Can Write Code, Pass Exams, and Generate Business Ideas', *The American Enterprise Institute*, 16 December. Available online: https://www.aei.org/technology-and-innovation/meet-chatgpt-the-ai-chatbot-that-can-write-code-pass-exams-and-generate-business-ideas/ (Accessed 12 August 2023).
30 Weaver, W. (1949), 'The Mathematics of Communication', *Scientific American*, 181: 11–15. Available online: https://monoskop.org/images/4/48/Weaver_Warren_1949_The_Mathematics_of_Communication.pdf (Accessed 12 August 2023), 12.
31 Wright, H. C. (1985), 'Shera as a Bridge between Librarianship and Information Science', *The Journal of Library History (1974–1987)*, 20 (2): 137–56.
32 Jesse H. Shera as quoted in Roszak, T. (1986), *The Cult of Information: The Folklore of Computers and the True Art of Thinking*, London: Paladin Grafton Books, 52.
33 United Nations Security Council (2023), International Community Must Urgently Confront the New Reality of Generative, Artificial Intelligence, Speakers Stress as Security Council Debates Risks, Rewards [Press release] *UNSC*, 18 July. https://press.un.org/en/2023/sc15359.doc.htm (Accessed 2 October 2023).
34 Kasparov, G. (2018), *Deep Thinking*, London: John Murray.
35 Schmidt, E., and Cohen, J. (2014), *The New Digital Age: Reshaping the Future of People, Nations and Business*, London: John Murray.
36 Ball, S. (2008), *The Education Debate*, London: The Policy Press, 110.
37 Ibid., 110.

38 Hillman, V. (2022), 'Edtech Procurement Matters: It Needs a Coherent Solution, Clear Governance, and Market Standards', Social Policy Working Paper 02-22, London: LSE Department of Social Policy. Available online: https://www.lse.ac.uk/social-policy/Assets/Documents/PDF/working-paper-series/02-22-Hillman.pdf (Accessed 15 August 2023).
39 Roszak, *The Cult of Information*.
40 *New York Times* archives (1960), 'Decisions from Computers Envisioned', *New York Times Archives*.
41 Fazackerley and Helm (2023), 'Children without a Bed Aren't Going to Be Interested in School'.
42 Postman, N. (1995), *The End of Education: Redefining the Value of School*, New York: Vintage Books, 46.
43 EU EdTech Alliance (2023), 'Time for Action: Making Edtech a Key Driver in the European Digital Education Ecosystem', *EU EdTech Alliance*, 26 March. Available online: https://digitaleducationstakeholderforum.eu/public/uploads/Time-for-action-making-EdTech-a-key-driver-in-the-European-digital-education-ecosystem.pdf (Accessed 15 August 2023).
44 Ibid., 6.
45 Roszak, *The Cult of Information*, 9.
46 Selwyn, Neil (2022), *Education and Technology: Key Issues and Debates*, London, UK: Bloomsbury, 2.
47 Weiser, M. (1991), 'The Computer of the 21st Century', *Scientific American*, 265: 94–104. https://doi.org/10.1038/scientificamerican0991-94, 94.
48 Sheff, D. (1985), 'Playboy Interview: Steven Jobs', *Playboy*, 1 February. Available online: https://allaboutstevejobs.com/verbatim/interviews/playboy_1985 (Accessed 15 August 2023).
49 Weiser, 'The Computer of the 21st Century', 4.
50 Ibid.
51 Williamson, B. (2021), 'Digital Policy Sociology: Software and Science in Data-Intensive Precision Education', *Critical Studies in Education*, 62 (3): 354–70. https://doi.org/10.1080/17508487.2019.1691030.
52 Zuboff, *The Age of Surveillance Capitalism*, 20–1.
53 Watters, A. (2022), *Teaching Machines: The History of Personalized Learning*, Cambridge, MA: MIT Press.
54 Fulghum, R. (1986), *All I Really Need to Know I Learned in Kindergarten*, New York: Ballantine Books.
55 Means, A. J. (2018), *Learning to Save the Future: Rethinking Education and Work in an Era of Digital Capitalism*, London: Routledge.
56 Fouad, N. S. (2022), 'The Security Economics of EdTech Vendors' Responsibility and the Cybersecurity Challenge in the Education Sector', *Digital Policy, Regulation and Governance*, 24 (3): 259–73.
57 See, for example, the Jacobs Foundation, the Institute for Education Sciences https://ies.ed.gov/ncee/wwc/WhatWeDo. The Bill & Melinda Foundation and the Edtech Labs of University College London.

58 UNESCO (2023), *Technology in Education: Tool on Whose Terms?*, Paris: UNESCO. Available online: https://www.unesco.org/gem-report/en/technology (Accessed 3 September 2023).
59 https://op.europa.eu/en/publication-detail/-/publication/0d219a7a-76dd-11ee-99ba-01aa75ed71a1#_publicationDetails_PublicationDetailsPortlet_pa (Accessed 3 September 2023).
60 https://joint-research-centre.ec.europa.eu/scientific-activities-z/education-and-training/well-being-education_en (Accessed 3 September 2023).
61 Hillman, V. (2019), *Creative Explorations through the Use of Digital Devices for Self-Organised Learning in the Classroom*. Education Research Monograph Series, Msida: University of Malta.
62 Alper, M. (2017), *Giving Voice: Mobile Communication, Disability and Inequality*, Cambridge, MA: MIT Press.
63 Illich, I. (2001) Tools for Conviviality. London: Marion Boyars.
64 Beckett, L. (2019), 'Under Digital Surveillance: How American Schools Spy on Millions of Kids', *The Guardian*, 22 October. Available online: https://www.theguardian.com/world/2019/oct/22/school-student-surveillance-bark-gaggle (Accessed 4 September 2023).
65 Turner, J. (2019), 'Tech Software Gaggle Finds Possible Pornographic Item on Chesterfield Schools Device', *NBC*, 8 March. Available online: www.nbc12.com/2019/03/08/tech-software-gaggle-finds-possible-pornographic-item-chesterfield-schools-device/ (Accessed 4 September 2023), para 5.
66 Kelly, H. (2019), 'School Apps Track Students from Classroom to Bathroom, and Parents Are Struggling to Keep Up', *The Washington Post*, 29 October. Available online: www.washingtonpost.com/technology/2019/10/29/school-apps-track-students-classroom-bathroom-parents-are-struggling-keep-up/ (Accessed 15 September 2023).
67 This was one of the best times in my life, working on *Phase* magazine for, by and with young people in my second home, Malta. It was a print publication, and I delivered to schools around the island who subsequently also welcomed me to research relating to the digital lives of children and young people and eventually my PhD. Here is an example of the winter copy: https://timesofmalta.com/article/school-has-lost-its-cool.262539 (Accessed 15 September 2023).
68 https://schoolgovernors.thekeysupport.com/the-governing-body/constitution-and-membership/governing-body-constitution/parent-governor-trustee-roles-and-responsibilities/ (Accessed 20 August 2023).
69 UK Department for Education (2017), *A Competency Framework for Governance*. UK Department for Education. Available online: https://assets.publishing.service.gov.uk/media/5a809e8740f0b62305b8c336/Competency_framework_for_governance_.pdf (Accessed 20 August 2023).
70 Woolcock, N. (2023), 'Schools Lament Faulty Oxford Entrance Tests', *The Times UK*, 21 October. Available online: https://www.thetimes.co.uk/article/schools-lament-faulty-oxford-entrance-tests-7c56hfw9j#:~:text=Oxford%20University%20candidates%20were%20unable,and%20useless%20levels%20of%20support (Accessed 21 October 2023).

71 Metz, C., and Wakabayashi, D. (2020), 'Google Researcher Says She Was Fired Over Paper Highlighting Bias in AI', *The New York Times,* 3 December. Available online: https://www.nytimes.com/2020/12/03/technology/google-researcher-timnit-gebru.html (Accessed 23 October 2023).

72 Mac, R., and Kang, C. (2021), 'Whistle-Blower Says Facebook 'Chooses Profits over Safety', *The New York Times,* 3 October. Available online: https://www.nytimes.com/2021/10/03/technology/whistle-blower-facebook-frances-haugen.html#:~:text=On%20Sunday%2C%20Frances%20Haugen%20revealed,before%20leaving%20in%20May%2C%20Ms (Accessed 23 October 2023).

73 Franceschi-Bicchierai, L. (2022), 'Facebook Engineers Admit They Don't Know What They Do with Your Data', *Vice,* 7 September. Available online: https://www.vice.com/en/article/qjk3wb/facebook-engineers-admit-they-dont-know-what-they-do-with-your-data (Accessed 23 October 2023).

74 Microsoft (n.d.), 'Digital Literacy'. Microsoft. Available online: https://www.microsoft.com/en-us/digital-literacy (Accessed 23 October 2023).

75 European Commission (2021), 'Digital Education Action Plan (2021–2027)', European Commission. Available online: https://education.ec.europa.eu/focus-topics/digital-education/action-plan#:~:text=The%20Digital%20Education%20Action%20Plan%20(2021%2D2027)%20is%20a,States%20to%20the%20digital%20age (Accessed 23 October 2023).

76 UK Department for Education (2020), 'Schools to Benefit from Education Partnership with Tech Giants | Thousands of Schools to Receive Technical Support to Start Using Google and Microsoft's Education Platforms' [Press Release], *UK Department for Education,* 24 April. Available online: https://www.gov.uk/government/news/schools-to-benefit-from-education-partnership-with-tech-giants#:~:text=Thousands%20of%20schools%20will%20benefit,be%20available%20for%20schools%20immediately (Accessed 23 October 2023).

77 Frischmann, B. M., and Selinger, E. (2018), *Re-engineering Humanity,* Cambridge, UK: Cambridge University Press.

78 US Chamber of Commerce Foundation (2014), 'Managing the Talent Pipeline: A New Approach to Closing the Skills Gap', US. *Chamber of Commerce, Centre for Education and Workforce,* 19 November. Available online: https://www.uschamberfoundation.org/sites/default/files/Managing%20the%20Talent%20Pipeline.pdf (Accessed 2 August 2023).

79 UK Department for Education (2021), 'DfE Outcome Delivery Plan: 2021 to 2022. Corporate Report', UK Department for Education. Available online: https://www.gov.uk/government/publications/department-for-education-outcome-delivery-plan/dfe-outcome-delivery-plan-2021-to-2022 (Accessed 8 September 2023).

80 European Commission (2020), *Communication – European Skills Agenda for Sustainable Competitiveness, Social Fairness and Resilience,* Brussels: European Commission. Available online: https://ec.europa.eu/migrant-integration/library-document/european-skills-agenda-sustainable-competitiveness-social-fairness-and-resilience_en (Accessed 23 October 2023).

81 Mantelero, A. (2022), *Beyond Data: Human Rights, Ethical and Social Impact Assessment in AI*. Berlin: Springer. Available online: https://doi.org/10.1007/978-94-6265-531-7.
82 United Nations (1989), *Convention on the Rights of the Child, United Nations*. Geneva: United Nations. Available online: http://www.ohchr.org/EN/ProfessionalInterest/Pages/CRC.aspx (Accessed 23 October 2023).
83 See Talbot, D. (2015), 'Lessons From the Digital Classroom', *MIT Technology Review*, 27 July. Available online: https://www.technologyreview.com/2015/07/27/248287/lessons-from-the-digital-classroom/ (Accessed 19 May 2024); Shadbolt, N. and Williams, M. (2023), Digital Education Strategy 2023-27. University of Oxford. Available online: https://www.ctl.ox.ac.uk/sites/default/files/ctl/documents/media/digital_education_strategy_2023-27_-_final_for_publishing_30_jan_2023.pdf (Accessed 19 May 2024); and see also, European Commission (2020) Digital Education Action Plan (2021-2027). Available online: https://education.ec.europa.eu/focus-topics/digital-education/action-plan (Accessed 19 May 2024).
84 UK Department for Education (2017), *A Competency Framework for Governance: The Knowledge, Skills and Behaviours Needed for Effective Governance in Maintained Schools, Academies and Multi-Academy Trusts*, UK Department for Education. Available online: https://assets.publishing.service.gov.uk/government/uploads/system/uploads/attachment_data/file/583733/Competency_framework_for_governance_.pdf (Accessed 23 October 2023). See, United Nations (n.d.), *What Is Good Governance?*, Geneva: UN. Available online: https://www.unescap.org/sites/default/files/good-governance.pdf; United Nations (n.d.), *About Good Governance*, Geneva: UN. Available online: https://www.ohchr.org/en/good-governance/about-good-governance (Accessed 23 October 2023).
85 See for example, Department for Education. (2023), 'EdTech Quality Frameworks and Standards Review', Available online: https://assets.publishing.service.gov.uk/media/6579d0ac0467eb001355f761/EdTech_quality_frameworks_and_standards_review.pdf (Accessed 19 May 2024); Hollow, D. (2021), '17 EdTech Frameworks and Who Needs to Know Them', *EdTech Hub*, 1 September. Available online: https://edtechhub.org/2021/09/01/17-edtech-frameworks-and-who-needs-to-know-them/ (Accessed 19 May 2024); and Barth, S., Ionita, D. and Hartel, P. (2023), 'Understanding Online Privacy—A Systematic Review of Privacy Visualizations and Privacy by Design Guidelines', *ACM Computing Surveys*, 55 (3), Article 63, pp. 1–37. Available online: https://doi.org/10.1145/3502288 (Accessed 19 May 2024).

Chapter 2

1 https://www.netsupportschool.com/classroom-management-instruction/?Ad=UK_Brand&gad_source=1.

2. Light, B., Burgess, J., and Duguay, S. (2018), 'The Walkthrough Method: An Approach to the Study of Apps', *New Media & Society*, 20 (3): 881–900. https://doi.org/10.1177/1461444816675438.
3. Grimes, S. M. (2015), 'Little Big Scene', *Cultural Studies*, 29 (3): 379–400.
4. NetSupport (2012), 'NetSupport School – Classroom Instruction and Monitoring Solution: Product Overview' [Video file] *YouTube*, 4 September. Available online: https://www.youtube.com/watch?v=e4g3Dqg6Dnc (Accessed 28 July 2023), 2:25.
5. NetSupport (2021), 'NetSupport School – A Teacher's Guide' [Video file] *YouTube*, 25 October. Available online: https://www.youtube.com/watch?v=HJSwz0uzAeQ.
6. Ibid., 1:03.
7. Anthology (n.d.), 'About Us', *Anthology*. Available online: https://www.anthology.com/about-us (Accessed 28 July 2023).
8. Veritas Capital (2022), 'Houghton Mifflin Harcourt Successfully Completes Sale to Veritas Capital', *Veritas Capital*. Available online: https://www.veritascapital.com/news-info/houghton-mifflin-harcourt-successfully-completes-sale-to-veritas-capital#:~:text=Houghton%20Mifflin%20Harcourt%20Company%20(%22HMH,a%20focus%20on%20technology%20companies (Accessed 28 July 2023).
9. *Federal Trade Commission* (2022), 'FTC-DOJ Merger Guidelines Listening Forum- Technology' [Video file] *FTC*, 12 May. Available online: https://www.ftc.gov/media/ftc-doj-merger-guidelines-listening-forum-technology-may-12-2022 (Accessed 28 July 2023), 12:15–16:55.
10. Anthology, 'About Us'.
11. Selwyn, N. (2022), *Education and Technology: Key Issues and Debates* (3rd ed), London: Bloomsbury Academic.
12. Ibid., 9–10.
13. Poell, T., Nieborg, D., and van Dijck, J. (2019), 'Platformisation', *Internet Policy Review*, 8 (94): 2.
14. Ibid.
15. Gulson, K., Sellar, S., and Webb, P. (2020), *Algorithms of Education: How Datafication and Artificial Intelligence Shape Policy*. Minnesota: University of Minnesota Press.
16. Kerssens, N. & van Dijck, J. (2022), 'Governed by Edtech? Valuing Pedagogical Autonomy in a Platform Society', *Harvard Educational Review*, 92 (2): 284–301. Available online: https://meridian.allenpress.com/her/article-abstract/92/2/284/483737/Governed-by-Edtech-Valuing-Pedagogical-Autonomy-in?redirectedFrom=fulltext (Accessed 20 August 2023).
17. Gulson, Sellar, and Webb, *Algorithms of Education*, 72.
18. Ibid., 76.
19. Ibid.
20. Using their Foundry platform, Palantir Technologies acted as the data processor under contract with NHS England to access the nation's

(aggregated) health data during the Covid-19 pandemic. See https://www.palantir.com/uk/healthcare/ (Accessed 20 August 2023).
21 EdTech applications such as Thrively, a platform used in the US K-12 education, measure 'how hopeful' a student is. The platform's algorithm first determines students' level of 'hopeful' by combining two components: students' 'agency', their determination to reach a goal, and 'pathways', students' routes to the goal. See https://www.thrively.com/ (Accessed 20 August 2023).
22 You can see their data factory designs here: https://www.palantir.com/platforms/foundry/ (Accessed 20 August 2023).
23 Frické, M. (2008), 'The Knowledge Pyramid: A Critique of the DIKW Hierarchy', *Journal of Information Science*, 35 (2): 131–42. doi:10.1177/0165551508094050.
24 Ibid.,136.
25 van Dijck, J. (2014), 'Datafication, Dataism and Dataveillance: Big Data between Scientific Paradigm and Ideology', *Surveillance & Society*, 12 (2): 197–208. doi:10.24908/ss.v12i2.4776.
26 Couldry, N., and Mejas, U. A. (2019), *The Costs of Connection. How Data Is Colonizing Human Life and Appropriating It for Capitalism*, Palo Alto, CA: Stanford University Press.
27 Cavoukian, A., and Castro, D. (2014), 'Big Data and Innovation, Setting the Record Straight: De-identification Does Work', Ontario, Canada: Information and Privacy Commissioner. Retrieved from https://www2.itif.org/2014-big-data-deidentification.pdf.
28 Solove, J. D., and Schwartz, P. M. (2020), *Consumer Privacy and Data Protection* (3rd ed.), New York, NY: Wolters Kluwer.
29 Bozkurt, A., Jung, I., Xiao, J., Vladimirschi, V., Schuwer, R., Egorov, G., and Paskevicius, M. (2020), 'A Global Outlook to the Interruption of Education Due to Covid-19 Pandemic: Navigating in a Time of Uncertainty and Crisis', *Asian Journal of Distance Education*, 15 (1): 1–126. doi:10.5281/zenodo.3878572.
30 U.S. Department of Education (2017), *Reimagining the Role of Technology in Education: 2017 National Education Technology Plan Update* (Report). Available online: https://tech.ed.gov/files/2017/01/NETP17.pdf.
31 UNESCO (2023), *Global Education Monitoring Report: Technology in Education,* UNESCO. Available online: https://www.unesco.org/gem-report/en.
32 Fontichiaro, K., and Oehrli, J. A. (2016, May/June), *Why Data Literacy Matters*. Available online: files.eric.ed.gov/fulltext/EJ1099487.pdf (Accessed 20 August 2023).
33 Stoilova, M., Livingstone, S., and Nandagiri, R. (2021), 'Data and Privacy Literacy: The Role of the School in Educating Children in a Datafied Society', in D. Frau-Meigs, S. Kotilainen, M. Pathak-Shelat, M. Hoechsmann, and S. R. Poyntz (eds.), *The Handbook of Media Education Research*, 413–25, Hoboken, NJ: John Wiley & Sons, Inc.

34 Bourdieu, P., and Passeron, J. C. ([2000]1977), *Reproduction in Education, Society and Culture* (2nd ed.), London: Sage Publications.
35 Bourdieu and Passeron, *Reproduction in Education*, 34.
36 Srnicek, N. (2017), *Platform Capitalism*, Cambridge, UK: Polity.
37 Srnicek, *Platform Capitalism*, 98.
38 Freire, P. (1970), *Pedagogy of the Oppressed*, London, UK: Penguin Group, 36.
39 Brunton, F., and Nissenbaum, H. (2015), *Obfuscation: A User's Guide for Privacy and Protest*, Cambridge, MA: MIT Press.
40 Citron, D. K., and Solove, D. J. (2021), 'Privacy Harms', (GWU Legal Studies Research Paper No. 2021-11), *Boston University Law Review*, 102 (2): 793–863. doi:10.2139/ssrn.3782222.
41 Skinner-Thompson, S. (2021), *Privacy at the Margins*, Cambridge, UK: Cambridge University Press.
42 Vèliz, C. (2021), *Privacy Is Power: Why and How You Should Take Back Control of Your Data*, London. UK: Bantam Press.
43 Warren, S. D., and Brandeis, L. D. (1890), 'The Right to Privacy', *Harvard Law Review*, 4 (5): 193–220. Available online: https://www.jstor.org/stable/1321160.
44 Richards, N. (2008), 'Intellectual Privacy (Working Paper)', *Texas Law Review*, 87: 387–445.
45 Ibid., 95.
46 Reidenberg, J. R., and Schaub, F. (2018), 'Achieving Big Data Privacy in Education', *Theory and Research in Education*, 16 (3): 263–79. doi:10.1177/1477878518805308.
47 Westin, A. F. (1968), *Privacy and Freedom*, New York, NY: Athenum.
48 Lanzing, M. (2019), '"Strongly Recommended" Revisiting Decisional Privacy to Judge Hypernudging in Self-Tracking Technologies', *Philosophy & Technology*, 32: 549–68. doi:10.1007/s13347-018-0316-4.
49 Mirsch, T., Lehrer, C., and Jung, R. (2017), 'Digital Nudging: Altering User Behaviour in Digital Environments', in *Proceedings of the 13th International Conference on Wirtschaftsinformatik (WI) 2017*. University of St. Gallen, St. Gallen, Switzerland, 634–48.
50 Yeung, K. (2015), '"Hypernudge": Big Data as a Mode of Regulation by Design', *Information, Communication & Society*, 20 (1): 118–36. doi:10.1080/1369118X.2016.1186713.
51 Mejtoft, T., Parsjö, E., Norberg, O., and Söderström, U. (2023), 'Design Friction and Digital Nudging', IVSP '23: Proceedings of the 2023 5th International Conference on Image, Video and Signal Processing. Available online: https://doi.org/10.1145/3591156.3591183, 183.
52 Tahaei, M., Frik, A., and Vaniea, K. (2021), 'Deciding on Personalized Ads: Nudging Developers about User Privacy', *USENIX Symposium on Usable Privacy and Security (SOUPS)*. doi:10.1145/3411763.3451805.
53 Freire, *Pedagogy of the Oppressed*, 31.
54 Skinner, B. F. (1974), *About Behaviourism*, New York: Vintage Books.

55 Dewey, J. ([1963]1938), *Experience and Education*, New York: Collier Books.
56 Bourdieu, P. (1986), 'Forms of Capital', in J. G. Richardson (ed.), *Handbook of Theory and Research for the Sociology of Education*, 241–58, Westport, CT: Greenwood.
57 Ibid., 36.
58 Johanes, P., and Lagerstrom, L. (2017), 'Adaptive Learning: The Premise, Promise, and Pitfalls', *ASEE Annual Conference and Exposition*, Conference Proceedings. doi:10.18260/1-2-27538. Available online: https://peer.asee.org/adaptive-learning-the-premise-promise-and-pitfalls (Accessed 1 September 2023).
59 Biesta, 'Why "What Works" Won't Work: Evidence-Based Practice and the Democratic Deficit in Educational Research'. Available online: https://doi.org/10.1111/j.1741-5446.2006.00241.x, p. 15.
60 Ibid., 17.
61 Ibid., 4.
62 Department for Education. (2023), Share Your Daily School Attendance Data. Available online: https://www.gov.uk/guidance/share-your-daily-school-attendance-data (Accessed: 10 May 2024); see also Department for Education. (2024), Guidance For Sharing Daily Pupil Attendance Data. Available online: https://assets.publishing.service.gov.uk/media/6643266d993111924d9d3383/Guidance_for_sharing_daily_pupil_attendance_data.pdf (Accessed: 10 May 2024).
63 Department for Education. (2023) Securing good attendance and tackling persistent absence. Available at: https://www.gov.uk/government/publications/securing-good-attendance-and-tackling-persistent-absence/securing-good-attendance-and-tackling-persistent-absence (Accessed: 10 May 2024).
64 Dencik, L., Redden, J., Hintz, A., and Warne, H. (2019), 'The "Golden View": Data-Driven Governance in the Scoring Society', *Internet Policy Review*, 8 (2). Available online: https://policyreview.info/articles/analysis/golden-view-data-driven-governance-scoring-society (Accessed 1 September 2023).
65 National Center for Education Statistics (NCES). (n.d.), About Us. Available online: https://nces.ed.gov/about/ (Accessed 14 May 2024), also see National Center for Education Statistics (NCES). (n.d.), Early Childhood Longitudinal Study (ECLS). Available online: https://nces.ed.gov/ecls/ (Accessed 14 May 2024).
66 See https://www.crunchbase.com/acquisition/renaissance-learning-acquires-nearpod–9a50425b (Accessed 13 September 2023).
67 See https://www.crunchbase.com/hub/acquired-edtech-companies (Accessed 13 September 2023).
68 Bourdieu and Passeron, *Reproduction in Education*, 34.
69 US Chamber of Commerce Foundation, 'Managing the Talent Pipeline: A New Approach to Closing the Skills Gap'.

70 US Chamber of Commerce (2015), 'Building the Talent Pipeline: An Implementation Guide', *US Chamber of Commerce Foundation: Centre for Education and Workforce*.
71 Marsh, J. (2010), *Childhood, Culture and Creativity: A Literature Review*. Newcastle: Creativity, Culture and Education. Available online: https://www.academia.edu/679206/Childhood_Culture_and_Creativity_A_Literature_Review (Accessed 13 September 2023), 45.
72 Le Galés, P. (2016), 'Performance Measurement as a Policy Instrument', *Policy Studies*, 37 (6): 508–20.
73 Shore, C., and Wright, S. (2015), 'Governing by Numbers: Audit Culture Rankings and the New World Order', *Social Anthropology/Anthropologie Sociale*, 23 (1): 22–8, 22.
74 Freire, P. ([1996]1970), *Pedagogy of the Oppressed*, London: Penguin Group, 35.
75 Ibid., *Pedagogy of the Oppressed*, 30.
76 Eliot, T. S. (1956), 'The Frontiers of Criticism', *The Sewanee Review*, 64 (4): 525–43, 525.
77 Brynjolfsson, E., and McAfee, A. (2014), *The Second Machine Age: Work, Progress, and Prosperity in a Time of Brilliant Technologies*, New York: W.W. Norton & Company.
78 Brynjolfsson, E., and McAfee, A. (2014), *The Second Machine Age: Work, Progress, and Prosperity in a Time of Brilliant Technologies*. New York: W.W. Norton & Company, Acknowledgements page.
79 Robinson, K. (2006) Do Schools Kill Creativity? Available online: https://www.ted.com/talks/sir_ken_robinson_do_schools_kill_creativity?language=en (Accessed: 2 September 2023).
80 Papert, S. (1993), *The Children's Machine: Rethinking School in the Age of the Computer*, New York: Basic Books, 37.
81 Yu, J., and Couldry, N. (2020), 'Education as a Domain of Natural Data Extraction: Analysing Corporate Discourse about Educational Tracking', *Information, Communication & Society*. https://doi.org/10.1080/1369118X.2020.1764604, 8.
82 Papert built on Jean Piaget's theory of constructivism, which posits that children learn in stages, by emphasizing that children actively construct their own knowledge. Initially, they experiment with information provided by teachers or experts, but ultimately, they learn by creating and making things, a concept Papert termed constructionism. This approach supports a 'sandbox' environment where children can explore and self-navigate various topics of interest, fostering other positive aspects of learning and development. However, two points must be noted. First, this underpins the neoliberal view that one is on their own and therefore solely responsible for their own learning successes and failures. The role of the institution and even the pedagogue are diminished. Secondly, Papert also showed an interest in observing and influencing behaviour through digital technologies. This perspective aligns more with behaviourism, involving behavioural engineering and conditioning, rather than self-directed learning or free will.

83 Picard, R. W., Papert, S., Bender, W., Blumberg, B., Breazeal, C., Cavallo, D., and Strohecker, C. (2004), 'Affective Learning – A Manifesto', *BT Technology Journal*, 22 (4): 253–69. https://doi.org/10.1023/b:bttj.0000047603.37042.33.
84 Ibid., 258.
85 Ibid.
86 Ibid.
87 Picard, R., and Scheirer, J. (2001), *The Galvactivator: A Glove That Senses and Communicates Skin Conductivity*, MIT Media Laboratory. Available online: https://vismod.media.mit.edu/pub/tech-reports/TR-542.pdf (Accessed 15 October 2023).
88 NetSupport (n.d.), 'NetSupport Version 14', n.p., para 2. Available online: https://www.netsupportsoftware.com/20200129supporting-student-and-teacher-wellbeing-with-technology/ (Accessed 28 July 2023).
89 Wise, M. (1995), *The Values of Precision*, Princeton, NJ: Princeton University Press.
90 Ajunwa, I. (2023), *The Quantified Worker: Law and Technology in the Modern Workplace*, Cambridge: Cambridge University Press.
91 Freire, *Pedagogy of the Oppressed*, 53.
92 Ibid., 58.
93 Deegan, J., and Martin, N. (2018), *Demand Driven Education: Merging Work and Learning to Develop the Human Skills That Matter*, Pearson: Pearson and JFF. Available online: https://www.pearson.com/content/dam/one-dot-com/one-dot-com/global/Files/about-pearson/innovation/open-ideas/DDE_Pearson_Report_3.pdf (Accessed 15 October 2023).
94 Zeide, E. (2017), 'The Structural Consequences of Big Data-Driven Education', *Engineering, Medicine, Computer Science*, 5 (2): 164–72.
95 Nielsen, R. K., and Ganter, S. A. (2022), *The Power of Platforms: Shaping Media and Society*, Oxford: Oxford University Press.
96 Declan, K., Kearnes, M., and Gulson, K. (2020), 'The Promise of Precision: Datafication in Medicine, Agriculture and Education', *Policy Studies*, 41 (5): 527–46.
97 Ibid., 2.
98 Centre for Digital Democracy (2022), 'Trade Regulation Rule on Commercial Surveillance and Data Security Federal Trade Commission', ANPR, R111004, *Centre for Digital Democracy*, 21 November. Available online: https://www.federalregister.gov/documents/2022/10/20/2022-22813/trade-regulation-rule-on-commercial-surveillance-and-data-security (Accessed 15 October 2023).
99 Selwyn, N., and Jandrić, P. (2020), 'Postdigital Living in the Age of Covid-19: Unsettling What We See as Possible', *Postdigital Science and Education*, 2 (3): 989–1005. https://doi.org/10.1007/s42438-020-00166-9.
100 Nielsen and Ganter, *The Power of Platforms*.

101 Iliadis, A. and Russo, F. (2016), 'Critical Data Studies: An Introduction', *Big Data & Society*, 3 (2). https://doi.org/10.1177/2053951716674238.
102 Ibid., 1.
103 Yousif, M. (2015), 'The Rise of Data Capital', *IEEE Cloud Computing*, 2 (2): 4.
104 Gillespie, T. (2014), 'The Relevance of Algorithms', in T. Gillespie, P. J. Boczkowski, and K. A. Foot (eds.), *Media Technologies: Essays on Communication, Materiality, and Society*, Cambridge: MIT Press, 167–94.
105 Zuboff, *The Age of Surveillance Capitalism*.
106 Graham, M. (2015), 'Information Geographies and Geographies of Information', *New Geographies* 7: 159–66.
107 Iliadis and Russo, *Critical Data Studies*.
108 Perry-Hazan, L., and Birnhack, M. (2018), 'The Hidden Human Rights Curriculum of Surveillance Cameras in Schools: Due Process, Privacy, and Trust', *Cambridge Journal of Education*, 48 (1): 47–64.
109 Hope, A. (2009), 'CCTV, School Surveillance and Social Control', *British Educational Research Journal*, 35 (6): 891–907.
110 In 2022, the Dutch Data Protection Authority proposed Chromebooks and Google Workspace for Education ban in schools as Google failed to comply with regulation around transparency and protecting children's data privacy. Although Google subsequently improved its privacy measures, Google Search remains banned from use: Available online: https://www.bleepingcomputer.com/news/security/chrome-use-subject-to-restrictions-in-dutch-schools-over-data-security-concerns/ (Accessed 2 November 2023). Germany has imposed bans: Available online: https://www.itp.net/commsmea/20197-apple-google-and-microsoft-clouds-banned-in-schools-in-germany, and Denmark: https://www.datatilsynet.dk/presse-og-nyheder/nyhedsarkiv/2022/jul/datatilsynet-nedlaegger-behandlingsforbud-i-chromebook-sag.
111 Australia was among the early adopters of laws designed to compel Google and Facebook to compensate news providers, aiming to balance the playing field for local news entities in the wake of tech giants' monopolistic competition. Learn more here: https://techcrunch.com/2020/03/09/australia-sues-facebook-over-cambridge-analytica-fine-could-scale-to-529bn/ (Accessed 2 November 2023).
112 Bietti, E. (2023), 'A Genealogy of Digital Platform Regulation', *7 Georgetown Law Technology Review*, 1 (2023): 1–67.
113 Human Rights Watch (2023), 'Governments Harm Children's Rights in Online Learning', Available online: https://www.hrw.org/news/2022/05/25/governments-harm-childrens-rights-online-learning (Accessed 17 July 2023).
114 Ibid.
115 Google Play Store (2021), *Microsoft Teams*. Google. Available online: https://web.archive.org/web/20210411070441/https://play.google.com/store/apps/details?id=com.microsoft.teams (Accessed 3 October 2023), n.p.

116 Microsoft (2021), *Microsoft Privacy Statement*. Microsoft. Available online: https://web.archive.org/web/20210303004921/https://privacy.microsoft.com/en-us/privacystatement (Accessed 3 October 2023).
117 Federal Trade Commission (FTC), 'FTC Will Require Microsoft to Pay $20 Million over Charges It Illegally Collected Personal Information from Children without Their Parents' Consent', [Press Release].
118 NOYB. (2024), Microsoft Violates Children's Privacy, Blames Your Local School. Available online: https://noyb.eu/en/microsoft-violates-childrens-privacy-blames-your-local-school (Accessed: 4 June 2024), n.p.
119 Ibid.
120 Broussard, M. (2023), *More Than a Glitch: Confronting Race, Gender, and Ability Bias in Tech*, Cambridge, MA: MIT Press.
121 Ibid., 12.
122 The World Bank (n.d.), 'Global Education Evidence Advisory Panel', The World Bank. Available online: https://www.worldbank.org/en/topic/teachingandlearning/brief/global-education-evidence-advisory-panel (Accessed 3 October 2023).
123 Sullivan, E. T. (2021), 'How Much Does the US Spend on Edtech? No One Knows, and That's a Problem', *EdSurge,* 22 March. Available online: *https://www.edsurge.com/news/2021-03-22-how-much-does-the-u-s-spend-on-edtech-no-one-knows-and-that-s-a-problem* (Accessed 22 October 2023).
124 Davis, R. M. (2019), 'K-12 Districts Wasting Millions by Not Using Purchased Software, New Analysis Finds', *EdWeek Market Brief,* 14 May. Available online: https://marketbrief.edweek.org/marketplace-k-12/unused-educational-software-major-source-wasted-k-12-spending-new-analysis-finds/.
125 Mathewson, T. G., and Butrymowicz, S. (2020), 'Edtech Companies Promise Results, but Their Claims Are Often Based on Shoddy Research', *The Hechinger Report,* 20 May. Available online: https://hechingerreport.org/ed-tech-companies-promise-results-but-their-claims-are-often-based-on-shoddy-research/ (Accessed 22 October 2023).
126 Sullivan, *How Much Does the US Depend on Edtech?*
127 Couldry, N., and Mejias, U. (2019), *The Costs of Connection: How Data Is Colonising Human Life and Appropriating It for Capitalism*. Stanford: Stanford University Press.
128 Kerssens and van Dijck, *Governed by Edtech?*, 284.
129 Williams and Gilbert (2022), *Hegemony Now: How Big Tech and Wall Street Won the World (and How We Win It Back)*, London: Verso, 171.
130 Ibid.
131 Ibid.
132 Ibid., 172.
133 Ibid.
134 Weiser, 'The Computer of the 21st Century', 94.

Chapter 3

1. Eliot, T. (1933), *The Use of Poetry and the Use of Criticism: Studies in the Relation of Criticism to Poetry in England*, London: Faber and Faber Ltd., 148.
2. Ball, S. (2008), *The Education Debate*, Bristol: The Policy Press.
3. Nussbaum, M. C. (2009), 'Tagore, Dewey, and the Imminent Demise of Liberal Education', in H. Siegel (ed.), *The Oxford Handbook of Philosophy of Education*, 52–66, Oxford: Oxford University Press.
4. Ball, *The Education Debate*.
5. Theodore, N., Peck, J., and Brenner, N. (2011), 'Neoliberal Urbanism: Cities and the Rule of Markets', in S. Watson and G. Bridge (eds.), *The New Blackwell Companion to the City*, New Jersey: Wiley, 15.
6. Hall, S. (2011), 'Thatcher, Blair, Cameron – The Long March of Neoliberalism', *Soundings*, May (No 48). Gale Literature Resource Centre. Available online: https://go.gale.com/ps/i.do?id=GALE%7CA287386101&sid=googleScholar&v=2.1&it=r&linkaccess=abs&issn=13626620&p=LitRC&sw=w&userGroupName=anon%7Ea22aea93&aty=open-web-entry (Accessed 1 November 2023).
7. Klein, N. (2008), *The Shock Doctrine*, London: Penguin Press.
8. Robertson, S. (2002), *Changing Governance/Changing Equality? Understanding the Politics of Public-Private-Partnerships in Education in Europe*, Bristol: Department of Education, University of Bristol, 2.
9. Ibid.
10. Mazzucato, M., and Collington, R. (2023), *The Big Con: How the Consulting Industry Weakens Our Businesses, Infantilizes Our Governments and Warps Our Economies*, London, UK: Penguin Press.
11. Ibid., 25.
12. Maes, T., and Preston-Whyte, F. (2022), 'E-Waste It Wisely: Lessons from Africa', *SN Applied Sciences*, 4 (3). Available online: https://doi.org/10.1007/s42452-022-04962-9.
13. Means, A. (2018), *Learning to Save the Future: Rethinking Education and Work in an Era of Digital Capitalism*, New York, NY: Routledge.
14. Ibid., 12.
15. Ball, *The Education Debate*, 22.
16. Slater, D., and Tonkiss, F. (2001), *Market Society: Markets and Modern Social Theory*, New Jersey: Wiley.
17. See Thompson, K. (2023), 'The Cruel Optimism of Educational Technology Teacher Ambassador Programs', *Power and Education*, 0 (0). https://doi.org/10.1177/17577438231164717.
18. Ball, *The Education Debate*, 23.
19. Ibid., 23.
20. Foucault, M. (1979), *Discipline and Punish*, Harmondsworth: Peregrine, 186.
21. Ibid.

22 Peters, M. A., Jandrić, P., and Means, A. J. (eds.) (2019), *Education and Technological Unemployment*, Singapore: Springer.
23 Hall, *Thatcher, Blair, Cameron*, 45.
24 Ibid.
25 Peters, Jandrić, and Means, *Education and Technological Unemployment*.
26 Ball, *The Education Debate*, 110–11.
27 Ibid.
28 Ibid., 43.
29 Ibid.
30 Ibid., 44.
31 Foucault, M. (2009), *Security, Territory, Population: Lectures at the College de France 1977–78*, New York: Palgrave Macmillan, 365.
32 Ball, S. (2013). *Foucault, Power, and Education*, London: Routledge, 140.
33 Ibid., 115.
34 Lowe, R. (1998), 'The Educational Impact of the Eugenics Movement – Eugenics and the Declining Birth Rate in Twentieth-Century Britain', *International Journal of Educational Research*, 278): 647–60.
35 Loutas, N., Kamateri, E., Bosi, F., and Tarabanis, K. (2011), 'Cloud Computing Interoperability: The State of Play', in *Proceedings of the 2011 3rd IEEE International Conference on Cloud Computing Technology and Science*, 752–7. Available online: https://doi.org/10.1109/CloudCom.2011.116.
36 Michael, A., Armando, F., Rean, G., Anthony, D. J., Randy, H. K., Andrew, K., Gunho, L., David, A. P., Ariel, R., Ion, S., and Matei, Z. (2010), 'A View of Cloud Computing', *Commutations of the ACM*, 53 (4): 50–8. Available online: https://cacm.acm.org/magazines/2010/4/81493-a-view-of-cloud-computing/fulltext?mobile=false (Accessed 26 September 2023).
37 Gulson, Sellar, and Webb, *Algorithms of Education*, 4.
38 Stengers, I. (2021), 'Putting Problematization to the Test of Our Present', *Theory, Culture and Society*, 38 (2): 71–92. Available online: https://journals.sagepub.com/doi/abs/10.1177/0263276419848061 (Accessed 26 September 2023).
39 National Centre for Education Statistics (2019), 'Statewide Longitudinal Data System Topical Webinar Summary: Infrastructure Series 3: Data Lakes, Data Science, and Preparing an SLDS to Meet Emerging Data Needs', *National Centre for Education Statistics*. Available online: https://slds.ed.gov/services/PDCService.svc/GetPDCDocumentFile?fileId=34963.
40 CEDS (n.d.). *CEDS Standards*. CEDS [Computer Software]. Available online: https://github.com/CEDStandards/CEDS-Elements (Accessed 26 September 2023).
41 UK Department for Education (2010), 'Education, Skills and Children's Services: Interoperability Review', *UK Department for Education*, 2 August. Available online: https://assets.publishing.service.gov.uk/government/uploads/system/uploads/attachment_data/file/181165/DFE-00523-2010.pdf (Accessed 26 September 2023).

42 Bill and Melinda Gates Foundation (n.d.), 'Foundation Invests in Research and Data Systems to Improve Student Achievement – Bill and Melinda Gates Foundation'. Available online: https://www.gatesfoundation.org/ideas/media-center/press-releases/2009/01/foundation-invests-in-research-and-data-systems-to-improve-student-achievement (Accessed 26 September 2023).

43 Ho, S. (2018), 'Bill Gates Calls for More Global Education Assessments Data', *Associated Press*, 18 September. Available online: https://apnews.com/article/b69709de17f5472bac4b8c7aca4badcb (Accessed 26 September 2023).

44 Bill and Melinda Gates Foundation (2007), *Landscape Review: Education Data*. The Parthenon Group. Available online: https://docs.gatesfoundation.org/documents/landscape-review-education-data.pdf (Accessed 26 September 2023), 5.

45 Access 4 Learning (A4L) (2015), 'Introducing the Access 4 Learning Community – The SIF Association Matures to Address Not Only Data Management but Data Usage for Learning', *PRLog*, 20 May. Available online: https://www.prlog.org/12457789-introducing-the-access-4-learning-community.html (Accessed 28 September 2023).

46 Gulson, Sellar, and Webb, *Algorithms of Education*, 76.

47 Ibid.

48 Shapiro, C., and Varian, H. (1999), *Information Rules: A Strategic Guide to the Network Economy*, Boston: Harvard Business School Press, 13.

49 Gulson, Sellar, and Webb, *Algorithms of Education*, 86.

50 Agre, P. E. (1994), 'Surveillance and Capture: Two Models of Privacy', *The Information Society: An International Journal*, 10: 101–27.

51 Common Education Data Standards (n.d.), 'Related Efforts', *CEDS*. Available online: https://ceds.ed.gov/relatedInitiatives.aspx (Accessed 28 September 2023), n.p.

52 Common Education Data Standards (2021), 'CEDS Data Warehouse: Expansion Project', *CEDS*. Available online: https://ceds.grads360.org/#communities/ceds-osc/workgroups/ceds-dw-expansion (Accessed 28 September 2023), 3.

53 InnovateEDU (2021), 'InnovateEDU's Project Unicorn Releases Inaugural School Data Interoperability Update', *InnovateEDU*. Available online: https://www.innovateedunyc.org/internal-news.

54 Bulger, M., McCormick, S. M., and Pitcan, M. (2017), *The Legacy of InBloom*. Data & Society Research Institute.

55 Data Quality Campaign (2021), 'It's Time to Make Linked Data Work for K-12 Leaders', *DQC*. Available online: https://chiefsforchange.org/wp-content/uploads/2021/11/It's-Time-to-Make-Linked-Data-Work-for-K-12-Leaders.pdf (Accessed 28 September 2023), n.p.

56 Ibid.

57 CDC has been funded by the Bill and Melinda Gates Foundation. See Gates Foundation (2019), 'Committed Grants: Chiefs for Change', Available

online: https://www.gatesfoundation.org/about/committed-grants/2019/10/inv004270 (Accessed 28 September 2023).
58 Hillman, V., and Esquivel, M. (2023), 'The "Solution Stack" of a Neoliberal Inferno Apparatus: A Call for Teacher Conscience', *Postdigital Science and Education*, 1–22. doi:10.1007/s42438-023-00442-4.
59 Chiefs for Change (2021), 'The Role of Governance in Supporting Learner Pathways', *Chiefs for Change*. Available online: https://chiefsforchange.org/resources/?r-category=61 (Accessed 2 October 2023).
60 National Centre for Education Statistics (NCES) (2019), 'SLDS Topical Webinar Summary: Infrastructure Series 3: Data Lakes, Data Science, and Preparing an SLDS to Meet Emerging Data Needs', *NCES*, 26 August. Available online: https://slds.ed.gov/services/PDCService.svc/GetPDCDocumentFile?fileId=34963 (Accessed 2 October 2023).
61 Bailey, J., Carter, C. S., Schneider, C., and Ark, V. T. (2015), 'Data Backpacks: Portable Records and Learner Profiles', Digital Learning Now: Smart Series. Available online: http://digitallearningnow.com/site/uploads/2012/10/Data-Backpacks-FINAL.pdf (Accessed 2 October 2023), 2.
62 UK Department for Education (2021), 'Skills for Jobs: Lifelong Learning for Opportunity and Growth', White Paper, January 2021. Available online: https://assets.publishing.service.gov.uk/government/uploads/system/uploads/attachment_data/file/957856/Skills_for_jobs_lifelong_learning_for_opportunity_and_growth__web_version_.pdf (Accessed 2 October 2023).
63 Virginia Business Higher Education Council (2021), 'Growth 4 VA: A Campaign of the Virginia Business Higher Education Council'. Available online: https://growth4va.com/wp-content/uploads/2021/09/2021Policy.pdf (Accessed 2 October 2023).
64 Workforce Training and Education Coordinating Board (WTECB) (2019), 'Future of Work Task Force 2019 Policy Report', *WTECB*, December. Available online: https://www.wtb.wa.gov/wp-content/uploads/2019/12/Future-of-Work-2019-Final-Report.pdf (Accessed 2 October 2023). See also Workforce Training and Education Coordinating Board (2021), 'House College and Workforce Development Committee: Overview'. Available online: https://app.leg.wa.gov/committeeschedules/Home/Document/226010#toolbar=0&navpanes=0 (Accessed 2 October 2023).
65 GO Virginia Foundation (2020), 'Virginia Growth and Opportunity Foundation'. Available online: https://govirginia.org/about/go-virginia-foundation/ (Accessed 4 October 2023).
66 Lundie, D., Zwitter, A., and Ghosh, D. (2022), 'Corporatized Education and State Sovereignty', *Brookings*. Available online: https://www.brookings.edu/articles/corporatized-education-and-state-sovereignty/ (Accessed 4 October 2023).
67 US Chamber of Commerce Foundation (CCF) (n.d.), *Talent Pipeline Management*. CCF. Available online: https://www.uschamberfoundation.org/talent-pipeline-management (Accessed 4 October 2023).

68 Ball, *The Education Debate*, 63.
69 Illich, I. ([1978] 2009), *The Right to Useful Unemployment*, London: Marion Boyars Publishers Ltd.
70 Ibid., 11.
71 Illich, I., and Verne, E. (1976), *Imprisoned in the Global Classroom*, London, UK: Writers and Readers Publishing Cooperative.
72 Hillman, V., and Bryant, J. (2023), 'Families' Perceptions of Corporate Influence in Career and Technical Education through Data Extraction', *Learning, Media and Technology*, 48 (3): 401–14, doi:10.1080/17439884.2022.2059765.
73 See https://www.amazonfutureengineer.com.
74 Robinson, D., and Bunting, F. (2021), *A Narrowing Path to Success? 16–19 Curriculum Breadth and Employment Outcomes*, Education Policy Institute, the Royal Society. Available online: https://epi.org.uk/wp-content/uploads/2021/09/EPI-Royal_Society-16-19-report.pdf (Accessed 7 October 2023).
75 Hampf, F., and Woessmann, L. (2016), 'Vocational vs General Education and Employment Over the Life-Cycle: New Evidence from PIAACC', *CESifo Economic Studies*, 63 (3): 255–69.
76 Eurofound (2018), *Automation, Digitisation and Platforms: Implications for Work and Employment*, Luxembourg: Publications Office of the European Union.
77 CCF, *Talent Pipeline Management*.
78 European Commission (EC) (2020), 'European Commissions: Questions and Answers', *EC*. Available online: https://ec.europa.eu/commission/presscorner/detail/en/qanda_20_1197 (Accessed 7 October 2023), 8.
79 See the Brazilian Open Education Initiative and Kerssens, N., Nichols, T. P., and Pangrazio, L. (2023), 'Googlization(s) of Education: Intermediary Work Brokering Platform Dependence in Three National School Systems', *Learning, Media and Technology*, 1–14. https://doi.org/10.1080/17439884.2023.2258339.
80 https://dxtera.org/about-us/ (Accessed 12 October 2023).
81 https://www.broadbandcommission.org/wp-content/uploads/2023/10/Broadband-Commission-Working-Group-on-Data-for-Learning-Report.pdf (Accessed 20 October 2023).
82 https://dxtera.org/news/news-dxtera-joins-digital-education-hub-community-of-practice/ (Accessed 12 October 2023).
83 https://globaleducationcoalition.unesco.org/members (Accessed 12 October 2023).
84 Williamson, B. (2020), 'New Pandemic Edtech Power Networks', *Techlash*. Available online: https://der.monash.edu/wp-content/uploads/2020/06/TECHLASH-01-COVID-education.pdf (Accessed 12 October 2023), 19–20.
85 Digital and data strategies for the UK are similar to texts found in EU and US policy papers. See the UK National Data Strategy: https://www.gov.uk/government/publications/uk-national-data-strategy/national-data-

strategy#the-data-opportunity and the European Digital Education Action Plan: https://education.ec.europa.eu/focus-topics/digital-education/action-plan. The data narrative is not promoted in education but everywhere. Here is former prime minister's think-tank, the Tony Blair Institute, endorsing the transformation of agriculture through data https://www.institute.global/insights/tech-and-digitalisation/transforming-agriculture-through-data-insights-from-malawi and digital education https://www.institute.global/insights/public-services/future-of-learning-delivering-tech-enabled-quality-education-for-britain with little critical thought.

86 American Workforce Policy Advisory Board (AWPAB) (2019), 'White Paper on Interoperable Learning Records: Data Transparency Working Group', *AWPAB*, September. Available online: https://www.commerce.gov/sites/default/files/2019-09/ILR_White_Paper_FINAL_EBOOK.pdf (Accessed 12 October 2023).
87 AWPAB, *White Paper on Interoperable Learning Records,* 14.
88 U.S. Chamber of Commerce Foundation (CCF), 'Managing the Talent Pipeline: A New Approach to Closing the Skills Gap'.
89 U.S. Department of Commerce (2019), 'Interoperable Learning Records Landscape Inventory', *U.S. Department of Commerce*. Available online: https://www.commerce.gov/sites/default/files/2019-12/AWPAB_ILR_Inventory_Nov2019.pdf (Accessed 24 October 2023), 1.
90 Hillman, and Esquivel 'The "Solution Stack" of a Neoliberal Inferno Apparatus: A Call for Teacher Conscience'.
91 McGraw Hill (n.d.), 'Making Learning More Accessible'. Available online: https://www.mheducation.com/prek-12/explore/integration-services.html (Accessed 24 October 2023).
92 Ibid., n.p.
93 1EdTech (2022), 'IMS Global Learning Consortium Becomes the 1EdTech Consortium' [Press Release], *1EdTech*, 25 May. Available online: https://www.1edtech.org/article/ims-global-learning-consortium-becomes-1edtech-consortium#:~:text=Today%2C%20IMS%20GLobal%20Learning%20Consortium,new%20brand%2C%201EdTech™%20Consortium (Accessed 24 October 2023).
94 IMS Global. Consortium (2020), 'TrustEd Apps.: Security Trust for Your Digital Learning Ecosystem', IMS Global Consortium. Available from: https://www.imsglobal.org/sites/default/files/webinars/webinar_ims_trusted_apps_100620.pdf (Accessed 6 November 2023), 20.
95 See http://www.imsglobal.org/home (Accessed 6 November 2023).
96 1Edtech (n.d.), 'Join the Brightest Minds in Education and Technology', 1EdTech. Available online: https://www.1edtech.org/about/membership/supplier (Accessed 3 November 2023).
97 U.S. Department of Commerce, 'Interoperable Learning Records Landscape Inventory', 49.
98 Ibid., 50.

99 Ibid., 26.
100 Hillman, and Esquivel, 'The "Solution Stack" of a Neoliberal Inferno Apparatus: A Call for Teacher Conscience'.
101 Prometheus-X. (n.d.), 'Welcome to Prometheus-X', *Prometheus-X*. Available online: https://dataspace.prometheus-x.org (Accessed 4 November 2023).
102 Prometheus-X. (n.d.), 'Vision', *Prometheus-X*. Available online: https://dataspace.prometheus-x.org/fundamentals/vision (Accessed 4 November 2023).
103 Lessig, L. (2000), *Code and Other Laws of Cyberspace*, New York: Basic Books.
104 Prometheus-X. (n.d.), 'Personalised Skills Matching', *Prometheus-X*. Available online: https://dataspace.prometheus-x.org/use-cases/skills/personalised-skills-matching (Accessed 4 November 2023).
105 Lewis, S., Sellar, S., and Lingard, B. (2016), 'PISA for Schools: Topological Rationality and New Spaces of the OECD's', *Global Educational Governance*, 60 (1): 27–57.
106 Ball, S. J. (ed.) (2017), *Educational Policy Major Themes in Education*. Volume 1, New York, NY: Routledge, 8.
107 Means, *Learning to Save the Future*, 25.
108 Ball, S. J. (2013), *Foucault, Power and Education*, New York, NY: Routledge, 134.
109 Lazzarato, M. (2009), 'Neoliberalism in Action: Inequality, Insecurity and the Reconstitution of the Social', *Theory, Culture and Society*, 26 (6): 109–33.
110 Bourdieu, P. (1998), *Acts of Resistance: Against the New Myths of Our Time*, Cambridge: Polity Press, 85.
111 Moore, M. (2019), 'The Gig Economy: A Hypothetical Contract Analysis', *Legal Studies*, 39 (4): 579–97. See also Stuart, D. (2020), 'The Rise of Casual Worker Puts Us All at Risk', *The Jacobin,* 23 August. Available online https://jacobinmag.com/2020/08/casual-work-australia-part-time-jobs (Accessed 6 November 2023).
112 Moret, S. [@StephenMoret] (2019), 'How Did Virginia Win Amazon HQ2? Other States Pitched Incentives; We Pitched Our Educated Workforce' [Tweet]. Twitter, 18 July. Available online: https://twitter.com/chamberrva/status/1151859322483335168 (Accessed 6 November 2023).
113 Bourdieu, *Acts of Resistance*, 98.
114 Ibid., 99.
115 Falk, C. (1999), 'Sentencing Learners to Life: Retrofitting the Academy for the Information Age', *Theory, Technology and Culture*, 22 (1–2): 19–27.
116 Roszak, *The Cult of Information*, 79.
117 Biesta, G. (2022). 'The Aim of Education in an Age of Measurement' [video] YouTube: https://www.youtube.com/watch?v=dQs-cKpO0LI (Accessed 6 November 2023), 8:50. Biesta's speech was during the

fifteenth Anniversary of *Encyclopaedia – Journal of Phenomenology* held in Bologna, 15 October 2022. Available online: https://encp.unibo.it/article/view/16908/15973.
118 Ibid., 10:01.
119 Ibid., 10:35.

Chapter 4

1   Joe Jackson interview with Bono, lead musician of the Irish rock band U2, is available here: Available online: https://www.hotpress.com/music/the-magical-mystery-tour-2613077 (Accessed 8 September 2023). Here I refer to the song's fourth verse.
2   Ibid, n.p.
3   Audi (2022), 'Vorsprung durch Technik Turns 50'. *Audi*, March 24. Available online: https://www.audi.ca/ca/web/en/inside-audi/innovation-and-technology/vorsprung-durch-technik-turns-50.html (Accessed 20 September 2021).
4   Broussard, *More than a Glitch*, 2–3.
5   Ibid.
6   https://www.vice.com/en/article/akvmke/facebook-doesnt-know-what-it-does-with-your-data-or-where-it-goes (Accessed 8 September 2023).
7   Google (2017), The Story of AlphaGo: The First Computer Program to Defeat a Go World Champion. *Google Arts & Culture*. Available online: https://artsandculture.google.com/story/the-story-of-alphago-barbican-centre/kQXBk0X1qEe5KA?hl=en (Accessed 8 September 2023).
8   Knight, W. (2017), No One Really Knows How the Most Advanced Algorithms Do What They Do. That Could Be a Problem. *MIT Technology Review*. https://www.technologyreview.com/2017/04/11/5113/the-dark-secret-at-the-heart-of-ai/ (Accessed 8 September 2023).
9   Morozov, E. (2013), *To Save Everything, Click Here'*, New York: Public Affairs.
10 Plumb, R. K. (1958), Computer Develops Capacity to 'Learn', New York Times Archives (Accessed 8 September 2023). Published January 4, 1958.
11 Rahm, L. (2019), *Educational Imaginaries: A Genealogy of the Digital Citizen*, Linköping: Linköping University Press.
12 Gulson, K. N., and Witzenberger, K. (2022), 'Repackaging Authority: Artificial Intelligence, Automated Governance and Education Trade Shows', *Journal of Education Policy*, 37 (1): 145–60. https://doi.org/10.1080/02680939.2020.1785552.
13 Selwyn, N. (2022), *Education and Technology: Key Issues and Debates*, London: Bloomsbury Academic, 147.
14 Broussard, *More Than a Glitch*, 12.
15 Ibid., 12.

16 Barocas, S., Hardt, M., and Narayanan, A. (2019), *Fairness and Machine Learning: Limitations and Opportunities* [Online Book] *Fairmlbook.org*. Available online: http://www.fairmlbook.org, 1.
17 Ibid.
18 CENTURY Tech (2020), 'CENTURY Home Learning Learner Introduction' [YouTube video]. Available online: https://www.youtube.com/watch?v=dDHl89apiSE (Accessed 8 September 2023).
19 Broussard, M. (2020), 'When Algorithms Give Real Students Imaginary Grades', *The New York Times*, 8 September. Available online: https://www.nytimes.com/2020/09/08/opinion/international-baccalaureate-algorithm-grades.html#:~:text=How%20did%20this%20happen%3F,exams%20because%20of%20the%20pandemic (Accessed 8 September 2023).
20 Berland, M., and Garcia, A. (2024), The Left Hand of Data — Designing Education Data for Justice. Cambridge, MA: The MIT Press.
21 Berland, M., and Garcia, A. (2024), The Left Hand of Data. MIT Press, Cambridge, MA.
22 Biesta, G. J. J. (2015), 'What Is Education For? On good Education, Teacher Judgement, and Educational Professionalism', *European Journal of Education*, 50 (1): 75–87.
23 Broussard, *When Algorithms Give Real Students Imaginary Grades*.
24 Barocas, Hardt, and Narayanan, *Fairness and Machine Learning: Limitations and Opportunities*, 1–2.
25 Sylvester, R. (2021), 'The AI Revolution Can Supercharge Learning in Schools', *The Times UK*, 26 November. Available online: https://www.thetimes.co.uk/article/the-ai-revolution-can-supercharge-learning-in-school-xnv0vql8r (Acccessed 8 September 2023).
26 Fischer, C., Pardos, Z. A., Baker, R. S., Williams, J. J., Smyth, P., Yu, R., Slater, S., Baker, R., and Warschauer, M. (2020), 'Mining Big Data in Education: Affordances and Challenges', *Review of Research in Education*, 44 (1): 130–60. https://doi.org/10.3102/0091732X20903304.
27 Arthur, W. B. (2009), *The Nature of Technology: What It Is and How It Evolves*, New York, NY: Simon & Schuster, 21.
28 McNamara, D. S., Graesser, A. C., McCarthy, P., and Cai, Z. (2014), *Automated Evaluation of Text and Discourse with Coh-Metrix*, Cambridge: Cambridge University Press. Also see https://soletlab.asu.edu/coh-metrix/.
29 Ibid.
30 Pennebaker, J. W., Boyd, R.L., Jordan, K., and Blackburn, K. (2015*), The Development and Psychometric Properties of LIWC2015*, Austin, TX: University of Texas at Austin.
31 Lan, A. S., Vats, D., Waters, A. E., and Baraniuk, R. G. (2015), 'Mathematical Language Processing: Automatic Grading and Feedback for Open Response Mathematical Questions', in *Proceedings of the Second ACM Conference on Learning at Scale*, 167–76. Association for Computing Machinery. https://doi.org/10.1145/2724660.2724664.

32 Cooper, S., Nam, Y. J., and Si, L. (2012), 'Initial Results of Using an Intelligent Tutoring System with Alice', in *Proceedings of the 17th ACM Annual Conference on Innovation and Technology in Computer Science Education*, 138–43. Association for Computing Machinery. https://doi.org/10.1145/2325296.2325332.

33 Price, T. W., Dong, Y., and Barnes, T. (2016), 'Generating Data-Driven Hints for Open-Ended Programming', *Educational Data Mining*. Available online: https://api.semanticscholar.org/CorpusID:14468405.

34 Demmans Epp, C., Phirangee, K., and Hewitt, J. (2017), 'Talk with Me: Student Pronoun Use as an Indicator of Discourse Health', *Journal of Learning Analytics*, 4 (3): 47–75. Available online: https://learning-analytics.info/index.php/JLA/article/view/5341.

35 Peralta, M., Alarcon, R., Pichara, K., Mery, T., Cano, F., and Bozo, J. (2018), 'Understanding Learning Resources Metadata for Primary and Secondary Education', *IEEE Transactions on Learning Technologies*, 11 (4): 456–67.

36 Yang, Yz., Zhong, Y., and Woźniak, M. (2021), 'Improvement of Adaptive Learning Service Recommendation Algorithm Based on Big Data', *Mobile Network Applications*, 26: 2176–87.

37 Crossley, S., Liu, R., and McNamara, D. (2017), 'Predicting Math Performance Using Natural Language Processing Tools', in *Proceedings of the Seventh International Learning Analytics & Knowledge Conference*, 339–47. *Association for Computing Machinery*. Available online: https://doi.org/10.1145/3027385.3027399.

38 Allen, L. K., Mills, C., Jacovina, M. E., Crossley, S., D'Mello, S., and McNamara, D. S. (2016), 'Investigating Boredom and Engagement during Writing Using Multiple Sources of Information: The Essay, the Writer, and Keystrokes', in *Proceedings of the Sixth International Conference on Learning Analytics & Knowledge*, 114–23. *Association for Computing Machinery*. https://doi.org/10.1145/2883851.2883939.

39 Raso, F., Hilligoss, H., Krishnamurthy, V., Krishnamurthy, V., Bavitz, C., and Kim, L. Y. (2018), 'Artificial Intelligence & Human Rights: Opportunities & Risks', Berkman Klein Centre Research Publication No. 2018-6. Available online: https://ssrn.com/abstract=3259344.

40 Davies, C., Ebbels, S., Nicoll, H., Syrett, K., White, S., and Zuniga-Montanez, C. (2023), 'Supporting Adjective Learning by Children with Developmental Language Disorder: Enhancing Metalinguistic Approaches'. *International Journal of Language & Communication Disorders*, 58 (2): 629–50. https://doi.org/10.1111/1460-6984.12792.

41 Ding, Y., Riordan, B., Horbach, A., Cahill, A., and Zesch, T. (2020), 'Don't Take "nswvtnvakgxpm" for an Answer: The Surprising Vulnerability of Automatic Content Scoring Systems to Adversarial Input', in *Proceedings of the 28th International Conference on Computational Linguistics*, 882–92. Barcelona, Spain. Available online: https://aclanthology.org/2020.coling-main.76.

42 Fortnite Sensay (2021), 'DreamBox Hack Still TikTok' [YouTube video]. Available online: https://www.youtube.com/watch?v=j1Idc2RpSis 00:17.
43 Khosravi, H., Buckingham Shum, S., Chen, G., Conati, C., Tsai, Y. S., Kay, J., Knight, S., Martinez-Maldonado, R., Sadiq, S., and Gašević, D. (2022), 'Explainable Artificial Intelligence in Education', *Computers and Education: Artificial Intelligence*, 3: 100074. https://doi.org/10.1016/j.caeai.2022.100074.
44 Selwyn, N., Hillman, T., Bergviken Rensfeldt, A., and Perrotta, C. (2023), 'Digital Technologies and the Automation of Education – Key Questions and Concerns', *Postdigital Science & Education*, 5: 15–24. https://doi.org/10.1007/s42438-021-00263-3, 20.
45 Hassija, V., Chamola, V., and Mahapatra, A. (2024), 'Interpreting Black-Box Models: A Review on Explainable Artificial Intelligence', *Cognitive Computation*, 16: 45–74. Available online: https://doi.org/10.1007/s12559-023-10179-8.
46 Ibid.
47 Ibid., 20.
48 Wachter, S., Mittelstadt, B., and Floridi, L. (2017), 'Why a Right to Explanation of Automated Decision-Making Does Not Exist in the General Data Protection Regulation', *International Data Privacy Law*, 7 (2): 76–99. https://doi.org/10.1093/idpl/ipx005.
49 Field, H. (2021), 'At Stanford's "Foundation Models" Workshop, Large Language Model Debate Resurfaces', *Emerging Tech Brew*.
50 Blodgett, S. L., and Madaio, M. (2021), 'Risks of AI Foundation Models in Education', *arXiv*. Available online: https://arxiv.org/abs/2110.10024.
51 Wachter, Mittelstadt, and Floridi, 'Why a Right to Explanation of Automated Decision-Making Does Not Exist in the General Data Protection Regulation'.
52 Edwards, L., and Veale, M. (2017), 'Slave to the Algorithm? Why a "Right to an Explanation" Is Probably Not the Remedy You Are Looking For', *Duke Law & Technology Review*, 16: 18–84.
53 Information Commissioner's Office (ICO) (2023), 'The Information Commissioner's Response to the Government's AI White Paper', *ICO*. Available online: https://ico.org.uk/media/about-the-ico/consultation-responses/4024792/ico-response-ai-white-paper-20230304.pdf.
54 Ibid., 19.
55 Djeffal, C., and Hitrova, C. (2021), 'Recommender Systems and Autonomy: A Role for Regulation of Design, Rights, and Transparency', *Indian Journal of Law and Technology*, 17 (1) 3: 1–52. Available online: https://repository.nls.ac.in/ijlt/vol17/iss1/3.
56 Gilliard, C. (2018), 'Friction-Free Racism', *Real Life*, 15 October. Available online: https://reallifemag.com/friction-free-racism/, n.p.
57 Veale, M. (2020), 'A Critical Take on the Policy Recommendations of the EU High-Level Expert Group on Artificial Intelligence', *European Journal of Risk Regulation*, 11 (1): 1–10. doi:10.1017/err.2019.65, 4.

58 UNICEF (2021), 'Nearly 240 Million Children with Disabilities around the World, UNICEF's Most Comprehensive Statistical Analysis Finds', *UNICEF*, 9 November. Available online: https://www.unicef.org/press-releases/nearly-240-million-children-disabilities-around-world-unicefs-most-comprehensive#:~:text=NEW%20YORK%2C%2010%20November%20 2021,%2Dbeing%2C%20the%20report%20says (Accessed 9 September 2023).
59 World Health Organisation (2023), 'Deafness and Hearing Loss: Key Facts', *WHO*, 27 February. Available online: https://www.who.int/health-topics/hearing-loss#tab=tab_2 (Accessed 9 September 2023).
60 Federal Communications Commission (2021), '21st Century Communication and Video Accessibility Act (CVAA)', *FCC*, 27 January. Available online: https://www.fcc.gov/consumers/guides/21st-century-communications-and-video-accessibility-act-cvaa (Accessed 9 September 2023).
61 FCC News (2021), 'Pluto and ViacomCBS Will Pay $3.5 Million Penalty for Violation of Accessibility Rules', *FCC News*, 29 September. Available online: https://docs.fcc.gov/public/attachments/DOC-376155A1.pdf (Accessed 10 September 2023).
62 European Parliament, Council of the European Union (2019), Directive (EU) 2019/992 of the European Parliament and of the Council of 17 April 2019 on the Accessibility Requirements for Products and Services. PE/81/2018/REV/1. Available online: http://data.europa.eu/eli/dir/2019/882/oj (Accessed 10 September 2023).
63 See the Web Accessibility Initiative, https://www.w3.org/WAI/standards-guidelines/wcag/.
64 Broussard, *More than a Glitch*, 70.
65 Dewey, J. ([1938] 1963), *Experience and Education*, New York: Collier Books.
66 Vygotsky, L. S. (1978), *Mind in Society: The Development of Higher Mental Process*, Cambridge, MA: Harvard University Press.
67 Vygotsky, L. (2012), *Thought and Language – Revised and Expanded Edition*, ed. and transl. E. Hanfmann, G. Vakar and A. Kozulin, Cambridge, MA: MIT Press, 256.
68 Gee, J. P. (2014), *How to Do Discourse Analysis: A Toolkit*, London: Routledge.
69 Johanes, and Lagerstrom, 'Adaptive Learning: The Premise, Promise, and Pitfalls'.
70 Turkle, S. (2015), *Reclaiming Conversation*, New York: Penguin Press, 319.
71 Rasskin-Gutman, D. (2010), *Chess Metaphors: Artificial Intelligence and the Human Mind*, transl. Deborah Klosky. Available online: https://web.mit.edu/6.034/wwwbob/kasparov-article.pdf (Accessed 24 September 2023), 4.
72 Brynjolfsson and McAfee, *The Second Machine Age*.
73 https://dictionary.cambridge.org/dictionary/english/efficiency (Accessed 24 September 2023).
74 DreamBox (2023), 'Troubleshooting Tips: Computer', *DreamBox*, 2 September. Available online: https://support.dreambox.com/s/article/Troubleshooting-Tips-Computer#:~:text=Clear%20your%20browser%20

cache&text=This%20can%20cause%20the%20DreamBox,takes%20less%20than%20five%20minutes (Accessed 24 September 2023).
75 Taylor, A. (2018), 'The Automation Charade', *Logic(s)*, 1 August. Available online: https://logicmag.io/failure/the-automation-charade/ (Accessed 20 October).
76 Molina, E. (2021), 'Challenges Teachers Encounter When Integrating Technology in a Culturally, Linguistically, and Diverse High School' [Doctoral dissertation] *Nova Southeastern University*. Available online: https://nsuworks.nova.edu/cgi/viewcontent.cgi?article=1345&context=fse_etd (Accessed 20 October).
77 Johnson, A. M., Jacovina, M. E., Russell, D. E., and Soto, C. M. (2016), 'Challenges and Solutions When Using Technologies in the Classroom', in S. A. Crossley, and D. S. McNamara (eds.), *Adaptive Educational Technologies for Literacy Instruction*, New York: Routledge, 13–29.
78 Klein, A. (2022), 'Tech Fatigue Is Real for Teachers and Students. Here's How to Ease the Burden', *Education Week*, 8 March. Available online: https://www.edweek.org/technology/tech-fatigue-is-real-for-teachers-and-students-heres-how-to-ease-the-burden/2022/03 (Accessed 20 October).
79 Brown, E. R., and Culora, A. (2021), *Independent Analysis of the Relationship between Sparx Math and Maths Outcomes*. Technical report. Rand Europe, 10–11.
80 Brown, and Culora, *Independent Analysis*, 14.
81 Ibid.
82 Yu, and Couldry, 'Education as a Domain of Natural Data Extraction Analysing Corporate Discourse about Educational Tracking'. doi:10.1080/1369118X.2020.1764604.
83 Smith, L. T. (2012), *Decolonizing Methodologies: Research and Indigenous Peoples* (2nd ed.), London: Zed Books.
84 Hall, S. (ed.) (1997), *Representation: Cultural Representations and Signifying Practices*. London: SAGE Publications, 3. Available online: https://eclass.aueb.gr/modules/document/file.php/OIK260/S.Hall%2C%20The%20work%20of%20Representation.pdf.
85 Hill, J. (2023), 'Priya Lakhani, Founder of EdTech AI Firm Century', *Schools Week*, 14 March. Available online: https://schoolsweek.co.uk/ceos-mission-to-make-ai-a-force-for-good-in-classrooms/ (Accessed 10 September 2023).
86 Blair, T., and Hague, W. (2023), *A New National Purpose: Innovation Can Power the Future of Britain*. Tony Blair Institute for Global Change. Available online: https://institute.global/policy/new-national-purpose-innovation-can-power-future-britain (Accessed 23 October 2023).
87 Hillman, V. (2022), 'The State of Cybersecurity in Education: Voices from the Edtech Sector' [Working Paper]. London: London School of Economics & Political Science. Available online: https://www.lse.ac.uk/media-and-communications/assets/documents/research/working-paper-series/WP72.pdf (Accessed 23 October 2023).
88 Westervelt, E. (2015), 'Meet the Mind-Reading Robo Tutor in the Sky'. *NPR*, 13 October. Available online: https://www.npr.org/sections/

ed/2015/10/13/437265231/meet-the-mind-reading-robo-tutor-in-the-sky#:~:text=%22He%20is%20overselling%20the%20kind,he%20is%20selling%20snake%20oil.%22 (Accessed 23 October 2023).
89 See here https://www.wiley.com/en-gb/education/alta.
90 Kolowich, S. (2013), 'The New Intelligence', *Inside the Higher Ed*, 24 January. Available online: https://www.insidehighered.com/news/2013/01/25/arizona-st-and-knewtons-grand-experiment-adaptive-learning#ixzz2adIDKPLD (Accessed 23 October 2023).
91 See here https://stockanalysis.com/stocks/pwsc/market-cap/#.
92 Apple (2001), 'Apple to Acquire PowerSchool', *Apple*, 14 March. Available online: https://www.apple.com/newsroom/2001/03/14Apple-to-Acquire-PowerSchool/ (Accessed 10 September 2023).
93 Apple (2006), 'Pearson to Acquire PowerSchool', *Apple,* 25 May. Available online: https://www.apple.com/newsroom/2006/05/25Pearson-to-Acquire-PowerSchool/ (Accessed 12 October 2023).
94 Feathers, T. (2022), 'This Private Equity Firm Is Amassing Companies That Collect Data on America's Children', *The Markup*, 11 January. Available online: https://themarkup.org/machine-learning/2022/01/11/this-private-equity-firm-is-amassing-companies-that-collect-data-on-americas-children (Accessed 12 October 2023), n.p.
95 Full list of companies per industry sector, see here https://www.vistaequitypartners.com/companies/portfolio/.
96 For a list of subsidiaries of PowerSchool Holdings, Inc. see here https://www.sec.gov/Archives/edgar/data/1835681/000119312521107673/d24413dex211.htm.
97 Ménard, J. (2022), 'PowerSchool: The Path to Dominate the K-12 Market', *ListEdTech,* 23 February. Available online: https://listedtech.com/blog/powerschool-the-path-to-dominate-the-k-12-market/#:~:text=Under%20the%20ownership%20of%20Vista,well%2Dknown%20career%20readiness%20solutions (Accessed 12 October 2023), n.p.
98 Yu, and Couldry, *Education as a Domain of Natural Data Extraction.*
99 van Ark, B. (2016), 'The Productivity Paradox of the New Digital Economy', *International Productivity Monitor*, Centre for the Study of Living Standards, 31: 3–18.
100 MIT Initiative on the Digital Economy (2019), 'Analysis: The Productivity Paradox, Digital Abundance and Scarce Genius', *MIT Initiative on the Digital Economy*, 28 March. Available online: https://ide.mit.edu/insights/analysis-the-productivity-paradox-digital-abundance-and-scarce-genius/ (Accessed 17 October 2023), n.p.
101 Marconi, F. (2020), *Newsmakers,* New York: Columbia University Press.
102 Broussard, *More than a Glitch,* 9.
103 Gitelman, L. (ed.) (2013), *Raw Data Is an Oxymoron*, Cambridge, MA: MIT Press.

Chapter 5

1. This is a great book that can be read with, to or by children and young people: Jolie, A., and van Bueren, G. (2021), *Know Your Rights and Claim Them: A Guide for Youth*, London: Andersen Press, 15.
2. Couldry, N. (2010), *Why Voice Matters: Culture and Politics after Neoliberalism*, London: SAGE Publications, 2.
3. Ibid.
4. Lundy, L. (2007), '"Voice" Is Not Enough: Conceptualising Article 12 of the United Nations Convention on the Rights of the Child', *British Educational Research Journal*, 33 (6): 927–42. doi:10.1080/01411920701657033.
5. International Digital Accountability Council (IDAC) (2020), 'Privacy in the Age of Covid: An IDAC Investigation of Covid-19 Apps', https://digitalwatchdog.org/wp-content/uploads/2020/07/IDAC-COVID19-Mobile-Apps-Investigation-07132020.pdf (Accessed 27 October 2023).
6. Article 5 of UNCRC (UNCRC).
7. Druin, A. (2002), The Role of Children in the Design of New Technology. *Behaviour and information technology*, 21(1): 1–25. https://doi.org/10.1080/01449290110108659.
8. Barron, R. (2020), 'The Student Voice on a Token Economy System at Whole-School Level', HDip. diss., Dublin: Dublin Business School, School of Arts. https://esource.dbs.ie/bitstream/handle/10788/4015/hdip_geoghegan_c_2020.pdf?sequence=1&isAllowed=y (Accessed 27 October 2023).
9. United Nations (1989), Convention on the Rights of the Child. Adopted and opened for signature, ratification and accession by General Assembly Resolution 44/25 of 20 November 1989. Available online: https://www.unicef.org.uk/wp-content/uploads/2016/08/unicef-convention-rights-child-uncrc.pdf (Accessed 10 October 2023).
10. Lansdown, G. (2005), *The Evolving Capacities of the Child*, Florence: United Nations Children's Fund (UNICEF). https://www.unicef-irc.org/publications/pdf/evolving-eng.pdf (Accessed 27 October 2023).
11. eNACSO (2016), 'When Free Isn't: Business, Children and the Internet', http://www.enacso.eu/wp-%20%20content/uploads/2015/12/free-isnt.pdf (Accessed 27 October 2023).
12. Lievens, E., Livingstone, S., McLaughlin, S., O'Neill, B., and Verdoodt, V. (2018), 'Children's Rights and Digital Technologies', in T. Liefaard and U. Kilkelly (eds.), *International Human Rights of Children*, 487–513, Berlin: Springer.
13. Ibid., 3.
14. Varadan, S. (2019), 'The Principle of Evolving Capacities under the UN Convention on the Rights of the Child', *The International Journal of Children's Rights*, 27 (2): 306–38. doi:10.1163/15718182-02702006.
15. On participatory digital democracy, see Fuchs, C. (2021), 'The Digital Commons and the Digital Public Sphere: How to Advance

Digital Democracy Today', *Westminster Papers in Communication and Culture*, 16 (1): 9–26. doi:https://doi.org/10.16997/wpcc.917.
16. Fortin, J. (2009), *Children's Rights and the Developing Law*, Cambridge: Cambridge University Press.
17. United Nations General Assembly. (1989), Convention on the Rights of the Child, Available online: https://www.ohchr.org/en/professionalinterest/pages/crc.aspx (Accessed 29 October 2023), 3.
18. Van Der Hof, S., Lievens, E., Milkaite, I., Verdoodt, V., Hannema, T., and Liefaard, T. (2020), 'The Child's Right to Protection against Economic Exploitation in the Digital World', *The International Journal of Children's Rights*, 28 (4): 833–59. https://doi.org/10.1163/15718182-28040003, 841.
19. United Nations Committee on the Rights of the Child (UNCRC) (2021), 'Convention on the Rights of the Child: General Comment No. 25 (2021) on Children's Rights in Relation to the Digital Environment', *UNICEF*, 2 March. Available online: https://www.unicef.org/bulgaria/en/media/10596/file (Accessed 29 October 2023).
20. Breiter, A., and Hepp, A. (2018), 'The Complexity of Datafication: Putting Digital Traces in Context', in A. Hepp, A. Breiter, and U. Hasebrink (eds.), *Transforming Communications – Studies in Cross-Media Research*, 387–405, Cham: Palgrave Macmillan.
21. Bailey, J., Laakso, M., and Nyman, L. (2019), 'Look Who's Tracking', *Informaatiotutkimus*, 38 (3–4): 20–44.
22. Csikszentmihaly, M. (2013), *Creativity: The Psychology of Discovery and Invention*, New York: Harper Perennial Modern Classics.
23. Clements, D. H., and Nastasi, B. (1993), 'Electronic Media and Early Childhood Education', in B. Spodek (ed.), *Handbook of Research on the Education of Young Children*, New York: Macmillan, 251–75.
24. Amabile, T. M., and Gitomor, J. (1984), 'Children's Artistic Creativity: Effects of Choice in Task Materials', *Personality and Social Psychology Bulletin*, 10 (2): 209–15.
25. Loveless, A. (2003), 'Creating Spaces in the Primary Curriculum: ICT in Creative Subjects', *The Curriculum Journal*, 14 (1): 5–21.
26. Freire, P. (1970), *Pedagogy of the Oppressed*, London: Penguin Group, 30.
27. Runco, M. A. (2004), 'Creativity', *Annual Review of Psychology*, 55: 657–87.
28. Craft, A. (2001), 'Little c: Creativity in Craft', in A. Craft, B. Jeffrey, and M. Liebling (eds.), *Creativity in Education*, 45–61, London: Continuum.
29. Common Sense Media (2016), 'The Common Sense Census: Plugged-In Parents of Tweens and Teens', Common Sense Media. Available online: https://www.commonsensemedia.org/sites/default/files/uploads/research/common-sense-parent-census_whitepaper_new-for-web.pdf.
30. Jensen, M., George, M. J., Russell, M. R., and Odgers, C. L. (2019), 'Young Adolescents' Digital Technology Use and Adolescents' Mental Health

Symptoms: Little Evidence of Longitudinal or Daily Linkages', *Clinical Psychological Science*, 1–18. https://doi.org/10.1177/2167702619859336.
31 Vygotsky, L. (2004), 'Imagination and Creativity in Childhood', *Journal of Russian and East European Psychology*, 42 (1): 7–97.
32 Russ, S. W. (2003), 'Play and Creativity: Developmental Issues', *Scandinavian Journal of Educational Research*, 47 (3): 291–303.
33 Amabile, T. M. (1996), *Creativity in Context*, Boulder, CO: Westview Press.
34 Feldman, D. H., Csikszentmihalyi, M., and Gardner, H. (1994), 'Changing the World: A Framework for the Study of Creativity', *The Journal of Mind and Behaviour*, 16 (1): 99–101.
35 Csikszentmihaly, *Creativity*.
36 Loveless, A., and Williamson, B. (2013), *Learning Identities in a Digital Age: Rethinking Creativity, Education and technology*, New York: Routledge.
37 Resnick, M. (2017), *Lifelong Kindergarten: Cultivating Creativity through Projects, Passion, Peers, and Play*, Cambridge: The MIT Press.
38 Gee, J. P. (2007), *What Video Games Have to Teach Us about Learning and Literacy*, New York: Palgrave Macmillan.
39 https://www.nasa.gov/apps/.
40 https://merlin.allaboutbirds.org.
41 https://www.inaturalist.org.
42 Tondeur, J., Braak, J. Van, and Ertmer, P. A. (2017), 'Understanding the Relationship between Teachers' Pedagogical Beliefs and Technology Use in Education: A Systematic Review of Qualitative Evidence', *Educational Technology Research & Development*, 65 (3): 555–75. https://doi.org/10.1007/s11423-016-9481-2.
43 Light, Burgess, and Duguay, 'The Walkthrough Method', 881–900.
44 Team Thrively (2020), 'Welcome to Thrively: Overview' [YouTube video], *Team Thrively*. Available online: https://www.youtube.com/watch?v=VUSvhUVmK_U.
45 Ibid., 00:18.
46 Hooper, L., Livingstone, S., and Pothong, K. (2022), *Problems with Data Governance in UK Schools: The Cases of Google Classroom and ClassDojo*, London, UK: Digital Futures Commission, 5Rights Foundation.
47 Team Thrively, 'Welcome to Thrively: Overview', 00:35. Accessed 24 October 2023.
48 Barbovschi, M., Green, L. and Vandoninck, S. (eds) (2013), 'Innovative Approaches for Investigating How Children Understand Risk in New Media', *Dealing with Methodological and Ethical Challenges*, London: EU Kids Online, London School of Economics and Political Science.
49 Office of Communications (OFCOM) (2022), 'Children and Parents: Media Use and Attitudes Report 2022', *OFCOM*, 30 March. Available online: https://www.ofcom.org.uk/__data/assets/pdf_file/0024/234609/childrens-media-use-and-attitudes-report-2022.pdf (Accessed 29 October 2023), 78.

50 Mourlam, D., DeCino, D. A., Newland, L. A., and Strouse, G. A. (2020), '"It's Fun!" Using Students' Voices to Understand the Impact of School Digital Technology Integration on Their Well-Being', *Computers & Education*,159: 104003. https://doi.org/10.1016/j.compedu.2020.104003.

51 Selwyn, N., Nemorin, S., and Johnson, N. F. (2020), 'The "Obvious" Stuff: Exploring the Mundane Realities of Digital Technology Use in School', *Digital Education, Review*, 37(June 2020). http://greav.ub.edu/der/, 5.

52 Moya, A. A., and Damşa, C. (2023), 'Affordances and Agency in Students' Use of Online Platforms and Resources Beyond Curricular Boundaries', *Learning, Media and Technology*, 48 (4): 685–700. doi: 10.1080/17439884.2023.2230124.

53 Kosmas, P., and Zaphiris, P. (2021), 'Improving Students' Learning Performance through Technology-Enhanced Embodied Learning: A Four-Year Investigation in Classrooms', *Education and Information Technologies* (2023) 28: 11051–74.

54 Pothong, K., and Livingstone, S. (2023), *Children's Rights through Children's Eyes: A Methodology for Consulting Children*. Digital Futures Commission, 5Rights Foundation, 12.

55 Pothong, and Livingstone, *Children's Rights through Children's Eyes*, 12.

56 Ibid., 13.

57 Wang, G., Zhao, J., Van Kleek, M., and Shadbolt, N. (2023), '"Treat Me as Your Friend, Not a Number in Your Database": Co-designing with Children to Cope with Datafication Online', in *Proceedings of the 2023 CHI Conference on Human Factors in Computing Systems (CHI '23)*, 23–8 April 2023, Hamburg, Germany (21 pages). ACM, New York, NY, USA. https://doi.org/10.1145/3544548.3580933.

58 Wang et al., 'Treat Me as Your Friend, Not a Number in Your Database'.

59 Ibid.

60 Smahel, D., Wright, M. F., and Cernikova, M. (2015), 'The Impact of Digital Media on Health: Children's Perspectives', *International Journal of Public Health*, 60: 131–7. https://doi.org/10.1007/s00038-015-0649-z.

61 Lundy, L., Byrne, B., Templeton, M., and Lansdown, G. (2019), *Two Clicks Forward and One Click Back: Report on Children with Disabilities in the Digital Environment*, Council of Europe. https://rm.coe.int/two-clicks-forward-and-one-click-back-report-on-children-with-disabili/168098bd0f, 11.

62 Alper, *Giving Voice*, 23.

63 Ibid., 23.

64 Selwyn, N. (2016), 'Digital Downsides: Exploring University Students' Negative Engagements with Digital Technology', *Teaching in Higher Education*, 21 (8): 1006–1021. doi:10.1080/13562517.2016.1213229, 442.

65 Federici, R. A., and Skaalvik, E. M. (2014), 'Students' Perception of Instrumental Support and Effort in Mathematics: The Mediating Role of Subjective Task Values', *Social Psychology of Education*, 17 (3): 527–40.

66 Porumbescu, G., Bellé, N., Cucciniello, M., and Nasi, G. (2017), 'Translating Policy Transparency into Policy Understanding and Policy Support: Evidence from a Survey Experiment', *Public Administration*, 95 (4): 990–1008.
67 Leeming, D. (ed.) (2001), *A Dictionary of Asian Mythology*, London: Oxford University Press.
68 Moro, C., Phelps, C., Redmond, P., and Štromberga, Z. (2020), 'HoloLens and Mobile Augmented Reality in Medical and Health Science Education: A Randomised Controlled Trial', *British Journal of Educational Technology*, 52 (2): 680–94. https://doi.org/10.1111/bjet.13049.
69 Asia Society/OECD (2018), *Teaching for Global Competence in a Rapidly Changing World*, New York: OECD Publishing. https://doi.org/10.1787/9789264289024-en.
70 Farley, H. (2011), 'The University of Queensland's Virtual World Religion Bazaar Project', in *Teaching Arts and Science with the New Social Media*, Bingley: Emerald Group Publishing.
71 McClean, P., Saini-Eidukat, B., Schwert, D., Slator, B., and White, A. (2001), 'Virtual Worlds in Large Enrollment Science Classes Significantly Improve Authentic Learning', in J. A. Chambers (ed.), *Selected Papers from the 12th International Conference on College Teaching and Learning*, 111–18, Jacksonville, FL: Center for the Advancement of Teaching and Learning, Florida State College at Jacksonville.
72 Pereira, J. (2010), \AVALON to Shakespeare: Language Learning and Teaching in Virtual Worlds', *Teacher Development and Education in Context: A Selection of Papers Presented at IATEFL 2010 by the British Council*, S. Sheehan, London: British Council, 94–7.
73 Farley, *The University of Queensland's Virtual World Religion Bazaar Project*.
74 Nearpod (2023), 'NearPod VR – Introducing Virtual Field Trips' [Video file]. Available online: https://vimeo.com/143698022.
75 Aspire East Palo Alto Phoenix Academy, public school reviews, available online: https://www.publicschoolreview.com/aspire-east-palo-alto-phoenix-academy-profile.
76 See Karl M. Kapp on gamification of learning and instruction and a balanced view of learning and literacy in video game playing, James Paul Gee.
77 Meta (n.d.) 'Learn', *Meta*. Available online: https://www.oculus.com/horizon-worlds/learn/?locale=en_GB (Accessed 18 September 2023).
78 YouTube (2022), 'Lacoste x Minecraft: Croco Island Trailer' [YouTube video]. Available online: https://www.youtube.com/watch?v=P0l30wtuS_U (Accessed 18 September 2023).
79 Microsoft (2016), 'Minecraft: Education Edition Is Released to Help Children Learn in Schools', *Microsoft News Centre UK*, 3 November. Available online: https://news.microsoft.com/en-gb/2016/11/03/minecraft-education-edition-released-help-children-learn-schools/ (Accessed 18 September 2023).
80 Microsoft (2016), 'A New Minecraft Could Help Your Child Do Better at School', *Microsoft News Centre UK*, 10 June. Available online: https://news.

microsoft.com/en-gb/2016/06/10/24883/#sm.001ppd4ga12rmdq2qxw1kfvn1nbdr (Accessed 18 September 2023).
81 Cohen, D. (2020), 'PacSun Goes Back to School with Snapchat AR Lens', *Adweek*, 23 September. Available online: https://www.adweek.com/brand-marketing/pacsun-goes-back-to-school-with-snapchat-ar-lens/ (Accessed 18 September 2023).
82 Driver, R. (2021), 'Ralph Lauren Dives into Digital Fashion with Zepeto', *Fashion Network*, 26 August. Available online: https://uk.fashionnetwork.com/news/Ralph-lauren-dives-into-digital-fashion-with-zepeto,1328258.html (Accessed 18 September 2023).
83 Wang, G., Zhao, J., Van Kleek, M., and Shadbolt, N. (2022), '"Don't Make Assumptions About Me!": Understanding Children's Perception of Datafication Online', *Proc. ACM Human-Computer Interaction*, 6 (CSCW2) Article 419. https://doi.org/10.1145/3555144.
84 Ofcom (2022), 'Children and Parents: Media Attitudes Report 2023', *Ofcom*, 30 March. Available online: https://www.ofcom.org.uk/research-and-data/media-literacy-research/childrens/children-and-parents-media-use-and-attitudes-report-2022.
85 Livingstone, S., Bulger, M., Burton, P., Day, E., Lievens, E., Milkaite, I., and De Wolf, R. (2022), 'Children's Privacy and Digital Literacy across Cultures: Implications for Education and Regulation', in L. Pangrazio, and J. Sefton-Green (eds.), *Learning to Live with Datafication: Educational Case Studies and Initiatives from across the World*, 184–200. https://doi.org/10.4324/9781003136842-11.
86 Ibid., 189.
87 Ibid., 189–90.
88 Pangrazio, L., and Selwyn, N. (2018), '"It's Not Like It's Life or Death or Whatever": Young People's Understandings of Social Media Data', *Social Media Society*, 4 (3). https://doi.org/10.1177/2056305118787808, 4.
89 Ibid., 6.
90 Bailey, Laakso, and Nyman, 'Look Who's Tracking', 20–44.
91 Jaunzems, K., Holloway, D. J., Green, L., and Stevenson, K. J. (2019), 'Very Young Children Online: Media Discourse and Parental Practice', in L. Green, D. J. Holloway, K. J. Stevenson, and K. Jaunzems (eds.), *Digitizing Early Childhood*, 16–27, Newcastle upon Tyne: Cambridge Scholars Publishing.
92 Breiter and Hepp, 'The Complexity of Datafication', 387–405.
93 Pandey, N., and Pal, A. (2020), 'Impact of Digital Surge during Covid-19 Pandemic: A Viewpoint on Research and Practice', *International Journal of Information Management*, 55: 102171. doi:10.1016/j.ijinfomgt.2020.102171.
94 Baby, A., and Kannammal, A. (2020), 'Network Path Analysis for Developing an Enhanced TAM Model: A User-Centric E-Learning Perspective', *Computers in Human Behaviour*, 107: 106081.
95 Pedrosa, A. L., Bitencourt, L., Fróes, A. C. F., Cazumbá, M. L. B., Campos, R. G. B., de Brito, S. B. C. S., and Simões e Silva, A. C. (2020), 'Emotional,

Behavioural, and Psychological Impact of the Covid-19 Pandemic', *Frontiers in Psychology*, 11: 566212.
96 Ketelhut, S., Röglin, L., Martin-Niedecken, A. L., Nigg, C. R., and Ketelhut, K. (2022), 'Integrating Regular Exergaming Sessions in the ExerCube into a School Setting Increases Physical Fitness in Elementary School Children: A Randomized Controlled Trial', *Journal of Clinical Medicine*, 11 (6): 1570. https://doi.org/10.3390/jcm11061570.
97 Gottschalk, F. (2019), *Impacts of Technology Use on Children*, Paris: OECD Education Working Papers. https://doi.org/10.1787/8296464e-en.
98 Stieber, D. (2022), America's Teachers Aren't Burned Out. We Are Demoralized, 14 February, EdSurge. Available online: https://www.edsurge.com/news/2022-02-14-america-s-teachers-aren-t-burned-out-we-are-demoralized (Accessed 12 November 2023).
99 Pangrazio, L. and Selwyn, N. (2018), '"t's Not Like It's Life or Death or Whatever": Young People's Understandings of Social Media Data', *Social Media + Society*, 4 (3): 1–9. https://doi.org/10.1177/2056305118787808.
100 Seldon, A. (2018), *The Fourth Education Revolution: Will Artificial Intelligence Liberate or Infantilise Humanity?*, Buckingham, UK: University of Buckingham Press.
101 Mahieu, R. L. P., Asghari, H., and van Eeten, M. (2018), 'Collectively Exercising the Right of Access: Individual Effort, Societal Effect', *Internet Policy Review*, 7 (3). https://doi.org/10.14763/2018.3.927, 15.
102 Zuboff, *The Age of Surveillance Capitalism*.
103 Schneier, B. (2006), 'Commentary: The Eternal Value of Privacy', *WIRED*, May 18. Available online: http://www.wired.com/news/columns/1,70886-0.html (Accessed 11 October 2023).
104 Solove, D. J. (2007), '"I've Got Nothing to Hide" and Other Misunderstandings of Privacy', *San Diego Law Review*, 44: 745. GWU Law School Public Law Research Paper No. 289. Available online: https://ssrn.com/abstract=998565, 767.
105 Quoted in Solove (2007), Bartow, A. (2006), 'A Feeling of Unease about Privacy Law', University of Pennsylvania Law Review, 52. Available online: https://scholarship.law.upenn.edu/penn_law_review_online/vol155/iss1/6, 768.
106 Masur, P. K. (2020), 'The Politics of Privacy: Communication and Media Perspectives to Privacy Research', *Media and Communication*, 8 (2): 2183–439. doi:10.17645/mac.v8i2.2855.
107 Pangrazio, L., and Selwyn, N. (2020), 'Towards a School-Based Critical Data Education', *Pedagogy, Culture & Society*, 29 (3): 431–48. doi:10.1080/14681366.2020.1747527.
108 Oehrli, J. A. and Fontichiaro, K. (2016), 'Why Data Literacy Matters', *Journal of Youth Services in Libraries*, 44 (5): 21–27. Available online: https://eric.ed.gov/?id=EJ1099487.
109 Stoilova, Livingstone, and Nandagiri, 'Data and Privacy Literacy', 413–25.

Chapter 6

1. William, E. H. (1888), *Invictus*, Poetry Foundation. Available online: https://www.poetryfoundation.org/poems/51642/invictus.
2. Cuban, L. (2002), *Oversold and Underused: Computers in the Classroom*, Cambridge, MA: Harvard University Press.
3. Selwyn, and Jandrić, 'Postdigital Living in the Age of Covid-19', 989–1005.
4. Crisp, W. (2023), 'Met to Increase Intelligence Gathering in London Schools Amid Israel-Gaza Tensions', *The Guardian*, 29 October. Available online: https://www.theguardian.com/uk-news/2023/oct/29/met-increase-intelligence-gathering-london-schools-amid-gaza-tensions (Accessed 29 October 2023).
5. Strathern, M. (2000), 'Introduction: New Accountabilities', in *Audit Cultures Anthropological Studies in Accountability, Ethics and the Academy*, London: Routledge, 1–18.
6. Lingard, B., Nixon, J., & Ranson, S. (eds.) (2008), *Transforming Learning in Schools and Communities: The Remaking of Education for a Cosmopolitan Society*. London: Continuum, 47.
7. Bauman, Z. (1991), *Modernity and Ambivalence*, Oxford: Polity Press, 11.
8. https://www.worldbank.org/en/topic/education/overview#:~:text=Education%20is%20a%20human%20right,to%20ensure%20equity%20and%20inclusion (Accessed 29 October 2023).
9. https://www.worldbank.org/en/publication/human-capital/publication/collapse-recovery-how-covid-19-eroded-human-capital-and-what-to-do-about-it (Accessed 29 October 2023).
10. OECD (2018), *The Future of Education and Skills: Education 2030*, Paris: OECD, Available online: https://www.oecd.org/education/2030/E2030%20Position%20Paper%20(05.04.2018).pdf (Accessed 10 September 2023).
11. Cuban, L. (2004), *Oversold and Underused: Computers in the Classroom*, Cambridge, MA: Harvard University Press.
12. As quoted in Postman, N. (1994), *The Disappearance of Childhood*, New York: Vintage Books, 17.
13. Ibid.
14. Ibid.
15. Prout, A. (2011), 'Taking a Step Away from Modernity: Reconsidering the New Sociology of Childhood', *Global Studies of Childhood*, 1 (1): 4–14.
16. Prout, A. (2008), 'Participation, Policy and the Changing Conditions of Childhood', in B. Lingard, J. Nixon, and S. Ranson, *Transforming Learning in Schools and Communities: the Remaking of Education for a Cosmopolitan Society*, 288–301, London: Continuum, 288.
17. Ibid., 288.
18. As quoted in Prout, *Participation, Policy and the Changing Conditions of Childhood,* 290. Freeman, R. (1999), 'Recursive Politics: Prevention, Modernity and Social Systems', *Children and Society*, 13 (4): 232–41.

19 Ibid., 290.
20 World Economic Forum (WEF) (2020), 'Schools of the Future: Defining New Models of Education for the Fourth Industrial Revolution', *WEF*, January. Available from: https://www3.weforum.org/docs/WEF_Schools_of_the_Future_Report_2019.pdf (Accessed 12 September 2023), 6.
21 Gardner, H., and Davies, K. (2013), *The App Generation: How Today's Youth Navigate Identity, Intimacy, and Imagination in a Digital World*, New Haven: Yale University Press.
22 See evidence, as exemplified by the UK Children's Commissioner's findings on children's exposure to pornography: https://www.childrenscommissioner.gov.uk/resource/a-lot-of-it-is-actually-just-abuse-young-people-and-pornography/; On grooming, harassment, risk of harm to children online and online radicalization, among other issues, see: https://assets.publishing.service.gov.uk/media/5bf8721fed915d17d20fc7bc/Literature_Review_Final_October_2017.pdf and www.gov.uk/government/groups/uk-council-for-child-internet-safety-ukccis. That said, global initiatives, advocating for child's rights and driving new legislation to address these issues and safeguard children on the internet, continue actively.
23 Jenkins, H. (2008), *Convergence Culture: Where Old and New Media Collide*, New York: NYU Press. See also boyd, d. (2011), *A Networked Self: Identity, Community, and Culture on Social Network Sites*, New York: Routledge.
24 Organisation for Economic Co-operation and Development (2018), *Idea Exchange: The Future of Education*, Paris: OECD. Available online: https://one.oecd.org/document/EDU/EDPC(2018)4/en/pdf#:~:text=Curriculum%20overload.&text=As%20a%20result%2C%20students%20often,to%20'quality%20learning%20time', 6.
25 Eurostat (2022), *Archive: Being Young in Europe Today – Demographic Trends*, Brussels: Eurostat. Available online: https://ec.europa.eu/eurostat/statistics-explained/index.php?title=Being_young_in_Europe_today_-_demographic_trends&oldid=575085#Europe.E2.80.99s_demographic_challenge.
26 Office for National Statistics (2021), *Population Estimates for the UK, England and Wales, Scotland and Northern Ireland: Mid-2019*, Office for National Statistics. Available online: https://www.ons.gov.uk/peoplepopulationandcommunity/populationandmigration/populationestimates/bulletins/annualmidyearpopulationestimates/mid2019estimates.
27 Prout, *Participation, Policy and the Changing Conditions of Childhood*, 298.
28 Ibid.
29 As quoted in Prout, *Participation, Policy and the Changing Conditions of Childhood*, 298. See Christensen, P. H. (1994), 'Children as the Cultural Other', *KEA: Zeitschrift für Kulturwissenschaften*, 6: 1–16.
30 Bourdieu, P. (1980), *The Logic of Practice*, Stanford, CA: Stanford University Press.
31 Bourdieu, and Passeron, *Reproduction in Education, Society and Culture*, 6.
32 Ibid.

33 Nash, R. (1990), 'Bourdieu on Education and Social and Cultural Reproduction', *British Journal of Sociology of Education*, 11 (4): 431–47.
34 Ibid., 436.
35 Ibid. See translator's note, xxiii–xxvi.
36 Shapiro, and Varian, *Information Rules: A Strategic Guide to the Network Economy*.
37 Postman, N., and Weingartner, C. (1973), *The School Book: For People Who Want to Know What All the Hollering Is About*, New York: Dell Publishing, 99–103.
38 Undergoing training for a postgraduate certificate in higher education with the department of education at Goldsmiths College, UK.
39 Biesta, 'What Is Education For? On Good Education, Teacher Judgement, and Educational Professionalism', 75–87, 77.
40 Sana, F., Weston, T., and Cepeda, N. J. (2013), 'Laptop Multitasking Hinders Classroom Learning for Both Users and Nearby Peers', *Computers & Education*, 62: 24–31. https://doi.org/10.1016/j.compedu.2012.10.003.
41 May, K. E., and Elder, A. D. (2018), 'Efficient, Helpful, or Distracting? A Literature Review of Media Multitasking in Relation to Academic Performance', *International Journal of Educational Technology in Higher Education*, 15 (1): 1–17. https://doi.org/10.1186/s41239-018-0096-z.
42 Bailey, J., Carter, S., Schneider, C., and Ark, T. (2013), 'Portable Records and Learner Profiles', COGNIA. Available online: https://source.cognia.org/issue-article/portable-records-and-learner-profiles/ (Accessed 15 October 2023), n.p.
43 Ibid.
44 Shadmy, T. (2019), 'The New Social Contract: Facebook's Community and Our Rights', *Boston University International Law Journal*, 37, SSRN: https://ssrn.com/abstract=3238665.
45 Baudrillard, J. (1994). Simulacra and simulation. Ann Arbor: University of Michigan Press.
46 Hanushek, E. A., and Woessmann, L. (2007), 'The Role of Education Quality for Economic Growth', World Bank Policy Research Working Paper No. 4122. Available online: SSRN: https://ssrn.com/abstract=960379.
47 Lingard, B., and Rizvi, F. (2010), *Globalizing Education Policy*, New York: Routledge, 2–3.
48 Lingard and Rizvi, *Globalizing Education Policy*, 3.
49 Cuban, L. (2004), *The Blackboard and the Bottom Line: Why Schools Can't Be Businesses*, Cambridge, MA: Harvard University Press, 47.
50 Ibid., 49.
51 Ball, *The Education Debate*, 63.
52 Ball, S. J. (2013), *Foucault, Power, and Education*, New York: Routledge, 76.
53 For an extensive exploration of the history of neoliberalist free-market ideology, you can refer to Burgin, A. (2012), *The Great Persuasion: Reinventing Free Markets Since the Depression*, Cambridge, MA: Harvard University Press; Harvey, D. (2007), *A Brief History of Neoliberalism*, Oxford: Oxford University Press.

54 Ball, *The Education Debate*, 43.
55 Ibid., 44.
56 See for more https://www.undp.org/governance/public-sector-reform.
57 See for example, Matovich, I., & Esper, T. (2023), Following New Philanthropy by Network Ethnography: How Did the Varkey Foundation Land and Expand in Latin America? *ECNU Review of Education*, 6(4): 541–567. https://doi.org/10.1177/20965311231168422, and Bishop, M. and Green, M. (2015), Philanthrocapitalism Comes of Age. In: A. Nicholls, R. Paton, and J. Emerson, eds. Social Finance. Oxford: Oxford Academic. Available online: https://doi.org/10.1093/acprof:oso/9780198703761.003.0005.
58 https://www.amazonfutureengineer.co.uk.
59 https://grow.google/intl/uk/google-career-certificates/.
60 Skinner, B. F. (1985), 'Cognitive Science and Behaviorism', *British Journal of Psychology*, 76: 291–301. https://doi.org/10.1111/j.2044-8295.1985.tb01953.x.
61 Dewey, J. ([1933] 1960), *How We Think: A Restatement of the Relation of Reflective Thinking to the Educative Process*, Lexington, MA: D. C. Heath and Company.
62 Dewey, *Experience and Education*.
63 Marsh, J. (2010), *Childhood, Culture and Creativity: A Literature Review*, Newcastle upon Tyne: Creativity, Culture and Education, Available online: https://www.creativitycultureeducation.org/wp-content/uploads/2018/10/CCE-childhood-culture-and-creativity-a-literature-review.pdf, 45.
64 Piaget, J. (1964), 'Cognitive Development in Children: Piaget Development and Learning', *Journal of Research in Science Teaching*, 2: 176–86.
65 Vygotsky, L. (1978), 'Interaction between Learning and Development', in M. Gauvain and M. Cole (eds.), *Readings on the Development of Children*, 34–40, New York: Scientific American Books.
66 Dewey, *How We Think*, 36.
67 Johanes and Lagerstrom, 'Adaptive Learning: The Premise, Promise, and Pitfalls'.
68 Zeide, 'The Structural Consequences of Big Data-Driven Education', 164–72.
69 Johanes and Lagerstrom, *Adaptive Learning*.
70 Shapiro and Varian, *Information Rules*, 2.
71 Ibid., 14.

Chapter 7

1 Wu, T. (2016), *The Attention Merchants*, New York: Alfred A. Knopf Inc.
2 Gilbert, J., and Williams, A. (2023), *Hegemony Now: How Big Tech and Wall Street Won the World (and How We Win It Back)*, London: Verso, xii–xiii.
3 As quoted in Gilbert, and Williams, *Hegemony Now*.
4 Gilbert, and Williams, *Hegemony Now*, xiii.
5 Ball, *The Education Debate*, 101.

6 As quoted in Wilkins, A., and Olmedo, A. (eds.) (2018), *Education Governance and Social Theory: Interdisciplinary Approaches to Research*, Bloomsbury: London, 5.
7 Wilkins, and Olmedo, *Education Governance and Social Theory*,17.
8 Ibid.
9 Lingard, B., Martino, W., and Rezai-Rashti, G. (2016), 'Testing Regimes, Accountabilities and Education Policy: Commensurate Global and National Developments', *Journal of Education Policy*, 28 (5): 539–56.
10 Ball, *The Education Debate*, 101.
11 Ibid., 30.
12 Carmona, S., and Ezzamel, M. (2007), 'Accounting and Accountability in Ancient Civilizations: Mesopotamia and Ancient Egypt', *Accounting, Auditing and Accountability Journal*, 20 (2): 179–209.
13 Carruthers, B. G., and Espeland, W. N. (1991), 'Accounting for Rationality: Double-Entry Bookkeeping and the Rhetoric of Economic Rationality', *American Journal of Sociology*, 97 (1): 31–69. http://www.jstor.org/stable/2781637.
14 Piattoeva, N., and Boden, R. (2020), 'Escaping Numbers? The Ambiguities of the Governance of Education through Data', *International Studies in Sociology of Education*, 29: 1–2, 1–18. doi:10.1080/09620214.2020.1725590.
15 Hood, C. (1989), 'Public Administration and Public Policy: Intellectual Challenges for the 1990s', *Australian Journal of Public Administration*, 48 (4): 346–58.
16 Piattoeva, and Boden, *Escaping Numbers*, 4.
17 Ibid.
18 Power, M. (1996), *The Audit Explosion*, London: White Dove Press. Available online: https://demos.co.uk/wp-content/uploads/files/theauditexplosion.pdf.
19 Kak, A., and West, S. M. (2023), 'AI Now 2023 Landscape: Confronting Tech Power', AI Now Institute, 11 April. Available online: https://ainowinstitute.org/2023-landscape, 9.
20 Power, *The Audit Explosion*.
21 Ibid.
22 Ibid., 34.
23 Bowker, G. C., and Star, S. L. (1999), *Sorting Things Out*, MIT Press.
24 Ibid., 299.
25 Children's Commissioner (2020), 'Too Many At-Risk Children Are Still Invisible to Social Care', *Children's Commissioner*, Briefing, January. Available online: https://assets.childrenscommissioner.gov.uk/wpuploads/2021/01/cco-too-many-at-risk-children-are-still-invisible-to-social-care.pdf (Accessed 15 November 2023).
26 European Commission (2021), *Digital Education Action Plan 2021–2027: Resetting Education and Training for the Digital Age*, Brussels: European Commission. Available online: https://education.ec.europa.eu/focus-topics/digital-education/action-plan#:~:text=The%20Digital%20Education%20

Action%20Plan%20(2021%2D2027)%20is%20a,States%20to%20the%20 digital%20age (Accessed 15 November 2023), 8.
27 Ibid., 8.
28 https://www.ncbi.nlm.nih.gov/pmc/articles/PMC7344032/.
29 Mazzuccato, M., and Collington, R. (2023), *The Big Con: How the Consulting Industry Weakens Our Businesses, Infantilises Our Governments and Warps Our Economies*, London: Penguin Random House.
30 Ibid., 207.
31 Ibid.
32 https://www.broadbandcommission.org/working-groups/data-for-learning/job-board-data-governance/#:~:text=Data%20governance%20 is%20crucial%20for,privacy%2C%20and%20compliance%20with%20laws (Accessed 21 November 2023).
33 https://groundshifts.substack.com/p/edtech-research-predictions-for-2023 (Accessed 21 November 2023).
34 https://www.edsurge.com/news/2022-06-23-schools-are-looking-for-evidence-from-their-edtech-are-companies-ready-to-provide-it (Accessed 21 November 2023).
35 As quoted in Mazzucato, and Collington, *The Big Con*; Cornell, B., and Damodaran, A. (2020), 'Valuing ESG: Doing Good or Sounding Good?', *NYU Stern School of Business,* 20 March. Available online: https://papers.ssrn.com/sol3/papers.cfm?abstract_id=3557432 (Accessed 21 November 2023), 228.
36 https://dl.acm.org/doi/10.1145/3502288.
37 Trucano, M. (2016), *SABER-ICT Framework Paper for Policy Analysis: Documenting National Educational Technology Policies around the World Over Time.* World Bank Education Technology & Innovation: SABER-ICT Technical Paper Series (#01), Washington, DC: The World Bank. Available online: https://www.edu-links.org/sites/default/files/media/file/Documenting%20national%20educational%20technology%20policies.pdf.
38 UNESCO (2011), *UNESCO ICT Competency Framework for Teachers* (version 2.0), Paris: UNESCO. Available online: https://unesdoc.unesco.org/ark:/48223/pf0000213475.
39 Rivas, A. (2021), *The Platformisation of Education: A Framework to Map the New Directions of Hybrid Education Systems*, Paris: UNESCO, International Bureau of Education. Available online: https://unesdoc.unesco.org/ark:/48223/pf0000377733.
40 OECD (2022), *PISA 2021 ICT Framework*, Paris: OECD. Available online: https://www.oecd.org/pisa/sitedocument/PISA-2021-ICT-framework.pdf.
41 CoAction Learning Lab (2019), 'Framework for Stakeholder Inclusion in the Technology Planning Process', The Pennsylvania State University. Available online: https://coaction.psu.edu/inclusion-framework/.
42 Punya, M. (2019), 'Considering Contextual Knowledge: The TPACK Diagram Gets an Upgrade', *Journal of Digital Learning in Teacher*

Education, 35 (2): 76–8. Available online: https://doi.org/10.1080/21532974.2019.1588611.
43. Magana, A. J. III. (2019), 'Disruptive Classroom Technologies', Oxford Research Encyclopaedia of Education,1–28. doi:10.1093/acrefore/9780190264093.013.423. Available online: https://maganaeducation.com/wp-content/uploads/2020/11/Magana-Disruptive-Classroom-Technologies.pdf, 1.
44. Trust, T. (2018), '2017 ISTE Standards for Educators: From Teaching with Technology to Using Technology to Empower Learners', *Journal of Digital Learning in Teacher Education*, 34 (1): 1–3. doi:10.1080/21532974.2017.1398980.
45. ISTE (2023), *Teacher Ready: Edtech Product Evaluation Guide*, ISTE. Available online: https://cms-live-media.iste.org/ISTE_Edtech_Product_Evaluation_Guide_2023_v1023.pdf?_ga=2.164533247.1752817368.1699653248-824124001.1699653248.
46. ISTE (2020), *The Five Pillars for Edtech Procurement*, ISTE. Available online: https://cdn.iste.org/www-root/PDF/EL%20January%202020-weboptimized.pdf.
47. ISTE (2023), 'EdTech Providers: Accelerate Your Impact with ISTE', *ISTE*. Available online: https://iste.org/edtech-providers.
48. https://www.educateventures.com/consultancy (Accessed 21 November 2023).
49. https://iste.org/become-a-member?_ga=2.128260428.1752817368.1699653248-824124001.1699653248 (Accessed 21 November 2023).
50. http://www.aurora-institute.org/wp-content/uploads/national-standards-for-quality-online-teaching-v2.pdf (Accessed 21 November 2023).
51. https://fcit.usf.edu/matrix/ (Accessed 21 November 2023).
52. Foerster, M., Gourdin, A., Huertas, E., Möhren, J., Ranne, P., and Roca, R. (2019), 'Framework for the Quality Assurance of E-Assessment', *TESLA (European Horizon Project, Report,* H2020-ICT-2015/H2020-ICT-2015 Agreement Number: 688520). Available online: https://www.enqa.eu/wp-content/uploads/D4.7-Framework-screen-TeSLA-2606.pdf (Accessed 21 November 2023).
53. The European Centre for Standardisation (2023), *Age Appropriate Digital Services Framework*, CEN. Available online: https://www.cencenelec.eu/news-and-events/news/2022/workshop/2022-03-28-digitalservices/ (Accessed 21 November 2023).
54. http://tpack.org (Accessed 21 November 2023).
55. For EdTech frameworks based on their creators, features and uses, see Cherner, T. & Mitchell, C. (2021) Deconstructing EdTech frameworks based on their creators, features, and usefulness, Learning, Media and Technology, 46(1): 91-116. DOI: 10.1080/17439884.2020.1773852.
56. https://edtech.digitalpromise.org (Accessed 21 November 2023).

57 Safer Technologies 4 Schools. (2023), Safer Technologies 4 Schools Vendor Guide Version 2023.2. Available online: https://st4s.edu.au/st4s-vendor-guide/ (Accessed 27 November 2023).
58 https://www.nis-2-directive.com/ (Accessed 21 November 2023).
59 https://www.statista.com/statistics/1273188/cybersecurity-standards-usage-control-systems/ (Accessed 21 November 2023).
60 UNICEF (2021), Child Rights Impact Assessment: Template and Guidance for Local Authorities. Child Rights Impact Assessment - Child Friendly Cities & Communities. 1 July. Available online: https://www.unicef.org.uk/cfc.
61 European Committee for Standardization (CEN) and European Committee for Electrotechnical Standardization (CENELEC). (2023), Age-Appropriate Digital Services Framework, https://www.cencenelec.eu/news-and-events/news/2023/eninthespotlight/2023-09-14-cwa-18016-children-protection-online/ (Accessed, 9 September 2023).
62 Kalliomeri, R., Mettinen, K., Ohlsson, A-M., Soini, S. and Tulensalo, H. (2023), *Child-centered design*. Save the Children. Available online: https://www.pelastakaalapset.fi/lapsilta-opittua/wp-content/uploads/sites/80/2023/09/save_the_children_child-centered_design.pdf (Accessed 10 September 2023).
63 TECH TRANSFORMED (2019), Consequence Scanning: An Agile Event for Responsible Innovators, Available online: https://doteveryone.org.uk/project/consequence-scanning/ (Accessed 10 September 2023).
64 D4CR (2022), *Design Principles* (Version 2.0), *Children's Design Guide*. Available online: https://childrensdesignguide.org/wp-content/uploads/2022/07/D4CR-Design-Principles-2.0-2022-07-12.pdf (Accessed 10 September 2023).
65 https://onlinelibrary.wiley.com/doi/full/10.1002/poi3.255 (Accessed 21 November 2023).
66 IEEE (2021), 'Standard for an Age-Appropriate Digital Services Framework Based on the 5 Rights Principles for Children', in *IEEE Std 2089–2021*, 30 November, 1–54. doi:10.1109/IEEESTD.2021.9627644.
67 Elliott, L. (2023), 'Top Economists Cal for Action on Runaway Global Inequality', *The Guardian*, 17 July. Available online: https://www.theguardian.com/inequality/2023/jul/17/top-economists-call-for-action-global-inequality-rich-poor-poverty-climate-breakdown-un-world-bank#:~:text=Failure%20to%20tackle%20the%20widening,200%20leading%20economists%20have%20said. (Accessed 10 October 2023).
68 https://www.ftc.gov/legal-library/browse/federal-register-notices/commercial-surveillance-data-security-rulemaking.
69 https://williamjnovak.com/assets/final-page-proofs-of-public-utility-chapter.pdf.
70 https://eprints.qut.edu.au/216577/.

71 Dreamforce (2023), 'Dreamforce 2023 Main Keynote' [YouTube video]. Available online: https://www.youtube.com/watch?v=Ew-xxNhhscU (Accessed 10 October 2023), 23:22.
72 https://www.theguardian.com/education/2023/jan/09/third-of-englands-teachers-who-qualified-in-last-decade-have-left-profession (Accessed 10 October 2023).
73 https://www.amazon.co.uk/Demoralized-Santoro-author-Berliner-Foreword/dp/1682531325 (Accessed 10 October 2023).
74 https://www.theguardian.com/education/2023/jan/29/tell-us-which-schools-could-collapse-labour-will-force-ministers-to-reveal-data (Accessed 10 October 2023).
75 https://www.theguardian.com/education/2022/nov/10/children-not-eligible-for-free-school-meals-going-hungry-say-teachers (Accessed 10 October 2023).
76 UNESCO (2023), *Technology in Education: A Tool on Whose Terms?* Global Education Monitoring Report, Paris: UNESCO. Available online: https://www.unesco.org/gem-report/en.
77 Ibid.
78 UNESCO, *Global Education Monitoring Report*.
79 Kim, B. C., Chen, P.-Y., and Mukhopadhyay, T. (2011), 'The Effect of Liability and Patch Release on Software Security: The Monopoly Case', *Production and Operations Management*, 20 (4): 603–17.
80 Hillman, V. (2022), 'The State of Cybersecurity in Education: Voices from the Edtech Sector'.
81 Ibid.
82 See here https://privacy.a4l.org/geps/
83 Safer Technologies for Schools Assessment (ST4S) (2021).
84 Hillman, (2022) Edtech Procurement Matters.
85 Nielsen, and Ganter, *The Power of Platforms*, 159.
86 UNESCO, *Global Education Monitoring Report*.
87 Hillman, V (2022) Edtech Procurement Matters.
88 https://aftersurveillance.net/higher-education-surveillance-observatory-some-initial-thoughts/.
89 See updates here: https://ico.org.uk/about-the-ico/information-commissioner-s-response-to-the-data-protection-and-digital-information-bill/.
90 https://bills.parliament.uk/bills/3322 (Accessed 28 November 2023).
91 https://ico.org.uk/about-the-ico/media-centre/news-and-blogs/2022/11/department-for-education-warned-after-gambling-companies-benefit-from-learning-records-database/#:~:text=In%20June%202022%20John%20Edwards,million%20in%20this%20specific%20case (Accessed 28 November 2023).
92 https://ico.org.uk/about-the-ico/media-centre/news-and-blogs/2022/11/department-for-education-warned-after-gambling-companies-benefitfrom-learning-records-database/#:~:text=In%20June%202022%20

John%20Edwards,million%20in%20this%20specific%20case (Accessed 28 November 2023).
93 Data Protection Act (2018). Available online: https://www.legislation.gov.uk/ukpga/2018/12/section/123/enacted (Accessed: 27 November 2023).
94 DCMS & Home Office (2020) Online Harms White Paper. Available at: https://www.gov.uk/government/consultations/online-harms-white-paper/online-harms-white-paper (Accessed: 27 November 2023]
95 United Nations (1990) Convention on the Rights of the Child. Available at: https://www.ohchr.org/en/instruments-mechanisms/instruments/convention-rights-child
96 Hillman, 'EdTech Procurement Matters: It Needs a Coherent Solution, Clear Governance and Market Standards'.
97 UNESCO, *Technology in Education*.
98 Information Commissioner's Office (ICO) (2021), 'The UK General Data Protection Regulation (UK GDPR)'. Available online: https://ico.org.uk/for-organisations/dp-at-the-end-of-the-transition-period/data-protection-and-the-eu-in-detail/the-uk-gdpr/ (Accessed 28 November 2023).
99 Hillman, V. (2022), 'Bringing in the Technological, Ethical, Educational and Social-Structural for a New Education Data Governance', *Learning, Media and Technology*, 48 (1): 122–37, https://doi.org/10.1080/17439884.2022.2052313.
100 United States Department of Education (2011). *Family Educational Rights and Privacy Act* (FERPA), 34 CFR Part 99. Available online: https://www.govinfo.gov/content/pkg/FR-2011-12-02/pdf/2011-30683.pdf.
101 ICO (2023), Children's Code Evaluation. Available online: https://ico.org.uk/media/about-the-ico/documents/childrens-code/4025494/childrens-code-evaluation-report.pdf (Accessed 27 November 2023).
102 Hooper, L., Livingstone, S., and Pothong, K. (2022), Problems with data governance in UK schools: the cases of Google Classroom and ClassDojo. Digital Futures Commission, 5Rights Foundation.
103 Hillman, V. (2022). Edtech Procurement Matters.
104 In June 2025, the European Union has set out to implement the European Accessibility Act. This means that all 'businesses selling products and services covered by the Act must check the national laws and regulations transposing the European Accessibility Act in their country for compliance requirements'. Businesses will have three years to ensure that their products and services comply with the common EU accessibility requirements. See more: https://ec.europa.eu/social/main.jsp?catId=1202&intPageId=5581&langId=en.
105 Hillman, V. (2022). Edtech Procurement Matters.
106 Hillman, 'Bringing in the Technological, Ethical, Educational and Social-Structural for a New Education Data Governance', 122–37.
107 Access 4 Learning Community (A4L.org). (2020). Student Data Privacy Consortium (SDPC) Rules of Governance 2020. Available online: https://cdn.ymaws.com/www.a4l.org/resource/resmgr/files/sdpc-publicdocs/sdpc_rules_of_governance2020.pdf (Accessed 10 November 2023).

108 Zeide, 'The Structural Consequences of Big Data-driven Education', 164–72.
109 Palfrey, Q., Good, N., Ghamrawi, L., Monge, W., and Boag, W. (2020), 'Privacy Considerations as Schools and Parents Expand Utilization of EdTech Apps during the Covid-19 Pandemic', International Digital Accountability Council. Available online: https://digitalwatchdog.org/wp-content/uploads/2020/09/IDAC-Ed-Tech-Report-912020.pdf.
110 https://www.hrw.org/news/2022/05/25/governments-harm-childrens-rights-online-learning.
111 International Digital Accountability Council, 'Privacy in the Age of Covid: An IDAC Investigation of Covid-19 Apps'.
112 Hillman, V. (2022). Bringing in the technological, ethical, educational and social-structural for a new education data governance. Learning, Media and Technology, 48(1), 122–137. https://doi.org/10.1080/17439884.2022.2052313
113 Hooper, Livingstone, and Pothong, *Problems with Data Governance in UK Schools*.
114 Federal Trade Commission (2019), 'Google LLC and YouTube, LLC'. Available online: https://www.ftc.gov/legal-library/browse/cases-proceedings/172-3083-google-llc-youtube-llc.
115 Shadmy 'The New Social Contract: Facebook's Community and Our Rights', 319.
116 Ibid., 309.
117 Rousseau, J. J. (1998), *The Social Contract*, Ware: Wordsworth Classics.
118 Hillman, V. (2022). Bringing in the technological, ethical, educational and social-structural for a new education data governance. Learning, Media and Technology, 48(1), 122–137. https://doi.org/10.1080/17439884.2022.2052313, p.128
119 Agbo, C., Mahmoud, H. Q., and Eklund, J. M. (2019), 'Blockchain Technology in Healthcare: A Systematic Review', *Healthcare*, 7 (2): 56. doi:10.3390/healthcare7020056.
120 Sweeney, K. (2019), *An Operational Data Governance Framework for New Zealand Government*, Wellington: Stats NZ.
121 Federal Trade Commission. (1999), Children's Online Privacy Protection Act of 1998 (COPPA). [Online]. Available online: https://www.ftc.gov/system/files/2012-31341.pdf.
122 *The Family Educational Rights and Privacy Act (FERPA)* (20 U.S.C. § 1232g; 34 CFR Part 99). Available online: https://www2.ed.gov/policy/gen/guid/fpco/ferpa/index.html.
123 Hillman, V. (2022), Bringing in the technological, ethical, educational and social-structural for a new education data governance. Learning, Media and Technology, 48(1), 122–137. https://doi.org/10.1080/17439884.2022.2052313, p. 127.
124 Information Commissioner's Office (2020), 'Statement on the Outcome of the ICO's Compulsory Audit of the Department for Education',

Department for Education. Available online: https://ico.org.uk/about-the-ico/news-and-events/news-and-blogs/2020/10/statement-on-the-outcome-of-the-ico-s-compulsory-audit-of-the-department-for-education/.

125 National Schools Interoperability Program (NSIP) (020), 'National Education Risk Assessment: Vendor Guide', NSIP, March 20. Available online: https://www.nsip.edu.au/sites/nsip.edu.au/files/National%20Education%20Risk%20Assessment%20Vendo%20Guide%20v2.3.pdf.r (Accessed 28 November 2023).

126 Synced (2020), 'Machine Unlearning: Fighting for the Right to Be Forgotten', *Synced Review*. Available online: *https://medium.com/syncedreview/machine-unlearning-fighting-for-the-right-to-be-forgotten-c381f8a4acf5* (Accessed 28 November 2023).

127 Swart, C. (2023), 'The Further Education Sector and Its Use of Artificial Intelligence – Can Regulation Alleviate Concerns?' [MA thesis], Brighton: University of Sussex.

128 Mantelero, A. (2022), *Beyond Data: Human Rights, Ethical and Social Impact Assessment in AI*, The Hague: Springer.

129 https://teachmateai.com.

130 https://www.khanmigo.ai.

131 Bietti, 'A Genealogy of Digital Platform Regulation', 1–67.

132 The drive for evidence of what works with digital technologies in education has spurred yet another market that increasingly blurs the lines between academia and industry. The market of evidence-based gathering and agenda setting has launched commercial avenues for further promotion and brokering between schools and vendors, but also more digitization and drive for standardization of digital models for education globally. For example, media production of the marketization of digital education imaginaries are the EdTech fairs, trade shows, conventions and exhibitions organized all around the world. Such trade shows and expos are key venues where education and technology policy actors, IT industry players, technology advocates, policymakers, and teachers convene, interact, and exchange knowledge. Researchers highlight the significance of these gatherings in supporting EdTech as these events can influence discourse as well as policy. See Player-Koro, C., Rensfeldt, A.B., and Selwyn, N. (2018), 'Selling Tech to Teachers: Education Trade Shows as Policy Events', Journal of Education Policy, 33(5): 682–703. https://doi.org/10.1080/02680939.2017.1380232. Also, see Forsman, M., Forsler, I., Opermann, S., Bardone, E., and Pedaste, M. (2023), 'Future Classrooms and Ed-Tech Imaginaries. Notes From the Estonian Pavilion at EXPO 2020 and beyond', Learning, Media and Technology, 49(1): 133–46. https://doi.org/10.1080/17439884.2023.2237875 . On brokering, see Ortegón, C., Decuypere, M., and Williamson, B. (2024), 'Mediating Educational Technologies: Edtech Brokering between Schools, Academia, Governance, and Industry', Research in Education. https://doi.org/10.1177/00345237242242990.

133 Hillman, V., Esquivel, M., Gonsales, P., Johnston, S-K. & Ogu, E.C. (2023), Global transformations, local choices: Navigating the impacts of Artificial Intelligence on education. In: Brazilian Network Information Centre, ed. ICT in Education: Survey on the Use of Information and Communication Technologies in Brazilian Schools. Brazilian Internet Steering Committee. Available online: https://cetic.br/media/docs/publicacoes/2/20231122132216/tic_educacao_2022_livro_completo.pdf [Accessed 18 June 2023].
134 https://teachmateai.com.
135 Hillman, 'EdTech Procurement Matters: It Needs a Coherent Solution, Clear Governance and Market Standards'.
136 Decuypere, M., Hartong, S., Brandau, N., Joecks, L., Loft-Akhoondi, A., Ortegón, C., Tierens, T., and Vanermen, L. (2024), 'Maneuvering Constellations of Valuation: A Critical Investigation of the Edtech Startup Sector', *Critical Studies in Education*. https://doi.org/10.1080/17508487.2024.2362196.
137 Aulner, F., and Chee, F. Y. (2021), 'Google Loses Challenge against EU Antitrust Ruling, $2.8 Billion Fine', *Reuters*, 11 October. Available online: https://www.reuters.com/technology/eu-court-upholds-eu-antitrust-ruling-against-google-2021-11-10/ (Accessed 29 November 2023).
138 Alcanara, C., Schaul, K., Vynck, G., and Albergotti, R. (2021), 'How Big Tech Got So Big: Hundreds of Acquisitions', *The Washington Post*. Available online: https://www.washingtonpost.com/technology/interactive/2021/amazon-apple-facebook-google-acquisitions/ (Accessed 29 November 2023).
139 Lotteries, and Gaming Authority (2018), *Legislation and Regulations*. Available online: https://www.mga.org.mt/legislations-regulations/.
140 See International Monetary Fund (2018), Malta: Selected Issues, IMF, Volume 2018, issue 020. Available online: https://www.elibrary.imf.org/downloadpdf/view/journals/002/2018/020/article-A003-en.pdf; and also Malta Gaming Authority. (2017), Annual Report 2017. Available online: https://www.mga.org.mt/app/uploads/Annual-Report-2017.pdf.
141 Watters, A. (2023), *Teaching Machines: The History of Personalised Learning*, Cambridge, MA: MIT Press.
142 Kramer, D. I. A., Guillory, E. J., and Hancock, T. J. (2014), 'Experimental Evidence of Massive-Scale Emotional Contagion through Social Networks', *Proceedings of the National Academy of Sciences of the United States of America*, 111 (24): 8788–90. https://doi.org/10.1073/pnas.1320040111.

Chapter 8

1 Boxtel, C. J. V., Santoso, B., and Edwards, I. R. (2008), *Drug Benefits and Risks: International Textbook of Clinical Pharmacology*, Amsterdam: IOS Press.

2   Griffin, J. P. (2004), 'Venetian Treacle and the Foundation of Medicines Regulation', *British Journal of Clinical Pharmacology*, 58 (3): 317–25. doi:10.1111/j.1365-2125.2004.02147.x.
3   Rägo, L., and Santoso, B. (2008), 'Drug Regulation: History, Present and Future', in C. J. V. Boxtel, B. Santoso, and I. R. Edwards (eds.), *Drug Benefits and Risks: International Textbook of Clinical Pharmacology*, Amsterdam: IOS Press.
4   The Online Safety Bill, following the tragic case of Molly Russell, a fourteen-year-old girl who took her own life as a result of being exposed to self-harming content on social media, the much-delayed bill has finally been passed as an Act in the UK. Available online: https://bills.parliament.uk/bills/3137/news.
5   Tidy, J. (2023), 'Worldcoin: Sam Altman Launches Eyeball Scanning Crypto Coin', *BBC News*, 25 July. Available online: https://www.bbc.co.uk/news/technology-66128111.
6   Hillman, V., Forshaw, B., and Parmar, N. (forthcoming), 'Re-thinking EdTech Governance: A Socio-technical Audit Logic Model in Practice', *Computers and Education*.
7   Lessig, L. (2000), Code and Other Laws of Cyberspace, New York: Basic Books.
8   Mazzucato, and Collington, *The Big Con*.
9   Ibid., 230–1.
10 See great work from the Ranking of Digital Rights, which analyses extensively the policies of some of the biggest technology and telecommunications companies. However, in light of the advancement in AI, the question is how effective this effort is in protecting data from being exploited even when privacy and security measures are addressed. See RDR here: https://rankingdigitalrights.org.
11 https://dictionary.cambridge.org/dictionary/english/governance#.
12 Wilkins, A. and Gobby, B. (2021), 'Governance and Educational Leadership: Studies in Education Policy and Politics', in S. Courtney, H. Gunter, R. Niesche, and T. Trujillo (eds.), *Understanding Educational Leadership: Critical Perspectives and Approaches*, 309–23, London: Bloomsbury.
13 Ibid.
14 Ibid., 3.
15 Ibid., 4.
16 Ibid., 3.
17 Wilkins, and Gobby, 'Governance and Educational Leadership'.
18 Clarke, J., and Ozga, J. (2012), 'Working Paper 4: Inspection as Governing', Available online: http://jozga.co.uk/GBI/tag/working-paper/, p. 1 (Accessed 22 November 2023). Cited in: Wilkins, A., and Olmedo, A. (eds.) (2019), *Education Governance and Social Theory: Interdisciplinary Approaches to Research*. London: Bloomsbury Academic, 9.
19 https://www.iso.org/obp/ui/en/#iso:std:iso-iec:17065:ed-1:v1:en.
20 https://www.coe.int/en/web/civil-society/democratic-governance.

21 https://www.coe.int/en/web/civil-society/democratic-governance.
22 https://www.ohchr.org/en/good-governance/about-good-governance.
23 Wilkins, A., and Olmedo, A. (eds.) (2019), *Education Governance and Social Theory: Interdisciplinary Approaches to Research*, London: Bloomsbury Academic, 3.
24 Kooiman, J., and Jentoft, S. (2009), 'Meta-Governance: Values, Norms and Principles, and the Making of Hard Choices', *Public Administration*, 87 (4): 818–36.
25 Wilkins, and Olmedo, *Education Governance and Social Theory*.
26 Gulson, Sellar, and Webb, *Algorithms of Education*.
27 https://www.statista.com/outlook/dmo/eservices/online-gambling/worldwide.
28 Statista (2023), 'Online Education Worldwide', Statista.com. Available online: https://www.statista.com/outlook/dmo/eservices/online-education/worldwide#:~:text=Revenue%20in%20the%20Online%20Education,US%24239.30bn%20by%202027 (Accessed 29 November 2023).
29 HolonIQ (2021), 'Education Technology in 10 Charts', *HolonIQ*. Available online: https://www.holoniq.com/edtech-in-10-charts.
30 Ibid.
31 https://www.gamblingcommission.gov.uk/licensees-and-businesses/licences-and-fees.
32 The Malta Gaming Authority (MGA). (2023), The Malta Gaming Authority Annual Report. Available online: https://www.mga.org.mt/app/uploads/Annual-Report-2022.pdf.
33 https://www.gamblingcommission.gov.uk/statistics-and-research/publication/young-people-and-gambling-2019.
34 https://nationalcollege.com/news/online-gambling-and-young-people-understanding-the-risks#:~:text=The%202019%20Young%20People%20%26%20Gambling,Becoming%20easily%20agitated.
35 Ding, K., and Li, H. (2023), 'Digital Addiction Intervention for Children and Adolescents: A Scoping Review', *International Journal of Environmental Research and Public Health*, 20 (6): 4777. doi: https://doi.org/10.3390/ijerph20064777.
36 That said, habit-forming behaviour is not always negative. However, the problem with many digital applications and social media platforms in particular is that they drive habit formation that does not prioritize individuals' well-being and best interests.
37 More about the book and author see here https://www.nirandfar.com/about-nir-eyal/.
38 Aston, J., Davies, E., Guijon, M., Lauderdale, K., and Popov, D. (2022), 'The Education Technology Market in England', Research Report, London: Department for Education. Available online: https://assets.publishing.service.gov.uk/government/uploads/system/uploads/attachment_data/file/1117067/Edtech_market_in_England_Nov_2022.pdf (Accessed 29 November 2023).

39 Ibid., 264.
40 Kim, Chen, and Mukhopadhyay, 'The Effect of Liability and Patch Release on Software Security: The Monopoly Case', 603–17.
41 Information Commissioner's Office (2020), 'About the Code', Information Commissioner's Office. Available online: https://ico.org.uk/for-organisations/uk-gdpr-guidance-and-resources/childrens-information/childrens-code-guidance-and-resources/age-appropriate-design-a-code-of-practice-for-online-services/about-this-code/ (Accessed 29 November 2023).
42 https://5rightsfoundation.com/uploads/Letter_5RightsFoundation-Breaches oftheAgeAppropriateDesignCode.pdf.
43 Hillman, *Bringing in the Technological, Ethical, Educational and Socio-Structural for a New Education Data Governance.*
44 The EU Accessibility Act (Directive 2019/882) requires that everyday products and services should be accessible to people with disabilities. The focus of the Act is on digital technologies. As such, the Act covers products and services like computers and operating systems, smart phones and other communication devices, e-books and other audio-visual media services. See more here: https://ec.europa.eu/social/main.jsp?catId=1202&intPageId=5581&langId=en.
45 This module is informed through the review of some of the following resources: https://ico.org.uk/for-organisations/uk-gdpr-guidance-and-resources/artificial-intelligence/guidance-on-ai-and-data-protection/ai-and-data-protection-risk-toolkit/, https://www.irishstatutebook.ie/eli/2019/act/5/enacted/en/htmlhttps://ico.org.uk/privacy-design; https://ico.org.uk/for-organisations/uk-gdpr-guidance-and-resources/ and https://gdpr-info.eu.
46 https://sdpc.a4l.org/gess/.
47 Such requirements are informed by reviewing the most recent EU legislative package, including https://osf.io/preprints/socarxiv/gj2kf/, https://digital-strategy.ec.europa.eu/en/library/ethics-guidelines-trustworthy-ai, https://doi.org/10.1007/978-94-6265-531-7,https://ec.europa.eu/info/fundingtenders/opportunities/docs/2021-2027/horizon/guidance/ethics-by-design-and-ethics-of-use-approaches-for-artificial-intelligence_he_en.pdf, https://standards.ieee.org/industry-connections/ec/autonomous-systems/, https://www.oecd-ilibrary.org/docserver/6ff2a1c4-en.pdf?expires=1690979884&id=id&accname=guest&checksum=9D06D22A9FF2801ABCB80DE5A10CB19A (on OECD's AI principles see also https://oecd.ai/en/ai-principles).
48 See the Education Alliance Finland's assessments: https://educationalliancefinland.com.
49 See for instance ErasmusPlus (2020), 'SELFIE Helper and Pedagogical Innovation Assistant (SHERPA)', Brussels: European Commission. Available online: https://ec.europa.eu/programmes/erasmus-plus/projects/eplus-project-details/#project/612867-EPP-1-2019-1-EL-EPPKA3-PI-FORWARD and Directorate-General for Education, Youth, Sport, and Culture (2019), 'Assessment of Tools and Deliverables under the Framework for European Cooperation in Education and Training (ET2020)', Final report. Luxembourg: Publications Office of the European Union.

50 International Digital Accountability Council (IDAC), 'Privacy in the Age of Covid: An IDAC Investigation of Covid-19 Apps'.
51 Collier, K. (2022), 'Illinois College, Hit by Ransomware Attack, to Shut Down', *NBC News*. Available online: https://www.nbcnews.com/tech/security/ransomware-attack-covid-combine-shutter-illinois-college-rcna24905.
52 Levin, D. A. (2022), 'The State of K-12 Cybersecurity: Year in Review – 2022 Annual Report', *K12 Security Information Exchange* (K12 SIX). Available online: https://www.k12six.org/the-report.
53 Cyber Security Works (2022), 'Why Should Schools Prioritise Cybersecurity?' [Blog post], 4 July. Available online: https://cybersecurityworks.com/blog/why-should-schools-prioritize-cybersecurity-1.html.
54 Department for Digital, Culture, Media and Sport (2022), 'Cyber Security Breaches Survey 2022', *Department for Digital, Culture, Media and Sport*. Available online: https://assets.publishing.service.gov.uk/government/uploads/system/uploads/attachment_data/file/1064445/Education_annex_-_cyber_security_breaches_survey_March_2022__WEB_.pdf.
55 Singer, N. (2022), 'A Cyberattack Illuminates the Shake State of Student Privacy', *The New York Times*, 31 July. Available online: https://www.nytimes.com/2022/07/31/business/student-privacy-illuminate-hack.html (Accessed 12 October).
56 See more here: https://www.ucledtechlabs.com.
57 https://ico.org.uk/media/action-weve-taken/4022280/dfe-reprimand-20221102.pdf.
58 Cohen, J. (2019), *Between Truth and Power*, Oxford: Oxford University Press, 171.
59 Mantelero, *Beyond Data Privacy*.
60 Broussard, *More Than a Glitch*, 163.
61 HolonIQ (2023), Education Technology in 10 Charts. Available online: https://www.holoniq.com/edtech-in-10-charts (Accessed 21 November 2023).
62 Williamson, B., & Komljenovic, J. (2022), Investing in imagined digital futures: the techno-financial 'futuring' of edtech investors in higher education. *Critical Studies in Education*, 64(3): 234–249. https://doi.org/10.1080/17508487.2022.2081587
63 Although Byju, India's most valuable EdTech startup, valued by investors at over $22 billion, is now considered 'worth nothing'. See the Economist (2022), Can the ed-tech boom last? https://www.economist.com/business/2022/02/19/can-the-ed-tech-boom-last?ppccampaignID=18151738051&ppcadID=&utm_medium=cpc.adword.pd&utm_source=google&ppccampaignID=18156330227&ppcadID=&utm_campaign=a.22brand_pmax&utm_content=conversion.direct-response.anonymous&gad_source=1&gclsrc=ds, and Singh, M. (2024), BlackRock has Slashed the Value of Stake in Byju's Once Worth $22B, to Zero, 7 June, TechCrunch. Available

64. As quoted in Broussard, 158. McGuiness, T. D., and Schank, H. (2021), *Power to the Public: The Promise of Public Interest Technology*, Princeton, NJ: Princeton University Press.
65. Broussard, *More Than a Glitch*, 158.
66. 'One can find schools' values typically on their websites. Some of the listed values have been taken from UK and US schools.
67. van Dijck, J., Bogaerts, G.-J., and Zuckerman, E. (2023), 'Creating PublicSpaces. Centring Public Values in Digital Infrastructures', *Digital Government: Research and Practice*, 4 (2), Article 9. Available online: https://doi.org/https://dl-acm-org.proxy.library.uu.nl/doi/pdf/10.1145/3582578.
68. Ibid.
69. Zuboff, *Surveillance Capitalism*.
70. van Dijck, Bogaerts, and Zuckerman, *Creating PublicSpaces*, 5.
71. Ibid., 6,7.
72. Kerssens, N., and Dijck, J. V. (2021), 'The Platformisation of Primary Education in The Netherlands', *Learning, Media and Technology*, 46 (3): 250–63.
73. https://unstats.un.org/sdgs/report/2017/goal-04/.
74. Couldry, and Mejias, *The Costs of Connection*.
75. Suleyman, M. (2023), *The Coming Wave: AI, Power and the 21st Century's Greatest Dilemma*, 10, London: The Bodley Head.
76. Bourdieu, *Acts of Resistance*, 82.
77. Cowen, T. (2013), *Average Is Over: Powering America beyond the Age of the Great Stagnation*, New York, NY: Dutton.
78. Bourdieu, *Acts of Resistance*, 98.
79. Ibid.
80. Gray, M. L. and Suri, S. (2019), *Ghost Work: How to Stop Silicon Valley from Building a New Global Underclass*, Boston: Houghton Mifflin Harcourt, ix.
81. Katz, L., and Krueger, A. (2016), 'The Rise and Nature of Alternative Work Arrangements in the United States', 1995–2015. NBER Working Paper series, No. 226667, National Bureau of Economic Research, Cambridge, MA, September 2016. Available online: https://www.nber.org/system/files/working_papers/w22667/w22667.pdf.
82. Beckett, L. 2019, 'Under Digital Surveillance: How American Schools Spy on Millions of Kids', *The Guardian*, 22 October. Available online: https://www.theguardian.com/world/2019/oct/22/school-student-surveillance-bark-gaggle (Accessed 29 November 2023).
83. https://www.indeed.com/cmp/Gaggle/reviews?fjobtitle=Student+Representative.
84. https://www.tandfonline.com/doi/abs/10.1080/17439884.2022.2059765?journalCode=cjem20.
85. Cowen, in Means, *Learning to Save the Future*, 47–8.

86 Marcuse, H. (1964), *One-Dimensional Man*, Boston: Beacon. Available online: https://www.marcuse.org/herbert/pubs/64onedim/odm6.html#:~:text=In%20the%20construction%20of%20the,become%20fungible%20objects%20of%20organization.
87 https://jacobin.com/2015/03/education-technology-gates-erickson.
88 Postman, and Weingartner, *The School Book*.
89 Richtel, M. (2011), 'At Waldorf School in Silicon Valley, Technology Can Wait', *New York Times*, 22 October. Available online: https://www.nytimes.com/2011/10/23/technology/at-waldorf-school-in-silicon-valley-technology-can-wait.html?pagewanted=all&_r=0 (Accessed 29 November 2023).
90 Martin, L. H., Gutman, H., and Hutton, P. H. (1988), *Technologies of the Self: A Seminar with Michel Foucault*, London: Tavistock. Available online: https://monoskop.org/images/0/03/Technologies_of_the_Self_A_Seminar_with_Michel_Foucault.pdf (accessed 28 November 2023), 12.
91 Freire, *Pedagogy of the Oppressed*.
92 United Nations (2020), Digital Cooperation Roadmap. Available online: https://www.un.org/en/content/digital-cooperation-roadmap/assets/pdf/Roadmap_for_Digital_Cooperation_EN.pdf (Accessed 22 November 2023).
93 United Nations (2021), Common Agenda Report. Available online: https://www.un.org/en/content/common-agenda-report/assets/pdf/Common_Agenda_Report_English.pdf (Accessed 22 November 2023); see also https://giga.global.
94 See https://www.gatesfoundation.org/our-work/programs/global-growth-and-opportunity/global-education-program, https://www.globalpartnership.org, and https://mastercardfdn.org/#:~:text=The%20Mastercard%20Foundation%20works%20with,their%20leadership%20and%20contributions%20matter.
95 https://www.itu.int/itu-d/sites/partner2connect/.
96 As an aside, there are opinions opposing to the argument that corporations prioritize their own profit and growth. Such opinions are critical of governments' systematic failures in tackling all kinds of problems – from climate change to poverty – and instead propose that we should all hope for the generosity of the rich through their philanthrocapitalism, see Bishop, M. and Green, M. (2008), *Philanthrocapitalism: How Giving Can Save the World*. London: A & C Black Publishers. However, on what do these wealthy individuals and their philanthropy base which problem should be attended to first? What happens if their generosity doesn't succeed? This idea undermines the very foundations of societies, and the dignity, freedoms and rights of individuals.

Index

A
Access 4 Learning (A4L) Community 68, 69
Accessible Portable Item Protocol (APIP) 79
ACE Learner Success Lab 81
adaptive
　digital systems 104, 135
　learning 21, 48, 94, 99, 100, 103, 109
　software 93
　technologies 15, 161
Affective Learning – a Manifesto 45
Adaptive Learning Market Acceleration Program (ALMAP) 161
Africa 60
age of measurement 85
Age of Synthetic Existence 11
age-appropriate design code 176, 184, 185, 205
agonistic-political 198
AI Now Institute 169
Algorithms of Education: How Datafication and Artificial Intelligence Shape Policy 67
All I Ever Needed I Learned in Kindergarten 16
Allen, Laura 97
Alper, Meryl 129
AlphaGo 90
Alta 109
Altman, Sam 195
Amazon 20, 30, 52, 73, 74, 85, 193
　Future Engineer 159
　Mechanical Turk 218
ambassadorship, ambassadorships 61, 159, 175
American Workforce Policy Advisory Board (AWPAB) 78
American Workforce Policy Paper 77
Anatolia 195
Android 82
Anglo-American
　and Western 165
　contexts 16, 63, 64, 125, 218
　educational systems 107
Anthology 26–30, 204, 207
　SafeAssign 28
Apothecary Wares, Drugs and Stuffs 195
Apple 3, 14, 20, 109, 162
　iOS 82
Application Programming Interfaces 82
Arthur, Brian 95
Artificial intelligence (AI) 8, 67, 83
　infused automation 96, 99, 165
　integrated products 190
　narrow AI 92
Asana 27
Aspire Palo Alto Phoenix Academy 131
ASU + GSV Summit 175
audit, auditing, auditors 10, 17, 141, 43, 60, 109, 111, 112, 141, 142, 147, 169, 173, 180, 186, 192, 193, 202, 203, 208, 210, 212, 214
　culture 23, 197, 201, 204, 209
　-to-license 211
augmented reality (AR) 121, 130, 133
Australia/Australian 48, 53, 55, 57, 67, 68, 69, 86, 126, 158, 169, 175, 180, 189, 220
Australian Online Formative Assessment 57
Australia's Safer Technologies 4 Schools (ST4S) 175, 180

automated, automation, automating 45, 84, 89, 93, 96, 102, 111, 188, 215
   activity 219
   decisions, decision-making 92, 94
   future(s) 91, 218
   grading 97, 190
   systems 100, 101
avatar 35, 98, 131, 132, 215

B
Badgr 80
Ball, Steven J. 10, 35, 63, 64, 65, 84, 158, 167
banking skills 218
Barocas, Solon 93, 94
Bartow, Anne 139
Baudrillard, Jean 154
behaviour 46, 47, 50, 82, 95, 105, 111, 115, 123, 129, 133, 137, 148, 152, 154, 161, 188, 196, 198, 217
   change 68
   dispositions 149
   management 41, 96, 116
   manipulation 53
   model 159
   modification 138, 139, 215
   patterns 71, 153
   tracking 118, 135
behaviourism, behaviourist 35–7, 121, 160
Between Truth and Power 211
Biesta, Gert 7, 37, 38, 85–6, 151–5, 199
Bill and Melinda Gates Foundation 161
Black and Brown students 102
Black Mirror 98
Blackboard 20, 26, 27, 47, 82
Blair, Tony 109
Boden, R. 168
Bogaerts, Geert-Jan 213
Boolean formats 188
bootstrapping 5, 52
Bourdieu, Pierre 31–6, 84, 85, 148, 149, 216, 217

Bowker, Geoffrey C. 170
Brin, Sergey 9
British Naturalist Society 122
Broadband Commission 75
Broussard, Meredith 54, 89, 92, 93, 102, 110–2, 211, 212
Bryant, Jeff 74
Brynjolfsson, Erik 43
Burning Glass Technologies 80

C
California Consumer Privacy Act 175
Cambridge, Massachusetts 184
   school district 186, 189
Cambridge Analytica 135
career and technical education (CTE) 73–5
Carmona, Salvador 168
Castañeda, Isabel 102 (*see also* Broussard, Meredith)
Century Tech 98, 108, 109, 204
Chalkable 110
ChatGPT 8, 105–6, 191, 216
Chicago School, The 158, 217
Chiefs for Change (CFC) 70
child, children 1–23, 27, 29–39, 42–56, 60, 66, 70–9, 86, 89–91, 95, 101–2, 106–8, 110–49, 152–63, 165–66, 169–78, 182–4, 186–9, 191–4, 196–7, 201, 203, 205, 206, 209, 215, 217–21
childhood 4, 22, 39, 113, 129, 143, 144–8, 155, 162
   obesity 137
children's basic human rights, children's rights 18, 29, 52, 113–18, 120, 125, 127, 129, 130, 135, 145, 153, 173–5, 178, 182, 183, 184, 196, 203, 205, 206, 221
children's digital rights 118, 127
Children's Machines: Rethinking School in the Age of the Computer, The 44, 46
Children's Online Privacy Protection Act (COPPA) 116, 189

Cisco 60, 73, 74, 174
Class Dojo 20, 41, 95, 121
ClassLink 26
cognitive offloading 130
Coh-Metrix 96
Cohen, Jared 9
Cohen, Julie 211
Collington, Rosie 60, 172, 173, 196, 197
commodification of knowledge 61
common data standards 30
Common Education Data Standard (CEDS) 68, 70 (*see also* US CEDS Data Warehouse)
Communication and Video Accessibility Act (CVAA) 102
competency-based learning 80
computer merchants 4, 13, 168 (*see also* Roszak, Theodore)
computing 44
Concentric Sky 80
conservative economic and social policy 158
constructionism 45
constructivist, constructivism 36, 43, 45, 159, 160
consultation fatigue 115
convivial/conviviality 18, 38, 41, 114
Core Learning Exchange 80
Cornell Lab 121
corporatocracy 59
Costs of Connection: How Data Is Colonising Human Life and Appropriating It for Capitalism, The 55
Couldry, Nick 55, 114, 216
Council of Europe 200
Counter Terrorism and Security Act 2015 4
Covid-19 3, 50, 52, 60, 75, 112, 125, 135, 142, 143, 170, 178
Cowen, Tyler 218
cradle-to-career 40, 57, 81, 83–6, 110, 220

CrashCourse 126
Credential Engine 81
credential/credentialing 22, 55, 61, 72, 74–8, 80, 81, 83, 116, 122, 162, 153, 218
Croco Island 132
Crossley, Scott 97
Csikszentmihalyi, Mihaly 106
Cuban, Larry 157
Cubberley, Ellwood 155, 156, 159
curriculum 5, 18, 44, 73, 79, 85, 106, 112, 142, 159, 192
  decisions 34, 42
  design 171
  development 31, 110
  expertise 70
  flexibility 74
  modification 56
  universal 148
customer relationship management (CRM) 27, 28, 31, 168, 213
cyberattacks 106, 209
cyberpunk 89
Cyprus 193

D

Darwin/Darwinian 106, 217
data lake 28, 30, 78, 153
data literacy 138, 139
data privacy impact assessments 208
Data Privacy Officer (DPO), DPOs 184–6, 208
Data Protection Act 184
Data Protection and Digital Information Bill, the 183
Data Quality Campaign 70
datafication 8, 11, 29, 32, 34, 42, 45, 47, 50, 52, 63, 65, 66, 67, 76, 77, 122, 128, 135, 139, 142, 157, 172
dataveillance 32
DeepMind 90, 91, 216
Demmans Epp, Carrie 96
Dennett, Daniel 90

desocialization 101
Dewey, John 36, 154, 156, 159, 160
diagnostic, diagnostics 66, 85, 153, 180
  assessment 94
  proposals 142
  results 100
  test 98
DigCompOrg conceptual framework 207
digital badges 41, 203
digital economy 21, 61, 110
Digital Education Hub 75
digital libraries 220
digital skill, digital skills 91, 119, 120, 139, 170, 171, 172
Digital Promise 175
digital twins 31
digital/data backpacks 70, 152, 153
digitized classroom 8, 17, 21, 22, 29, 31, 47, 51, 54, 56, 66, 85, 113, 115, 118, 120, 130, 137, 145, 147, 155, 187, 199, 218
disability, disabilities 18, 102, 124, 129, 135
Disappearance of Childhood, The 144
Disneyland 154
DreamBox 98, 105, 108
Dublin's Factory 89
dummy data 70
Dutch PublicSpaces initiative 213
DXtera Institute 75, 175

E
E-waste 60
EdTech Evidence Exchange 55
EdTech procurement 17, 22, 175, 180, 181, 183, 186, 208
Education and Technology: Issues and Debates 92
education data governance 182
education/educational
  benefits 38
  capital 84 (*see also* human capital education)
  community 75, 215
  content 100
  crisis 59
  data 20, 22, 28, 36, 37, 39, 49, 67, 68, 69, 70, 77, 103, 110, 153, 159, 160, 161, 162, 173, 182, 188, 189
  domain(s) 127, 203
  ecosystems 14
  effectiveness 92
  evidence 54 (*see also* Global Education Evidence Advisory Panel of the World Bank)
  experience 15, 123
  governance 23, 31, 38, 40, 66, 69, 83, 92, 111, 151, 166, 167, 201
  institutions 5, 7, 23, 55, 56, 62, 64, 73, 76, 79, 80, 82, 87, 109, 133, 141, 149, 156, 158, 163, 169, 172, 177, 180, 186, 187, 197, 198, 208, 211, 213, 214, 218
  leadership 198, 199
  materials 27, 79
  needs 13, 52, 55, 127, 150, 193
  policy 4, 6, 66, 91, 107, 119, 151, 157, 195, 198
  problems 61, 85
  processes 8, 9, 15, 20, 22, 30, 32, 42, 48, 49, 75, 121, 142, 161, 191
  proposals 76
  purpose 130
  reform 59
  research 115
  resources 72
  scholars 118
  sector 60, 139, 184, 202
  security standard 207 (*see also* global education security standard)
  settings 16, 18, 28, 181, 185
  software 82, 209
  stakeholders 28, 206, 215
  statistics 39

systems 10, 29, 32, 35, 42, 48, 53, 57, 62, 79, 85, 91, 97, 107, 156, 158, 165, 166, 192, 197, 218
technologies 5, 6, 8, 15, 183
theory 18
values 208
Effective Learning by Fostering Innovation through Educational Technology 207
Einstein 106
Electronic Learning 3
Elliot, T. S. 41, 59
Embodied Cognition Theory 127
embodied learning 127
environmental, social and governance (ESG) 173, 196, 199
Ericson, Megan 218
EU Director General for Innovation, Digital Education and International Cooperation 193
EU Edtech Alliance 211
EU Joint Research Council 136
EU NIS2 Directive 175, 207
European Accessibility Act 102
European Commission 170
European Union (EU) 3, 17, 55, 60, 100, 175, 176, 220
evolving capacities 115, 117, 145
Exergames 127
existential 11
Expl*AI*nations 98
EY 146
Eyal, Nir 203
Ezzamel, Mahmoud 168

F
Facebook 2, 20, 50, 52, 60, 75, 90, 181, 193, 213
Fairness and Machine Learning: Limitations and Opportunities 93
Family Computing magazine, The 2
Family Educational Rights and Privacy Act, The 179, 189
Fantasy worlds 131
Fauxtomation 106
Federal Communications Commission (FCC) 102
Federal Trade Commission (FTC) 27, 54, 176
Five Pillars for Edtech Procurement 174 (*see also* EdTech procurement)
flexploitation 84
Fouad, Noran 205
Foucault, Michel 62, 67, 219
Foundry 31
Framework for Stakeholder Inclusion 174
frameworks 102, 187, 209
Freeman, Richard 145
Freire, Paulo 33, 35, 41, 42, 120, 220
Frické, Martin 31
Frontiers of Criticism 43
Fulghum, Robert 16
Future of Education and Skills 2030 143 (*see also* OECD)

G
Gaggle 122, 217
Gambling Act of 2005 202
gambling-style games 202
games 127
gamification 65, 121, 131, 132
Ganter, Sarah Anne 50
Gates, Bill 70 (*see also* Parthenon Group *and* Adaptive Learning Market Acceleration Program)
Foundation 68, 161
Gateways Initiative 3, 220
GDP 202
GEM Report 178, 181
General Comment No. 25 184
General Data Protection Regulation (GDPR) 99, 100, 176, 178, 183–5, 190, 206
General Trust 2
Gervais, Ricky 141

Gibraltar 193
gig, gig worker 84, 85, 218
GIGA 3, 220
Gilbert, Jeremy 56
global, globalist, globalization 60, 61, 63, 143, 158, 165, 221
Global Education Coalition 75
Global Education Evidence Advisory Panel of the World Bank 54
Global Education Privacy and Security Standard (GEPS) 180
Global Education Security Standard 180, 207 (*see also* Global Education Privacy and Security Standard)
Global North 10, 22
Global Partnership for Education 220
Gobby, Brad 198, 199
good school/bad school 147
Google 3, 15–20, 28, 30, 34, 50, 52, 60, 75, 82, 90, 103, 134, 135, 154, 162, 181, 193, 213, 219
  accreditation programs 159
  Chromebooks 122
  classroom 26, 27, 187, 217
  Data Studio 27
  Earth Tour Guide 122
  Google Ideas 9
  Workspace for Education 185
governance
  and control 77
  by distraction 165, 166
  by numbers 168
  data 182
  effective 19, 206
  fragmented 195
  frameworks 102, 187, 209
  materials 27, 79
  mechanism 64, 189
  methods 69
  modes of 30
  of edtech 16, 130, 201
  of education 75, 111, 167, 172
  of the digitisation of education 23
  players 31
  proposals 22
  school x
  social and 173, 196 (*see also* environmental, social and governance)
  structures 22, 134
  synthetic 67
GovernorHub Knowledge Body 19
Gray, Mary 217
Great Depression, The 157
Gulson, Kalevro, Sellar, Sam, Webb, Taylor 30, 67, 69, 70, 92, 201

H

habitus 11, 33, 40, 148, 149
Hague, Lord William 109
Hall, Stuart 59, 62
Hardt, Moritz 93, 94
Hassabis, Demis 90
hegemony, hegemonic 56, 188
  imperatives 166
  power 165
Hegemony Now: How Big Tech and Wall Street Won the World (and How We Win It Back) 56
hidden pedagogy of oppression 33, 41 (*see also* Freire, Paulo)
Hint Factory 96
Hispanic 131
HolonIQ 202
Hooked: How to Build Habit-Forming 203
Hub 75 (*see also* Digital Education Hub)
Hub Integration Testing Service (HITS) 69
human capital education 84
human capital investment 218
human rights 2, 13, 17, 18, 22, 29, 33, 97, 101, 106, 122, 113–18, 129, 178, 183, 184, 185, 190, 200, 206, 208, 209, 221
Human Rights Ethical and Social Impact Assessment (HRESIA) 190

Human Rights Watch 52, 113, 208
humane-by-design 128
hyper-meritocracy 217
hyper-specialized 74
hyperreality 154

I
IBM 60, 73
   Watson 10
Illich, Ivan 18, 72, 73
Illuminate Education 209
IMS Global/1Edtech 68, 80, 174, 175
   (*see also* TrustEd Apps Rubric)
   Data Privacy Seal 79
   Global Learning Consortium 79
iNaturalist 122
Indiana 81
Information Commissioner's Office (ICO) 38, 183–5
Information Society Services (ISS) 184, 185, 205
Instagram 121
institutional inefficiencies 157
intelligent tutoring systems, intelligent tutors (ITS) 35, 37, 45, 47, 94, 96, 98, 109
International Data Accountability Council, The 208
International Monetary Fund 60
International Organisation for Standardisation (ISO) 199
International Society for Technology in Education (ISTE) 175
   ISTE Edtech Product Evaluation Guide for Teachers 174
interoperability 21, 30, 31, 66–72, 79, 82, 83, 123, 189, 208
Interoperable Learning Records (ILR) 77, 78
invisible student 99

J
Japan, Japanese 2, 105
JavaScript 10

Jentoft, Svein 201
Job Insecurity Is Everywhere Now 216

K
K-12
Kasparov, Garry 9
Kerssens, Niels 56
Keynesian welfarism 59
Khan Academy 191
   Khanmigo 216
kids in crisis 19
kinect-based educational games 127
Knewton 109
know your customer 202
knowledge model 36, 37
Kooiman, Jan 201
Korczak, Janusz 113

L
Labour Party 158
Lacoste 132
landscape 60, 142
Large Language Models (LLMs) 8, 126
Latin America 60
leaderboards 40
leadership 198, 199
leap motion 127
learning 25, 120
   activities 1
   app, applications 16, 136, 160
   choices 152
   community 124
   environment, environments 10, 142, 143, 171
   experience 20, 126, 130, 162, 182
   games 98
   gains 153
   information systems 2
   lifelong 216
   loss 143
   management 26, 27
   model, models 159, 190
   needs 7, 22, 206 (*see also* workforce needs)

opportunities 74
outcome, outcomes 7, 20, 108, 127, 160, 161
output 82
path, pathways 105, 155
platform, platforms 3, 34, 107, 109
poverty 143
process, processes 103, 160, 161, 165
project-based 112
records 81
sciences 15
skills 178
styles 175
subject 119
technologies 103, 172
theories 35
through play 121
trajectory 34
virtual 35
Learning Management Systems (LMSs) 27, 28, 126
Learning Tools Interoperability standards (LTI) 68
Lego 6, 104
Lessig, Laurence 82, 196
Lexis games 127
license to operate 201
Lingard, Bob 156
Linguistic Inquiry 96
longitudinal data, databases 22, 41
Louis Vuitton 132
low- and middle-income regions 107
Lundy, Laura 114, 115

M

machine learning (ML) 19, 38, 46, 92, 93, 111, 112, 123, 172, 190
Mahieu, René L. P. 139
Malta 193, 202
Malta Gaming Authority 202
Mantelero, Alessandro 190
Marcuse, Herbert 218
marketing 3, 22, 39, 54, 89, 106, 107, 110, 131, 132, 146, 179, 219, 221

Mazzuccato, Mariana 60, 172, 173, 196, 197
McAfee, Andrew 43
McGraw Hill 79
McKinsey 146
Means, Alexander J. 61, 84, 85, 218
mechanisms of change 167
Media Lab, The 45–7, 122
Mejias, A. Ulises 55, 216
Merlin Bird ID 121
Meta 20, 60, 75, 132, 193
metapolicies 220
Metaverse 5, 131
Microsoft 2–3, 13, 19–20, 30, 50–4, 60, 68, 133, 154, 162, 174, 187
 Power BI 27
 Teams for Education 82
Minecraft 132, 133
Minority Report 98
MIT 45
Mithridates VI 195
mixed reality (MR) 130, 131
models 31
 assessment 190
 data 11, 68, 82
 global(ist) 192
 ML 111, 112
 predictive 93
Monmouth County 90
Moodle 82
More Than a Glitch: Confronting Race, Gender, and Ability Bias in Tech 54
Mozart 106
Mr P ICT 190, 192
Multi Academy Trusts 211
multiple intelligences 123

N

Narayanan, Arvind 93, 94
NASA 121
Nash, Roy 149
Nation at Risk: The Imperative for an Educational Reform, A 59

National Assessment Program – Literacy and Numeracy (NAPLAN) 69
National Council for the American Worker (NCAW) 78
National Student Clearinghouse (NSC) 81
national testing data 153
natural language processing (NLP) 95, 96, 97, 98
Nearpod 20, 39
    VR Lessons 131, 132 (*see also* Virtual Reality)
Neoliberal Revolution 59
neoliberal/neoliberalism/ neoliberalist 16, 40, 56, 59, 62, 64, 65, 84–6, 114, 157, 158, 165, 168, 176, 180, 216, 218, 221, 233
Netherlands 213, 214
NetSupport/NetSupport School 25–9, 41, 47, 95, 138
network 81 (*see also* Strada Education Network)
New National Purpose: Innovation Can Power the Future of Britain, A 109
New York Times digital archive 90
New Zealand 175, 185
Newton 106
NextLevel Jobs 81
Nielsen, Rasmus Kleis 50
Nike 132
NIST 175
normative power 154, 188
Northern Italy 168
NOYB 54
nudging/hyper-nudging 34, 41, 42, 51, 187
Nussbaum, Martha 59
Nvidia (*see also* Nvidia Canvas) 6, 90

O
O'Neil, Kathy 112
Odyssey 195

Office of Communications, The 125
Olmedo, Antonio 167, 201
OneRoster® 26, 79
online gambling 193, 197, 201–4, 208
Open AI 195
Organisation for Economic Cooperation and Development (OECD) 60, 143, 146, 158, 159
othering 108

P
P-20W 70
PacSun 133
Page, Larry 9
Palantir Technologies 31
Papert, Seymour 43–7
Paris 132
Parthenon Group 68
participation gap 118, 129
pathways 20
Pearson 110, 193
pedagogy/pedagogic 4, 66, 70, 75, 151, 161, 172, 173, 197, 208
    action and work 33, 38, 40
    and commercial value 25
    authority/authorities 20, 35, 49, 148
    autonomy 56
    critical 33
    failure 52
    interventions 51, 103
    methodologies 18, 99
    of oppression 41, 42
    power 32
    practice/s 149, 201
    value 192, 204, 205
Peralta, Manuel 96
performativity 10, 38, 41, 49, 65, 66, 85, 158
    drive 159
    in education 48
    measures 74
personalized bubble domes 15
personalized, personalization 101, 152
    experiences 27, 119

instruction 35, 97
learning 66, 95, 102
learning platform 107
of education 45
recommendations 41
personas 11
Pharmacopoeias 195
philanthrocapitalism 159
Piaget, Jean 44, 45
Piattoeva, Nelli 168
Picard, Rosalind W. 46, 47
PK-20 data 207
Platform Gateways 220
platform power, power of platforms 50, 51, 56, 57
platformization 30, 74, 76, 77
player protection 202
plug-and-play architecture 80
policy, policymakers 4, 12, 16–18, 39, 40, 63–7, 79, 80, 122, 125, 128, 129, 137, 140, 142, 158, 174, 193, 196, 220
actors 69, 82
and business 76
and federal funding 73
and governance 38
and regulation 89
assessments 208
context 184
decisions 20
discourse 45
drive, drives 22, 91
functions 202
incentives 179
instruments 159
measures 21
options 102
perspectives 11
principle 117
privacy 53
ranks 75
reports 108
solutions 60
speak 86
structures 84
Postman, Neil 12, 144, 219
Power, Michael 169
Power of Platforms: Shaping Media and Society, The 50
PowerSchool 2, 20, 109, 110, 147, 190
practices 56, 112
predictive 74
capabilities 28, 31, 123, 201
diagnostic 85
models 93
policing 39
systems 139
Price, Thomas W. 96
PriceWaterhouseCoopers 146
prison 1, 49, 144, 169
privacy, data privacy 19, 20, 23, 42, 55, 98, 127, 130, 138–40, 186, 194, 210, 211, 213
activists 17
agreements 154
and civil liberties 117
and ethical practices 48
and exploitation 52
and safety 44
and security requirements 197
and security risks 18, 68, 76, 177
by-design 174, 176
consultants 173
frameworks 181
impact assessments 185, 208
in education 178
loss 16, 33, 35
measures 179
officers 180
protection 187, 190
rules 125
settings 214
privacy-by-design 174, 176, 182
production bottleneck 110
productivity targets 63
Program for International Student Assessment (PISA) 159
ICT Framework 174
programmable machines 11, 41

progress in understanding mathematics assessment (PUMA) 107
project management tools (PMTs) 27, 168
Prometheus X 82, 83
Prout, Alen 145, 147
psychometric profiles 109
public interest technology 112, 212
pupil voice 114
Python 218

Q
Question & Test Interoperability (QTI) 79

R
R Studio 10
Rahm, Lina 91
Ralph Lauren 133
randomized controlled trials (RCT) 17
Raso, Filippo, A. 97
React Native 82
recommender systems 101
Renaissance Learning 39
reproduction, (re) production 13, 32, 33, 62, 84, 86, 148, 149, 151, 165 (*see also* Bourdieu, Pierre)
Richards, Neil 34
Rights Protection Act (*see also* Family Educational Rights Protection Act)
Rizvi, Fazal 156
Roadmap for Digital Cooperation 220 (*see also* United Nations)
Robinson, Sir Ken 43
Roblox 132, 133
robot, robotic 101, 190, 195
Rockefeller Foundation, The 220
Roszak, Theodore 11, 13, 85
Rousseauan 188
Russia, Russian 44

S
SABER-ICT 174
salesforce 27
Save the Children 113
Schmidt, Eric 9
Schneier, Bruce 139
SchoolMateAI 190
schoology 110, 190
Schools Interoperability Framework (SIF) 68, 69
Schools of the Future: Defining New Models of Education for the Fourth Industrial Revolution 143 (*see also* World Economic Forum)
Science Technology Engineering and Mathematics (STEM) 74, 96, 218
scratch 122
screen time, time on their screens 4, 26, 136, 137, 142, 146, 192
Second Machine Age: Work, Progress, and Prosperity in a Time of Brilliant Technologies, The 43
Second World War 113
Secretary General of the United Nations 220
security standard 207 (*see also* Global Education Security Standard)
seek 122
SeeSaw 95
self-driven learning 43, 46
self-reinforcement learning 90
Selwyn, Neil 13, 29, 92, 130
settings 16, 18, 28, 181, 185
Shakespearian 11
Shapiro, Carl 69
Shera, Jesse H. 8, 9
Silicon Valley 57, 219
skill deficiencies 83
Skillful Indiana 81
skills of the future 22
Snapchat 121, 133

social confluence 15
software-as-a-service (SaaS) 30
Solar System Exploration 121
Solove, Daniel J. 139
SparkNotes 126
sparks 124, 125
Sparx Maths 107, 108
special educational needs 127
stakeholders 28, 206, 215
Stanford University 155
Star, Susan Leigh 170
Star Walk 2 121
Strada Education Network 81
strategy of devolution 158
student information system (SIS) 26, 28, 68, 72, 79, 110
Sub-Saharan Africa 60
Suleyman, Mustafa 216
Suri, Siddharth 217
surveillance 8, 15, 16, 18, 19, 32, 34, 47, 48, 52, 54, 95, 119, 122, 135, 137, 139, 142, 145, 176, 213
symbolic violence 33, 35, 36, 38, 40, 41, 108, 160 (*see also* Bourdieu, Pierre)
synthetic
  economy 218
  ecosystems 14
  existence 11
  governance 67, 201
  world 11
systemic retrenchment 172

T
Tahaei, Mohammad 34
Taj Mahal, The 132
talent pipeline 40, 75, 78, 119
  tanagement 71
Taming of the Shrew 11
Taylor, Astra 105
Taylor, Frederick Winslow, Taylorism 168
Teacher Match 110
Teaching and the Computer 3

Teaching Machines: The History of Personalised Learning 15
tech fatigue 106
technochauvinism 54, 89
Technological, Pedagogical, and Content Knowledge (TPAC) framework 174, 175
technologies 5, 6, 8, 15, 183
technology-enhanced embodied learning environments 127
Tekscan 47
Tesla 90
theoretical learning models 35
three-dimensional environments 131
thrively 95, 123, 124, 125, 147
token, tokens 51, 139, 203
  economy 116
Topalov, Veselin 104
trajectory 34
TrustEd Apps Rubric 79, 80
Turkle, Sherry 103

U
U2 90–2
UK Cyber Essentials 175
UK Daily Mail (*see also* General Trust) 2
UK Department for Education 38, 183, 186
UK the Office for Standards in Education, Children's Services and Skills (Ofsted) 38
UN Convention on the Rights of the Child (UNCRC) 114, 116, 118, 184
Unboxit 127
unethical practices 2, 208, 215
UNICEF 102, 113, 175
United Nations 178, 220
  Human Rights Office of the High Commissioner (OHCHR) 200
  Millennial Summit 216

United Nations Educational, Scientific and Cultural Organisation (UNESCO), 17, 60, 178, 211
   ICT Competency Framework for Teachers 174
   Global Education Coalition 75
United Nations Human Rights Office of the High Commissioner (OHCHR) 200
United Nations Millennial Summit 216
Universal plugin SDKs 82
University College London Edtech Labs 210
US CEDS Data Warehouse 70
US Chamber of Commerce Foundation 57, 75, 81
US Department of Education 70
US Department of Labour 70
US Federal Trade Commission 2
US Health and Human Services 70
US National Centre for Education Statistics (NCES) 39

V
Van Der Hof, Simone 116
Van Dijck, José 56, 213
Varian, Hal 69
Veale, Michael 102
Veritas Capital 27, 30
Verne, Etienne 73
vertical hegemony 188
Very Large online Platforms/VLOPs 52
ViacomCBS 102
Virginia 55, 71, 85
virtual reality, VR 127, 130
virtual worlds 6, 130, 131
Vista Equity Partners 110

Vorsprung durch technik 89
Vygotsky, Lev 102

W
walkthrough method/methodology 25, 123
Watters, Audrey 15
Weaver, Warren 8
Web3 media 131
Weingartner, Charles 219
Weiser, Mark 14, 57
Why Voice Matters: Culture and Politics after Neoliberalism 114
Wii 127
Wiley & Sons 109 (*see also* Knewton)
Wilkins, Andrew 168, 198, 199, 201
Williams, Alex 56
Williams, Raymond 166
Williamson, Ben 75
Witzenberger, Kevin 92
Wonde 38
workforce 22, 59, 71, 72, 73, 77, 78, 80–6, 142, 157, 159, 217
World Atlas 122
World Bank, The 54, 60, 61, 174, 211
World Economic Forum (WEF) 61, 143

X
xAI 98, 100
Xbox 2

Y
YouTube 121

Z
Zepeto 133
Zooropa 89, 90
Zuboff, Shoshana 15
Zuckerman, Ethan 213